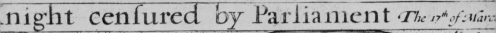

...n Giles was brought
...thought
...was comitted,
...e ſhould be fitted
...at hee had done;
...here to runne;
...baniſht quite
...a Knight
...roul'd
...eat contrould.

Nowe beinge cenſur'd banniſhed and gone,
With penſive ſpeech. thus may hee mourne alone;
Woe worthe the time when firſt on Innes I thought
For private gaines when I their hindrance ſought;
Thoſe Monopolies curſed bee with ſhame,
Which have my reputation thus made lame:
My Honours which hath turn'd to other ſtyles
From St. Mompeſſon vnto poore lame Giles;
Yett haultinge nowe before, me thinks I ſee
Some in the way of haultinge after mee.

Hoe fellowe Giles ſtay for vs yett a while
For heere, wee come, although behinde a mile.

...enry laſt
...they paſſ

...why you knowe, our gracious Kinge is bent
...ve his faithfull ſubiects all content;
...e love is due, hee lovingly doth ſhow't,
...e mercies meete by pardon many know't,

By rendringe Iuſtice vnto great and ſmall,
The ſmale ones trippe & great ones downe right fall,
Oh what more needs a Loyall Subiect crave
Then mercy, love, and juſtice choice to have.

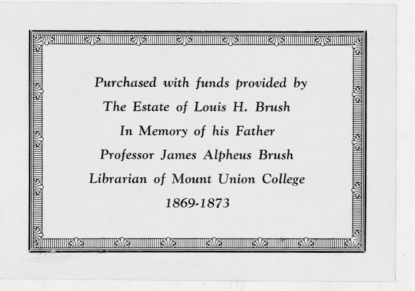

The Amazing Career of
SIR GILES OVERREACH

EDMUND KEAN as SIR GILES OVERREACH in the last scene of *A New Way to Pay Old Debts*, from the painting by George Clint, A.R.A., at the Garrick Club

THE AMAZING CAREER OF
SIR GILES OVERREACH

Being the Life and Adventures
Of a Nefarious Scoundrel who for three centuries
Pursued his Sinister Designs
In almost all the Theatres
Of the British Isles and America

The whole comprising
A HISTORY OF THE STAGE

By ROBERT HAMILTON BALL

PRINCETON & LONDON

To be had from most booksellers, or from the printers and publishers,
Princeton University Press, corner of William and Charlton
Streets, Princeton, New Jersey, and Sir Humphrey
Milford at the *Oxford University Press*, London

MCMXXXIX

uGE

The tail-piece at the conclusion of the volume is from a letter in the Folger Shakespeare Library. The vignette used on the front cover is from Dibdin's London Theatre.

PRINTED AT PRINCETON UNIVERSITY PRESS
PRINCETON, NEW JERSEY, U. S. A.

FIRST EDITION

TO
MY MOTHER
AND FATHER

"Actors are the best commentators
on the poets."

— *Hazlitt*

PREFATORY REMARKS

STAGE-HISTORY is a comparatively new field for scholarship, and only recently has its importance been realized. Drama exists only in the theatre. Whatever its literary value, a play unproduced is not drama; the dramatist writes for the stage. Our final judgment of a play, therefore, must be based, not merely on its qualities as literature, but on its effect in the theatre, and it is only through a study of stage-history that we can arrive at sound criticism. This does not mean that the literary element should be neglected; that every play which succeeds on the stage is a great play, or that every unsuccessful one is without merit. It does mean that we must approach the play through the theatre to attain a full understanding of its qualities as a work of dramatic art.

It is my purpose in this book to approach Philip Massinger's *A New Way to Pay Old Debts* purely from the point of view of the theatre, to examine it on the basis of presentation, acting, and review. Without such examination I do not see how we have grounds for thinking we understand a professional playwright who was working for the theatre. *A New Way to Pay Old Debts* has had an amazing stage-history. It has been presented, as far as I can ascertain, more often than any other English play of its age excepting only some of Shakespeare's. I wish to show to what extent it has held the stage, why it has been so popular, and how this contributes to criticism.

On the other hand I did not write this book *only* to find out whether *A New Way to Pay Old Debts* is a good play. It becomes a focus by means of which we may see other things clearly as well. I have tried to present a more or less unified view of the English and American stage, to distinguish the conditions of one period from another, of one country from another, to make each important actor stand out as a separate and recognizable entity, to comment as topics appear worthy of commentary, in short to make a contribution to stage-history which will be of value, regardless whether the reader is a specialist in Massinger or particularly interested in Massinger's masterpiece.

Finally I have written the book to please myself.

> I wolde go the myde way
> And write a book between the tway,
> Somewhat of lust, somewhat of lore.

As a child I was fascinated by the theatre; next I passed through a period of disillusion, the inevitable result of a persistent desire to go "back-stage," where the romance becomes reality; I have now reached "the everlasting yea," where "behind the scenes" is a country, real but stimulating, peopled with men and women to whom the smell of grease-paint is as the breath of life, and theatrical setting the landscape of the world.

The importance of the leading character of Massinger's play has led me to employ the device of a fantastical biography of Sir Giles Overreach. Instead of adhering to strict chronological sequence of performance, I have grouped the presentations under the actors, and then treated these groups chronologically according to the date of each actor's *first* performance of the part. I have hoped by this method partially to escape the danger of mere cataloguing, and to present a unified view of the actors who are responsible for the continued success of the play. With productions in languages other than English I have not been concerned. Presentations in the United States have been separated from those in Great Britain, though many actors played in both, in order to show the theatrical conditions peculiar to each, and to allow the reader to scan an ever changing theatrical diorama without a break in continuity.

This study does not pretend to be complete. To list every performance of *A New Way to Pay Old Debts* would be impossible, even if it were desirable. It would necessitate more travel than a scholar can afford, and more research than could be accomplished in any reasonable length of time. I have been content to deal in the main only with large theatrical centers, though I have noted performances elsewhere when the information came to hand, and to correct many inexact and erroneous statements which are likely to be accepted as facts. That I have myself made no mistakes, I do not dare to hope. The facilities for theatrical research are not centralized. This has made necessary a great deal of copying, sometimes at second hand, into which error is always wont to intrude, and the acceptance of some statements which I have not always been able personally to verify. The number of books I have had to consult, only a small fraction of which turned out to be of any value, has occasionally forced me to use indices, possibly incomplete; and the number of playbills and newspapers I have had to examine should in part palliate any faults in the examination. I regret that it has been necessary to include so many footnotes, but since theatrical memoirs, biographies, and histories are notoriously inaccurate, I could only resort to full documentation.

Acknowledgments are due to so many that I can mention only a few: Professor Thomas Marc Parrott, whose sound scholarship and constructive criticism have been of great assistance; Professor Donald Clive Stuart, who for many years has stimulated my studies in the theatre; Mrs. J. D. Hall of the Harvard Theatre Collection, who put that amazing repository at my disposal, and who knows so much about this book that she should have written it herself; the late Mr. John Drew, Mr. Walter Hampden, and Mr. Roy Day of The Players; Professor George C. D. Odell, whose fine example I have done my best to follow; the late Mr. William Seymour, of whose theatrical collection I have the honor to be curator; Mr. Martin K. Bovey, who as a graduate student at Harvard University generously abandoned a study similar to mine and gave me his notes; the staffs of many libraries, in particular of Princeton University; many friends who, unsolicited, have sent me information, or consulted, spared neither time nor trouble; and especially to my wife, whose encouragement in the face of obstacles has meant more than she knows.

R.H.B.

Princeton, New Jersey

TABLE OF CONTENTS

LIST OF ILLUSTRATIONS

PART I

A NEW WAY TO PAY OLD DEBTS
IN GREAT BRITAIN

CHAPTER I

THE HATCHING OF A CORMORANT

THIS book is the biography of a character who actually never lived. Sir Giles Overreach, though he was drawn from life, did not spring into being until he was conceived in the fertile brain of a Jacobean dramatist, Philip Massinger. He is the chief personage in the play, *A New Way to Pay Old Debts;* it is he, chiefly, who has made the play successful; in many respects he is the play. There is therefore some justification for treating the stage-history of this old drama as a sort of fantastical biography of Sir Giles Overreach, who, though born early in the seventeenth century, can hardly be said to have died, since he has persistently reappeared in various manifestations and transformations as he has been interpreted by the actors who merged their identity with his.

James VI of Scotland ascended the throne of England in 1603 with practically the full consent of the nation. His gentlemanly qualities, his liberality in dispensing rewards, his decision to make no sweeping changes in the ministry hid for a time his impatience with details, his arrogance, his insistence on royal prerogatives in the face of popular opposition. Yet the history of his reign is the history of a coming revolution, and it is necessary to trace the events which made him unpopular in order to understand the conditions which made "Cormorant Overreach" possible. Elizabeth's strong central government, inherited from her Tudor ancestors, had been successful in a succession of crises because of her own ability and personality. In less troublous times could a Stuart from Scotland make his will felt and at the same time control the House of Commons?

Two pressing questions greeted James almost at once, the official attitude towards Spain and the matter of religious toleration. James elected for peace with Spain and imprisoned the leader of the hostile party, Sir Walter Raleigh, on a charge of treason. Not content with a mere decision in the Hampton Court Conference in

1604, the new King exploded in anger and bitterly alienated the milder Puritans who had petitioned for minor relaxations in the rules and orders of the Established Church. The bishops were delighted, but the House of Commons on the whole disapproved. Moreover it received with disfavor the King's scheme for a union with Scotland. Financial difficulties increased the dissatisfaction, and the session concluded with a quarrel. Others of James's policies too did not entirely win approval. Having remitted the recusancy fines in the first year of his reign, he banished all Catholic priests from London in 1604 and restored the fines a year later; the revelation of the Gunpowder Plot increased the persecution of the Catholics. The confiscation of Irish counties and their resettlement by colonists, partly Scotch, did not add to his popularity. Unable to obtain from Commons the naturalization of Scottish subjects in England, James succeeded in having his judges declare all those born after his accession legally naturalized, an ominous sign of the use of legal power when opposed by popular opinion.

But the irritation of Commons was most clearly visible in matters financial. James was the reverse of thrifty, his tastes were expensive; unlike Elizabeth he had a family to support, his favorites had to be rewarded. Money he needed and money he could not have without a grant from Commons, unless he had recourse to impositions more sweeping than those which had been demanded by Elizabeth. James decided to add further duties, but in 1606 a merchant named Bate challenged the imposition on currants. The Court of Exchequer decided for the King, and since the Commons' Petition of Grievances was to no avail, James added new impositions in 1608. Finally, since these would not balance the budget, Parliament was called in 1610 to consider the situation. It agreed to provide the King with a certain revenue in return for the surrender of harsh feudal rights, but before the Great Contract was consummated, the matter of impositions raised its head and a resolution of the House of Commons declared them illegal. James hedged over the summer vacation, further disputes arose at the next session, and the King wrathfully dissolved his first Parliament, determined so far as possible to rule without it. Though his want of money drove him in 1614 to call a new Parliament, the House insisted on the discussion of impositions, and, after a few weeks, this too was dissolved. In desperation James renewed negotiations for a profitable Spanish marriage for his son, dickering with a Catholic King who was England's hereditary enemy.

James was a virtuous man but not always a wise one. Most of all he felt he needed an attractive companion who would take some of the burdens off his shoulders and dispense his patronage. His first choice had been Robert Carr, Earl of Somerset, who with his wife was found guilty of the murder of Sir Thomas Overbury in 1616. His next was George Villiers, who had been appointed a gentleman of the bedchamber and knighted in 1615, and who subsequently became Earl, Marquis, and Duke of Buckingham, and virtual ruler of England. Buckingham had few political principles other than a primary one, to become an increasingly powerful favorite of the King's to whom all must bow down who wished to soar. His sudden rise, his airs and his arrogance, his self-assurance and the servility he demanded disgusted men of independent judgment, alienated the older nobility, and made the common people distrust him. Neither the King nor Buckingham, who was his mouthpiece, gained caste in the affair of the Palatinate. The third Parliament, summoned in 1621 to vote supplies for the war, found James dilatory and erratic, and a disappointed Commons began to criticize domestic policy and royal prerogative. One of the prime sources of grievance was the monopolies.

The monopolies were nothing new in England. In order to encourage home manufacture and at the same time to regulate commerce, the Crown permitted certain people to hold the sole right to manufacture various articles or to regulate licensing. Because abuses had crept in, the subject had been thoroughly discussed in Parliament in 1601 and the Queen had graciously revoked the more obnoxious patents and declared that the legality of others might be tested in the law courts. In 1603 it had been adjudged in the case of Darcy *v.* Allen that a monopoly was illegal, but the law had not been rigidly enforced, and patents continued to be sold and passed about. In spite of the protests of Parliament in 1606, 1610, and 1614, James's need for money had led him in the last year to widen the field. As Buckingham came into power, many of the monopolies passed through his hands to his friends or relatives, and it was generally believed that they made enormous sums for themselves and the Crown by extortionate practices. An attack on the monopolies was therefore an attack on Buckingham. Commons, discreetly enough, attacked indirectly: it lit on Sir Giles Mompesson.[1]

Born in Wiltshire in 1584, Giles Mompesson matriculated at Hart Hall, Oxford, on October 24, 1600, but never took a university degree. He married about 1612 Catherine St. John, whose sister was already the wife of Edward Villiers, half-brother to the subsequent Duke of Buckingham. This connection was to prove of great value to him in his later political life. Encouraged and supported by George Villiers, Mompesson was elected to Parliament in 1614 for Great Bedwin. He was not long in reaping his own profit. Two years later he proposed to the favorite a scheme which might benefit both the Crown and himself, namely the creation of a commission to license inns. Inns would be brought under strict control, mine host would be prevented from charging exorbitantly, the impoverished exchequer would be enriched, and the commissioners would, of course, deduct a percentage for themselves. Villiers was in favor of the project, but there was some question of its legality. Attorney-General Bacon, when consulted, suggested the appointment of three judges to confer with him as referees. This was accordingly done. The judges reported unanimously in favor of the commission, and the patent was drawn up and sealed by the King's special direction, with Mompesson nominated as one of the commissioners. It was stipulated that four-fifths of the money received from licenses were to be paid in to the Treasury, but the original charge was left to the discretion of the commissioners. Meanwhile, in November of 1616, Mompesson was knighted by James at Newmarket to give authority to his office. Bacon was pleased that the corruption and dishonesty prevalent in the inns would now be definitely checked and that by the acquisition of knighthood Mompesson might "the better fight with the Bulls and the Bears, and the Saracen's Heads, and such fearful creatures."

[1] Though I have used primary sources and made a number of additions, my account of Sir Giles Mompesson follows those of Sir Sidney Lee in the *DNB* and Samuel R. Gardiner's monumental *History of England from the Accession of James I to the Outbreak of the Civil War*, which has also furnished the historical data. Except in case of additions, therefore, I have omitted bibliography in the footnotes.

Unfortunately Bacon had not judged his man correctly. No sooner was Sir Giles in power than he began to exercise his privileges with a vengeance. To quote Sir Sidney Lee, "he charged exorbitant fees, exacted heavy fines from respectable innkeepers for trifling neglect of the licensing laws, and largely increased the number of inns by granting, on payment of heavy sums, new licenses to keepers of houses that had been closed on account of disorderly conduct." There were of course protests and outcries. Mompesson, however, was clever enough to keep his sinister practices from the knowledge of those in power. If murmurs reached them, they were considered merely what was to be expected from indignant criminality as a result of the now greater strictness. He was intimate with both Buckingham and Bacon, the latter frequently discussing with him matters of revenue at conferences both public and private. In October of 1618, Mompesson's unflagging zeal in carrying out the Crown's designs was rewarded by his addition to an already existing commission whose duty it was to punish all those who without a license engaged in the manufacture of gold and silver thread. Moreover Bacon and Montague suggested to James a new plan by which "goldsmiths and silkmen might be required to enter into bonds not to sell their wares to unlicensed persons." This was accepted and passed on to the commissioners. With righteous enthusiasm which was well assumed, Mompesson and Francis Michell, his associate, called five silk-mercers before the commission and warned them that unless the bonds were sealed, "all the prisons in London should be filled, and thousands should rot in prison." Again there were murmurs of disapprobation but they seem not to have affected Mompesson or his associates, and Bacon upheld his judgments. In 1619 he acted as clerk of the council, and surveyor of the profits of the New River Company; in 1620 he was licensed to convert coal and other fuel (except wood) into charcoal.

However, Mompesson's extortion and tyranny could not last. Public feeling against the monopolies blew into a storm of protest. Bacon advised the withdrawal of some of the patents, but Buckingham persisted. In February of 1621, a committee of the whole House of Commons began an investigation into the patent for licensing inns. Witnesses were not lacking to prove that Mompesson, himself a member of the House, had perverted the King's patent to his own ends. Realizing that he had overreached himself, Sir Giles admitted his errors, but it was too late. He was vigorously examined; evidence was produced that he had threatened a justice of the peace because the latter had tried to close a disreputable house; that one of his agents had succeeded by a ruse in spending the night at an alehouse and then had fined the host for keeping a stranger overnight without an innkeeper's license. Sir Francis Michell in various instances had used his offices to support the extortionate practices of Mompesson. Coke reported to the House that Sir Giles, the original projector of the patent for licensing inns, had prosecuted thirty-three hundred and twenty innkeepers for technical breaches of obsolete statutes, and that in one county alone he had licensed sixteen inns which had previously been shut down as disorderly. His conduct as commissioner for other patents had been equally reprehensible. Mompesson was committed to the care of the sergeant-at-arms, and while charges accumulated, Commons asked the Lords for a conference to determine his punishment. On March 3, Sir Giles received permission to enter his wife's room, whence he escaped through the window and succeeded in reaching France though all ports were notified and a proclamation was issued for his arrest. He was at once expelled from his seat in the House, and a full account of his offenses was sent to the Lords. In a joint meeting on March 27 the Lord Chief Justice pronounced sentence upon him. He was to be degraded from knighthood and perpetually outlawed; his testimony was not to be received in court and he was exempt from all general pardons; he was to be imprisoned during his life and forbidden to approach within twelve miles of the court; his property was to be confiscated and he was to be fined £10,000; and finally he was forever to be held an infamous person.

Two items which concern Mompesson are important enough to deserve quotation. The first of these is a letter from Lord Zouch to Francis Wilford, lieutenant of Dover Castle, which gives orders for the apprehension of Mompesson and a description of him: "He is a little man of a black swart complection with a little black beard and of the age of about fourtie yeares."[2] The second reveals the public attitude towards Mompesson. It is stated in the *Manuscripts of the House of Lords* that "the 26th of March [is] to be kept wholly by general sermons over England to declare the king's honour and justice and the deliverance of the subject from the oppression of Mompesson and his agents."[3]

It is plain enough that Mompesson had become a monster in the public eye. A rare print compared him to the popularly notorious Sir Richard Empson, collector of taxes and fines with Edmund Dudley under Henry VII, and the names were similar enough to provoke an anagram.[4] He was charged with having mercilessly trodden on those less fortunate and more honest than himself, and with having filled his coffers with dishonest gains. The print mentioned above is in three divisions. In the first Mompesson is seen approaching an inn, The Bell, a devil's head in a patent box under one arm, and a patent in his hand. The landlady stops his entrance; on the sign of her inn is written:

> Fye S[r] Giles my bell doe not disgrace
> Pluck 'm not downe except you take his place

Sir Giles replies:

> Your signe shall downe for this

Above is a label inscribed:

> This craftie GILES through faire & false pretences
> Committinge, for redressinge foule offences
> From Tapsters tubs, from Innes moist droppinge quills
> And other crafts, with Coyne his cofers fills
> For greedie gaine hee thrust the weake to wall,
> And thereby gotte himselfe the divell and all,
> His name MO-EMPSONS Annagrame doth make

[2] *Manuscripts of the Corporation of Rye*, Historical Manuscripts Commission (London, 1892), p. 159.

[3] Fourth Report of the Royal Commission on Historical Manuscripts, Part I (London, 1874), p. 121.

[4] *The description of GILES MOMPESSON, late Knight censured by Parliament the 17th of March A° 1620.* See the *Catalogue of Prints and Drawings in the British Museum*, Division I, Political and Personal Satires (London, 1870), Vol. I, pp. 55-6. The *Catalogue* makes numerous errors of transcription. I have kept the original spelling but modernized the letters and resolved *n*-contractions.

> And Empsons courses also did hee take;
> Oppression sore hee used where hee went
> As yet not thinkinge of a Parliament.

The second picture represents Mompesson in flight, the devil whispering in his ear, "Shift for thy selfe." In the distance he is seen climbing down a rope from a second-story window and galloping off. The label reads:

> But Parliament once call'd then Giles was brought
> Unto account, contrary to his thought:
> There to the Serjeant⁵ ward hee was committed,
> Which made him much to feare, hee should be fitted
> For all those former wrongs, that hee had done;
> Which from his keeper made him here to runne;
> Hee outlawde therefore was and bannish't quite
> And also judg'd to be no more a Knight:
> Not only so but infamous inroul'd,
> Although (before) hee Justice seat controul'd.

The third picture shows Mompesson limping away on crutches with his patent box empty. Two other men on crutches hail him:

> Hoe, fellowe Giles stay for us yett a while
> For heere wee come, although behinde a mile.

Empson and Dudley are seen hobbling away.

> In first yeare of Kinge Henry last
> By Parliament to death they past

On the label above we read:

> Nowe being censur'd bannished and gone,
> With pensive speech, thus may hee mourne alone;
> Woe worthe the time when first on Innes I thought
> For private gaines when I their hindrance sought;
> Those Monopolies cursed bee with shame,
> Which have my reputation thus made lame:
> My Honours which hath turn'd to other styles
> From Sʳ Mompesson unto poore lame Giles;
> Yett haultinge nowe before, me thinks I see
> Some in the way of haultinge after mee.

¶ By the King.

¶ A Proclamation for the finding out and apprehending of
Sir *Giles Mompeſſon* Knight.

 Hereas Sir *Giles Mompeſſon*, Knight, being Convented
before our Commons house of Parliament, and there questio-
ned for many hainous offences and misdemeanours, to the into-
lerable grieuance of our good and louing Subiects, the great
dishonour of Our Person, and scandall of Our gouernment,
hath out of the guilt of his owne conscience, as it is to be presu-
med, whilest hee was there vnder examination, and for feare of
condigne punishment, which might bee inflicted vpon him for
the same, made an escape out of the custody of the Sergeant of
that house, to whom by their Order hee was committed, for se-
curitie of his person to be forth comming, vpon occasion of further triall.

Wee therefore, out of Our knowen and wonted zeale to Iustice, and out of Our tender
and princely care, that offenders of so foule a nature as this seemeth to be, vnder whose op-
pressions Our louing Subiects do so much suffer, to our great griefe and displeasure, when
we are truely informed thereof, may not escape and auoyd the hands of Iustice, but that to
the terroue and example of others, they may be brought forth to receiue their Triall, Censure and punishment according to their demerits; Doe hereby straightly charge and command, all and euery Our Lieutenants, Deputy-Lieutenants of any County within
this Our Realme, Maiors, Sheriffes, Iustices of Peace, Customers, Comptrollers, Sear-
chers, and other Officers of Our Ports, Constables, Headboroughs, and all other Our Officers and louing Subiects whatsoeuer, within Liberties or without, to vse all possible di-
ligence and indeuour, for the searching and finding out of the sayd Sir Giles Mompesson, in any
part of this Our Realme, and him to apprehend, and safely to conuey and bring vnto Our
Tower of London, and there to deliuer him into the hands of the Lieutenant of Our
Tower, to bee safely kept, vntill further order be taken by the House of Parliament for proceeding against him. And this Our Royall Commandement to bee forthwith carefully
executed, by all and euery Our said Officers, and others to whom it may in any wise apper-
taine, vpon paine of Our High displeasure; And as they will answere the contrary at their
vttermost perils.

Giuen at Our Palace of Westminster the third of March, in the eighteenth yeere of Our Reigne of
Great Britaine, France, and Ireland.

God saue the King.

¶ Imprinted at London by ROBERT BARKER, and IOHN BILL,
Printers to the Kings most Excellent Maiestie.

M. DC. XX.

"A Proclamation for the finding out and apprehending of
Sir *Giles Mompesson* Knight"

At the bottom of the print are the following verses:

> All you which Monopolies seeke for gaines,
> And faire pretences turne to other straines;
> Example take by Giles Mompessons fall,
> Least honie sweet soone turne to bitter gall.
> Which to prevent, see that you undertake
> None other thinge, but such as sure may make
> A benefite to commonwealth and Kinge,
> Which will you wealth and honour also bringe.
> For why you knowe, our gracious Kinge is bent
> To give his faithfull subjects all content;
> Where love is dwe, hee lovingly doth show't,
> Where mercies meete by pardon many know't,
> By rendringe Justice unto great and small,
> The smale ones trippe & great ones downeright fall,
> Oh what more needs a Loyall Subject crave
> Then mercy, love, and justice choice to have.

Sir Giles Mompesson rose with Buckingham; involved in his fall was a greater man, Lord Chancellor Bacon. Buckingham himself, his relatives, and friends had supported the monopolies and profited by them. When he saw himself in danger, he turned first against Mompesson, then against the referees responsible for the patents, and finally against his implicated brothers. By some nimble side-stepping he escaped impeachment, and a royal proclamation on March 30, 1621 cancelled the more hateful patents. Bacon, however, as referee for the monopolies was now held in distrust and suspicion by the House of Commons. Though it withdrew an inquiry into the conduct of the referees, his association with Buckingham counted heavily, and when charges of bribery were made against him, it sent them to the Lords. Buckingham supported his friend until he found himself in political danger, and then as usual followed his own interests. Though there is no evidence that it had ever affected his decisions, it became increasingly clear that Bacon had accepted money and presents during the progress of suits, and he was finally stripped of office and disgraced. In 1624 the Statute of Monopolies, with certain exceptions, made internal monopolies illegal. And James, who had tried to rule without Parliament, found Parliament stronger than he.

A large section of the aristocracy, brought up in the Elizabethan tradition, disapproved of the King's pacifistic and unparliamentary policies. Prominent in this group was William Herbert, third Earl of Pembroke. His views were often diametrically opposed to those of James, but since he was wealthy and popular, the King found it expedient to conciliate him, though he never loved him. Although Herbert opposed alliance with Spain, the King gave him in 1616 the office of Lord Chamberlain, for which his intelligence and amiability made him particularly fit. On the other hand, this preferment did not affect Pembroke's political views. He distrusted Buckingham and almost immediately clashed with him over patronage. In 1621, he supported the House of Commons in its demand for an inquiry into the monopolies, and disapproved of James's failure to defend the Palatinate. His protests against the dissolution of Parliament brought from Buckingham the charge that he wished to insult the King. In 1623 he courageously attacked the favorite's opinions with regard to Spain, and though a reconciliation was effected, he was soon at open variance with him in the French marriage negotiations and joined the parliamentary opposition. In short, Pembroke was in many respects anti-court, and in almost all respects anti-Buckingham.

Arthur Massinger, the father of the dramatist, was a gentleman in the service of the House of Pembroke at Wilton. Highly regarded by the second Earl, he undertook numerous confidential missions of trust, was retained by William Herbert, and held an honorable position with the family until his death in 1603.[5] His son, Philip, was born at Salisbury in 1583, and there can be little doubt that the Pembroke family early took an interest in him. Gifford conjectures that he may have been educated at Wilton,[6] and it is not unlikely that he acquired there a taste for theatrical representations. In 1602 he entered St. Alban's Hall, Oxford, according to Anthony à Wood "patronized" by the Earl of Pem-

---

[5] For biographical data on Arthur Massinger, see Chelli, pp. 39-41; Robert H. Ball, *MLN*, June 1931, Vol. XLVI, pp. 399-400; Mark Eccles, *TLS*, July 16, 1931, p. 564.

[6] Vol. I, p. xxxix; all references are to the second edition (1813) of *The Plays of Philip Massinger*; throughout this study, quotations from Massinger's plays other than *A New Way to Pay Old Debts* are from Gifford's text. Cunningham, p. viii, suggests that Massinger was a page to the Countess of Pembroke.

broke.[7] *The Bondman* was dedicated to Pembroke's brother, Philip Herbert, Earl of Montgomery: "However I could never arrive at the happiness to be made known to your lordship, yet a desire, born with me, to make a tender of all duties and service to the noble family of the Herberts, descended on me as an inheritance from my dead father. . . . The consideration of this encouraged me (having no other means to present my humblest service to your honour) to shroud this trifle under the wings of your noble protection. . . . When it was first acted, your lordship's liberal suffrage taught others to allow it for current, it having received the undoubted stamp of your lordship's allowance. . . ." Massinger's epistle dedicatory of *A New Way to Pay Old Debts* was to Robert, Earl of Carnarvon, whose wife was the daughter of Philip Herbert. Two of the dramatist's poems draw more closely the bonds which tied him to the House of Pembroke :[8] *The Copie of a Letter written upon occasion to the Earle of Pembroke Lo: Chamberlaine,* a plea for patronage addressed to William Herbert; and *Sero sed Serio,* "To the Right Honourable my most singular Lord and Patron, Philip Earl of Pembroke and Montgomery, Lord-Chamberlain of His Majesty's Household, &c. upon the deplorable and untimely Death of his late truly noble son, Charles Lord Herbert, &c," the poet's debt

> . . . being more
> Than they could owe, who since, or heretofore,
> Have labour'd with exalted lines to raise
> Brave piles, or rather pyramids of praise
> To Pembroke and his family. . . .

And finally Aubrey adds that the fourth Earl gave the playwright a pension of twenty or thirty pounds a year, which was continued to his wife after his death.[9]

Among the dramatists of his time, Philip Massinger was peculiarly apt to reflect in his plays the political conditions which surrounded him, and more apt than most to make his comments on

[7] *Athenae Oxonienses* (London, 1815), Vol. II, p. 655.

[8] Ms., G, 2, 21, pp. 554-9, Trinity College, Dublin, printed by A. B. Grosart, *Engl. Stud.*, Vol. XXVI, pp. 4-6; Percy Simpson, *Athenaeum*, September 8, 1906, p. 273; Cruickshank, pp. 208-11; Ms. British Museum, King's Library, Catalogue 1734, 18A XX, No. 4, printed by Cunningham, pp. 628-9.

[9] *Natural History of Wiltshire* (London, 1847), p. 91.

them. These views were, naturally enough, in agreement with those of the Earl of Pembroke. Over sixty years ago, Gardiner suggested that references to Gisco in *The Bondman* applied unmistakably to Buckingham; that *Believe As You List,* originally refused a license "because it did contain dangerous matter, as the deposing of Sebastian, King of Portugal, by Philip II, and there being a peace sworn twixt the Kings of England and Spain," reflected negotiations with Spain in regard to the Palatinate; and that *The Maid of Honour* contained a thinly disguised reproach of James's insufficiency in the Thirty Years War.[10] This is not a question of mere allusion, more or less satirical, to contemporary events or customs, though there is plenty of this in Massinger; it is a question of a dramatist's planning a play in such a way as to make a forthright protest, of building on social and political foundations. King Charles himself read *The King and the Subject* and marked against one passage, "This is too insolent, and to be changed." I do not mean to imply of course that Massinger was in any sense a conspirator, but that he expressed popular views, even though contrary to those of the King and his favorite, with singular courage and independence.[11]

It can therefore hardly be considered surprising that Massinger should concern himself with the monopolies.[12] In Act II, scene iii, of *The Bondman,* licensed December 3, 1623, there is evidence that he was already cognizant of extortion by patents, even so far as to refer definitely to the monopoly on gold thread:

> Observe but what a cozening look he has!—
> Hold up thy head, man; if, for drawing gallants
> Into mortgages for commodities, cheating heirs
> With your new counterfeit gold thread, and gumm'd velvets,
> He does not transcend all that went before him,
> Call in his patent.

In the industrial monopolies, business men were usually responsible for originating designs which could be turned into profits for

[10] *Contemporary Review,* August 1876, Vol. XXVIII, pp. 496-507.
[11] See on this subject, Chelli, pp. 318-28.
[12] On the economic chaos of the reign of James I and its reflection in the drama with special reference to the monopolies, see Knights, particularly pp. 71-88, 124-6, 134-6, 173-6, 200-27, 233-4, 259-69, 273-92.

themselves and the court. These projectors Massinger bitingly took
to task in Pulcheria's speech in Act I, scene ii, of *The Emperor of
the East,* licensed March 11, 1631; nor does the Crown itself escape:

> Projector, I treat first
> Of you and your disciples; you roar out,
> All is the king's, his will above his laws;
> And that fit tributes are too gentle yokes
> For his poor subjects: whispering in his ear,
> If he would have their fear, no man should dare
> To bring a salad from his country garden,
> Without the paying gabel; kill a hen,
> Without excise: and that if he desire
> To have his children or his servants wear
> Their heads upon their shoulders, you affirm
> In policy 'tis fit the owner should
> Pay for them by the poll; or, if a prince want
> A present sum, he may command a city
> Impossibilities, and for non-performance,
> Compel it to submit to any fine
> His officers shall impose. Is this the way
> To make our emperor happy? can the groans
> Of his subjects yield him music? must his thresholds
> Be wash'd with widows and wrong'd orphans' tears,
> Or his power grow contemptible?

But though these references are deliberately "near a late and sad
example," they are not architectonic. One might expect that Massinger would employ the monopolies or some of the leading figures
involved in them as part of the basic structure of a play. And that
is precisely what Massinger did in *A New Way to Pay Old Debts,*
when he took the notorious Sir Giles Mompesson and transformed
him into Sir Giles Overreach.[13]

It is not possible to state precisely when Massinger's *A New Way
to Pay Old Debts* was first produced. It was entered on the Station-
ers' Registers "under the hands of Sir Henry Herbert and Master
Aspley" on November 10, 1632; and the first and only Quarto was
"Printed by E.P. [Elizabeth Pursloe] for Henry Seyle" in 1633,
"As it hath beene often acted at the Phoenix in Drury-Lane, by the

---

[13] The relation between Overreach and Mompesson was first noted by Gifford, Vol. III, pp. 517 *ff.*

Queenes Maiefties feruants." Since Massinger seems to have become definitely connected with the King's Company in 1629 if not
earlier,[14] we may confidently assign the first production to a period
before that date. Various allusions in the play to a state of war
strengthen this view, for peace with France was declared in April
1629, and with Spain in 1630. On the other hand, we may assume
from a reference in Act I, scene ii, ll. 25-8 that the play was written
after the first of July, 1625, when Breda, besieged for ten months,
surrendered to Spinola; and it could not have been produced before
December 1625, when Queen Henrietta's Company reopened the
Phoenix, previously occupied by Princess Elizabeth's men and
closed since May on account of the plague.[15] The date of first production falls therefore between 1625 and 1629. Allowing a certain
amount of time for Massinger to write the play, and considering
the nature of the reference to the siege of Breda, which is the more
apt the sooner after the event, I am inclined to give the first production of the play the approximate date of 1626.[16]

At first sight it seems a bit odd that Massinger's play should not
be publicly produced until five years after the climax of Mompesson's career. On the other hand, the Statute of Monopolies was not
passed until 1624, and possibly so thoroughgoing an exposure had
best attend a propitious hour. Moreover the continuance of Sir
Giles's unsavory reputation would still make *A New Way to Pay
Old Debts* of topical importance in 1626. For one thing, Mompesson, in spite of severe prohibitions, had succeeded in returning to

---

[14] Chelli, pp. 345-6.

[15] All references are to the edition by A. H. Cruickshank. For an account of
Queen Henrietta's Company and the Phoenix, see Murray, Vol. I, pp. 265-70;
Adams, pp. 348-68.

[16] Although he does not definitely reject a later date, A. K. McIlwraith, *MLR,*
Vol. XXVIII, pp. 431-8, has recently stated the case for 1621. I am not primarily
concerned here with this question, but it must be pointed out that if the earlier
date is accepted, some of the difficulties inherent in this chapter are automatically
removed, since it is no longer necessary to explain the gap between Mompesson's
sentence and the production of the play. I should much rather, therefore, be content with 1621. Unfortunately, though Professor McIlwraith's arguments are
careful and ingenious, I am not prepared to reject, as he does, the reference to
Spinola and the fall of Breda as a later interpolation. Ward, Vol. III, p. 21,
thinks that the lines from Act III, scene i, which refer to the extent of the falcon's
flight in one day, are echoed by similar lines in Act I, scene iii, of *The Roman
Actor.* He, therefore, dates the play before *The Roman Actor,* which was licensed October 11, 1626.

England for periods of various duration, and in 1623 had the colossal audacity "to put his patents for alehouses, &c., in execution, they not having been abrogated by Act of Parliament."[17] The popular feeling which resulted from this would certainly keep Mompesson's name alive. At length Sir Giles seems to have been successful in evading orders to leave the country, or else the voice of authority sank to a whisper, for from 1630 he lived in retirement in Wiltshire, where he is mentioned as late as 1651. Even here he contrived to make himself unpopular, as we learn from a letter from Sir John Kyrle to Sir John Coke, Knight, principal secretary to his Majesty, dated April 6, 1631 :[18]

> Sir Giles Mompesson making his repair to Wilton to the house of Sir Giles Bridges did then and there in the behalf of the Lady Villiers consult and devise how and which way he might best improve a good part of the Forest of Dean called Mailscott, which they pretend was given by King James to Sir Edward Villiers. It was at length agreed by Sir Giles and his associates to inclose it, which was begun, and he eftsoones put men to work to dig for coals. The foresters grieved with this attempt of his, some twenty persons threw part of the inclosure in again, not without opprobrious words uttered by them against the said Mompesson, whom they termed to be an odious projector. All this did not qualify him, for he notwithstanding put men eftsoons on work there to dig for coals. This did stir up and exasperate their giddy brains, and seconded their first attempt by sound of drum and ensigns in most rebellious manner, carrying a picture or statue apparelled like Mompesson and with great noise and clamour threw it into the coalpits which the said Sir Giles had digged. On the 5th April the commoners in a new fury assembled together with sound of drums, ensigns displayed, and in warlike manner did enter into the Forest and then and there without any resistance have committed many insolent and fearful parts, by breaking open the inclosures, destroying a ropehouse, burning some houses, and proclaimed that they would assemble again upon Saturday next, being Easter eve, with a far greater power to finish their work. The number assembled were (as is conceived) 3,000.

[17] *Calendar of State Papers*, Domestic, 1623-1625, Entry July 12, 1623, p. 13. Chamberlain to Carleton.

[18] *Manuscripts of the Earl Cowper, K.G. preserved at Melbourne Hall, Derbyshire*, Historical Manuscripts Commission (London, 1888), Vol. I, pp. 429-30.

The gap between the investigation and sentence of Sir Giles Mompesson and the production of Massinger's play should therefore excite no wonder. At least ten years after the decline of his power, Mompesson's name was anathema, and we need no further explanation to discover why Sir Henry Moody in his prefatory verses commended the playwright for having found a plot "so proper to the time."[19]

When the character of Sir Giles Overreach was acted on the stage, it must have been perfectly evident to a good many of his audience whence Massinger had drawn the basic characteristics. Both bear the name Sir Giles, a name apparently so despised that its application would be immediately recognizable and so familiar in its attachment to one person that it would be as plain a means of identification as, say, John D. is today. Mompesson of course gives way to the "humours" name of Overreach, which describes both characters equally well. Both are to the popular eye cruel extortioners, selfish, pitiless, trampling on the poor, scheming, remorseless villains. Certainly the references in the play to commissions[20] must have had to those hearing it an ominous sound. Both Mompesson and Overreach have subservient justices who work for the ends of their masters in defiance of equity and law.[21] Moreover, Overreach, through his henchmen, so controls Tapwell, an alehouse keeper, that the latter refuses to allow Wellborn to set foot in his house, until the orders are countermanded. Note also that Tapwell's is a place of ill repute ("As the receiving of stolne goods, and bawdrie"—Act IV, scene ii, l. 12) and yet through the connivance of Overreach it remains open—actually the kind of practice which

---

[19] Pembroke, whose seat was at Wilton, became warden of the Forest of Dean in 1608. My colleague, Dr. Fredson T. Bowers, reminds me that Thomas Randolph refers to Mompesson (edition W. C. Hazlitt, Vol. I, p. 16; Vol. II, p. 456) in *Aristippus* and *Hey for Honesty*, both produced at Cambridge after Randolph's matriculation in 1624, further evidence that at the quarter century and later, Mompesson's "persecution of innocent tapsters" was still news.

[20] Act I, scene ii, l. 42; I, iii, l. 26; II, i, ll. 1-22; III, ii, l. 306.

[21] On Michell, see William Carr in the *DNB*. He was justice for Middlesex; "stimulated by the activity of Mompesson, he exercised his powers corruptly and with considerable harshness for two years, thereby incurring great odium." Gifford also suggests (Vol. III, pp. 517 *ff.*) that Michell's clerk may have sat for the portrait of Marrall; Professor McIlwraith in the article already cited (pp. 433-4) gives additional evidence for the relationship between Michell and Greedy.

we found associated with Sir Giles Mompesson's name—until Wellborn influences Justice Greedy to call in the license and tear down the sign (Act IV, scene ii, ll. 60-2, 76-9). We have seen that Massinger had close connections with Pembroke, who supported the inquiry into the monopolies, and that he had already referred in *The Bondman* to one of the patents of which Mompesson was commissioner. Last, remember that Massinger was of a prominent Salisbury family, and that Mompesson was closely connected with Wiltshire and that his mother came from Salisbury, and you have added reason for Massinger's interest in the man and for his knowledge of the circumstances. It can be fairly stated that in broad outlines Sir Giles Mompesson and Sir Giles Overreach are recognizably similar.

If, however, certain basic traits appear both in the historical figure and the dramatic character, it is not to be assumed that the two figures are identical. Massinger did not attempt to present Mompesson with photographic exactness. He copied from life only with rough preliminary strokes; the detail was filled in with his own imagination. Overreach is not in office, and there are no specific references in this play to the patents with which Mompesson was connected. There is no story concerning Mompesson which is similar to the plot of *A New Way to Pay Old Debts.* The resemblances are basic and suggestive, generalities upon which the playwright impressed his own art to form an individual creation, resemblances having to do with certain straight lines of character rather than the labyrinthine elements of the story by which the character is revealed.

It seems clear that the main features of the plot by which Sir Giles Overreach was to be revealed were suggested to Massinger by Thomas Middleton's popular play, *A Trick to Catch the Old One,* first published in 1608. In both plays an extortionate uncle, after having done his nephew out of his lands, is gulled by the nephew; in both it is the supposed affection of a rich widow for the nephew which supplies the bait; in both the uncle restores his nephew to favor and pays off his creditors; in both, in short, a spider is caught in a web of his own weaving. Moreover, the resemblance does not end there. There is evidence in plenty that in language, situations, and the development of ideas, Massinger followed the earlier dramatist.[22] Yet when all is said, one is struck more by the difference between the two plays than by their resemblance. The tone of the plays is not the same, the effects produced are at variance, the major characters are not alike. And especially the importance of the characterization of Sir Giles Overreach and *his* importance to the play heighten the dissimilarities and give the impression that the point of departure was his character and the rest only a means of expressing it. We must remember too that gulling was a favorite theme of the Elizabethans, and one which, dramatically at least, came to them from Latin comedy. It is therefore illogical and misleading to speak of *A Trick to Catch the Old One* as the *source* of *A New Way to Pay Old Debts,* and equally misleading and illogical to think of the latter play as primarily an adaptation or alteration of the earlier work, in spite of the fact that they have a common theme, and in part a common method. It should not be entirely forgotten, moreover, that Throate in Lording Barry's *Ram Alley* is tricked in much the same way as Sir Giles, Hoard, and Lucre.[23] Finally, therefore, all that need be and should be said is that Massinger, casting about for the means by which Sir Giles was to be circumvented, remembered *A Trick to Catch the Old One,* used it, and improved upon it. We must not fail to give Massinger credit because, like many playwrights of his time, he refashioned for his own purposes material from an earlier play, nor fail to see the originality in his attack. The details, the characterizations in general, the methods, the emphasis, the ends seem largely to be the work of Massinger himself.[24]

In summary then the antecedents of the subject of our biography are the character of Sir Giles Mompesson, the extortionate commissioner of patents, and the dramatist, Philip Massinger, who

[22] For an elaborate study of the relationship between the two plays, see Marston Balch, *The Dramatic Legacy of Thomas Middleton*, Chap. II. (Unpublished Harvard doctoral dissertation, 1930.)

[23] Curiously enough, Ram Alley is mentioned in Massinger's play (Act II, scene ii, l. 123)—not that this is significant!

[24] For a more conventional statement of the relationship, see Emil Koeppel, "Quellen-Studien zu den Dramen George Chapman's, Philip Massinger's und John Ford's, *Quellen und Forschungen* . . . , Vol. LXXXII, pp. 137-40. According to Koeppel, the whole intrigue is borrowed from Middleton; Mompesson is relegated to one sentence of a footnote on the ground that Gifford's suggestion, though interesting, cannot be checked.

reworked the historical figure into the dramatic character, and who, though he must acknowledge indebtedness to Middleton, was the principal architect for the plot in which his leading character was to live and move and have his being.

Since we are to trace the life of Sir Giles Overreach, we must endeavor to find his first embodiment, the first means by which he was presented in flesh and blood on the stage. Who were the actors who took part in this production? Is it possible to pick out from them that one who first presented in reality what the imagination of Philip Massinger had conceived as Sir Giles Overreach?

In the first place it is clear enough from the title-page that *A New Way to Pay Old Debts* was presented by Queen Henrietta's Company at the Phoenix, or, as it was sometimes called, the Cockpit, in Drury Lane. Fortunately six extant plays acted by this company include partial casts. These plays, all produced between 1626 and 1636, are Shirley's *Wedding,* Davenport's *King John and Matilda,* Massinger's *Renegado,* Heywood's *Fair Maid of the West* (Parts I and II), and Nabbes' *Hannibal and Scipio.*[25] It appears from these actor-lists and from Wright's *Historia Histrionica*—I quote from the latter—that "Those of principal note at the Cock-pit, were Perkins, Michael Bowyer, Sumner, William Allen, and Bird, eminent actors, and Robins[on], a comedian."[26] It is reasonable to suppose therefore that the original representative of the part of Sir Giles Overreach is to be found among these actors.

It seems to me most logical to assume that Richard Perkins was the man for whom we are seeking. Wright mentions him first in his list; he was certainly the most eminent and the best known of the company. That he was a player of considerable experience by the time *A New Way to Pay Old Debts* was produced is plain, since he was a member of Worcester's Company as early as 1602. After this group became Queen Anne's Company, numerous references indicate his prominence. When John Webster's *White Devil* was printed in 1612, the playwright took the occasion in an appended note to commend the actors who had presented his play, "whereof

[25] For these actor-lists, see Murray, Vol. I, pp. 265-70; for what is known about the actors, see Nungezer, *A Dictionary of Actors . . , s.v.*
[26] pp. 4-5.

as I make a generall acknowledgment, so in particular I must remember the well approved industry of my friend Maister Perkins, and confesse the worth of his action did crowne both the beginning and end." At the funeral of Queen Anne on May 13, 1619, he attended as a representative of her London company. The company thereafter became the Players of the Revels at the Red Bull, and in 1622 Perkins is mentioned as one of the "chief players."[27] When it was disbanded in 1623, Perkins went over to the King's Company and sometime after the death of James, whose funeral he attended, he became a member of the company which produced *A New Way to Pay Old Debts*. With Queen Henrietta's Company, according to the actor-lists previously cited, he played Sir John Belfare in Shirley's *Wedding*, Fitzwater in Davenport's *King John and Matilda*, Captain Goodlack in Heywood's *Fair Maid of the West*, and Hanno in Nabbes' *Hannibal and Scipio*. In *King John and Matilda*, it is specifically mentioned that his "action gave grace to the play." Heywood's prologue to the 1633 edition of Marlowe's *Jew of Malta* makes it plain that he played Barabas in the revival of that play by the Queen's Company at the Cockpit. When the company was reorganized in 1637 by amalgamation with the Revels Company at Salisbury Court, Perkins apparently became one of the managers, a position retained until the closing of the theatres. He has been identified with the Richard Perkins whose death is recorded in 1650 in the register of St. James, Clerkenwell. He contributed prefatory verses to Heywood's *Apology for Actors*, calling him his "loving friend and fellow." Dulwich College, appropriately enough, has his portrait.[28] Obviously Perkins was a person of some importance and an actor of the first rank.

Besides his eminence in the profession, moreover, the list of his known parts contributes evidence that it was most likely he who first acted Sir Giles. A man of middle age, he was evidently suited to play fathers as his line. *The Wedding*, and *King John and Matilda*, the two plays having actor-lists nearest in time to the production of *A New Way to Pay Old Debts*, both presented him in this type of rôle. Moreover that he acted the heavy part of Barabas constitutes further testimony. And last, none of the other actors of

[27] Adams (ed.), *Herbert*, p. 63.
[28] Warner, p. 207.

the company appears to be so fitted or so disposed to play such a part as Sir Giles Overreach. Unless other evidence is forthcoming, Mr. Richard Perkins must make his bow as the first representative of Massinger's extortioner.

To assign the other actors of the company to parts in the first production may be a pleasant game, but so sparse and contradictory is the evidence that it can be only a game. Michael Bowyer's line appears to have been the young but matured first lover, though distinctly not the juvenile lead. He therefore may have played Wellborn or Lord Lovell. In the latter event John Sumner was perhaps the Wellborn. William Allen in at least two cases played villains, but apparently he is neither a lover nor a father; very hesitantly, I conjecture that he acted Marrall. Since William Robinson was known as a comedian, it is easy to assume that he may have played Justice Greedy—easy but perhaps misleading, for two centuries later Munden preferred Marrall. As a possible juvenile lead, John Young may have been Allworth. Since Hugh Clark is known to have played two leading female parts, perhaps we can assign him to Lady Allworth; since he could play Hubert in *King John and Matilda* about 1629, he seems to have been older than the average heroine and therefore more suited to this part than to the younger and less important Margaret. This last may have been acted by Edward Rogers, Theophilus Bird, or John Page, with the guesses in that order.

That the play was popular in Massinger's own time there can be little doubt. The title-page of the Quarto tells us that it was "often acted," and the commendatory verses are extravagantly eulogistic. Thomas Jay's lines, it is true, praise the dramatist more than this particular work, but Sir Henry Moody's verses are directly on "his comoedie." The latter say in part (the reader should repunctuate):

> Tis a rare charity, and thou couldst not
> So proper to the time have found a plot:
> Yet whilst you teach to pay, you lend, the age
> We wretches live in; that to come, the stage,
> The thronged audience that was thither brought
> Invited by your fame, and to be taught
> This lesson. All are growne indebted more,
> And when they looke for freedome ran in score.

Fortunately, however, we do not have to depend merely on the evidence of the Quarto. We know from the *Account Books of the Clifford Family* that the play was on the stage in 1635.[29] Under that year is the following item: "To a certeyne company of roguish players who represented 'A New Way to Pay Old Debts'. . £1.0.0." This production was at Skipton Castle, the seat of the Cliffords. Murray comments: "On the same visit they seem to have played *The Knight of the Burning Pestle,* in which they were assisted by one 'Adam Gerdler, whom my Lord sent for from York to act a part.' As both these plays are mentioned as acted by the Queen's company in London, there can be little doubt that the players performing them before Lord Clifford were the Queen's travelling company."

On May 10, 1636, the London theatres were ordered closed because of the ravages of the plague, and except for a short interval in February of the following year they remained closed until October 2, 1637. By this time the Queen's Company had been disbanded or, to be more accurate, the majority of the actors had united themselves with the Revels Company at Salisbury Court. The company thus formed continued to be called the Queen's. Meanwhile Christopher Beeston's boys had taken over the Cockpit, at least two of the actors of the old Queen's Company, Theophilus Bird (Bourne) and Ezekiel Fenn, and apparently the Queen's Company's plays. On August 10, 1639, was issued an order giving William Beeston, who had taken over the management from Christopher, the acting rights to forty-five plays, and prohibiting all other companies from using them. This order was probably made necessary because the new Queen's Company at Salisbury Court still continued to act some of the old Queen's Company's plays. Among those mentioned in the order are five included in the Massinger corpus: *The Bondman, The Renegado, The Great Duke of Florence, The Maid of Honour,* and *A New Way to Pay Old Debts.* In 1640 William Beeston was removed from the management of the company and William Davenant was appointed his successor. The company, under Davenant, acted at the Cockpit

[29] Murray, Vol. II, pp. 104-5, 255; the remainder of this chapter is summarized from Murray, Vol. I, pp. 267-9, 367-70.

until the closing of the theatres, in 1642. We have of course no direct evidence of any definite performance of *A New Way to Pay Old Debts* by Beeston's or Davenant's company, but since the play is specifically mentioned in the order of August 10, 1639, it is highly probable that it was acted intermittently until the beginning of the Puritan interregnum.

CHAPTER II

RUSTICATION AND RETURN

A FTER the Restoration, Sir Giles Overreach, not unlike many precociously popular children, suffered temporary neglect. His very wickedness was considered uncouth, deficient in those elements of wit and subtlety which the time demanded. Sensitive as always, this loss of attention seriously affected his health, and he went into a state of decline so dangerous that his life hung in the balance. Physicians, recognizing that the case was psychological, could do nothing for him. In short, there was little if any indication that the man, if he survived at all, would ever again seriously affect a large number of people, or be thought anything more than an awkward country knight between whom and "true Gentry" there was "a strange Antipathie." Sir Giles at court or in a London drawing-room would have seemed a subject for crushing ridicule, more fatal than a sword thrust.

A New Way to Pay Old Debts was not reprinted until 1744. Among the plays allotted to Killigrew in 1668/9 are seven by Massinger: *The Duke of Milan, The Unnatural Combat, The Guardian, The Bashful Lover, The Emperor of the East, The Fatal Dowry,* and *The Roman Actor,* but there is no mention of *A New Way to Pay Old Debts.*[1] *The Renegado, The Roman Actor, The Virgin Martyr,* and *The Bondman* were all definitely produced in London in Restoration times, the last a popular success, but London ignored Sir Giles Overreach.[2]

---

[1] For this list see Nicoll, *Restoration Drama,* Appendix B, p. 315. I assume that *The Guardian* was Massinger's play rather than Cowley's, since the latter was produced by the Duke's Company.

[2] Adams (ed.) *Herbert,* pp. 116-18; Downes (ed. M. Summers), *Roscius Anglicanus,* pp. 18, 161-3; McAfee, *Pepys on the Restoration Stage,* pp. 116, 118. On the whole subject of presentation and adaptation of Massinger's plays in the Restoration period, see James G. McManaway, *ELH,* December 1934, Vol. I, pp. 276-304. J. H. Wilson in his *Influence of Beaumont and Fletcher on Restoration Drama,* p. 126, has been curiously misled. A play attributed to Aphra Behn called *The Debauchee, or the Credulous Cuckold* was acted at Dorset Garden in 1677 (Genest, Vol. I, pp. 206-7). It was revived at Drury Lane on August 4, 1708, as *The Debauchee, or a New Way to Pay Old Debts* (Genest,

Nor was *A New Way to Pay Old Debts,* in any proper sense of the word, "adapted" for Restoration audiences, though matter from it is possibly or plainly borrowed in a number of instances. Some years ago Professor Saintsbury, and lately Montague Summers, pointed out that the incident of the disappearing ink by which Lady Cheatly cozens her creditors in Shadwell's *A. True Widow* (1678) bears certain resemblances to the trick by which Sir Giles is over-reached in *A New Way to Pay Old Debts.*[3] It is of course possible that some sort of an idea may have been given to Shadwell by Massinger's play; it is however necessary to point out that in Shadwell the ink is plainly of the type which fades until it is illegible, while in Massinger, though the incident is not entirely clear, Marrall seems to have tampered with the ink of already composed documents in order to erase the words. When one considers the multifarious possibilities of what *might* have been the source of the incident in Shadwell, whether from literature or life, it is surely being much too positive to say that *A New Way to Pay Old Debts* "would undoubtedly seem" to have provided it.

Chelli points out a vague resemblance between Massinger's plays and Mrs. Behn's *The City Heiress* (1682).[4] Mrs. Behn's piece is really a noose for Whigs and Commonwealth, and only a part of it bears any resemblance to *A New Way to Pay Old Debts.* Sir Timothy Treat-all, "an old seditious knight," cuts off his profligate Tory nephew, Tom Wilding, who has eloped with Mrs. Charlot Gettall, a city heiress, and made her his mistress. Tom wishes to persuade Sir Timothy that he is about to marry her and by appearing to come into wealth to obtain possession of certain papers of Sir Timothy's which make everything over to him. To that end he succeeds in inserting into Sir Timothy's house another mistress from his apparently inexhaustible supply, Diana, who is disguised as Mrs. Charlot. But Sir Timothy does not turn over the papers, which later have to be stolen, and he marries the supposed heiress,

Vol. II, p. 405). Wilson therefore gives revivals of Massinger's play in 1677 and 1708. As a matter of fact *The Debauchee* is an adaptation of Brome's *Mad Couple Well Match't.*

[3] Saintsbury (ed.), *Shadwell,* p. 121; Summers (ed.), *Shadwell,* Vol. III, p. 280. See *A True Widow,* Act III, scene i; *A New Way to Pay Old Debts,* Act IV, scene ii, ll. 122-9; Act V, scene i, ll. 183-93, 322-34.

[4] Chelli, *Étude,* p. 285, n. 1.

which was not in accord with Tom's original plan. The ending is typical: Sir Timothy is made ridiculous, Tom weds the real Mrs. Charlot, and his friend Sir Charles Merriwell, who is only bold when pot-valiant, marries Lady Galliard, a widow whom Tom has seduced. The plot is all very bawdy and considerably more complicated than my summary would indicate. So characteristic is it of a certain type of Restoration play that it is difficult to see here any real indebtedness to Massinger; at the most it shows the most superficial kind of borrowing, and I frankly doubt whether there is even that.

There can be little doubt, however, that Sir Giles Overreach provided inspiration—if one can call it that—for the character of Sir Marmaduke Seldin in John Lacy's *Sir Hercules Buffoon; or the Poetical Squire,* produced at Dorset Garden in 1684.[5] Sir Marmaduke storms at his daughter, Mariana, when she objects to his proposal to appropriate his wards' fortune (Act I, scene i); is deceived by her and her sister, Fidelia, who feign compliance with his wish that they impersonate the heiresses (Act II, scene i); protests that he wishes to marry her to Lord Arminger only to set her "upon the highest pinnacle of pride" (Act II, scene v); arranges for Fidelia to be fashionably dressed for the deception (Act III, scene i); after Lord Arminger is introduced, leaves him alone with Mariana, who explains that there are reasons why she cannot marry him (Act IV, scene i), and reveals to him the plot (Act IV, scene ii); when his machinations are betrayed, stabs Mariana, is disarmed of his sword, swears revenge (Act V, scene ii), and loses his mind (Act V, scene iii). Throughout these scenes, the language and minor business are reminiscent of those in the corresponding scenes of *A New Way to Play Old Debts.*[6] In short there is evidence aplenty of the appropriation of material from the earlier play; and if one doubted that Lacy had Massinger before him, the doubts would be removed by the obvious borrowings from *The City Madam* as well.

Edward Ravenscroft, too, seems definitely to have made use of characters and incidents from *A New Way to Pay Old Debts,* this

---

[5] So dated by Nicoll, *Restoration Drama,* p. 367; Summers, *Bibliography,* p. 83, says April-May 1682.

[6] Act III, scene ii; V, i.

in *The Canterbury Guests: or, A Bargain Broken,* acted at the Theatre Royal, Drury Lane, in September, 1694, and printed in the following year. The play, as Genest pointed out long ago, is decidedly eclectic, Massinger being only one of the playwrights from whom Ravenscroft has borrowed.[7] The plot need not concern us in detail. Alderman Furr brings his daughter, Jacinta, to Canterbury to marry old Sir Barnaby Buffler, whose humour it is to speak in proverbs. Jacinta is loved by Lovell, Sir Barnaby's half-brother; her cousin, Hillaria, attracts the attention of Lovell's dissolute friend, Careless. The contract, witnessed by Justice Greedy, is signed by the unwilling Jacinta and Sir Barnaby, whose sister meanwhile forms with the humorous sea-captain, Durzo, the third pair of lovers. From then on the plot gives way to the usual series of farcical scenes with the ladies and gallants precariously distributed, and with the inevitable Restoration wenches more embroiling the fray. In the end, Sir Barnaby and Furr, convinced of Jacinta's guilt, give over her roguish innocence to Lovell, and the other pairs of lovers are properly, though cynically, united.

This brief résumé makes it clear that the plot bears little or no likeness to that of *A New Way to Pay Old Debts.* The relationship lies in certain of the minor characters and incidents. The name, Lovell, may have been borrowed from Massinger. Sir Barnaby's scrivener, Dash, acts at table much like Marrall at Lady Allworth's dinner, from which scene the incident is obviously borrowed. Resemblances between Careless and Wellborn, Furr and Sir Giles are too minor to provoke comment. Justice Greedy, however, in character and in action is plainly enough Massinger's figure of the same name. As Sir Giles would say, "Some fury's in that gut." As in the earlier drama, Greedy is appointed to make arrangements for the feasting and exults in his absolute authority in his temple, the kitchen; like his forerunner, he is impatient of any delay in sitting down to table; he insists on interrupting an important consultation to complain that the cook will not obey his orders; and finally, at the wedding dinner for which he has so carefully prepared, the arrival of extra guests makes it necessary for him to

[7] Genest, Vol. II, pp. 57-8. I am indebted, however, to Dr. J. G. McManaway of the Folger Library for pointing out to me the relationship between the two plays.

eat elsewhere. Patently Justice Greedy is Justice Greedy. The play, however, is an isolated instance and seems not to have been revived. Justice Greedy, like his more distinguished companion, was wasting away.[8]

Only one man apparently did what he could to minister to the failing health of Sir Giles; that man was in all probability the somewhat eccentric and altogether extraordinary George Jolly.[9] Jolly first emerges from obscurity as the leader of a band of strolling players in Germany in 1648. English himself and at first with English actors, he presented plays in various sections of Germany intermittently until 1660. He had employed actresses in his troupe as early as 1654, the first English manager to do so, though the ladies and indeed most of his company by this time were probably Germans. Jolly has another claim to distinction in that his company played before Charles II at Frankfort in 1655 as The King's Servants, an occurrence which doubtless explains the royal favor extended to him when he returned to England at the Restoration. Notwithstanding his previous sanctioning of a virtual monopoly of the English theatre by Davenant and Killigrew, Charles on December 24, 1660, granted full power to Jolly to form a company of his own and erect a theatre. Consequently Jolly got together a company of players and hired the Cockpit, and later the theatre

---

[8] Since I shall not return later to the subject of borrowing from *A New Way to Pay Old Debts*, it may be well to point out here that the *Biographia Dramatica*, Vol. III, p. 140 (and see A. Nicoll, *A History of Late Eighteenth Century Drama*, p. 113) gives Justice Greedy in Massinger's play as the source of Sir Gregory Craveall (Famish) in *The Peruvian*, acted at Covent Garden on March 18, 1786 (Genest, Vol. VI, p. 397). *The Peruvian* is of furious unimportance, but I am somewhat skeptical of the relationship. It is true that the source of the main plot is Marmontel's *L'Amitié à l'Epreuve*, as the anonymous authoress herself states, and that the character in question is not to be found there; it is also true that Craveall has to a certain extent the eating humor. On the other hand, the point is made little of in the play, Sir Gregory's greatest indulgence being apparently in taking a cup of chocolate; his character of the gouty old fool with pretensions to love is not at all like that of Greedy; and, besides, to show that two people overindulge their appetites is not sufficient grounds for establishing their relationship. The authoress, by the way, expressly states of the comic scenes of the play of which Sir Gregory is a part that they are "merely Children of the Writer's fancy." They are such silly children that I am inclined to take her word.

[9] For George Jolly, see J. Leslie Hotson, *The Commonwealth and Restoration Stage*, pp. 167-96.

in Salisbury Court. Of course, Davenant and Killigrew were not entirely satisfied with the new trinity. They conceived the idea of renting Jolly's grant from him, and pushing him out into the country where he could not interfere. This they did on December 30, 1662; two days later Jolly received letters of authorization to raise a company of players to act outside London. Soon after Jolly had departed for the provinces, Davenant and Killigrew represented to the King that they had *bought* his warrant, that they would therefore like to have it revoked and a new one made out to them, so that they might have a complete monopoly, and permission to build a third playhouse to be used as a nursery for training actors for the two regular companies. Needless to say, when Jolly heard of this business, there were indignant protests. It is hardly to my purpose to go into the matter in detail; suffice it to say that Jolly finally regained some of his rights, and became manager of the Nursery, where no doubt he was preposterously cheated by both Davenant and Killigrew.

It was while George Jolly was touring in the provinces, however, that his company probably played *A New Way to Pay Old Debts*,[10] Dr. Edward Browne, the eldest son of Sir Thomas Browne, records in his notebook that he saw "at the Kings Armes Norwich" the following plays: *"Tu quoque, Pinner of Wakefield, Girle worth Gold, Tis pity Shee is a whore, The little Thiefe,* and *A new way to pay old debts;* also *The fair quarrell, Ignoramus,* and *Mulialses."*[11] The list is undated but entries begin at least in the summer of 1662 and cannot be later than the spring of 1664, when Browne left for the Continent. We know that when he graduated from Trinity College, Cambridge, in 1663, he returned to Norwich. Now early in 1663 George Jolly and his provincial company also appeared at Norwich, and on April 15 received permission to play "at the Kings armes in this Citty." On August 3, a second entry in the Mayor's Court Book records that Jolly and his troupe received permission to play five weeks longer. It would appear, then, that the company acted at Norwich from the middle of April until sometime in September 1663. In all probability therefore it

---

[10] Bernard M. Wagner, "George Jolly at Norwich," *RES,* October 1930, pp. 449-52.
[11] British Museum, Ms. Sloane 1900.

was a part of George Jolly's *repertoire* that Dr. Edward Browne recorded in his notebook; at any rate it is there we find the only record of the acting of *A New Way to Pay Old Debts* in the Restoration period. The admission, incidentally, appears to have been 1s. 6d.

A glance at the other plays named by Browne in his list may be significant. *"Tu quoque"* is of course the play usually known as *Greene's Tu Quoque* because of the success of the actor, Thomas Greene, in the part of Bubble; it was apparently written by Jo. Cooke and produced in 1611. *"Pinner of Wakefield"* is *George a Greene,* usually ascribed to Robert Greene and performed sometime before 1593. *"Girle worth Gold"* is merely the subtitle of Heywood's *Fair Maid of the West.* Ford's tragedy of incest needs no identification. *"The little Thiefe"* is the second title for Fletcher's *The Nightwalker,* an early comedy of intrigue touched up by Shirley and printed in 1640. Middleton's and Rowley's *A Fair Quarrel* was printed in 1617. *Ignoramus,* by George Ruggle, was produced before the King at Cambridge in 1615. *"Mulialses"* is presumably John Mason's *Muleasses the Turk,* presented in 1607. Surely it is plain that *A New Way to Pay Old Debts* is in strange and strangely assorted company. *The Nightwalker* sounds a distinctly Restoration note, and the satire of *Ignoramus,* translated into English, might still be effective, but why in these times such old stuff as *Greene's Tu Quoque,* why a play in praise of English yeomanry, why the distinctly Elizabethan *Fair Maid of the West* and the extravagantly melodramatic *Muleasses the Turk?* The point is that Jolly was producing the successes of a past era for the consumption of provincial audiences not yet ready for the polished wit and cynical urbanity of Restoration London. The inclusion of *A New Way to Pay Old Debts* among Jolly's plays, therefore, interesting though it may be, is no indication that it enjoyed any popularity in the theatrical center. It means, on the contrary, that Sir Giles Overreach was vacationing in the country with a few old-fashioned fellows who understood him, because he found himself outmoded in his native London.

The explanation for the almost complete disappearance of *A New Way to Pay Old Debts* is not far to seek, and the subject needs no learned disquisition. To take the whole Restoration period in one paragraph, the play was simply not one which a typical London audience would have enjoyed. Massinger is not distinguished by an amoral suavity. There is a world of difference between this drama and the comedy of manners, the comedy of humors, or the comedy of intrigue of the period. *A New Way to Pay Old Debts* is a comedy largely in that it has a happy ending for the virtuous characters and retribution for the unscrupulous. Except in its byplay it is somewhat grim. It is not meant primarily to be a picture of manners. Its purpose is to tell a highly edifying story about an extortioner. In that story there are definite characters and strong passions expressed in blunt language. Wit and grace are lacking; the intrigue does not exist for itself but for the plot; the dialogue is not "refined"; the play is moral rather than cynical, emotional rather than "artificial." That some of Massinger's tragedies and more heroic comedies were revived is another matter; there are similarities between Massinger and Otway. But Massinger is poles apart from the series of dramatists from Etherege to Congreve, from Shadwell to Aphra Behn, who, if they do not always represent the common fare of the Restoration theatre-goer, crystallize the comic impulses of the period. It would be much harder to account for the Restoration revival of *A New Way to Pay Old Debts* than it is to explain why it did not appear.

Nor was the play of any importance on the stage of the first half of the eighteenth century. The main types of comedy which characterized the Restoration were handed on to new dramatists who slowly modified their cynicism into a new gentility or their wit into farce. Ballad-opera, opera, burlesque, and pantomime became the most popular forms. There was as yet little revival of the earlier comedy, though Fletcher and his companions were ransacked for new situations. Criticism, dominated by neo-classic "rules," could not recommend Massinger's play. It had neither "decorum" nor "good taste"; it covered ground not proper to comedy; characters did not act according to logic or common sense; there is some question whether the rewards and punishments are fairly distributed. To make matters worse, *A New Way to Pay Old Debts* could not be judged even on the basis of the "irregular" comedy of Shakespeare. It is not until we come to criticism of the

"Romantic" period that the play is hailed with any enthusiasm. Audiences which cared little for the "rules" did not have a chance to see it; managers preferred to gamble on new or stock pieces rather than take chances on a play which seemed strangely out-of-date. The century was almost half over before Sir Giles Overreach made a timid public appearance.

A New Way to Pay Old Debts reached the boards again when David Garrick revived the play at Drury Lane in 1748. It was acted four times during the season: October 19, 20, and 21, 1748, and January 23, 1749.[12] What prompted Garrick to this presentation? Robert Dodsley in 1744 had included it in his first collection of old English plays;[13] since Garrick was one of the subscribers, it is likely that he read the play here and thought it might succeed.[14] By mid-century, Restoration comedy was fast fading from the picture, to be replaced by the image of the sentimental Muse. Possibly Garrick thought that the play had certain elements which would appeal to the changing taste: the reformed-rake episode, the young lovers in danger, the highly moral sentences of Lord Lovell. We shall find later that Kemble in his alteration cut Justice Greedy out of the last act and even gave Marrall a chance to lead a better life.[15] Moreover there was by this time a perceptible tendency towards Elizabethan revival, though this primarily concerned the Shakespearean comedies; Garrick was a leader in this tendency.

However, the extraordinary fact about this revival in the light of subsequent stage-history is that Garrick not only did not act Sir Giles Overreach but did not appear in the play at all. It is difficult to explain why the manager himself did not head the cast. Why did not he avail himself of the opportunity to create a character which might forever be associated with his name? I find it hard to believe that Garrick, who thought very well of himself indeed, feared that the task would be beyond his ability. Perhaps

---

[12] Genest, Vol. VI, pp. 259-60, 265.

[13] *A Select Collection of Old Plays*, London, 1744, Vol. VIII. *The City Madam, The Guardian, The Unnatural Combat*, and *The Picture* are in the same volume. For discussion, see Appendix, pp. 391-2. *A New Way to Pay Old Debts* was also issued separately in 1744 and reprinted by Dodsley in 1748 as "Acted at the Theatre-Royal in Drury-Lane."

[14] Straus, p. 65.

[15] Appendix, pp. 399-404.

it is most logical to assume that he did not realize the possibilities
before him, and was anxious not to appear in a play which might
be an unwelcome revival. Whatever the reason, however, Garrick
assigned Sir Giles to an unimportant and obscure actor named
Bridges, and cast the play as follows:[16]

Sir Giles Overreach	Bridges
Wellborn	Sowdon
Justice Greedy	Woodward
Allworth	King
(first time of his appearing in any character)[17]	
Marrall	Neale
Furnace	Blakes
Tapwell	Taswell
Lord Lovell	Havard
Lady Allworth	Mrs. Pritchard
Margaret	Mrs. Green
Froth	Mrs. Bridges

Garrick's first revival was definitely not a success. In the Harvard Theatre Collection, there is a curious unpublished manuscript
called *Tit for Tat, Etc., The first Season (and second) of Mr.
G-----k's Management,* in which a dissatisfied assistant treasurer
furnishes a cash account of the receipts for every night of Garrick's first two seasons as manager of Drury Lane. The figures are
revealing. The season of 1748-1749 began on September 29 with
Richard III to a house of £183.15.0. On October 18, when the play

[16] Genest, Vol. IV, pp. 259-60. Cruickshank is of course quite wrong when
he states (*Philip Massinger,* p. 124, n. 4): "The part of Sir Giles Overreach
has been taken by many of our great actors, notably Garrick, who revived it
in 1745." He has stated the facts correctly in the Appendix (p. 125) to his edition of the play. Frederick Hawkins in *The Theatre,* August 1, 1895, p. 73, gives
Bridges's first name as Thomas, on what evidence I do not know. He may have
confused him with the author of *Dido,* 1771 (Gilliland, Vol. I, p. 275). The
actor appeared at Drury Lane as early as September 19, 1743, and as late as
March 14, 1751. (See Genest, Vol. IV, *passim,* and Harvard clippings for his
characters.)

[17] The statement is equivocal and shows the difficulty of working with playbills. Tom King had previously acted in the provinces. Moreover, he had also
already appeared at Drury Lane, as the herald in *King Lear,* presumably on
October 8. If the statement is to be taken as true at all, it must mean either
the first time he acted in London a part which required characterization, or
the first time his name appeared on the bills.

was *The Provoked Wife,* the receipts were £124.10.0. Three performances of *A New Way to Pay Old Debts* followed:

October 19	£ 93.14.6
October 20	£ 95.00.0
October 21	£ 98.11.0

On the next night *The Fair Penitent* brought in £131.6.0. The receipts for October 19 indeed were the lowest of the season up to that date. Most of the entries are well over £100; the average, lowered by several costly failures, is £116.10.6 The last performance of the play was no more remunerative than the third:

January 23	£ 98.1.6

Financially, it is plain, *A New Way to Pay Old Debts* was in 1748-1749 a poor way to pay any debts, old or new.

The result was that except for a performance of the play at the White Swan, Norwich, by the Norwich Company in 1749,[18] it was ten years before *A New Way to Pay Old Debts* was acted again; and as this second attempt was probably for the benefit of Burton, Garrick very likely had little to do with it. It was played only once, on May 11, 1759. Genest gives a partial cast:[19]

Sir Giles Overreach	Burton
Wellborn	Palmer
Justice Greedy	Yates
Allworth	Holland
Lady Allworth	Mrs. Pritchard

It appears also that Mrs. Abington "got up the play of *A New Way to Pay Old Debts*" for her benefit at the Smock Alley Theatre, Dublin, in the spring of 1760.[20] Tate Wilkinson comments appropriately: "A strange play for Mrs. Abington to chuse it was! . . . but she made amends by other performances that evening."[21] The date was March 17, and I suppose she played Lady Allworth, but I have found no other information on the subject. I am also without information or confirmation of a performance of the play,

---

[18] Sybil Rosenfeld, "The Players in Norwich, 1710-1750," *RES*, July 1936, Vol. XII, p. 295.
[19] Genest, Vol. V, p. 551. Repetition: May 8, 1760.
[20] Hitchcock, Vol. II, pp. 31-2.
[21] Wilkinson, *Memoirs*, Vol. II, p. 76.

recorded by Canon Cruickshank, at the King Street Theatre, Birmingham, in 1762.[22]

In 1761 an anonymous essay, admittedly by George Colman, entitled *Critical Reflections on the Old English Dramatick Writers,* was prefixed to the second issue of Thomas Coxeter's four-volume edition of *The Dramatic Works of Philip Massinger.*[23] This essay, "addressed to David Garrick, Esq.," was an earnest plea for the revival of Massinger's plays on the stage. "Shakespeare has been transmitted down to us with successive Glories; and you, Sir, have continued, or rather increased, his Reputation. You have, in no fulsome Stream of Compliment, been stiled the Best Commentator on his Works: But have you not, like other Commentators, contracted a narrow, exclusive, Veneration of your Author? Has not the Contemplation of Shakespeare's Excellencies almost dazzled and extinguished your Judgment, when directed to other Objects, and made you blind to the Merit of his Cotemporaries? Under your Dominion, have not Beaumont and Fletcher, nay even Jonson, suffered a kind of theatrical Disgrace? And has not poor Massinger, whose cause I have now undertaken, been permitted to languish in Obscurity, and remained almost entirely unknown?"

To this appeal, Garrick was apparently deaf. He waited until October 21, 1769, before again producing *A New Way to Pay Old Debts,* and he made no attempt to revive any other plays by Massinger. Of the 1769 production Genest remarks: "This is the second or third time that Garrick revived this play without giving it a fair chance of success," meaning, I suppose, that he should have played Sir Giles himself.[24] And the editor of the *Biographia Dramatica* comments: ". . . whether from any fault in the per-

[22] Cruickshank (Edition), p. 130.

[23] Coxeter's edition had been published posthumously by Dell in 1759. The essay was "thrown together at the instance of Mr. Garrick, to serve his old subject Davies, who, converted from an actor into a bookseller, had purchased the remaining copies of Coxeter's *Reflections* as a Preface" (Colman, *Prose on Several Occasions, &c.,* preface to Vol. I, quoted by Page, p. 51); it was also issued separately in 1761, "Printed for T. Davies . . . , James Fletcher . . . , J. Merrill," reissued in revised form in 1763, and prefaced to Mason's edition in 1779. Colman, both as writer and manager, was an important factor in the revival of the older dramatists.

[24] Genest, Vol. V, p. 257.

formance, or want of taste in the audience, it did not meet with that success which might have been expected from its merit, and which some of its contemporaries, not possessed of more, have since received on a revival. We are the more inclined to believe that the want of success must have arisen from the performers, as it was acted in 1781, in a manner which showed it was deserving of the utmost applause."[25] The play ran three nights, the third perform- ance falling on October 27, 1769.[26] The actors were Love, Burton, Waldron, Palmer, Cautherley, J. Aiken, Moody, W. Palmer, Mrs. Hopkins, Miss Younge, and Mrs. Bradshaw. Genest gives the following cast as probable:[27]

Sir Giles Overreach	Burton
Wellborn	Palmer
Justice Greedy	Love
Marrall	Waldron
Allworth	Cautherley
Lord Lovell	J. Aiken
Lady Allworth	Mrs. Hopkins
Margaret	Miss Younge
Froth	Mrs. Bradshaw

It seems reasonable to suppose that the failure of *A New Way to Pay Old Debts* under the Drury Lane management of David Garrick can be attributed to Garrick's own lack of confidence in the play, and to the poor casting and inadequate acting consequent. Possibly too an audience veering from the Restoration comedy of manners and intrigue towards sentimental comedy was not ready for this serious comedy of Massinger's. But the Garrick revivals, while not in themselves successful, are significant for two reasons: first, because they were the first London revivals of Massinger's realistic comic drama; and second, because they paved the way for more important revivals, in which the value of *A New Way to Pay Old Debts* as an acting play was to be realized, and in which Sir Giles Overreach was to become a "star" part.

[25] *Biographia Dramatica*, Vol. III, p. 81.
[26] Genest does not give the date of the second performance. Cruickshank (Edition), p. 126, says it was on October 24.
[27] Genest, Vol. V, p. 257; I have not seen the playbill.

CHAPTER III

OVERREACH REDIVIVUS

HE was an actor of uncommon powers, and a man of the brightest intellect, formed to be the delight of society, and few indeed are those men of distinguished talents, who have been more prematurely lost to the world, or more lastingly regretted. What he was on the stage, those who recollect his Falstaff, Shylock, Sir Giles Overreach, and many other parts of the strong cast, can fully testify; what he was at his own fireside and in his social hours, all, who were within the circle of his intimates, will not easily forget."[1] Thus spoke Richard Cumberland of John Henderson, the first actor to *star* in *A New Way to Pay Old Debts*.

Henderson made his début on the stage as Hamlet on October 6, 1772, under Palmer at Bath, whither he had been sent by Garrick, who had no great faith in his powers. At this time he bore the pseudonym of Courtney. His reception was decidedly favorable, and he shortly after appeared as Richard III, Benedict, Macbeth, Bobadill, and on the 26th under his own name as Hotspur. Though his popularity soon brought him the appellation of "the Bath Roscius," he was not at first successful in his attempts to obtain a London engagement. Finally in the spring of 1777 he was secured by Colman, who had taken over the Haymarket from Foote. Here Henderson gained such favor that he is said to have made £4500 for his manager in thirty-six performances. He was then engaged by Sheridan for Drury Lane where he acted for two years, going to Covent Garden in 1778 in consequence of the coalition of the two companies. Here except for the usual provincial tours he acted until his death in 1785. Henderson in reality succeeded to the popularity of David Garrick. In widely dissimilar parts in both tragedy and comedy, he acted with fine intelligence, excelling particularly by reason of his elocution.[2]

[1] *Memoirs of Richard Cumberland* (ed. Henry Flanders), pp. 300-1.

[2] For accounts of John Henderson, see *Letters and Poems by the late Mr. John Henderson with anecdotes of his life by John Ireland*, London, 1786; [Thomas

I do not know who was responsible for this next revival of *A New Way to Pay Old Debts,* or what causes led to it; I can only indicate the possibilities. It was produced at Covent Garden under the management of Thomas Harris on April 18, 1781, for the benefit of Quick, who played Justice Greedy to the Sir Giles Overreach of Henderson. One of these three men must have seen the possibilities of the play as an acting vehicle. What brought the play to attention is conjectural. It may have been one of the Garrick revivals; Robert Dodsley's editions of 1744 and 1748, and Coxeter's edition of 1761 have already been mentioned, as well as Colman's plea for the recognition of Massinger. Two more editions had appeared previous to the Covent Garden revival: one was a heretofore unnoticed text issued by James Dodsley in 1770; the other was included in the four volume edition of Massinger by John Monck Mason in 1779.[3]

There is good reason to suspect, however, that it was Henderson himself who was instrumental in bringing about this revival; and, if so, to him must go the credit of being the first man in the eighteenth century to realize the dramatic power latent in the part of Sir Giles Overreach. That Henderson was at least partially acquainted with Massinger before this date is capable of proof. On November 10, 1779, he had acted in a version of *The Duke of Milan* at Covent Garden.[4] In the same year, though misdated 1789, had appeared *Some Account of the Life and Writings of Philip Massinger,* written by Thomas Davies and dedicated by "his much obliged and most obedient servant" to Dr. Johnson. The copy of this little book in the Harvard Library bears on the title-page the autograph inscription, "Mr. Henderson from T.

Davies], *A Genuine Narrative of the Life and Theatrical Transactions of Mr. John Henderson, commonly called the Bath Roscius,* 3rd ed., London, 1778. The following are good brief sketches of his career: Sinclair, "A Successor of David Garrick," *Scottish Historical Review,* Vol. I, pp. 306-13; Doran, *Annals of the English Stage,* Vol. III, pp. 144-53; and Joseph Knight's article in the *DNB,* Vol. XXV, pp. 399-401.

[3] A copy of the J. Dodsley edition, autographed T. Harris, is in the New York Public Library. Chelli, *Étude,* Bibl., p. 285 mentions a text issued by Barker and Son "with the Variations in the Manager's Book at the Theatre Royal" which he, following the British Museum, dates [1780]. The date is some twenty years too early; see Appendix, pp. 392-3.

[4] Genest, Vol. VI, p. 141.

Davies." It has not apparently been sufficiently realized how great were the services of Tom Davies to the cause of Massinger. He had already published Colman's *Critical Reflections* and Coxeter's edition; he now appears with a life of Massinger of his own composition, which, besides being issued separately, is included in Mason's four-volume edition, also one of his publications. Davies' life of Massinger is less interesting in the biographical part, which is gleaned principally from Anthony à Wood and Langbaine with the Ms. notes of John Oldys on Langbaine lent Davies by Reed of Staples Inn, than in a sentence from the opening paragraph, wherein it is stated that "though *Massinger's* claim to an eminent Rank amongst the English Dramatick Writers has never been contested . . . yet . . . the name of *Massinger,* till within these twenty Years, has been sunk in Obscurity, and almost buried in Oblivion." This in a book sent personally to Henderson would almost certainly set the actor to a perusal of Massinger's works with a view to possible revival. Now Henderson must have had more than an ordinary interest in Massinger. When his all too brief career was cut short by death a few years later, his personal library was sold at auction by T. and J. Egerton. In the catalogue of that sale are advertised Coxeter's four-volume edition as well as quartos of practically all of Massinger's plays.[5] It would seem logical to assume that Henderson, with his interest stirred by Davies, was responsible for the revival not only of *The Duke of Milan* but of *A New Way to Pay Old Debts* as well.

During the spring of 1781, Henderson acted Sir Giles five times; during the next theatrical season, five times; twice in the spring of 1783, and four times thereafter, all at Covent Garden.[6] On his first visit to Scotland in 1784 he also played the part; this

[5] Library of Congress, PN2598.H4D3.

[6] April 18, 1781; April 26, 1781; May 8, 1781; May 16, 1781; May 24, 1781; September 17, 1781; December 14, 1781; January 16, 1782; February 1, 1782; April 2, 1782; April 1, 1783; May 16, 1783; September 26, 1783; May 27, 1784; May 18, 1785; October 12, 1785. See Genest, Vol. VI, pp. 193, 220, 271, 386; the Theatrical Register in the *Gentleman's Magazine,* Vol. LI, pp. 155, 204, 404, 546; Vol. LII, pp. 35, 57, 162; Vol. LIII, pp. 308, 427, 880; Vol. LIV, p. 394; Vol. LV, pp. 382, 816; and the playbills. Neither Genest nor Cruickshank (Edition, p. 126) is complete.

was at Edinburgh on August 16.[7] The cast of the first Covent Garden performance follows:

Sir Giles Overreach	Henderson
Wellborn	Wroughton
Lord Lovell	Peile
Marrall	Wilson
Justice Greedy	Quick (bt.)
Allworth	Whitfield
Lady Allworth	Mrs. Inchbald
Margaret	Mrs. Lewis
Froth	Mrs. Pitt

For the production of September 17, 1781, the Lord Lovell was Lewis, the Lady Allworth Mrs. Yates, and the Margaret Miss Satchell, the last two marked "first time." Mrs. Inchbald again became the Lady Allworth and Davies took over the part of Lord Lovell for the performance of September 26, 1783. The playbill of May 27, 1784, shows Davies still in the cast with Fearon as Marrall and Mrs. Kemble as Margaret. This was not Tom Davies of course; he had retired from the stage in 1762. The Mrs. Kemble was Elizabeth Kemble, wife of Stephen and sister-in-law of the Miss Elizabeth Kemble at Drury Lane, afterwards as Mrs. Whitlock of some fame in the United States.

That Henderson's playing of the rôle of Sir Giles Overreach was a distinct success is attested by the passage from Cumberland's *Memoirs* already quoted. The *Biographia Dramatica* remarks: "Mr. Henderson's performance of Sir Giles Overreach in particular could not be too much commended," and the editor ranks his interpretation above Cooke's, whose popularity in the part will shortly be mentioned.[8] William Dunlap remembers Henderson's Sir Giles as being perfection itself.[9] James Boaden, biographer and admirer of John Philip Kemble, admits that Henderson's Sir Giles was far superior to Kemble's,[10] and Kemble himself wrote to Mrs. Inchbald, who had played Lady Allworth to Henderson's Overreach, asking for the particulars of his costume in the part and saying, "I shall be uneasy if I have not an idea of his dress,

[7] Dibdin, *Edinburgh Stage*, pp. 190-1.
[8] Vol. III, p. 81.
[9] Dunlap, *A History of the American Theatre*, p. 241.
[10] Boaden, *Kemble*, Vol. I, p. 132.

even to the shape of his buckles and what rings he wears."[11] Queen
Charlotte saw Henderson in *A New Way to Pay Old Debts* at a
command performance on April 26, 1781. Henderson it was who
released the flood-gates; hereafter no important actor could avoid
breasting the current of emotion which rushed through the character of Sir Giles. He was the first to turn the extortioner into a rôle
which a recognized star must essay.

In the same year in which John Henderson made his début in the
rôle of Sir Giles Overreach, an even greater actor attempted the
part. This was John Philip Kemble, who acted the leading character of *A New Way to Pay Old Debts* "for the first time" at the
Theatre Royal, Edinburgh, on July 30, 1781.[12] The partial cast
was as follows:[13]

Sir Giles Overreach .... Kemble
Arable .... Chalmers[14]
Justice Greedy .... Bailey
Wellborn .... Cummins
Margaret .... Mrs. Chalmers
Lady Allworth .... Miss Scarce

It is hardly necessary to inquire the reasons which led Kemble to
play Sir Giles. Kemble was both educated and intelligent and had
doubtless read Massinger along with other early dramatists; he

[11] Joseph Knight on Henderson in the *DNB*, Vol. XXV, p. 401.

[12] The standard life of Kemble is James Boaden's *Memoirs of the Life of John
Philip Kemble*, 2 vols., London, 1825, an interesting and valuable record not only
of the man and his career but also of the London stage of the period.

[13] Dibdin, *Edinburgh Stage*, p. 180. An article in the *Gentleman's Magazine*,
April 1783, Vol. LIII, pp. 309-10, seems to imply that Kemble had previously
acted Sir Giles at York: "About this time Mrs. Siddons accepted an invitation
to play at Bath; and Mr. Kemble became the hero of the theatre-royal in York.
Here he gave the town a comedy called 'Oh! it's Impossible.'—He next altered
and revived Massinger's 'New Way to pay old Debts,' and the year after, published a small collection of verses under the title of 'Fugitive Pieces.' " *Fugitive
Pieces* was published in 1780, which would place the revival before that date.
On the other hand, Dibdin said "for the first time" apparently because it had
been so stated on the bills; and I can find no record of any such performance.
Neither Boaden nor Tate Wilkinson refer to it. For Kemble's alteration, printed
in 1810, see Appendix, pp. 393-406.

[14] Arable is, I suppose, a misprint or a miscopying of Amble, though I do not
see why Dibdin should list so unimportant a character. Perhaps Dibdin means
Marrall. Chalmers, who played the part, later turns up as the first Sir Giles in
America; see Part II, pp. 169-72.

had already acted Paris in the scene of the Curia from *The Roman Actor* at York, and he later revived the play in a two-act form; in 1785 he played Adorni to the Camiola of his sister, Mrs. Siddons, in *The Maid of Honour*.[15] We have seen too that he knew of Henderson's success as Sir Giles Overreach.

Later in 1781, Kemble left Wilkinson's company to act under Daly at the new Smock Alley Theatre in Dublin, opening there on November 2 as Hamlet. During this Irish engagement he again played Sir Giles Overreach. Our informant is a writer in the *Gentleman's Magazine,* who indicates Kemble's success in the following terms: "Who can think it acting, when he expresses fear in Hamlet, courage in Henry V, joy in Sir Giles Overreach, horror in the Count of Narbonne, suspicion in King John, jealousy in Othello, and grief in Demetrius?" and later in the same article, "In Hamlet and the Count of Norbonne, Mr. Kemble seems to rise above himself, and in many others he has very uncommon merit, particularly in Sir Giles Overreach, Demetrius, Beverley, Orestes, Richard, Macbeth, and the Earl of Warwick."[16] It is to be remembered that this appeared in a London magazine before Kemble's début in that city.

Kemble first acted in London at Drury Lane on September 30, 1783; on November 4, his Sir Giles Overreach was exhibited for the first time to London playgoers. The bill shows the following cast:[17]

Sir Giles Overreach	Kemble
Wellborn	Palmer
Lord Lovell	Staunton
Marrall	Suett
Justice Greedy	Burton
Allworth	Bannister, jun.
Lady Allworth	Mrs. Ward
Margaret	Miss E. Kemble

15 Genest, Vol. VI, p. 335; Vol. VII, pp. 243-4.

16 *Gentleman's Magazine,* April 1783, Vol. LIII, p. 310.

17 See also Genest, Vol. VI, p. 298. Minor characters are omitted in the casts given hereafter unless there is some special reason for including them. I do not follow the playbills in printing the characters in the order of their social rank; nor do I, unless it is significant, preserve the variant spelling of the characters' names.

During the theatrical season of 1783-1784, Kemble played Sir Giles seven times.[18] According to the playbills Parsons supplanted Burton as Justice Greedy for the performance of January 26, 1784, and on May 26 of the same year Mrs. Inchbald was the Lady Allworth. The next season *A New Way to Pay Old Debts* was given twice, with Mrs. Ward again acting Lady Allworth on May 17, 1785.[19] The next three seasons, Kemble impersonated Sir Giles once each season.[20] The part of Justice Greedy was taken over by Quick on January 5, 1786. On January 13, 1787, Allworth was played by Lawrence, Margaret by Mrs. Brereton. On December 14, 1787, the Wellborn was Wroughten, the Allworth Whitfield, with the rest as before. This last performance took place shortly after Kemble's marriage to Mrs. Brereton, his Margaret in the play. Dr. Doran relates that the audience seized on a marked passage and laughed as they applauded to indicate they knew all about it. "Sir Giles remained grave and self-possessed."[21] Whether or not this facetiousness was annoying to Kemble I do not know, but with the exception of a performance during the same season, March 25, 1788, mentioned in *St. James's Chronicle; or British Evening Post,* he seems to have dropped the play at this point until 1810.

In the fall of 1788 Kemble succeeded King as the manager of Drury Lane, a post which except for a short interval he held until 1802. I can find no evidence that Kemble revived *A New Way to Pay Old Debts* during this period. He probably realized what will appear from later comment, that Sir Giles was not one of his most successful rôles, and decided to let the play rest. In 1803 Kemble took over Covent Garden, where Overreach had but lately been

[18] Genest, Vol. VI, p. 303 says six times but the Theatrical Register in the *Gentleman's Magazine* (Vol. LIII, pp. 956, 992; Vol. LIV, pp. 44, 148, 233, 394) lists performances on the following dates: November 14, 1783; November 17, 1783; December 4, 1783; January 26, 1784; February 9, 1784; March 18, 1784; May 26, 1784. Genest specifies only two of these (Vol. VI, pp. 295, 298). The casts of November 17, 1783 and December 4, 1783 were the same as that given above.

[19] November 2, 1784; May 17, 1785. See the Theatrical Register in the *Gentleman's Magazine,* Vol. LIV, p. 874; Vol. LV, p. 382, and the playbills.

[20] January 5, 1786; January 13, 1787; December 14, 1787. See Genest, Vol. VI, pp. 380, 430, 473, and the playbills. Succeeding records unless otherwise indicated are from the same sources.

[21] *Annals of the English Stage,* Vol. III, pp. 195-6.

impersonated by George Frederick Cooke, who continued to play the part under Kemble's management. Since the turbulent George Frederick had to be handled with gloves and since Sir Giles was one of his best parts, Kemble wisely abstained from challenging comparison and continued to let his own Sir Giles lapse. Two Sir Gileses in the same theatre would have been too much—especially when one of them was the brilliant but erratic Cooke. In the fall of 1810, however, Cooke went to America and remained there the rest of his life. In December of the same year, Kemble, emboldened perhaps by Cooke's success in the rôle and the increasing popularity of the play, resumed the part of Sir Giles and acted it intermittently thereafter.

Kemble's first performance of Overreach at Covent Garden came on December 29, 1810, with the following support:[22]

Sir Giles Overreach	Kemble
Wellborn	C. Kemble
Lord Lovell	Barrymore
Marrall	Munden
Justice Greedy	Liston
Allworth	Hamerton
Lady Allworth	Mrs. Weston
Margaret	Miss S. Booth

A fine cast, yet apparently the performance was not an outstanding success, for according to the playbills *A New Way to Pay Old Debts* was played only three times more that season, on January 4, February 21, and May 23, 1811. On the performance of February 21, Munden's son comments: "Mr. Kemble played Sir Giles Overreach, so long the property of Mr. Cooke; and Munden, Marrall. Mr. Kemble played Sir Giles with great discrimination, but his appearance and manners were too gentlemanly for the part. Overreach is a parvenu—an ill-bred, ferocious man: the coarse violence of Cooke was exactly suited to its delineation. Miss S. Booth played Margaret respectably, Kemble having taken great pains to instruct Miss Booth in the character."[23] Genest records another performance on January 17, 1812, with Marrall by Farley and

[22] Genest, Vol. VIII, p. 227, and the playbill. This was of course the new Covent Garden Theatre.
[23] *Memoirs of Munden*, p. 190.

Lady Allworth by Mrs. Powell, the rest of the cast as before.[24] A playbill shows Kemble's Sir Giles at Edinburgh on March 3, 1813:

Sir Giles Overreach .... Kemble
Wellborn .... Siddons
Lord Lovell .... Grant
Marrall .... Terry
Justice Greedy .... Russell
Allworth .... Jones
Lady Allworth .... Mrs. M'Namara
Margaret .... Mrs. H. Siddons

The performance was repeated on March 12.[25] There was another at Covent Garden on November 15, 1814:[26]

Sir Giles Overreach .... Kemble
Wellborn .... Conway
Lord Lovell .... Barrymore
Marrall .... Terry
Justice Greedy .... Blanchard
Allworth .... Hamerton
Lady Allworth .... Mrs. Renaud
Margaret .... Miss S. Booth

And then Kemble made a great mistake: he dared to provoke comparison between his restrained and coldly intelligent acting of the part and the almost hysterically emotional interpretation of the greatest Sir Giles in the history of the stage, Edmund Kean.

Kean had first presented his Sir Giles to a London audience at Drury Lane on January 12, 1816. When Kemble played Overreach at Edinburgh on March 30, the reviewer in *The Theatrical Inquisitor,* who had seen Kean's London success in the part, began the practice of comparison, though it was not yet odious:[27]

Mr. Kemble played Sir Giles Overreach for the first and only time during his engagement. The eminent success of Mr. Kean in this character, rendered Mr. Kemble's performance of it particularly interesting. The scenes with his daughter and Lord Lovell, are by far the best parts of Mr. Kemble's performance. He evidently found himself unable to enter into the spirit of the con-

[24] Genest, Vol. VIII, p. 288, and the playbill.
[25] Lockhart, *Scott,* Vol. IV, pp. 57-9.
[26] Genest, Vol. VIII, p. 475, and the playbill.
[27] *The Theatrical Inquisitor and Monthly Mirror,* Vol. VIII, pp. 318-19.

cluding scene, in which Sir Giles's reason is overthrown. He passed it over with a sort of sober acting. In the kind affection with which Sir Giles pretends to receive his nephew in the presence of Lady Allworth; Mr. Kemble is peculiarly happy; he gave an astonishing effect to the exclamation—

"—My nephew—

"Faith, you've been too long a stranger."

Mr. Kemble was tolerably well supported in this character. The Wellborn of Mr. Jones was a very good performance, Mr. James played Marrall in a very correct style, and Miss Dyke was well fitted for the quiet Margaret; but Russell would have been a better Justice Greedy had he been more anxious to show the character according to nature than in its most ludicrous aspect; in short, he overacted it.

On April 26, 1816, Kemble appeared as Sir Giles at Covent Garden, with the cast last printed.[28] William Hazlitt, who had been enthusiastic over Kean's playing of the rôle, reviewed Kemble in *The Examiner* of May 5; from his criticism I quote portions:[29]

. . . We never saw signs of greater poverty, greater imbecility and decrepitude in Mr. Kemble, or in any other actor: it was Sir Giles in his dotage. It was all "Well, well" and "If you like it, have it so," an indifference and disdain of what was to happen, a nicety about his means, a coldness as to his ends, much gentility and little nature. Was this Sir Giles Overreach? Nothing could be more quaint and out of the way. Mr. Kemble wanted the part to come to him, for he would not go out of his way to the part. He is, in fact, as shy of committing himself with nature, as a maid is of committing herself with a lover. All the proper forms and ceremonies must be complied with, before "they two can be made one flesh." Mr. Kemble sacrifices too much to decorum. . . .

The outrageousness of the conduct of Sir Giles is only to be excused by the violence of his passions, and the turbulence of his character. Mr. Kemble inverted this conception, and attempted to reconcile the character by softening down the action. He "aggravated the part so, that he would seem like any sucking dove." For example, nothing could exceed the coolness and *sangfroid*

---

[28] Genest, Vol. VIII, p. 552, and the playbill.

[29] A. R. Waller and Arnold Glover (eds.), *The Collected Works of William Hazlitt*, Vol. VIII, pp. 302 *ff*. Hazlitt implies in certain statements which I have not quoted that Kemble was forced into the part against his will by the other proprietors; I find no evidence for this view.

with which he raps Marall on the head with his cane, or spits at Lord Lovell: Lord Foppington himself never did any commonplace indecency more insipidly. The only passage that pleased us, or that really called forth the powers of the actor, was his reproach to Mr. Justice Greedy: "There is some fury in that *Gut*." The indignity of the word called up all the dignity of the actor to meet it, and he guaranteed the word, though "a word of naught," according to the letter and spirit of the convention between them, with a good grace, in the true old English way. Either we mistake all Mr. Kemble's excellencies, or they all disqualify him for this part. Sir Giles *hath a devil*; Mr. Kemble has none. Sir Giles is in a passion; Mr. Kemble is not. Sir Giles has no regard to appearances; Mr. Kemble has. . . . With all his faults, he has powers and faculties which no one else on the stage has; why then does he not avail himself of them, instead of throwing himself on the charity of criticism? Mr. Kemble has given the public great, incalculable pleasure; and does he know so little of the gratitude of the world as to trust to their generosity?

And Kemble did not play Sir Giles again! Hawkins tells us, perhaps from his imagination, that at this performance, the audience at first maintained a cold silence, and then bored by the monotony of the acting in contrast to Kean's fire, hissed. "The actor felt it deeply, and as he went off the stage murmured, 'It is time that I should retire.' He there and then expressed his determination to withdraw from the stage at the close of the following season."[30]

Classicism, it is plain, was fleeing from Romantic rage. Kemble had outlived the school of acting to which he belonged and which he helped to crystallize. Indeed his temperament and artistic sense did not fit him to act Massinger's extortioner. He was cool, restrained, thoughtful, intelligent, rather than fiery, impetuous, intuitive, and emotional. And the tradition of acting in which he had been educated was being destroyed by players like Kean and romantic critics like Hazlitt. But even if we admit that Kemble's histrionic training was against him in this rôle, on other standards he seems to have been below par. His biographer says: "With all my admiration of Kemble, I never thought his Sir Giles to be named with Henderson's. He had not the bustle, the ardour, the

[30] Hawkins, *Kean*, Vol. I, pp. 357-8. See also the review in *The Times* of April 27, 1816.

grasp of the man; and his exultation was not so triumphant as Henderson's."[31] Sir Walter Scott, who had seen Kemble play Sir Giles in Edinburgh on March 12, 1813, wrote to Joanna Baillie the following day comparing Kemble's interpretation unfavorably with Cooke's. Speaking of the scene between Sir Giles and Lord Lovell, he remarks, ". . . Kemble was too handsome, too plausible, and too smooth to admit its being probable that he should be blind to the unfavorable impression which these extraordinary vaunts are likely to make on the very person whom he is so anxious to conciliate."[32] "Requiring as it did," said Molloy, "varied display of passion, great facial expression, and subtle nervous force, the part was unsuited to the 'exhibition of elegantly disposed drapery' which was the great characteristic of Kemble's acting."[33] The statement is not fair to Kemble but none the less contains truth. It is hardly necessary to quote further to show that Kemble was too stately for the terrific bursts of passion which sweep through the character of Sir Giles Overreach. He was probably what the modern reviewer would call "adequate," but it was necessary to be more with Henderson at one end of his career, Cooke in the middle, and Kean at the other end. However, it takes little from the fame of one of the greatest actors of all time that he failed to realize one character totally unsuited to his histrionic genius.

Three or four minor revivals of *A New Way to Pay Old Debts* will serve as interlude between Kemble and Cooke. Charles Murray, from Norwich, played Sir Giles Overreach at Bath on October 8, 1785; Genest labels the performance "1st app." This actor was the son of Sir John Murray, of Broughton, Bart., who as secretary to the Pretender in the rebellion of 1745 was arraigned for high treason but finally pardoned by the King. Charles Murray was at first a surgeon's mate; he started acting professionally with Tate Wilkinson at York in 1775 under the name of Raymur. At Bath he became an established favorite, though I do not find him as Sir Giles again. At the time of his departure for London, a local critic wrote: "We shall lose in him a great actor—void of conceit or ostentation." He made his London début at Covent Garden on

[31] Boaden, Vol. I, p. 132.
[32] Lockhart, *Scott*, Vol. IV, pp. 57-9.
[33] Molloy, *Kean*, Vol. II, p. 25.

September 11, 1796, as Shylock, and became a member of the company; he reappears in this chronicle as a respectable Lord Lovell. Leigh Hunt says of him: "The genius of Mr. Murray is a correct mediocrity, and in his proper characters, which he seldom forsakes, he is natural and impressive. His person is not elegant nor is his countenance animated, but his manner is altogether interesting, and neither elegance of shape nor vivacity of feature are necessary to that kind of fatherly character, which it is his peculiar happiness to exhibit." Murray's daughter married Henry Siddons; his son was W. H. Murray, the Edinburgh manager.[34]

Our first amateur productions of *A New Way to Pay Old Debts* are recorded in *St. James's Chronicle* of 1787, where under date of April 14 and heading "News" it is stated: "The practice of acting plays in private will be the rage for the season. . . . The New Way to Pay Old Debts, is now rehearsing at two Ducal houses in Piccadilly." Sir Giles was coming up in the world. On April 19, 1796, the play, "altered from Massinger," was acted at Covent Garden for the benefit of Pope, who impersonated Sir Giles:

Sir Giles Overreach	Pope
Wellborn	Holman
Lord Lovell	Macready
Marrall	Powel
Justice Greedy	Quick
Allworth	Middleton
Lady Allworth	Mrs. Pope
Margaret	Miss Mansal

"all for the first time, except Quick." Genest, following the playbill, says "not acted 14 years."[35] This is an error, even if it applies only to Covent Garden; we have found Henderson playing Sir Giles there in 1785. The new Overreach, Alexander Pope, was a native of Cork, where be began acting. He came to Covent Garden in 1784, and after Henderson's death was for a few years the principal tragedian. When Holman resumed his position, Pope went to Edinburgh, but he later returned to the principal London theatres.

[34] Genest, Vol. VI, p. 417; Penley, *The Bath Stage*, p. 68; Hunt, *Essays on the Performers*, London, 1807, p. 42.

[35] Genest, Vol. VII, p. 271, and the playbill. Note the father of William Charles Macready as Lord Lovell.

Of good figure and fine voice, his countenance wanted expression, and his deportment, grace and dignity.[36]

George Frederick Cooke was a success on the London stage only after a long probation. If we may believe his own doubtful statements, he was born in 1756 and made his début as an actor twenty years later at Brentford. After two years of wandering, he appeared at the Haymarket but attracted little attention. This engagement was followed by more provincial strolling, which lasted until 1794, when he went to act in Dublin. Here he took part in a debauch which brought him so much disgrace that in a fit of drunkenness he enlisted in the army. Sickness fortunately kept him from being shipped to the West Indies, but he remained in the army until 1796, when his discharge was purchased by Manchester friends. The next year he reappeared in Dublin and during this engagement acted with Kemble. It was not until 1800 that he played at Covent Garden, but here at last he found success. By an effort of will he was able for a time to hold in check his vicious habits, though his audiences discovered only too soon that they could not depend on him. However, they were indulgent to the man because they admired the actor. As Richard, as Shylock, as Iago, as Kitely, he was conceded to have surpassed Kemble by virtue of his expression of the baser passions, his naturalness, and a voice of great range and power. With such characteristics it was to be expected that his Sir Giles Overreach would be a tremendous success, and these expectations were fulfilled.[37]

Cooke made his début as Sir Giles at Covent Garden on March 28, 1801, for the benefit of Lewis:

Sir Giles Overreach	Cooke
Wellborn	Lewis (bt.)
Lord Lovell	Murray
Marrall	Munden
Justice Greedy	Simmons
Allworth	H. Johnston
Lady Allworth	Miss Chapman
Margaret	Miss Murray

[36] On Pope, see *The Thespian Dictionary*; and Gilliland, *The Dramatic Mirror*.
[37] William Dunlap's *Life of George Frederick Cooke*, 2 vols., New York, 1813, written at Cooke's request and to which he contributed information, is the authority on this actor.

"How! Thunderstruck!"

GEORGE FREDERICK COOKE as SIR GILES OVERREACH, from the
painting by Singleton, engraved by C. Heath, Longman & Co., London

"being their first app. in those characters."[38] Munden's son, commenting on the performance, says, "He [Cooke] played with great discrimination and astonishing force."[39] According to Dunlap, "Mr. Cooke . . . added another wreath to his laurels." "In 'A New Way to Pay Old Debts' Mr. Lewis played Wellborn, and Mr. Cooke, Sir Giles Overreach, a character peculiarly suited to his genius and his powers. It is a highly colored picture by the author and Mr. Cooke's coloring was no less vivid and glowing in the representation. Arrogant and servile; haughty to inferiors, and fawning to those who are placed above him, by rank and fortune; daring and relentless, yet finally overpowered by the most frightful despair: this terrible portrait of unprincipled villainy, was by the talents of Cooke, rendered one of the most awfully impressive lessons which the drama ever presented."[40] The reviewer in *The Monthly Mirror* is no less enthusiastic: "March 28.—Mr. Lewis's Benefit—*A New Way to pay Old Debts*—was revived for the purpose of introducing Mr. Cooke in the character of Sir Giles Overreach, a character extremely well suited to that excellent performer's style of acting, and in which his powers are displayed to the happiest advantage. . . . The Wellborn of Mr. Lewis, and Munden's Marall are particularly good. Miss Murray is an interesting Margaret, and the deportment and gentlewomanly address of Miss Chapman appear to much advantage in the character of Lady Allworth. Simmons's Justice Greedy (which Mr. Fawcett's illness prevented him from playing), is highly entertaining, but he rather *buffoons* the part too much. . . . There are other plays of Massinger which would well repay the trouble and expense at which the managers might be at in reviving them. . . ."[41]

During the spring of 1801 Cooke played Sir Giles five times.[42] The cast remained the same except that Mrs. Glover superseded Miss Murray as Margaret. A Harvard playbill for May 7 brings us

[38] Genest, Vol. VII, p. 515, and the playbill.
[39] *Munden*, p. 96.
[40] Dunlap, Vol. I, pp. 177, 181-2.
[41] *The Monthly Mirror*, Vol. XI, p. 271.
[42] Genest, Vol. VII, p. 520, but he does not give the dates. There is in the Harvard Theatre Collection a dated list of Cooke's parts which is most helpful in tracing his performances (Extra-illustrated Dunlap's *Cooke*, Vol. V, p. 410). The dates were March 28, April 8, April 15, April 20, and May 7. All Cooke per-

directly to the performance with annotations by someone who was present: "Sir Giles Overreach by Mr. Cooke (one of his very best parts throughout); Lord Lovell by Mr. Murray (Very well); Justice Greedy by Mr. Simmons (too much grimace); Marall by Mr. Munden (Admirable); Allworth by Mr. H. Johnston (Rather tame); Wellborn by Mr. Lewis (Excellent); Lady Allworth by Miss Chapman (Extremely well); Margaret by Mrs. Glover (Very well but not equal to her sprightly comedy)." How little theatrical comment has changed!

During the summer of 1801, Cooke went to Edinburgh where he played Sir Giles twice.[43] The next theatrical season saw *A New Way to Pay Old Debts* only once at Covent Garden, on October 23, this time with Brunton as Allworth.[44] In the summer of 1802, Foote, the Plymouth manager, announced Cooke's engagement with a list of parts he was to play; Sir Giles is included among them.[45] He again played the rôle at Covent Garden on November 26, 1802, and on May 22, 1804, the latter for Murray's benefit with Mrs. St. Leger as Lady Allworth.[46] Genest records that Overreach was one of Cooke's characters during an engagement at Bath which began on March 27, 1806.[47] Cooke in his diary mentions a performance at Glasgow on June 26, 1806.[48] At Liverpool on September 10 of the same year, he took his benefit with this play; a playbill contributes the cast:

Sir Giles Overreach	Cooke (bt.)
Wellborn	Huddart
Lord Lovell	Wilkinson
Marrall	Penson
Justice Greedy	Blanchard
Allworth	Waring
Lady Allworth	Mrs. Harlowe
Margaret	Miss Norton

formances mentioned hereafter have been checked with this list, though I have often cited a more convenient reference; the list itself has been checked, whenever possible, with playbills and newspaper advertisements.

43 Dunlap, Vol. I, p. 186.
44 Genest, Vol. VII, pp. 549, 559.
45 Dunlap, Vol. I, p. 236.
46 Genest, Vol. VII, pp. 579, 623.
47 *ibid.*, Vol. VIII, p. 28.
48 Dunlap, Vol. I, p. 358.

In the spring of 1807 Cooke played Sir Giles twice at Covent Garden, on February 7 and April 21.[49] For a performance at Bath on January 18, 1808, the playbill shows the cast:

Sir Giles Overreach .... Cooke
Wellborn .... Cunningham
Lord Lovell .... Sedley
Marrall .... Lovegrove
Justice Greedy .... Gattie
Allworth .... Abbott
Lady Allworth .... Mrs. Marriott
Margaret .... Miss Jameson

Another bill shows that the same company played *A New Way to Pay Old Debts* at Bristol six nights later. Cooke acted Sir Giles again at Bath on December 3, 1808.[50] In his diary under date of January 28, 1809, is the following entry: "Acted Sir Giles Overreach well, in some parts extremely well; and had I not been disconcerted by the stupidity of some, it would have been a good whole. Certain plays are sadly neglected."[51] This was at the Haymarket with a cast which I take from the playbill:

Sir Giles Overreach .... Cooke
Wellborn .... Lewis
Lord Lovell .... Murray
Marrall .... Munden
Justice Greedy .... Simmons
Allworth .... Brunton
Lady Allworth .... Mrs. St. Leger
Margaret .... Miss Norton

Another bill shows the same cast for Cooke's benefit at the Haymarket on May 1; this was the Covent Garden company, burned out of its own theatre on September 20, 1808. At the end of the London season, Cooke acted three weeks at Liverpool, according to a playbill acting Sir Giles on June 15, 1809:

[49] Genest, Vol. VIII, p. 48, and the chronological list of Cooke performances in the Harvard Theatre Collection.
[50] Genest, Vol. VIII, p. 155.
[51] Dunlap, Vol. II, p. 96.

Sir Giles Overreach .... Cooke
Wellborn .... Rae
Lord Lovell .... Musgrave
Marrall .... Turpin
Justice Greedy .... Simmons
Allworth ....Jones
Lady Allworth .... Mrs. Weston
Margaret .... Mrs. Turpin

At the new Covent Garden Theatre on March 13, 1810, Cooke
made his last London appearance in *A New Way to Pay Old
Debts,* though at the time neither he nor his audience suspected it.
The playbill prints the now familiar cast except that Charles
Kemble has succeeded Lewis as Wellborn. On August 7 Cooke
played Sir Giles at Liverpool with Mrs. Stanley as Lady Allworth.[52] At Liverpool, however, Cooke's habits got him into
trouble with his audiences, and when the actor and manager,
Thomas Abthorpe Cooper, offered him twenty-five guineas a week
if he would come to the United States, he accepted, in spite of the
fact that he was still bound to Harris of Covent Garden. After a
deal of difficulty, since Cooke persisted in getting drunk on every
possible occasion, Cooper finally placed him on a ship which sailed
from Liverpool on October 4, 1810, for New York City, where
he arrived on the 16th of November, the first great English actor
to visit the New World.[53]

"A very judicious critic observed," says Genest, "that Cooke did
not play many parts well, but that he played those, which he did
play well, better than anybody else." And he lists as Cooke's best
parts Sir Pertinax Macsycophant, Iago, Richard III, Sir Giles
Overreach, Kitely, Shylock, and Sir Archy Macsarcasm.[54] Indeed
the testimony as to the success of Cooke's Sir Giles seems to be
unanimous, though several put him below Henderson in the rôle.
The *Biographia Dramatica* for example comments: ". . . Mr.
Cooke . . . though he may fall short of his predecessor just mentioned yet sustains the part with credit."[55] Boaden, always inclined

[52] Cruickshank (Edition), p. 130, following John Parker's communication in
The Times Literary Supplement of September 7, 1922.
[53] For Cooke's appearances as Sir Giles in America, see Part II, pp. 175-80.
[54] Genest, Vol. VIII, pp. 196-7.
[55] Vol. III, p. 81.

to underrate Cooke in order to exalt Kemble, remarks of Cooke's Overreach: "He played it as he did Richard, and there he was strictly right in everything he did. In the convulsive agony, however, he was only noisy; his face refused to supply what breath failed to utter. Still the exultation and the horror; alike, were perfect only in Henderson."[56] Others, however, do not temper their enthusiasm. *The Dramatic Censor* reviews one of his performances as follows:[57]

> The foundation of this character [Sir Giles Overreach], like that of his favorite one of Richard III, consists in strong passions, unprincipled ambition, and dark and daring designs; and we think Mr. Cooke's performance of it very masterly. When he came on the stage in the first act, he was so hoarse, that it was only by great exertions that he could make his voice audible; but in the succeeding scenes the spirit of the character animated him to such a degree, that the defect was scarcely noticed; and, at the conclusion, the little that remained of it seemed to be the natural effect of that frantic energy and unbroken resolution with which the bold and haughty mind of Sir Giles beholds all its projects dissipated, and its fondest designs reversed; he was borne off the stage amidst a tumult of applause which continued for some minutes.

When Sir Walter Scott saw Cooke in *A New Way to Pay Old Debts* I do not know, but on March 13, 1813, he wrote to Joanna Baillie: "I saw him [Kemble] play Sir Giles Overreach (the Richard III of middling life) last night; but he came not within a hundred miles of Cooke, whose terrible visage, and short, abrupt, and savage utterance, gave reality almost to that extraordinary scene in which he boasts of his own successful villainy to a nobleman of worth and honour, of whose alliance he is ambitious. Cooke contrived somehow to impress upon the audience the idea of such a monster of enormity as had learned to pique himself upon his own atrocious character."[58]

Three great actors, Henderson, Kemble, and Cooke, had now played Sir Giles, of whom only the second had failed to realize the character. Henceforth the part was alive, and nearly all the im-

[56] Boaden, Vol. II, p. 296.
[57] I copy from Ms. reviews in the Harvard Theatre Collection.
[58] Lockhart, Vol. IV, pp. 57-9.

portant stars—as well as many who twinkled most faintly—must have a try at it. A few of them perhaps surpassed the man who has just been discussed; yet somehow "the image of George Frederick Cooke, pointing with his long, lean forefinger and uttering Sir Giles's imprecation upon Marrall, never fades out of theatrical history."[59]

[59] Winter, *Shadows of the Stage*, First Series, pp. 73-4.

CHAPTER IV

THE LIGHTNING FLASHES

WITH Henderson and Kemble and Cooke, Sir Giles Over-reach came out of obscurity into the broad light of day. No longer skulking on his country estate or travelling unfrequented byways which only occasionally lead to London, he now found himself, not without some amazement, not only at home in the metropolis but on the verge of being the rage. It was not that his wickedness had abated one jot—indeed he became more villain-ous than ever—but that it was accepted as something real and vital which, however heinous, entitled him to respectful attention. To be passed over as not worthy of notice had been a condition he had not known how to combat, but to be hated was the very breath of life to him. Sir Giles actually began to swagger. In some dim recol-lection of the distant past, he remembered vaguely the furor he had once created; his heart warmed at the thought of becoming again popular in his unpopularity, a force of tremendous power. Secretly he thanked whatever gods he knew for those who had let loose emotions so long dammed up by court artifice and neo-classicism. He would show these Londoners, yes, all Great Britain and even those upstart Americans, a reincarnation of evil beyond their wild-est dreams. The only problem was to find someone to introduce him. Henderson and Kemble and Cooke had been very useful, but they had served their purpose and could now be discarded. He pondered long and anxiously, biding his time, finally made his choice, descended unexpectedly upon an obscure country tragedian called Edmund Kean.

A glamor attends the career of Edmund Kean such as surrounds that of no other actor. His life with its vicissitudes and successes is the most interesting of novels. Born under such doubtful cir-cumstances that even the identity of his mother is not certain, educated by the slings and arrows of outrageous fortune, a wanderer over the face of the earth, he attained histrionic triumphs which made him the toast of the noble and the fair, the recipient of the critics' superlatives, the very paragon of actors.

This is not the place to enter into an extended discussion of Kean's parentage. He was probably the son of Ann Carey, the scapegrace daughter of George Saville Carey, who was the son of the dramatist Henry Carey, in whom ran the noble blood of the great Lord Halifax. His father seems to have been either Aaron Kean, a tailor, or the latter's brother, Edmund, a clerk, with the probabilities in favor of Edmund. On the other hand Kean denied all this, proclaiming himself the son of Miss Tidswell, the actress who fostered him, by the Duke of Norfolk; *this* is denied by both parties concerned. The one important and indubitable fact is that he was born. Very likely this was in 1787. By turn a ballet-sprite, a tumbler at fairs, a packhorse for Ann Carey's pomatums, an amateur vagabond-player graduating to an "infant Roscius," "Master Carey, the Pupil of Nature," he had by 1804 become a professional strolling actor, whose complicated wanderings I shall not attempt to follow. In 1808, while acting at Cheltenham, he married a young Irish actress named Mary Chambers. Thereafter they loved and starved together, wandering, often by foot, from one engagement to another. Debt was followed by privation, and privation by gloom which Kean tried to cast off with drink. Two children born to them did not decrease their hardships. Such a life was for Kean, ambitious in spirit and conscious of powers always pointed at London, degrading and disheartening. At last Dr. Drury saw him act and reported to the Drury Lane committee; Arnold, the manager, was sent to Dorchester to see him play, and commenced negotiations to bring him to London. It was a long and, for the Keans, a painful process. Kean had neglected to tell Arnold that he was already engaged to Elliston for the New Olympic. The couple waited, despairing, sorrowing, hoping. Late in 1813 they went to London. Kean and Elliston and Arnold argued over the contracts, finally reached an agreement. Kean haunted the theatre with dogged persistence, claiming the trial which he hoped would change his luck. The other actors were scornful, the manager condescending, no one encouraging. At last he received grudging permission to play Shylock; undaunted by the open hostility at his innovations, he rehearsed. And on January 26, 1814, the obscure country tragedian made his appearance at Drury Lane before an audience which filled only a quarter of the huge house. What followed is familiar to all. Kean's new and vital and sardonic Shylock was received with rapturous applause by spectators who thrilled to his extraordinary intensity. His success was made. Richard III, Hamlet, Othello, Iago, and Luke (in *Riches,* an adaptation of Massinger's *City Madam*) followed in succession, of course with repetitions, with the free-list suspended and people clamoring for seats. The tide had turned and Edmund Kean, romantic actor *par excellence,* was the idol of London.[1]

It was in his third season at Drury Lane that Kean first gave his Sir Giles Overreach to a London audience, but he may have played the part before. I have been fortunate enough to find, among the clippings filed under Kean in the Harvard Theatre Collection, an interesting item which records, how truthfully it is impossible to say, what is evidently Kean's début in the rôle. Unfortunately there is nothing on the clipping to identify it, and my attempts to find the paper from which it was taken have proved fruitless. The clipping, which I quote entire, reads as follows:

Kean's First Success

Edmund Kean, the greatest of this century's actors, was, when a young man, employed in an extremely humble capacity on the boards. In 1803 he joined a strolling company in Scotland and continued with it for eleven years, at first, at least, as general property man and performer of subordinate parts. The following anecdote relating to this portion of his career I heard, upwards of fifty years ago, from Dr. Mounsey, Thornhill, Dumfriesshire. The company had been acting at Ayr and making very bad business, so that to work their way south to Dumfries it was necessary

---

[1] The literature on Edmund Kean is so vast in quantity that I can indicate here only a few sources. *The Life of Edmund Kean,* 2 vols., London, 1835, written anonymously by Brian Waller Proctor, is of importance for first hand information. For a long time the standard biography, largely because of its fullness rather than its authenticity, was F. W. Hawkins's *Life of Edmund Kean,* 2 vols., London, 1869. J. F. Molloy's *Life and Adventures of Edmund Kean,* 2 vols., London, 1888, is largely a popular rehash of the two above. A definitive biography has now at last appeared in Professor Harold N. Hillebrand's *Edmund Kean,* New York, 1933. This chapter was written before the publication of this book but has been corrected in the light of its fine clarity and distinguished scholarship. For further sources, readers are referred to Hillebrand.

for them to break up into separate sections. This gave Kean an opportunity of attempting parts for which he felt a calling but from which he had been hitherto debarred. His section reached the village of Thornhill and gave their entertainments in a barn with such properties as they had or could collect. The play for one evening was Massinger's "A New Way to Pay Old Debts," and Kean had managed to secure the part of Sir Giles Overreach (afterwards one of his masterpieces). At one portion of the performance, and when he was in the whirlwind of passion, he was suddenly interrupted by peal upon peal of uncontrollable laughter. Kean "piled up the agony," and all but tore the passion to tatters in his efforts to subdue the ill-timed merriment. In vain; the cachination waxed only louder. Disgusted, he turned to leave the stage, when the innocent cause of the disorder revealed itself to his eyes. The blanket, or whatever formed the back curtain, had dropped down, and exposed a half-clad member of the troupe painfully laboring to introduce his (or her) legs into a pair of sadly dilapidated silk stockings, whence his feet would insist on escaping through rents in this or that direction. The unconscious earnestness of the robing artist, whose back was towards the house, was too much for Kean also, and he, joining in the general "guffaw," rushed off the stage.

The Doctor used to say that this was the first occasion on which Kean was allowed a leading part, and constituted, therefore, his first real step toward advancement.

Whether this remarkable performance took place or whether it is merely the retrospective afterglow of Kean's later success in the part I do not know. The statement that he was with one strolling company from 1803 to 1814 is of course an error, and does not help towards the solution of the problem. I can see only one ray of light and that is very faint. In March 1806 Kean apparently was at Dumfries in a company managed by one Moss.[2] Is it possible that Kean, at that time about nineteen years of age, played Sir Giles under the circumstances mentioned above? Stranger things have happened of course—indeed we shall see them—yet I am inclined to think the performance alluded to, if it took place at all, occurred at some later date in his wanderings, a date which it is practically impossible to discover in view of the darkness which surrounds Kean's provincial strolling. Perhaps Kean played Sir

[2] Hawkins, Vol. I, p. 57.

Giles many times before his Drury Lane triumph, but these hypothetical performances too must remain a mystery.[3]

Almost two years after his first appearance as a star in a London theatre, Kean acted Sir Giles Overreach at Drury Lane. According to Hawkins,[4] it was due "to the taste and discrimination of Kean" himself that *A New Way to Pay Old Debts,* among other Elizabethan plays, was revived. This is made the more probable if Kean had already appeared in the play while on the road. The first performance was given on January 12, 1816, and proved to be one of the most amazing exhibitions in the history of the stage. The cast was as follows:[5]

Sir Giles Overreach .... Kean
Wellborn .... Harley
Lord Lovell .... Holland
Marrall .... Munden
Justice Greedy .... Oxberry
Allworth .... S. Penley
Lady Allworth .... Mrs. Glover
Margaret .... Mrs. Horn

and Froth by Miss Tidswell, whose relation to Kean has already been mentioned. I may be pardoned for quoting largely about this performance, since a paraphrase could not possibly be as graphic as the overwhelming testimony of contemporaries or of authoritative biographers.

Suppose we start slowly, mingling with some of the audience and getting their impressions. Henry Crabb Robinson was there, of course, but let him tell it himself:[6]

---

[3] Clapp in his *Record of the Boston Stage*, p. 172, makes the extraordinary but positive statement that when Kean was in Cherry's company at Swansea (and elsewhere) [1809-1811] "he achieved a succession of triumphs as Sir Giles Overreach," etc. I do not know the source of this statement, and I can find no evidence to this effect, but it may be true. See also Cotton, p. 31.

[4] Hawkins, Vol. I, p. 338.

[5] Genest, Vol. VIII, p. 524, and the bill.

[6] Thomas Sadler (ed.), *Diary, Reminiscences and Correspondence of Henry Crabb Robinson*, 2nd edition, London, 1869, Vol. II, p. 3.

Charles Lamb too must have seen Kean's Overreach for in August 1819, without referring to any particular performance, he comments on the acting of the part. He is really concerned with correcting an error of his in a previous criticism, so there is not much that is fit for our purpose; I reproduce therefore only part of one sentence: "When we consider the intense tone in which Mr.

I dined with the Colliers, and in the evening went to Drury Lane with Jane Collier and Miss Lamb to see "A New Way to Pay Old Debts," a very spirited comedy by Massinger. Kean's Sir Giles Overreach is a very fine piece of acting indeed. His rage at the discovery of the fraud in the marriage of his daughter is wrought to a wonderful height, and becomes almost too tragical. On the contrary, Munden, who also plays admirably the part of a knavish confidant, is infinitely comical, and in one or two instances he played too well, for he disturbed the impression that Kean was to raise by the equally strong effect of his own acting. Oxberry played Greedy, the hungry magistrate, pleasantly, and Harley was thought to perform Wellborn well; but he displeases me in this, that he seems to have no keeping. Sometimes he reminds one of Banister, sometimes Lewis, so that at last he is neither a character nor himself. Mrs. Glover was agreeable in playing Lady Allworth.

Whether Brian Waller Proctor saw this performance of January 12 I do not know, but we need not question the probity of his account in the main :[7]

But on the 12th of January, 1816, Massinger's play of "A New Way to Pay Old Debts" was revived; and here he [Kean] again produced a tremendous effect on the town by his performance of Sir Giles Overreach. . . . Kean acted Giles in his very best style: he kept close to the character, and indulged himself in few or none of those freaks or relaxations of manner, into which he occasionally broke in his other parts, and injured their integrity. His performance was vigorous, true, uniform, and complete. It was not so grand as his Othello, because the character does not admit of such grandeur; but the conclusion was as terrific as anything that has been seen upon the stage. It threw ladies in the side-boxes into hysterics, and Lord Byron himself into a "convulsion-fit." One veteran actress was so overpowered, by the last dying speech of Sir Giles, that she absolutely fainted upon the stage. All these things show more clearly than we can do, the surprising energy of Kean's acting. His success was equal to his merit. He performed the character seventeen times before the 9th

Kean thinks it proper (and he is quite as likely to be in the right as his blundering critic) to pitch the temperament of that monstrous character from the beginning, it follows but logically and naturally that where the wild, uncontrollable man comes to be baffled of his purpose, his passion should assume a frenzied manner. . . ." See Brander Matthews (ed.): *The Dramatic Essays of Charles Lamb*, pp. 258-9.

[7] Proctor, Vol. II, pp. 138-42.

Edmund Kean as Sir Giles Overreach, from the picture
by T. Wageman for Oxberry's *New English Drama*

of March [when *The Duke of Milan* was revived], and brought a prodigious sum of money into the Drury Lane treasury.

Kean exulted, as much as the humblest actor could do, at the applause that he forced from his audiences. The praise of individuals, however sincere or valuable, was nothing to that of the public. And to the praise of lords in particular, he seems to have been more than usually indifferent. When he returned home after his great triumph in Sir Giles Overreach, his wife met him at the door. "Well," said she, eagerly, "well,—what *did* Lord Essex think of it?" "D—n Lord Essex!" retorted the contemptuous tragedian. "The *pit* ROSE at me!"

The reviewer in *The Times* comments as follows:

"A New Way to Pay Old Debts" was revived at Drury Lane Theatre last night. This play, though occasionally brought into notice within the memory of those who still frequent the Drama, has, through some misfortune, or want of management—some failure in the acting, or corruption of the public feeling, never kept steady possession of the stage. We are happy to offer it as our decided judgment that it has now reappeared under such favorable circumstances as will ensure to the London audience a long course of rich and rational delight, and to the name of Massinger a full, however tardy, measure of justice. Of Mr. Kean's performance of the character of Sir Giles Overreach, we have some fear of being charged with the ordinary fault of exaggeration, if we attempt to convey to others our own conception of its excellence. We think it by many degrees his grandest and most noble effort. The character, indeed, belongs in the strictest sense, to tragedy; it is a vivid picture of terrific and untameable passions, leading to the commission of the most odious crimes. Shakespeare, perhaps, has scarcely ever sketched a more daring portrait. The subtle, malignant, and ironical oppressor; the hardy bravo that maintains by his sword the wrongs he offers—the miser, loaded with the spoils of triumphant avarice, dressing up to himself a second idol of ambition, that he may be refreshed by the acquisition of a double stimulus, to the accomplishment of further wickedness; all these are thrown together by a vigorous and luxuriant invention, and go to form, in the person of Sir Giles Overreach, a model which could only have sprung from a mind profoundly conversant in human nature, and gifted with an extraordinary power of generalizing and combining its observations. Mr. Kean gave to this character throughout a complexion of the deadliest hue. He gave it all its subtlety, coarseness, and ferocity. Tyrant and destroyer were written as legibly on his brow, as ever they sat on the countenance of Richard. His occasional relaxation into an assumed and designing levity was not the least striking instance of his skill, and was in frightful harmony with the schemes he meditated, and the passions he but half concealed. The tone of severe though almost involuntary sarcasm, with which he never failed to utter the title of "Lord," and the epithet "Right Honourable," had something in it strikingly characteristic of a spirit that mocked the puerility of its own ambition. His finest scenes were his first communication to his daughter of her intended marriage with Lord Lovell—his avowal to that Nobleman of his disdain for every upright principle, and moral obligation—and the last—in which his villanies were detected—his schemes disappointed—his nephew liberated from his gripe—and his daughter married, under the authority of his own signature, to Allworth. The variety, and at the same time the intensity of passion, which burned within him throughout this high-wrought scene, has never been surpassed by any actor. The whirlwind of rage and vengeance sweeping before it every creature within its reach—was succeeded by despair so terrible—and concluded by a torpor so fixed and shocking, that the look which accompanied his removal from the stage bore no resemblance to any thing we ever witnessed, except the expression which sometimes remains upon the human countenance when a violent death has imprinted there the image of its fatal agonies. As a proof of the force with which this impression was communicated by Mr. Kean to others beside ourselves, Mrs. Glover who stood near him immediately before he was carried off, was so far overcome by it, as to sink into a chair beside her. The other characters were respectably represented. Lady Allworth did not admit of much exertion, but Mrs. Glover gave it fully as much importance as belonged to it; her rebuke of a presuming servant was delivered with no common dignity and good sense. Munden's Marrall was in his best style of redundant, but irresistible humour. Harley was the Wellborn, which he played with less exuberance, and more like a gentleman than we had expected. His replies to his uncle in the concluding scene were delivered with spirit and feeling. Oxberry, in Justice Greedy; S. Penley, in Allworth; and Mrs. Horne, in Margaret, got through these subordinate parts without offending. This Play must surely become a favourite, and will, we trust, encourage the Managers to bring into circulation many other treasures from the same mine.

The Theatrical Inquisitor agrees with the reviewer in *The Times* that this is Kean's greatest part :[8]

Sir Giles Overreach as performed by Mr. Kean is a very superior piece of acting, his judgment is here displayed in all its wonted nicety, and his execution exceeds that of any character he has hitherto represented even without an exception in favour of Richard. Mr. Kean appears to have thrown his whole soul, as it were, into the part of Sir Giles, and the fruits of his efforts have been crowned with deserved success. In one or two instances, the force of his acting was most sensibly felt; and his genius shone forth with a splendour, which could not fail to be impressed upon the minds of the audience; his violent bursts of passion were succeeded by those calmer touches which form so essential a contrast, and give additional effect to the scene. In the interview with his daughter, whilst instructing her in what manner she is to receive the advances of Lord Lovell; he was particularly excellent. The sordid villain initiating virtue in the wiles of seduction; in order to gratify his unnatural, avaricious cravings, as beautifully portrayed by the author; had ample justice done to it by the execution of this great actor. He far surpasses what we have seen him before achieve; and indeed, those who would form a just estimate of Mr. Kean's talent, must witness his performance of Sir Giles Overreach.

A footnote states, "A handsome Cup is about to be presented to Mr. Kean by his brother Actors, as a compliment to his excellence in this character, to which Lord Byron, and several other distinguished theatrical Gentlemen, have contributed in a most liberal manner."

An even more graphic account of the conclusion is given by Hawkins :[9]

. . . Scream after scream reverberated through the solemn stillness of the house—a stillness now broken by the confusion caused by the removal of hysterical women; Lord Byron was seized with

[8] *The Theatrical Inquisitor and Monthly Mirror*, January 1816, Vol. VIII, pp. 71-2.
[9] Hawkins, Vol. I, pp. 343-7, 392. Much of Hawkins's account is either paraphrased or taken verbatim from the story in *The Times* already quoted. No acknowledgment is made for his undocumented borrowings. On Byron at this performance, see Thomas Moore (ed.), *Works of Lord Byron*, Vol. III, p. 77. There is also an interesting commentary in Byron's *Letters and Journals* (ed. Prothero), Vol. V, p. 90.

a sort of convulsive fit; the pit rose en masse; all parts of the house followed its example; and as hats and handkerchiefs were waved with unparalleled enthusiasm, thunders on thunders of applause swept over the theatre. But the effect of the actor's intensity was not confined to the audience; it had the extraordinary and unprecedented effect of communicating itself to the actors themselves. Mrs. Glover, an actress who, from her powerful intellect and long experience, might have been supposed proof against any species of dramatic illusion, fainted outright on the stage; Mrs. Horn staggered to a chair and wept aloud at the appalling sight; and Munden, who sustained Marall in a manner worthy of his leader, stood so transfixed with astonishment and terror, that he was taken off by the armpits, his legs trailing and his eyes riveted with a species of fascination on Kean's convulsed and blackened countenance. Once behind the scenes, however, and recalled to himself, the old comedian recovered. "My God!" he murmured to Harley, "is it possible?"

The performance over, Lord Byron rushed behind the scenes and grasped Kean's hand. "Great! great!" he exclaimed. "By Jove, that *was* acting."

Hawkins's exaggeration has obviously teased fact into fiction, as a comparison with any of the reviews already quoted shows at once. He has taken points here and there from various critiques and embellished them until the decoration has almost swallowed up the structure. But a comparison with the reviews also shows that a certain amount of what he says is based on fact, and that Kean's effect in this performance must have been tremendous. And it is exceedingly important to remember, as we try to discover exactly what *did* happen, that no contemporary, as far as I know, has ever denied in writing even the wildest of these accounts.[10]

Perhaps the most important critic who reviewed this performance of January 12, 1816 is William Hazlitt. His remarks appeared in *The Examiner* of January 14:[11]

[10] See also the letter (owned by W. J. Lawrence and printed by Hillebrand, pp. 158-9) by Mrs. Kean's sister, Susan Chambers, January 20, which reads in part: "Mrs. Glover got into strong histericks & many ladies fainted."

[11] A. R. Waller and Arnold Glover (eds.), *The Collected Works of William Hazlitt*, Vol. VIII, pp. 273-4. For general comment on the play and the character of Sir Giles Overreach, see Hazlitt's prefatory remarks to Oxberry's *New English Drama*.

We do not know any one now-a-days, who could write Massinger's Comedy of A New Way to Pay Old Debts, though we do not believe it was better acted at the time it was first brought out, than it is at present. We cannot conceive of any one's doing Mr. Kean's part of Sir Giles Overreach so well as himself. We have seen others in the part, superior in the look and costume, in hardened, clownish, rustic insensibility; but in the soul and spirit, no one equal to him. He is a truly great actor. This is one of his very best parts. He was not at a single fault. The passages which we remarked as particularly striking and original, were those where he expresses surprise at his nephew's answers, "His fortune swells him!—'Tis rank, he's married!" and again, where, after the exposure of his villanies, he calls to his accomplice Marall in a half-wheedling, half-terrific tone, "Come hither Marall, come hither." Though the speech itself is absurd and out of character, his manner of stopping when he is running at his foes, "I'm feeble, some widow's curse hangs on my sword,"[12] was exactly as if his arm had been suddenly withered, and his powers shrivelled up on the instant. The conclusion was quite over-whelming. Mr. Kean looked the part well, and his voice does not fail as it used to do. Mr. Munden's Marall was an admirable piece of acting, and produced some of the most complete comic contrasts we ever saw. He overdoes his parts sometimes, and sometimes gets into parts for which he is not fit: but he has a fine broad face and manner which tells all the world over. His manner of avoiding the honour of a salute from Lady Allworth, was a most deliberate piece of humour; and the account of the unexpected good fortune of young Welborn almost converts his eyes into saucers, and chokes him with surprises.

Mr. Oxberry's Justice Greedy was very entertaining, both from the subject and from his manner of doing it. Oxberry is a man of practical imagination, and the apparitions of fat turkies, chines of bacon, and pheasants dressed in toast and butter, evidently floated in rapturous confusion before his senses. There is nothing that goes down better than what relates to eating and drinking, on the stage, in books, or in real life. Mr. Harley's Welborn was indifferent, but he is upon the whole a very pleasant actor. Mrs. Glover, as Lady Allworth, puts on some very agreeable frowns; and Mr. Holland's Lord Lovell was one continued smile, without

---

[12] Here and elsewhere Hazlitt is quoting from memory or from a stage-version of the play.

any meaning that we could discover, unless this actor, after his disguise in the Beggar's Bush, was delighted at the restoration of his hat and feather.

After such reviews it is not surprising to discover that from January 12 to the end of the Drury Lane theatrical season, Kean played Sir Giles Overreach twenty-six times.[13] It became the rage to see Kean's Sir Giles. By February, a critic could write:[14] "In Sir Giles Overreach, we take pleasure to say it, Mr. Kean has acquired so high a reputation, not only with the public, but with his compeers, that his success has become the fashionable topic of the day; insomuch, that it supersedes the Englishman's darling theme of the weather, and the salute, *en passant* now is—not 'What a rainy day!'—but, 'Do tell me, have you seen Kean in Sir Giles Overreach?' "

Hazlitt was not content with one article on Kean's Sir Giles Overreach. A week after his review of the first performance, he wrote in *The Examiner*:[15]

> The admirable comedy of a New Way to Pay Old Debts continues to be acted with increased effect. Mr. Kean is received with shouts of applause in Sir Giles Overreach. We have heard two objections to his manner of doing the part, one of which we think right and the other not. When he is asked "Is he not moved by the orphan's tears, the widow's curse?" he answers—"Yes—as

[13] Genest, Vol. VIII, p. 524, but he mentions specifically only the first performance. Playbills and the advertisements in *The Times*, however, enable me to give the dates: January 12, 15, 19, 22, 26, 29; February 2, 5, 9, 12, 16, 19, 23, 26, 29; March 4, 7, 11, 14, 18, 21, 25; May 2, 6; June 17, 22. Mrs. Orger "in consequence of the sudden and severe Indisposition of Mrs. Horn," substituted for that lady for the performance of March 7; for a similar reason Gattie replaced Munden on March 18, 21, and 25; on May 2 and 6, Holland being ill, Kent played Lord Lovell; Bernard was the Allworth on May 6. Otherwise the cast remained the same.

[14] *The Critical Review*, Vol. III, Ser. V, p. 190.

This attitude naturally brought crowds to the theatre and money into the treasury. The two hundred eighteen nights of the season averaged £270 per night. Of the seven best nights, six were for Kean's *A New Way to Pay Old Debts*: January 29, £609.11; January 26, £608.3; January 22, £590.13; January 19, £581.6.6; January 15, £547.14.6; May 20 (*Bertram*), £524.16; February 12, £522.9 (*Reminiscences of Thomas Dibdin*, Vol. II, p. 102); but see also Hillebrand, p. 158.

[15] Waller and Glover, Vol. VIII, p. 277; or *The Examiner* for January 21, 1816.

rocks by waves, or the moon by howling wolves." Mr. Kean in speaking the latter sentence, dashes his voice about with the greatest violence, and howls out his indignation and rage. Now we conceive this is wrong: for he has to express not violence, but firm, inflexible resistance to it,—not motion, but rest. The very pause after the word *yes,* points out the cool deliberate way in which it should be spoken. The other objection is to his manner of pronouncing the word "Lord,—Right Honourable Lord," which Mr. Kean uniformly does in a drawling tone, with a mixture of fawning servility and sarcastic contempt. This has been thought inconsistent with the part, and with the desire which Sir Giles has to ennoble his family by alliance with a "Lord, a Right Honourable Lord."[16] We think Mr. Kean never showed more genius than in pronouncing this single word, *Lord.* It is a complete exposure (produced by the violence of the character), of the elementary feelings which make up the common respect excited by mere rank. This is nothing but a cringing to power and opinion, with a view to turn them to our own advantage with the world. Sir Giles is one of those knaves, who "do themselves homage." He makes use of Lord Lovell merely as the stalking-horse of his ambition. In other respects, he has the greatest contempt for him, and the necessity he is under of paying court to him for his own purposes, infuses a double portion of gall and bitterness into the expression of his self-conscious superiority. No; Mr. Kean was perfectly right in this, he spoke the word "Lord" *con amore.* His praise of the kiss, "It came twanging off— I like it," was one of his happiest passages. It would perhaps be as well, if in the concluding scene he would contrive not to frighten the ladies into hysterics. But the whole together is admirable.

Again the hysterics! Surely it is necessary to doubt no longer the tremendous effect of Kean's Sir Giles Overreach in the last scene.

Hawkins tells us of one bit of stage business which Kean used in this last scene, which was taken from an actual occurrence.[17] On one occasion, Kean witnessed a fight between a farmer and an actor whose name, curiously enough, was Giles. The farmer by superior strength easily overpowered his weaker antagonist, but Giles "remained unsubdued in spirit, and in a paroxysm of defeated wrath,

---

[16] See for example the critiques in *The News* of January 14, 1816; and *The Critical Review* of February 1816, Vol. III, Ser. V, pp. 189-91.

[17] Hawkins, Vol. I, p. 74, following without acknowledgment *Fraser's Magazine*, Vol. VII, pp. 734 *ff*.

which convulsed his whole frame and seemed all but to suffocate
him, he dragged open his shirt-collar, and tore it to ribands. This
incident was not lost upon Kean, who subsequently reproduced it
in the last scene of *A New Way to Pay Old Debts* when he appeared
as Overreach in London; and no one who saw him in that
character can ever forget the appalling sensations produced by his
manner as, with face livid, eyes distended, lips swollen and parted
at the corners, teeth set, and visage quivering, he dragged open his
shirt-collar and tore it to ribands." Here was realism indeed! It is
not so surprising that an audience, used to the classic acting of the
Kemble school, should be moved to an extraordinary pitch of
excitement.

On February 15, Hazlitt went again to see Kean play Sir Giles
Overreach, and contributed still another article on the subject to
The Examiner.[18] The article is exceedingly important because it
points out the difficulties which the size of the patent theatres
caused both the actors and contemporary dramatists. I will, I hope,
be pardoned the parenthesis if I remark that one of the reasons
why the early nineteenth century was so devoid of original plays
of any artistic merit is that the theatres were so large that only the
broad effects of pantomime and melodrama could reach the spectators in the back of the house. But to Hazlitt:

> We saw Mr. Kean's Sir Giles Overreach on Friday night from
> the boxes at Drury-Lane Theatre, and we are not surprised at
> the incredulity as to this great actor's powers, entertained by
> those persons who have only seen him from that elevated sphere.
> We do not hesitate to say, that those who have only seen him at
> a distance, have not seen him at all. The expression of his face
> is quite lost, and only the harsh and grating tones of his voice
> produce their full effect on the ear. The same recurring sounds,
> by dint of repetition, fasten on the attention, while the varieties
> and finer modulations are lost in their passage over the pit. All
> you discover is an abstraction of his defects, both of person, voice,
> and manner. . . . Mr. Kean's acting is not, we understand, much
> relished in the upper circles. It is thought too obtrusive and
> undisguised a display of nature. Neither was Garrick's at all
> relished at first, by the old Nobility, till it became the fashion to

[18] Waller and Glover, Vol. VIII, pp. 284-5; or *The Examiner* for February
18, 1816.

admire him. The court dresses, the drawing room strut, and the sing-song declamation, which he banished from the stage, were thought much more dignified and imposing.

Needless to say the fame of Kean's performances had spread, for, when in March he appeared at the Queen Street Theatre, Glasgow, then under the management of Harry Johnstone, who had gained for himself a considerable reputation by thrashing the Prince of Wales when he proved too attentive to his wife, the press was terrific. "When at last the portals were opened, a crush, which was mingled with shouts, cheers, and shrieks ensued. Men fought, women fainted, and were carried fainting in some instances into the theatre, unable to get out of the dense multitude."[19] I do not know whether Kean played *A New Way to Pay Old Debts* on this engagement but it is listed as among those dramas performed upon Kean's next visit to Glasgow in April.

Such an extraordinary exhibition of histrionic power as Kean's impersonation of Sir Giles Overreach demanded some equally extraordinary recognition, and the Drury Lane committee, adopting a suggestion of Mr. Justice Greedy Oxberry,[20] decided to present him with a silver cup, modelled on the famous Warwick vase, to cost three hundred guineas. Every member of the committee and company contributed with two exceptions, Munden and Dowton. The former was notably penurious, the latter jealous of Kean's success. One of the two, it matters little which,[21] when asked for his subscription, replied, "You may *cup* Mr. Kean if you like, but you don't bleed me." At the end of the season the cup was presented to Kean in the greenroom of the theatre. It bore the following inscription: "To Edmund Kean this vase was presented on the 25th day of June, 1816, by Robert Palmer, father of the

[19] Baynham, pp. 88-9, who is also the authority for the April performance of Sir Giles although he is a year early as to date.

[20] Oxberry later burlesqued Kean's last act of Sir Giles Overreach in Moncrieff's *Tereza Tompkins* at one of the minor theatres, which provoked a quarrel. See Colburn's *New Monthly Magazine* (1834), Vol. XLI, p. 58. On the play, see Genest, Vol. IX, pp. 174-5.

[21] My account is taken from Hawkins, Vol. I, pp. 378-82; Molloy, Vol. I, pp. 262-3; Hillebrand, p. 162. Hawkins tells the story of Dowton, Molloy of Munden, Hillebrand of Dowton. The introduction to French's acting edition agrees with Molloy. On the cup, see also Susan Chambers's letter (Hillebrand, pp. 158-9).

Drury Lane company, in the names of Right Hon. Lord Byron, Hon. Douglas Kinnaird, Right Hon. George Lamb, Chandos Leigh, Esq., S. Davies, Esq. [then follow the names of the company, fifty-two in number, Munden and Dowton being excluded], in testimony of their admiration of his transcendent talents, and more especially to commemorate his first representation of the character of Sir Giles Overreach on the 12th of January, 1816, when, in common with an astonished public, overcome with the irresistible power of his genius, they received a lasting impression of excellence, which twenty-six successive representations have served but to confirm."[22]

This is as good a place as any to state that from here on my catalogue of Kean's performances of Sir Giles must of necessity be incomplete. When an actor has played a part as many times as Kean played this one, it would be fruitless to expect to find records of all the performances. Therefore I must be content to note those I have discovered, warning the reader that I feel sure that there were many more which have escaped my search. Occasionally too I find hints of performances which no amount of pains has enabled me to date. One of Dr. Doran's manuscripts, for example, contains the following note:[23] "Mr. York, of Penzance, told us that Kean came with his yacht into Mount's Bay, and that he acted superbly Richard, Othello, and Sir Giles, at the Penzance Theatre, —which is now a carpenter's shop. 1871.", a reference which leaves me helpless. There are no annals of the Penzance Theatre, and none of Kean's biographers mentions a performance at that place. I can find no playbills to resolve the difficulty, and newspapers are inaccessible. Letters of inquiry brought no information.

The Drury Lane season over, Kean went to Bath, where as might have been expected, he played Sir Giles.[24] Genest records two performances, one on July 2, 1816, the other ten days later for Kean's benefit.[25] Stanley was the Wellborn, Mrs. Weston the Lady Allworth. At the performance on July 12, "when Kean was carried off in the last scene of the play, a Gentleman in the Pit

---

[22] I have levelled capitals and added punctuation.
[23] Doran, Vol. III, p. 399, editor's note.
[24] Hawkins, Vol. I, p. 382.
[25] Genest, Vol. VIII, p. 565.

called out for the Curtain to fall—this absurd notion was seconded by others, and the piece was brought to an abrupt conclusion—this was the more improper, as on the 2d of July Stanley had spoken the last speech particularly well."

On August 17, Kean played Sir Giles at Exeter where a newspaper critic commented in the following terms: "His acting surpassed all that could be conceived, and must be seen to be believed. The play abruptly ended on Sir Giles' removal from the stage; the audience wanted no more, and amidst tumultuous cheering and shouts of applause the curtain dropped."[26] Kean also played Sir Giles at Plymouth during the latter part of August,[27] and back at Drury Lane on September 21 with Lady Allworth by Mrs. Knight, repeated on the 28th.[28] Early in October he was in Edinburgh, playing Overreach on the 9th and 11th; the cast was as follows:[29]

Sir Giles Overreach	Kean
Wellborn	Jones
Lord Lovell	Trueman
Marrall	Mason
Justice Greedy	Finn
Allworth	Crook
Lady Allworth	Mrs. M'Namara
Margaret	Miss Dyke

Both the audience and the *Courant* were rapturous:[30]

But both these representations [Richard and Shylock] fall far short of the delineation of Sir Giles Overreach, which was given to us last night. It was in this tremendous display of the blackest and most savage workings of the soul, that the splendour of Mr. Kean's genius shone forth, outdazzling competition, and baffling every attempt at rivalry; and it is here that we are forced to relinquish even the effort to give any idea of his excellence, for while the language that aimed to describe it adequately would perhaps be charged with exaggeration, it would fall far below the truth. We really have not the courage to cope with the attempt.

26 Cotton, p. 41.
27 *Theatrical Inquisitor,* Vol. IX, p. 237.
28 Genest, Vol. VIII, p. 581, and advertisements in *The Times.*
29 Dibdin, pp. 274-5, and playbill.
30 *The Edinburgh Evening Courant,* Thursday, October 10, 1816.

It is a hideous character, and Kean aggravates every frightful lineament belonging to it. In the catastrophe, where all the pride and malice of the fiend are lapsed in the unmitigated bitterness of his rage and despair, he seemed to borrow his colouring from the nether world—so phrenzied and demoniacal were his ravings, so much more appalling was the terror of his silence. The acme of his frightful sufferings struck the ghastliness of dismay through the house. It will be recollected that his last words are—

> ". . . Shall I thus fall
> Ingloriously and yield? No: spite of fate,
> I will be forced to hell like to myself;
> Though you were legions of accursed spirits,
> Thus would I fly among you!"

In delivering these words, Kean attempts to draw his sword, and rushes madly among his enemies; but he has miscalculated the strength which his temporary energy had given him, and falls exhausted and insensible on the ground. Recovering from their amazement and horror, the bye-standers order him to be carried off, and his servants accordingly betake themselves to the performance of that office. At the moment when they are bearing him away, his senses slowly return—he slowly recovers his recollection, and with it all the demoniac fury of his remorseless nature. Its expression is confined, however, to his countenance, for every limb is chained up in impotence. His eyes kindle with renewed rancour, and he seems on the point of again springing upon his victims; but, at this moment of horrible interest, when fate and vengeance are glaring in his eyes, his physical powers utterly and at once forsake him, and his head drops lifeless on his chest. He is carried off.

The applause of the house here broke into shouts and hurras. They were too highly wrought to bear more, and the curtain was ordered to fall, leaving the play unfinished. Mr. Kean's triumph was complete.

Assuredly it must have been! Again his acting had stopped the play. It is worth pointing out here that in Walter Hampden's alteration of the play parts of the final scene are transposed in order to give Sir Giles the final curtain.[31] Evidently Kean should have used a similar arrangement. I must not fail to add that Candidus writing in the same issue of *The Courant* remarks in part: ". . . I have

[31] See Appendix, p. 415; see also p. 332.

seen Mr. Kean's Sir Giles Overreach, certainly the finest piece of theatrical representation as a whole that I have witnessed. . . . I had only one regret in witnessing this great display of genius, and it was that of seeing our old and distinguished favourite John Kemble left completely in the shade. He performed the same character on his last visit to this city, but compared to that I have witnessed, it dwindles into nothingness." Poor Kemble! The old order changeth. . . .

Kean's next recorded performance of Sir Giles was at Brighton on November 12, 1816,[32] whence he returned to Drury Lane where according to playbills and the advertisements in *The Times* he acted the part on November 21, November 28, and December 17, the Lady Allworth by Mrs. Knight and the rest as before. On the 27th of December, Mrs. Piozzi wrote from Bath to Sir James Fellowes:[33] "Mrs. Dimond offers me a place in her box to-night whence will be seen Massinger's horrible 'Sir Giles Overreach,' played by Mr. Kean. If he can stretch that hideous character as he does others, quite beyond all the authors meant or wished, it will shock us too much for endurance, though in these days people do require mustard to everything." She survived the performance, however, as is shown by her letter of January 4: "That I had not seen the great actor [Kean] in Sir Giles Overreach when last writing to Adbury is however perfect in my remembrance; he did it very finely indeed. A clear voice and dignified manner are not necessary to the character, and personal beauty would take off too much from one's aversion. I was well entertained, and caught no cold at all." On the 18th of January, we find Kean playing Sir Giles at Windsor.[34] Performances at Drury Lane on February 10, 18, March 22, April 25, and June 14, with Margaret by Mrs. Orger, the rest as before, conclude my London list for the season of 1816-1817.[35] Meanwhile according to the bills he had played the part at Edinburgh on April 8 and 12.

[32] Porter, p. 39.
[33] A. Hayward (ed.), *Autobiography, Letters and Literary Remains of Mrs. Piozzi*, Vol. II, pp. 354-6; see also Genest, Vol. VIII, p. 630.
[34] *The Theatrical Inquisitor and Monthly Mirror*, February, 1817, Vol. X, p. 158, quoting from *The Eton and Windsor Express*.
[35] Playbills and advertisements in *The Times*.

During the next theatrical season, Kean acted in *A New Way to Pay Old Debts* at least seven times at Drury Lane.[36] The cast for all the performances was as follows:

Sir Giles Overreach .... Kean
Wellborn .... Stanley
Lord Lovell .... Holland
Marrall .... Munden
Justice Greedy .... Oxberry
Allworth .... Penley
Lady Allworth .... Mrs. Knight
Margaret .... Mrs. Orger

Stanley, it will be noticed, has superseded Harley as Wellborn. Genest says:[37] "He was generally considered as playing the part better than Harley—it was out of Harley's line." On March 21, and April 9, 1818, Kean played Sir Giles in Edinburgh,[38] and the next day at Dumfries.[39] There is, however, one more performance this season still to be treated, though I shall let Francis Courtney Wemyss[40] treat it for me in his vivid way. Acting at Rochester in the late spring of 1818, he was first introduced to Kean. "The first time I ever saw him act, I played Wellborn, to his Sir Giles Overreach, in Massinger's Play of A New Way to Pay Old Debts. With the exception of my first appearance at Glasgow, I never suffered so much from stage fright; but his known kindness and affability, to actors of every grade, soon relieved me from my embarrassment. I supped with him after the performance, and from that hour, he became my friend. Many years afterwards, in Baltimore, I had the good fortune to extricate him from a most unpleasant and dangerous situation. But of this, hereafter,—if good reader, you can travel with me across the Atlantic." We shall see, if, good reader, you travel with *me* across the Atlantic!

[36] October 11 and 18, 1817; January 8 and 24, 1818; March 12, May 23, June 20, 1818. Playbills and advertisements in *The Times*.
[37] Genest, Vol. VIII, p. 634.
[38] Dibdin, p. 282; and playbills.
[39] I am indebted to Professor Harold N. Hillebrand for kindly sending me a list of provincial performances of Sir Giles Overreach by Kean, all copied from playbills, and hereafter to be referred to as "Hillebrand's notes"; Kean also played Dumfries in 1819 and 1822.
[40] Wemyss, p. 43.

Kean appeared as Overreach in four performances at Drury Lane in 1818-1819, H. Kemble succeeding Stanley as Wellborn for the last two.[41] I have record of only one Sir Giles during the summer, that at York on July 21, 1819.[42] The next season, after two performances at Drury Lane[43] with Wellborn this time going to Russell, Kean played Sir Giles at Bath on December 29, 1819. The cast I take from a playbill:

Sir Giles Overreach .... Kean
Wellborn .... Baker
Lord Lovell .... Rowbotham
Marrall .... Cunningham
Justice Greedy .... Smith
Allworth .... Horrebow
Lady Allworth .... Mrs. Pope
Margaret .... Miss Blanchard

Two more performances conclude the Drury Lane list for the season of 1819-1820.[44] Butler was the Justice Greedy for the first of these. Kean's Sir Giles was at Lynn, however, sometime in 1820; more specific I cannot be.[45]

Kean now purposed going to America, and Elliston reopened Drury Lane on August 15 to enable him to give farewell performances of his chief rôles. Sir Giles Overreach was his character on the 18th, the 24th, and the 31st with the following cast:[46]

Sir Giles Overreach.............................. Kean
Wellborn .... Russell
Lord Lovell .... Holland
Marrall .... Munden
Justice Greedy .... Oxberry
Allworth .... Penley
Lady Allworth .... Mrs. Egerton
Margaret .... Mrs. Edwin

[41] October 10, 1818; November 5, 1818; February 13, 1819; May 6, 1819. Playbills and advertisements in *The Times*.
[42] *The Theatre, or Dramatic and Literary Mirror*, Vol. II, p. 47.
[43] November 26, 1819; December 1, 1819; from the playbills.
[44] January 19, 1820; June 10, 1820. Playbills and advertisements in *The Times*.
[45] Burley, p. 133.
[46] Genest, Vol. IX, p. 39; playbills and advertisements in *The Times*. Hillebrand, p. 194, gives the theatre wrongly as the Haymarket.

Concluding his twenty-eight performances on the 16th of September with Richard III, Kean proceeded to Liverpool, whence after a short engagement he sailed for New York.[47]

In January 1820, Hazlitt published in *The London Magazine* the first of a series of essays on the drama.[48] In it he gives us valuable first-hand comments on Kean's Sir Giles as compared with Kemble's and Cooke's. Not so enthusiastic as his earlier reviews, it represents Hazlitt's opinion after mature reflection. He still, however, thinks Kean the greatest tragic performer on the stage:

> . . . His Sir Giles is his most equal and energetic character; but it is too equal, too energetic from the beginning to the end. There is no reason that he should have the same eagerness, the same *impetus* at the commencement as at the close of his career: he should not have the fierceness of the wild beast till he is goaded to madness by the hunters. Sir Giles Mompesson (supposed to be the original character) we dare say, took things more quietly, and only grew desperate with his fortunes. Cooke played the general casting of the character better in this respect: but without the same fine breaks and turns of passion. Cooke indeed, compared to Kean, had only the *slang* and *bravado* of tragedy. Neither can we think Mr. Kemble equal to him, with all his study, his grace, and classic dignity of form. He was the statue of perfect tragedy, not the living soul. Mrs. Siddons combined the advantage of form and other organic requisites with nature and passion: Mr. Kemble has the external requisites (at least of face and figure), without the internal workings of the soul: Mr. Kean has the last without the first, and, if we must make our election between the two, we think the *vis tragica* must take precedence of every thing else. Mr. Kean, in a word, appears to us a test, an *experimentum crucis,* to shew the triumph of genius over physical defects, of nature over art, of passion over affectation, and of originality over common-place monotony. . . .

Kean left the United States on June 4, 1821, and arrived at Liverpool on the 20th of July. On the 12th of December he again trod the boards as Sir Giles at Drury Lane:[49]

[47] Hawkins, Vol. II, pp. 148-50. For Kean's American performances, see Part II, pp. 184-9.

[48] Waller and Glover, Vol. VIII, pp. 383-92.

[49] Genest, Vol. IX, p. 144, and advertisements in *The Times.*

Sir Giles Overreach .... Kean
Wellborn .... Cooper
Lord Lovell .... Thompson
Marrall .... Munden
Justice Greedy .... Loveday
Allworth .... S. Penley
Lady Allworth .... Mrs. Knight
Margaret .... Mrs. Orger

The Theatrical Observer praised with some reservations:[50]

The first appearance, this season, of Mr. Kean in the character of *Sir Giles Overreach*, attracted a genteel and rather numerous audience here, last night.

Sir Giles is nothing more than a hideous *caricature* of a bad man: a rude out-line of covetousness, and of ambition in one of its lowest walks, which are not only unmasked, but loudly proclaimed by their possessor as the cherished qualities of his soul. In this there is more than a natural daring; it is fiend-like. And who is there, at present on the British stage, that can embody such feelings and give them all the diabolical expression they are susceptible of, like Mr. Kean?

This part, however, is not of a nature to afford him much scope for his peculiar talent, until the last act, when the overwhelming fury that breathes for the [*sic*] destruction of those who have outwitted him, but that only blasts his powers, and casts him raging to the earth, is wonderfully displayed.

We do not think Mr. Kean by any means equal to himself in several of the less impassioned scenes. He, there, frequently is quite lost to the due prominency of Sir Giles; and in *colloquial* passages too often forgets the *natural* for what he, perhaps, considers a more *effective* style. The effort of last night produced much applause towards the conclusion.

Surely this is almost damning with faint praise! On the 28th of the same month, he played the part at Brighton.[51] When Kean repeated Sir Giles at Drury Lane on May 16, the doubt seems to have passed, however, and the *Observer*[52] is unfeignedly enthusiastic: "He is unequalled in it by any one within memory." What an erratic genius the man was! At the end of the Drury Lane season, after taking a benefit on June 3 when he played Paris in the scene

[50] December 13, 1821, No. 35, p. 138.
[51] Porter, p. 49.
[52] May 17, 1822, No. 157, p. 626.

of the Curia from Massinger's *The Roman Actor*,[53] Kean went to
Bath where *A New Way to Pay Old Debts* was the bill on June 18,
with Wellborn by Vining. Curiously enough, "Kean did not attract
—he was much disgusted at his reception, and with good reason—
on this night the house was very bad—Kean was so cut up, that he
did not play in force till the last act."[54] Symptoms again? A tour
now followed with Kean making Birmingham his first stop; he
played Sir Giles there on June 27,[55] repeating his performance on
July 3.[56] *The Theatrical Looker-on* of July 1, 1822, comments as
follows: "The Sir Giles Overreach of Mr. Kean abounded
throughout with fine and masterly touches of genius; his scenes
with Marrall and Lord Lovell were wonderfully effective; as a
whole it was a most brilliant performance, and the reception it met
with from the audience altogether enthusiastic.—Mude, Butler,
Archer, Raymond, and Miss Middleton, did their best, and we left
the house in high good humour with them all." Continuing his
tour, Kean played Sir Giles at the New Theatre Royal, Dublin, on
July 27, 1822; the cast from the playbill:

Sir Giles Overreach	Kean
Wellborn	Talbot
Lord Lovell	Hamerton, Jun.
Marrall	Williams
Justice Greedy	Johnson
Allworth	Armstrong
Lady Allworth	Mrs. Vaughan
Margaret	Miss Curtis

[53] Genest, Vol. IX, p. 152; Hawkins, Vol. II, p. 198, who says Kean turned
over the entire proceeds of something over £500 to a fund for the relief of the
starving Irish; Hillebrand, p. 226, says the profits were £5.17.7.

[54] Genest, Vol. IX, p. 177.

[55] Cruickshank (Edition), p. 130 gives the date wrongly as June 25. According to *The Theatrical Looker-on*, Birmingham, June 24, 1822, Vol. I, No. 5,
p. 20, Kean commenced his Birmingham engagement on June 24 with *Richard III*.
According to the issue of July 1, 1822, Vol. I, No. 6, pp. 22-3, *The Merchant of
Venice, Brutus*, and *A New Way to Pay Old Debts* "followed in succession the
representation of Richard the Third." Consequently the play on June 25 was
The Merchant of Venice, with *A New Way to Pay Old Debts* falling on the
27th.

[56] *The Theatrical Looker-on*, July 8, 1822, Vol. I, No. 7, p. 26. The comment
is as follows: "Mr. Kean repeated the character of Sir Giles Overreach with
the same undiminished effect by which his genius has long distinguished it; this
is all that need be said respecting it."

In the latter part of August, he was at Edinburgh with *A New Way to Pay Old Debts,* according to the bills, the play on the 22nd and the 24th:

Sir Giles Overreach	Kean
Wellborn	Jones
Lord Lovell	Munro
Marrall	Mackay
Justice Greedy	Murray
Allworth	Denham
Lady Allworth	Mrs. Renaud
Margaret	Miss Eyre

An engagement at Dundee concluded the summer's travelling; here Kean played Sir Giles Overreach in October.[57]

During the season of 1822-1823 at Drury Lane, with Young somewhat in the way, Kean acted Overreach only once, November 16. The cast, which I take from the playbill, was as follows:[58]

Sir Giles Overreach	Kean
Wellborn	Cooper
Lord Lovell	Thompson
Marrall	Munden
Justice Greedy	Gattie
Allworth	Penley
Lady Allworth	Mrs. Knight
Margaret	Miss Smithson

The Theatrical Observer again comments on Kean,[59] and we find somewhat to our relief that "his acting, *throughout,* met with the most distinguished applause . . ."; the italics are mine. A playbill establishes a performance of *A New Way to Pay Old Debts* at Dublin on April 1, 1823. In Kean's next season at Drury Lane, this time with Macready as a rival, the cast for February 8, 13, and 19 was as before except that Archer was the Wellborn and Oxberry the Justice Greedy.[60] Hillebrand's notes contribute a per-

[57] Hawkins, Vol. II, p. 200.
[58] A portrait of Miss Smithson as Margaret may be found as frontispiece to one of the acting editions of John Cumberland, London, n.d. There is an interesting short account of Miss Smithson in Sherson, pp. 41-2; she later conquered Paris and married discord in Hector Berlioz.
[59] November 18, 1822, No. 315.
[60] Genest, Vol. IX, p. 233; and advertisements in *The Times.*

formance at Lincoln on May 1. A production at the Theatre Royal,
Dublin, on August 28, 1824, concludes—for me at least—the season, this from a playbill.

However, all was not as it should be. Kean had become involved
in an unfortunate *affaire* with a Mrs. Cox, whose husband brought
suit. The action "Cox *v.* Kean" was tried on the 17th of January,
1825, and needless to say the whole shoddy scandal immediately
became public property. The Court of King's Bench reached a
verdict which demanded eight hundred pounds from Kean.
Though there is no question of the fact of the *amour,* there is some
doubt as to the justice of the verdict since there is more than a
suspicion of connivance, but into the merits of the question we cannot go. In the minds of the general public and those organs of
public opinion, the newspapers, Kean had become a thing unclean,
no longer deserving a hearing. The result was that his performances of *Richard III* on January 24 and of *Othello* on the 28th
precipitated something like riots. While Kean was on the stage, the
tumult was deafening and the insults repeated. A manly curtain-
speech by Kean on the 28th seemed to have a beneficent effect, but
when he played Sir Giles on the 31st, "the play was got through
very nearly in dumb show."[61] Though there was now a perceptible
decline in the uproar which greeted the following performances,
hostility had shattered Kean's pride, humiliated him beyond extremes, and made him contemptuous and scornful of his audience.
Feeling himself an outcast, he turned sorrowfully to the provinces.
He apparently had staunch friends at Brighton where he acted in
the latter part of February: "So enthusiastic had the admirers of
Kean become, that when he appeared as Richard III, on the 23rd,
shouts of 'Kean! Kean! for ever!' resounded through the auditorium. His reception as Overreach (25th) was equally glowing."[62]
At London, the storm had somewhat subsided on March 10 when
his Sir Giles was again heard at Drury Lane.[63] Dublin, remembering how in 1822 Kean had contributed to the starving Irish, gave

[61] Hawkins, Vol. II, p. 242; Genest, Vol. IX, p. 289; and see the account in
The Times on the following day. Hillebrand, pp. 253-4 shows that they exag-
gerate.
[62] Porter, p. 52, and playbill on Hillebrand's list.
[63] Advertisements in *The Times*.

him a cordial reception in May and applauded his Overreach on the 30th.[64] Other cities, however, had not proved so generous and Kean, goaded to desperation, now definitely made plans, over which he had been vaguely brooding for some time, to leave England, never to return. With that end in view, we find him giving farewell performances at Drury Lane in June, *A New Way to Pay Old Debts* on the 22nd,[65] before an audience now somewhat mollified. Southampton applauded his Sir Giles in July,[66] Liverpool on August 24,[67] but Kean's mind was made up, and in September he sailed for America, where worse was to come.[68]

As we shall see later, Kean's second visit to the United States was not as happy as he had anticipated and he did not persist in his intention to spend the rest of his life in America. Early in 1827 we find him again at Drury Lane, with his audiences reconciled to him and applauding wildly his initial performance of Shylock. But Kean's strength was not what it had been, and the treatment he had received had subjected him to great nervous strain. His acting lost no whit of inspiration or intelligence, but the indomitable energy of his former days was gone, and after each performance he was physically worn out. Nevertheless he continued to play that part which required perhaps the most purely physical strength. His first performance of Sir Giles Overreach after his return to England came on January 25 with Cooper as Wellborn and Margaret by Miss Smithson; there were repetitions on February 8 and 27.[69] After a performance on March 17, 1827, at Dublin—I thank a playbill—we find him again at Drury Lane on May 24, when "he played the satanic hero of *A New Way to Pay Old Debts* with . . . beauty, energy, and grandeur,"[70] but Hawkins quotes Kean as saying, "My strength is gone; I cannot act Sir Giles as I used to." Rare playbills show performances at Leeds on July 11, 1827, with Allworth by a young gentleman named Phelps of whom we shall

---

[64] Hawkins, Vol. II, p. 246.
[65] Advertisements in *The Times*.
[66] Hawkins, Vol. II, pp. 247-8.
[67] Broadbent, p. 143, and the playbill.
[68] For Kean's reception and performances in the United States, see Part II, pp. 189-91.
[69] Genest, Vol. IX, p. 369; advertisements in *The Times*.
[70] Hawkins, Vol. II, pp. 291, 295.

hear more later; and at Liverpool on October 3. There having been some misunderstanding with Price, Kean now left the scene of his early London triumphs, Drury Lane, for Covent Garden. There he appeared as Sir Giles on October 25:[71]

Sir Giles Overreach	Kean
Wellborn	C. Kemble
Lord Lovell	Egerton
Marrall	W. Farren
Justice Greedy	Blanchard
Allworth	Raymond
Lady Allworth	Mrs. Faucit

Playbills tell us the Margaret was Miss Henry and add performances with the same cast for November 8, 15, December 19, and February 28, 1828.[72] In June, playing with the English company which had been assembled in Paris, Kean presented Sir Giles Overreach for the first time to French audiences. The theatre was the Odéon, the dates the 9th and 13th. In spite of his fast increasing debility, he apparently made something of a sensation in the part, and what a feather it must have been in the cap of the Romantics![73]

During his second season at Covent Garden, Kean played Sir Giles on October 23, 1828, with Lady Allworth by Miss Lacy, and Marrall by Meadows, the rest as before—so at least the playbill. An explosion of gas now compelled the closing of Covent Garden Theatre, and the company moved temporarily to the Lyceum, or as it was more often called, the English Opera House. Here *A New Way to Pay Old Debts* was played twice before Covent Garden reopened on December 4. These performances came on November 21 and December 1,[74] with the cast unchanged. Kean now went on tour, and we find him playing Sir Giles at Brighton on January 3,

[71] Genest, Vol. IX, p. 423, and the advertisement in *The Times* of date cited. Hawkins, Vol. II, p. 316 gives the date wrongly as October 24.

[72] I think Hawkins refers to the last performance when he says (Vol. II, p. 319): ". . . his [Kean's] physical energies were for the first time unable to execute his conception of the character," but he has dated it January 28 when the play was *Henry IV*. See *The Times* of dates cited.

[73] Hillebrand, p. 296; Borgerhoff, pp. 140-1.

[74] Playbills and advertisements in *The Times*, and review in *The Athenaeum* of December 3, 1828, p. 924.

1829.[75] The bill for a performance at Dublin on May 18, 1829, is so interesting that I cannot refrain from quoting:[76]

Theatre Royal, Dublin
Extraordinary Coalition of Talent!!
MR. KEAN,

Having recovered from the effects of the temporary indisposition under which he laboured, will have the honor of appearing on Monday next: and in order to remove any apprehension of disappointment, the subjoined Medical Certificate is submitted to the Public for the satisfaction of the numerous parties who have made application for places

"We certify that MR. KEAN is so far recovered from his severe attack of Gout, as to be able to perform SIR GILES OVERREACH on Monday night, the 18th instant."

"JOHN SPEER, M.D."
"JOHN STOKES"
Mr. KEAN, Jun.

Will also appear, in conjunction with his Father.

Gout? All spring Kean's dissipations had brought on a series of severe breakdowns. Was this intoxication, or illness, or both? One cannot help wondering. There is no wonder however that, with Edmund and Charles in the same play, "Every species of privilege (except the Public Press) [was] totally suspended." The cast was as follows:

Sir Giles Overreach	Kean
Wellborn	Kean, Junior
Lord Lovell	W. Johnstone
Marrall	Williams
Justice Greedy	Johnson
Allworth	M'Gill
Lady Allworth	Mrs. Balls
Margaret	Miss Kenneth

Hawkins tells us that "in May a total derangement of his [Kean's] system took place, and it was feared at the time that under any circumstances his reappearance on the stage was out of the question."[77] Poor shattered Kean! Yet in the latter part of July

---

75 Porter, p. 58.
76 I have reduced capitals and italics. See also Levey and O'Rorke, p. 21.
77 Hawkins, Vol. II, p. 333.

he was sufficiently recovered to play Sir Giles at Belfast, and on August 6 at Liverpool.[78]

In December 1829, Kean, dissatisfied with arrangements at Covent Garden where Fanny Kemble had just made her brilliant début as Juliet, returned to Drury Lane, opening there on the 2nd as Richard, and playing Sir Giles on the 9th and 18th:[79]

Sir Giles Overreach	Kean
Wellborn	Cooper
Lord Lovell	H. Wallack
Marrall	W. Farren
Justice Greedy	Webster
Allworth	J. Vining
Lady Allworth	Mrs. Faucit
Margaret	Miss Faucit

On February 11, 1830, he acted the part at The Theatre, Sheffield, with Phelps as Wellborn.[80] Hillebrand's notes tell me that Croydon saw Kean's Overreach on March 24. In July Kean was back in London playing Sir Giles at the Haymarket, a theatre at which with the exception of a few nights in 1819, he had not appeared since the summer season of 1806, when as a strolling player he acted minor parts there. The Haymarket performances, according to the bills, came on the 2nd and the 9th:

Sir Giles Overreach	Kean
Wellborn	Cooper
Lord Lovell	Thompson
Marrall	W. Farren
Justice Greedy	Williams
Allworth	Brindal
Lady Allworth	Mrs. Glover
Margaret	Mrs. Ashton

Kean now decided to revisit the United States, as he said, "to show those damned Boston people that I am not afraid to appear

[78] Hawkins, Vol. II, p. 333; Liverpool playbill.
[79] Genest, Vol. IX, p. 503, and advertisements in *The Times*.
[80] Playbill.

Extraordinary Coalition of Talent ! !

MR. KEAN,

Having recovered from the effects of the temporary indisposition under which he laboured, will have the honor of appearing on Monday next: and in order to remove any apprehension of disappointment, the subjoined Medical Certificate is submitted to the Public for the satisfaction of the numerous parties who have made application for places

" *We certify that Mr. KEAN is so far recovered from his severe attack of Gout. as to be able to perform SIR GILES OVERREACH on Monday night, the 18th instant.*"

" *Kingstown, May 15th.*"   **"JOHN SPEER, M. D."**

French street.   **"JOHN STOKES."**

Mr. KEAN, Jun.

Will also appear, in conjunction with his Father.
In addition to which, the celebrated

Mr. H. Johnston

Will have the honor of appearing in his popular character of RUGANTINO, in which he was most enthusiastically received on Saturday last.

This present MONDAY, May 18th, 1829, will be performed Massinger's play of

A NEW WAY
To Pay Old Debts

Sir Giles Overreach - - - - - - Mr. KEAN
Wellborn - - - - - - - - - Mr. KEAN, Junior.

Lord Lovel...Mr. W. JOHNSTONE.   Allworth...Mr MᶜGILL.
Justice Greedy... Mr. JOHNSON.   Marrall .. Mr. WILLIAMS.   Welldo...Mr. HAMERTON.
Order... Mr. COOKE.   Amble...Mr. O'ROURKE.   Furnace...Mr. AUSTIN.
Watchall... Mr. O'RYAN.   Tapwell... Mr. CUNNINGHAM.   Vintner... Mr. CHIPPENDALE.
Lady Allworth...Mrs BALLS.   Margaret...Miss KENNETH.
Abigail... Miss CRAWFORD.   Tabitha... Miss A. CRAWFORD.   Froth... Mrs. BURGESS.

The Evening's Performances will conclude with the celebrated Melo-Drama of

RUGANTINO

Rugantino (the Bravo) - - - Mr. H. JOHNSTON !
(*The original representative of this celebrated Character.*)
Beggarman - - - - - - Mr. H. JOHNSTON ! !
Friar - - - - - - - Mr. H. JOHNSTON ! ! !
Flodoardo - - - - - - Mr. H. JOHNSTON ! ! ! !
Duke of Milan - - - - Mr. H. JOHNSTON ! ! ! ! !

Andreas, Doge of Venice............Mr. CUNNINGHAM.
Lomellino......Mr. MELLON.   The Patriarch of Venice.. Mr. HAMERTON.   Parozzi ..Mr. COOKE.
Contarino................Mr. W. JOHNSTONE.   Falieri.......... ......Mr. BARRY.
Memmo............Mr. WILLIAMS.
Gonzaga...Mr. TURNER.   Stephano...Mr. ROSS.   Bertoldo...Mr. GREY.   Herald...Mr. O'ROURKE.
Rosabel's........ ....Miss HUDDART.
Camilla...Mrs. BURGESS.   Bettina....Miss CRAWFORD.   Laura...Miss MAHON.

Every species of privilege (except the Public Press) is totally suspended

J. CARRICK and SON, Printers, 29, Bachelors'-walk.

A KEAN PLAYBILL

before them again."[81] With this idea in mind, he gave a farewell benefit at the Opera House in the Haymarket (The King's Theatre) on July 19, 1830. On this night he played the fourth act of *Richard III*, the fourth act of *The Merchant of Venice*, the fifth act of *A New Way to Pay Old Debts*, the second act of *Macbeth*, and the third act of *Othello*, certainly a stupendous feat for anyone, especially anyone laboring under Kean's present physical handicaps. *The Times* of the following day reported "the largest concourse of people we ever saw assembled on any similar occasion." For the last act of *A New Way to Pay Old Debts* the playbill gives the following cast:

Sir Giles Overreach	Kean
Wellborn	J. Vining
Lord Lovell	Younge
Marrall	D. Rees
Allworth	J. Honner
Welldo	Fenton
Lady Allworth	Mrs. Knight
Margaret	Miss Chikini

On the 22nd he gave Sir Giles at Brighton.[82] Manchester saw his Overreach on August 6, Norwich on the 13th[83] whence he proceeded on his provincial tour to Yarmouth and Manchester. Here he fell dangerously ill, and by the time he had recovered and resumed his engagements, he had given up all thought of going to America.

Macready being in the way, Kean performed Sir Giles only once the next season at Drury Lane, on February 11; Talfourd writing in *The New Monthly Magazine* for March 1831, remarks:[84] "His Sir Giles is not so terrible as it was when it sent Lord Byron into hysterics, and made Mrs. Glover tremble; but it is sustained by a quiet consciousness of power, and superiority to principle or fear, and the deficiency of physical force in the last scene is supplied with consummate skill." A playbill gives the cast for *A New Way to Pay Old Debts* on May 13, 1831, at Edinburgh:

[81] Hawkins, Vol. II, p. 348.
[82] So at least Porter, p. 59; Hillebrand has 21st, when according to Porter the season opened with *Richard III*.
[83] Hillebrand's notes.
[84] March 1, 1831, Vol. 33, pt. III, p. 117.

Sir Giles Overreach .... Kean
Wellborn .... Hooper
Lord Lovell .... Bevan
Marrall .... Mackay
Justice Greedy .... Mason
Allworth .... Brindal
Lady Allworth .... Mrs. Stanley
Margaret .... Miss Penley

An even rarer bill and the advertisements in *The Times* tell of two strange performances a bit later—strange in that they were at the City Theatre, Milton Street, just opened as a playhouse. Macready was, it is evident, still occupying Drury Lane, Kean going swiftly downhill. Anyhow the dates are May 27 and June 1, and the cast— I had many times given it up for lost before I found a bill:

Sir Giles Overreach .... Kean
Wellborn .... Forde
Lord Lovell .... Cooke
Marrall .... Perry
Justice Greedy .... Manders
Allworth .... Courtney
Lady Allworth .... Mrs. Knight
Margaret .... Miss Pincott
Froth .... Mrs. Weston

A curious place for Kean to be acting but by no means a bad cast.

We next find Kean's Sir Giles at the Coburg, not yet named The Victoria or "Old Vic" nor so gentlemanly as at present. Tom Cobham was favorite there, as Kean soon found out to his dismay and indignation, exploding into a curtain-speech, not without courage, in which he remarked that he had never acted to such a set of ignorant, unmitigated brutes.[85] Nevertheless he remained to act

---

[85] John Booth, *The "Old Vic,"* pp. 28-30. The bills for Kean's engagement at the Coburg contain the following notice: "The Public are respectfully informed that a portion of the Pit will be fitted up with Stalls (4 s. each) as at the Opera, thus enabling Ladies and Gentlemen to be nearer the great Tragedian, than when in the Boxes." M. St. Clare Byrne points out (*Times Literary Supplement,* November 24, 1932, p. 888) that this is the first use of stalls for a series of ordinary dramatic performances in English. Later bills comment on the success of the innovation by which "every Master look and fine Tone of the Artist [is] to be distinctly seen and heard." In the light of Hazlitt's remarks on this subject in *The Examiner* of February 18, 1816, already quoted, this must have been of distinct benefit to Sir Giles.

Sir Giles there on July 6, though I think Cobham was not in the cast. *The Times* advertisement mentions only Serle as Wellborn, Miss Edmiston as Lady Allworth, and Miss Watson as Margaret.

Taking to the road, Kean was at the King's Theatre, Richmond, now under his management, toward the end of July, acting his extortioner on the 29th—we thank a playbill. Cruickshank says that Kean played Sir Giles at Birmingham in March and October of this year.[86] Maybe so; at any rate he was there on August 4, for I have seen the playbill. Perhaps it was at one of these performances that Kean, playing Sir Giles to a thin house, upon an allusion being made to the marriage of Margaret, replied to the stage suitor, "Take her, sir, and the Birmingham audience into the bargain."[87] On September 5 and September 30, 1831, his bodily strength now daily diminishing, Kean played Sir Giles at the Haymarket. The cast was as follows:[88]

Sir Giles Overreach	Kean
Wellborn	Cooper
Lord Lovell	H. Wallack
Marrall	W. Farren
Justice Greedy	Gattie
Allworth	Brindal
Lady Allworth	Mrs. Glover
Margaret	Mrs. Ashton

His Overreach was back at Richmond on October 26.[89] On December 23, 1831, at the Theatre Royal, Dublin,—so the playbill:

Sir Giles Overreach	Kean
Wellborn	King
Lord Lovell	Matthews
Marrall	Rees
Justice Greedy	Johnson
Allworth	Stanley
Lady Allworth	Mrs. Shuter
Margaret	Miss Chalmers

[86] Cruickshank (Edition), p. 130.
[87] Molloy, Vol. II, p. 132; Hawkins, Vol. II, p. 346. The latter says the story is told by Doran, but I cannot find the anecdote. This statement is credited to Barry Sullivan by Newton, p. 103.
[88] Playbill, and advertisements in *The Times*.
[89] Hillebrand, p. 317.

For his benefit at Dublin on January 2, 1832, Kean performed one act of each of his five favorite plays, as he had previously done at the King's Theatre on July 19, 1830. The bill shows a cast as above for the fifth act of *A New Way to Pay Old Debts*. On February 22, 1832, at Edinburgh:[90]

Sir Giles Overreach	Kean
Wellborn	Pritchard
Lord Lovell	Powell
Marrall	Mackay
Justice Greedy	Mason
Allworth	Faucit
Lady Allworth	Mrs. Stanley
Margaret	Mrs. Faucit

And when he played the last act for his benefit on the 27th, the cast was the same.[91] A Haymarket performance on June 13, advertised in *The Times,* brings the season to a close. Kean's Sir Giles was in the sere and yellow leaf.

Four more performances and this tedious cataloguing will be over. At the King's Theatre, Richmond, Sir Giles was exhibited on August 22, 1832. The next two performances are in London. At the Haymarket on October 5, 1832:[92]

Sir Giles Overreach	Kean
Wellborn	Elton
Lord Lovell	Haines
Marrall	Burton
Justice Greedy	Strickland
Allworth	Brindal
Lady Allworth	Mrs. Glover
Margaret	Mrs. Ashton

On November 16, 1832, Kean's Overreach tramped the boards of Drury Lane for the last time. A playbill shows the cast:

---

[90] Playbill; Hillebrand, p. 318.
[91] Playbill.
[92] Playbill. Edward William Elton had already played Sir Giles himself; see later, p. 114.

Sir Giles Overreach .... Kean
Wellborn .... Cooper
Lord Lovell .... Matthews
Marrall .... Farren
Justice Greedy .... Ayliffe
Allworth .... Brindal
Lady Allworth .... Mrs. Faucit
Margaret .... Miss Faucit

Only once more did Kean play Sir Giles—at Brighton on February 26, 1833.[93] His life was almost done. A physical wreck, he made his faltering farewell at Covent Garden on the 25th of March as Othello to his son's Iago and collapsed in the third act. On May 15, Kean died at Richmond. Whether or not during his last illness he recalled how proud he had felt when the pit rose at him on the night of his first London performance of Sir Giles Overreach—as Hawkins states[94]—I do not know, but it is a pleasant tale and deserves to be perpetuated; it makes a fitting end to the story of the successive impersonations of a villain by a genius.

It is said that Richard Brinsley Sheridan did not hold the Elizabethan dramatists in any great esteem, and that after his connection with Drury Lane had been severed, he rarely entered that theatre. "One night," says Munden's son,[95] "he was prevailed upon by Lord Essex to sit with his Lordship in his box to witness the performance of Kean in Sir Giles Overreach. At the conclusion of the play, Lord Essex begged of him to go into the greenroom. The actors flocked around the modern Congreve. In the scene of his former glory he was low and dejected. When Mr. Kean was introduced to him, every ear was awake, as it was supposed that Mr. Sheridan would pay him a compliment. The only remark he made was, 'Mr. Kean, I am sorry to see you in so bad a part.' "

Sheridan's views were certainly not echoed by the majority of his contemporaries. Genest, always prejudiced against Kean, says that Sir Giles was, next to Richard III, his best character.[96] A

---

[93] Porter, p. 62.
[94] Hawkins, Vol. II, pp. 386-7.
[95] *Munden,* pp. 240-50.
[96] Genest, Vol. VIII, p. 565.

writer in *Blackwood's* gives a pungent and stimulating criticism
of both the part and the actor :[97]

Sir Giles Overreach, if not the greatest, is certainly the most
perfect of all Mr. Kean's performances. It is quite faultless. The
character of Sir Giles Overreach is drawn with great force and
originality. It seems to have begun in avarice—blind and reckless
avarice; which, at the period of the play is become merged and
lost in intense personal vanity. He has glutted himself with wealth
till his very wishes can compass no more; and then, by dint of
gazing at *himself* as the creator of his boundless stores, avarice
changes into self-admiration; and he thenceforth lavishes as
eagerly to feed the new passion, as he had amassed to gratify the
old one. In delineating this latter part of the character, the author
has, by an admirable subtlety of invention, and a deep knowledge
of human nature, made Sir Giles build up an idol in the person
of his child, in which, by a self-deceit common to vulgar minds
(for his mind *is* a vulgar one notwithstanding its strength), he
worships his only god—himself. He is pleased to see her shining
in gold and jewels because she is *his* child; he hires decayed
gentry to do the menial offices of her house, because she is *his*
child;—nay, he even anticipates with delight the moment when
he shall have raised her to such a rank, that even *he* will be compelled to bow down before her; for, by an inconsistency which is
not uncommon in real life, while he regards titles *in others*
as empty names, *in her* they will appear to be substantial realities,
because she is *his* child.

Mr. Kean plays the first part of this character with a mixture of
gloom and vulgarity that is admirably original and characteristic.
And though we did not intend to have mentioned any particular
parts of the performance, we cannot help noticing the manner in
which he pronounces the titles of the person whom he wishes his
daughter to marry. It is always in a tone of derision and contempt,
which is but half concealed even when he speaks *to* "the lord."
At first sight it might appear inconsistent that Sir Giles should
feel contempt for rank and titles, and yet make them confessedly
the end and object of all his toils. "My ends—my ends are
compassed! I am all over joy!," he exclaims when he thinks he has
finally arranged his daughter's marriage with "the lord." But, on
reflection, it will be found to be one of the most refined parts of the
performance. We have before said, that part of Sir Giles's

[97] *Blackwood's Edinburgh Magazine,* April 1818, Vol. III, pp. 79-80.

character is a propensity to worship that *in himself* which *in others* he cannot help despising; and this half-contemptuous tone, when speaking of that which is the object of all his wishes, springs from the natural part of his character predominating over the artificial.

The last act of Mr. Kean's performance of Sir Giles Overreach is, without doubt, the most terrific exhibition of human passion that has been witnessed on the modern stage. When his plans are frustrated and his plots laid open, all the restraints of society are thrown aside at once, and a torrent of hatred and revenge bursts from his breaking heart, like water from a cleft rock, or like a raging and devouring fire that, while it consumes the body and soul on which it feeds, darts forth its tongue of flame in all directions, threatening destruction to everything within its reach.

It is a delight to read so fine a piece of criticism, and a pleasure to dust off its pages and bring it forth into the light for a more careful perusal. The writer has thought clearly and deeply in his armchair, but his mind has been illuminated to understanding by witnessing Kean's lightning-like acting of the figure he discusses. It is because we cannot be accorded such a privilege that the criticism becomes valuable. Understanding of Sir Giles Overreach comes from watching a genius represent the character which Massinger wrote for an actor. Literary criticism of the drama is dangerous and misleading, for out of the theatre a play loses much of its vitality, seems often indeed to be what it is not. Comprehension of the drama must spring from the stage on which it is presented, of dramatic character from the actor who impersonates it. So it is here. This man has seen Kean as Sir Giles, and henceforth the knight is no mere figure out of a book; he is alive. We owe the writer our thanks for communicating the experience of transformation, for having introduced us to reality.

The last scene of *A New Way to Pay Old Debts* is of course the most striking and thrilling one in the representation of the play and is therefore the object of most critical attention. But Kean's performance had quieter beauties which must not be forgotten. Dr. Doran, another writer undeservedly forgotten by the "scholar," says :[98] "In this last character [Sir Giles], all the qualities of Kean's

[98] Doran, Vol. III, p. 391.

voice came out to wonderful purpose, especially in the scene where Lovel asks him,[99]

> Are you not moved with the sad imprecations
> And curses of whole families, made wretched
> By your sinister practices?

to which Sir Giles replies:

> Yes, as rocks are
> When foamy billows split themselves against
> Their flinty ribs; or as the moon is moved
> When wolves with hunger pined, howl at her
> brightness

"I seem still to hear the words and the voice as I pen this passage; now composed, now grand as the foamy billows; so flute-like on the word 'moon,' creating a scene with the sound; and anon sharp, harsh, fierce in the last line, with a look upward from those matchless eyes, that rendered the troop visible, and their howl perceptible to the ear;—the whole serenity of the man, and the solidity of his temper, being illustrated less by the assurance in the succeeding words than by the exquisite music in the tone with which he uttered the word 'brightness.' "

In 1820 George Clint exhibited at the Royal Academy a picture of the last scene of *A New Way to Pay Old Debts* with Kean as Sir Giles Overreach. Kean, after repeatedly declining, had been persuaded to sit for it by his close friend, Reynolds, the engraver. When exhibited, the picture was so popular that a rail had to be placed in front of it to keep the crowd at a safe distance. It is the best illustration extant of Edmund Kean's acting in this play. We see Sir Giles, fury on his countenance, about to rush at his daughter with drawn sword, while the other characters cower in fear. The picture eventually came into the hands of Sir Henry Irving, who presented it to the Garrick Club, where it now hangs, a memorial to one of the most remarkable impersonations in theatrical history.[100]

[99] Dr. Doran is apparently quoting from memory of the Dibdin text. See Appendix, p. 409.

[100] Frederick Hawkins, "About a Picture at the Garrick Club," *The Theatre,* August 1, 1895, pp. 71-6.

Perhaps I cannot do better in ending this chapter than to quote the words of Henry Irving regarding Kean, and this, *his* part :[101] "As no bird but the eagle can look without blinking on the sun, so none but those who in the sacred privacy of their imaginations had stood face to face with the mightiest storms of human passion could understand such a performance. . . . [Kean] was not a scholar in the ordinary sense of the word, though Heaven knows he had been schooled by adversity, but I doubt if there ever was an actor who so thought out his part, who so clearly studied with the inward eye of the artist the waves of emotion that might have agitated the minds of the beings whom he represented."

[101] Irving, pp. 164-5.

CHAPTER V

TRIUMPHAL MARCH

SIR GILES was now at the height of his power in England. Edmund Kean had made his personality so recognized that his name was on the lips of all those who pretended to knowledge of the great and the bold. But like his prototype, the knight was never satisfied. For Kean and his predecessors he was thankful, would indeed have been grateful, if gratitude had not been so foreign to his nature. But his representatives, however worthy, were too few; he must have many ambassadors who would be constantly on duty to make his name feared and hated. Sir Giles with a seat on the apex of a pyramid wanted a base of larger dimensions. Higher he could not go, wider he would. He was not wise enough to realize that the broader his base, the less steep were the paths to his throne.

We are accustomed to think of Junius Brutus Booth as an American actor, and of course in the main that is what he was, but Booth did not come to the United States until after he had gained considerable fame—or notoriety—in England. Born in London in 1796, the son of a lawyer, he was well educated and had a decided taste for the arts. After trying painting, poetry, and sculpture, he at last found his *métier* in acting. Against his father's wishes, he made his début at Deptford in December of 1813 as Campillo in *The Honeymoon*. Returning from strolling on the Continent, he made efforts to obtain a London engagement, but, being unsuccessful, he accepted an offer from the Worthing and Brighton Theatres, managed by Thomas Trotter, for the summer of 1815. In the fall Booth finally succeeded in obtaining a place at Covent Garden, where he acted small parts for the season of 1815-1816. Dissatisfied, he returned to Trotter. Shortly afterwards an incident, connected with the very character which is the subject of this book, started him on the path to success.[1]

[1] Unless otherwise noted the details of the life of Junius Brutus Booth are taken from the following: *Passages, Incidents, and Anecdotes in the life of Junius Brutus Booth (The Elder)*, By His Daughter, New York, 1866; Asia

In the latter part of September 1816, Kean was scheduled to appear at Brighton for a short engagement, opening on the 28th as Sir Giles Overreach. Kean, however, failed to arrive, and at the last minute Booth was substituted for him in the part, "which he performed almost without preparation."[2] Because of Kean's failure to appear, "the house was but sparingly attended, and some hisses were heard upon the entrance of Mr. Booth, which his ulterior efforts converted into reiterated plaudits, and universal satisfaction."[3] "Murmurs of his 'presumption' and 'youthful ambition' died away altogether, and he was hailed by acclamations of delighted surprise."[4] Porter gives us a partial cast for this performance:[5]

71410

Sir Giles Overreach	Booth
Marrall	Vining
Justice Greedy	Butler
Lady Allworth	Miss Johannot
Margaret	Miss Norton

Further successes followed and Harris finally decided to give Booth a further trial at Covent Garden. Upon his arrival in London Booth discovered to his astonishment that he was announced to perform Richard III.

On February 12, 1817, Booth appeared at Covent Garden as Richard III. His resemblance to Kean was so marked that he divided the town into two camps, those who thought him merely an imitator, and those who thought they were both copying nature. At any rate Booth won a deserved success. But now events occurred for which it is hard to fix the blame. Booth thought Harris's offer of five pounds a week too small, and declined to accept it. Drury Lane received this news with enthusiasm; Kean called on Booth and attended him to the Drury Lane Committee

Booth Clarke, *The Elder and the Younger Booth* (American Actor Series), Boston, 1882; Edwin Booth, *Junius Brutus Booth* (in *Actors and Actresses of Great Britain and the United States,* ed. by Brander Matthews and Laurence Hutton, volume entitled *Kean and Booth, and Their Contemporaries,* New York, 1886).

[2] *The Theatrical Inquisitor and Monthly Mirror,* February 1817, Vol. X, p. 120.

[3] *ibid.,* April 1817, Vol. X, p. 244.

[4] Clarke, p. 12.

[5] Porter, p. 39, which also gives the date of the performance.

Room, where the latter hurriedly signed a contract for three years. Meanwhile Harris protested, and an audience which expected to see *Richard III* at Covent Garden with Booth in the title-rôle saw *Pizarro* without Booth. On the 20th of February, Kean and Booth acted Othello and Iago respectively at Drury Lane, and Booth began to realize that comparisons are odious. This impression was confirmed when he discovered that he was not to be allowed to act any of the parts to which Kean had priority of claim. That Kean was generous in order to bring about Booth's downfall seems likely. At any rate, Booth, young and inexperienced as he was, did not foresee the consequences of his change of theatres. At this time the actor received a communication from Harris which notified him that his engagement with Covent Garden was not legally broken. Booth, jumping at the chance to escape, did not appear at Drury Lane to play Iago, as announced on the bills, and the public was again disappointed. He now signed a contract to play at Covent Garden, and Drury Lane promptly filed a bill in chancery to prevent him from acting there. The petition was dismissed out of court, and on the 25th Booth tried to act Richard III at Covent Garden. The public, tired of the controversy and Booth's vacillation, greeted him with hisses and the play became pantomime. The storm gradually subsided, but for some time after Booth was cordially hated by a part of the London public, which proceeded to damn him on every possible occasion and in every possible way. This it is which explains the wide variance in the views of the critics who reviewed Booth's various London performances of that year, and which makes it difficult for the writer to estimate just how successful Booth was in his various impersonations.

Not only were Booth's audiences divided into factions for and against him, but there is some suspicion that there were hired bravos on both sides whose purpose it was to lead the applause or the hisses and to maintain their bought opinions by physical force. *The Theatrical Inquisitor* for March 1817[6] contains a letter

[6] *The Theatrical Inquisitor and Monthly Mirror,* March 1817, Vol. X, pp. 167-8. The letter itself is dated "March 2d, 1817" but this must be a misprint, for the playbill of March 8 states that when Booth played Sir Giles on that date, it was "his first appearance in that character," that is, his first London appearance. *The Times* of March 8, 1817 also says "first time."

entitled "Theatrical Fracas" which shows to what extent this was carried:

To the Editor of the Theatrical Inquisitor
Sir,

I beg through the medium of your entertaining and impartial Magazine, to give publicity to a growing evil in our theatrical exhibitions . . . the encreasing introduction of hired applause. . . .

I am led to these remarks by a circumstance which occurred a few nights since at Covent Garden Theatre, where the attraction of the evening was Sir Giles Overreach by Mr. Booth. I shall not invade your province by entering into any critique on the performance, though, permit me to remark, I thought the gentleman's genius, at least, equal to the *judgment* of his friends in the *second* circle, who, by subsequent conduct, proved they had not been much used to move in the *first*.

The play had proceeded to the part where Sir Giles rushes to his chest of writings, and produces the parchment. Here you must allow, Mr. Booth was guilty of a slight faux pas, by introducing a violent start, before it was possible he could have perceived that the deed was "a fair skin, without wax or words." At this ludicrous occurrence, an elderly gentleman, in a box adjoining to that in which I had been snugly seated, happened, involuntarily, I suppose, to laugh; and I might myself have been guilty of the same misdemeanor, but, being a peaceable character, I stood a little in awe of the applauding staves of my enthusiastic neighbors. Well, sir, this personage was immediately attacked, and insulted by several of the "bravos" seated near him. Some altercation ensued, and the laughing gentleman was ultimately saluted by the 1st Bravo with the polite epithet of "a d——d liar," when this affair, disgraceful to the boxes of perhaps the first theatre in the world, was transferred to the lobby . . .; my only motive in this letter is, to ascertain if it is correct conduct for the servants of the theatre, and their friends, admitted gratis, to molest any individual or that public by whom the said theatre is supported; or whether it will be in the power of a person, paying his money, to disapprove of a performance without standing a fair chance of foul play in being "knocked 'er the mazzard" by hired "bravos."

I am,
Mr. Editor,
Your obedient Servant,
A Passive Looker-On.

With such prejudices on both sides, it will be evident to the reader that it is exceedingly difficult to give a just estimate of Mr. Booth's Sir Giles at Covent Garden.

Booth played *A New Way to Pay Old Debts* three times in London, the performances falling respectively on March 8, March 13, and March 17.[7] The cast was as follows:

Sir Giles Overreach	Booth
Wellborn	C. Kemble
Lord Lovell	Barrymore
Marrall	Terry
Justice Greedy	Blanchard
Allworth	Connor
Lady Allworth	Mrs. Faucit
Margaret	Miss S. Booth

Sally Booth had, by the way, previously suggested to Junius Brutus that he spell his name with an "e," since she did not wish to be mistaken for a relative.[8] I select the review in *The Times* as perhaps the most nonpartisan:[9]

Mr. Booth appeared on Saturday night . . . in the part of *Sir Giles Overreach,* in the comedy of *A New Way to Pay Old Debts.* It has more than once fallen to our lot to offer our tribute of admiration to the extraordinary excellence of Mr. Kean's performance of this character. With the impression which these qualifications produced upon us still fresh in our recollection, it is, perhaps, no small praise to say at once, that Mr. Booth's execution of the task more than answered our expectations. Indeed, the very first remark that must have suggested itself to every spectator who had seen both competitors, was the similitude between their respective efforts—a similitude which tinged the greater part of the performance, and which was still evidently the work of nature rather than the result of imitation. Mr. Booth's manner is somewhat more subdued; and his style chiefly differed from his rival's in having less pretension, and in exhibiting fewer of those sudden flashes of brilliancy for which he is distinguished from every other tragedian. We have not leisure at present to point out particular blemishes; they were, in fact, more considerable in their number

[7] Playbills, and the advertisements in *The Times.*
[8] Clarke, p. 11.
[9] *The Times,* March 10, 1817. I cannot account for the variation in the quoted lines.

—From the Theatre Collection, New York Public Library

JUNIUS BRUTUS BOOTH as SIR GILES OVERREACH

than striking from their magnitude, and we prefer for the present the more agreeable employment of selecting one or two of his more prominent excellencies. It was in the scene where he prepares with such anxious solicitude, and with such singular disregard of morality, his daughter for the courtship of Lord Lovel, that his higher faculties began to manifest themselves. The stateliness of his pride, and the directness of his ambition, were portrayed with splendid colouring; and his avowal, that all his toils were directed to the establishment of his daughter's grandeur, whilst his conduct betrays an utter absence of every tender affection, was pronounced with a force and dignity which were best appreciated in the unanimous plaudits of the audience. We are desirous also of noting one merit of another kind—we mean the just and impressive delivery of such passages as are rather the flights of poetry than the exponents of ideas or feelings conducive to the action of the piece, and which depend entirely on gracefulness of gesture, and harmony of modulation. We may instance the following lines, in which the hero of the fable describes his own savage insensibility to the tears and cries of his victims :—

"Yes, as the rock when foaming billows break
"Against its flinty ribs: or as the moon,
"Which holds her steady course tho' hungry wolves
"Howl at her brightness."

The latter scenes of the play have been considered the *chef d'oeuvre* of Mr. Kean: and they were those in which the success of Mr. Booth likewise deserves best to be recorded. The subjection of a stern spirit by a continued series of disappointments defeating the most deeply laid schemes, and blasting hopes long cherished in the heart, will ever form a grand subject in the hands of a skilful artist. In Mr. Booth's delineation we had nothing to regret. The multitude of emotions by which he is alternately exalted to energy and oppressed to weakness, were figured, not only in his wild and hurried action, but in the more powerful flexibilities of his countenance. The final defection of his spirits was followed by the universal acclamations of the house; and we do not recollect an example of such significant testimonies of approbation offered on announcing a second appearance to a performer for his discharge of a character which a living predecessor had already made peculiarly his own.

So much for justice; if the reader craves amusement, he may find it in *The Theatrical Inquisitor* for April, where is printed the following "proclamation," dated March 23:[10]

Whereas it hath been humbly represented unto us, The Theatrical Inquisitor, that between the hours of seven and ten o'clock in the evening of Saturday, the 6th instant, Sir Giles Overreach, knt. was stopped in his journey through Covent Garden Theatre, and inhumanely murdered:[11]

And whereas, Junius Booth the younger, now of Queen-street, Bloomsbury, comedian, stands charged upon oath on a violent suspicion of having wilfully and feloniously attempted to kill and murder Richard Plantagenet, Duke of Gloucester, on Wednesday, the 12th day of February last; and the said Junius Booth also stands charged, on vehement suspicion, with having committed divers other high and atrocious theatrical offences; now, putting these specific charges together,

For the more speedy apprehending and bringing to justice the said Junius Booth for the offences aforesaid, The Theatrical Inquisitor is hereby pleased, acting in the name, and on behalf of his readers, to promise to any person or persons who shall apprehend, or cause to be apprehended, the said Junius Booth, the sum of Five Hundred thanks, to be paid by the Commissioners of the Editor's Treasury, upon the said Junius Booth being apprehended and lodged in any one of the Monthly Magazines.

—Inquisitor General—

The Morning Post emphasizes the similarity of the impersonations of Sir Giles Overreach by Booth and Kean:[12] "Less marked when in close and direct comparison, at a distance from each other they seemed cast in the same mould. This similarity extended to their minds, and consequently to their general style of action, and therefore few who, beholding Mr. Booth, could not have fancied that Kean stood in all his excellency before them." But in one bit of stage-business, Booth made an effort at realism which was an innovation. In the last scene, "one of the attendants who held him was furnished with a sponge filled with blood (rose pink), which he, unseen by the audience, squeezed into his mouth, to convey the idea of his having burst a blood-vessel." Macready was scorn-

---

[10] *The Theatrical Inquisitor and Monthly Mirror,* April 1817, Vol. X, p. 279.
[11] The date should be Saturday, the 8th.
[12] In lieu of the paper itself I quote from Molloy, Vol. II, p. 23.

ful: "It is not by such means as these that the dramatic poet is to find support from the artist."[13]

During Passion Week Booth played in Woolwich, giving his Sir Giles Overreach on April 5.

Sir Giles Overreach .... Booth
Wellborn .... Beverly
Lord Lovell .... Huddart
Marrall .... Lynch
Justice Greedy .... Frimbley, Jun.
Allworth .... Allen
Lady Allworth .... Miss Elliot
Margaret .... Miss Sidney

We should like to have heard the "Very Comical Song by Mr. Booth," advertised in the bill. "From a Woolwich correspondent to a London morning paper," Booth's daughter, Mrs. Clarke, takes the following:[14] "Mr. Booth was received by a full and elegant auditory. In the character of *Sir Giles* his claims to eminence were not only not equivocal, but fully established. In the last act more particularly his astonishingly striking display of the variedly agonized and frantic feelings with which *Sir Giles* is agitated at the failure to his schemes, came home to the feelings of all, and reiterated plaudits spoke the approbation of a crowded theatre." On May 15, during a short engagement, Booth played in *A New Way to Pay Old Debts* at Bath.[15] Oulton informs us[16] that "his King Richard was hissed by the Bath critics, and his Sir Giles Overreach and Sir Edward Mortimer were equally disliked." Either Bath audiences were more discriminating than those of Woolwich, or Rumor flew there more quickly. From Bath Booth proceeded to Liverpool, where on May 23 *A New Way to Pay Old Debts* was the bill with the following actors taking part:[17]

---

[13] Sir Frederick Pollock (ed.), *Macready's Reminiscences* . . . , Vol. I, p. 141.
[14] Clarke, pp. 45-6.
[15] Genest, Vol. VIII, p. 632.
[16] Oulton. This reference is from Vol. II of the series of 1818, p. 355.
[17] "Mr. Booth of the Theatre Royal, Covent Garden, is engaged at this Theatre for Nine Nights Only, and will have the honor of making his first appearance on this stage this present Friday, May 23, 1817."—from the playbill.

Sir Giles Overreach	Booth
Wellborn	Cooper
Lord Lovell	Bass
Marrall	Loveday
Justice Greedy	Tayleure
Allworth	Lombe
Lady Allworth	Mrs. Aldridge
Margaret	Mrs. Payne

Doubtless the cast was the same when the play was repeated on June 4.[18] August found Booth at Newcastle, making, says the bill, his "first appearance on this stage," as Sir Giles Overreach, on the 4th:

Sir Giles Overreach	Booth
Wellborn	Johnson
Lord Lovell	Mercer
Marrall	Villars
Justice Greedy	Kilner
Allworth	Pope
Lady Allworth	Mrs. Pope
Margaret	Miss Vining

I find no more performances of *A New Way to Pay Old Debts* until July of 1818, though doubtless there were many, if Booth persisted in this custom of opening his engagements as Sir Giles. A playbill of July 8, 1818, Theatre Royal, Edinburgh, which is reprinted by Booth's daughter,[19] states that Booth played Sir Giles with great success the preceding night, and that the play would be repeated on Saturday. This gives us performances on July 7 and July 11. A month later, August 5, Hull saw Booth's impersonation of Massinger's extortioner. The playbill of the next day tells us that "Mr. BOOTH's success last Night, in the character of SIR GILES OVER-REACH could only be equalled by that, which, on Monday Evening, attended his representation of RICHARD the THIRD; on both occasions, in obedience to the will of the audience, the Performances were abruptly terminated

---

[18] Cruickshank (Edition), p. 130, from John Parker (*The Times Literary Supplement*, September 7, 1922, No. 1077, p. 569), who refers to Captain W. Jaggard.

[19] *Passages, Incidents, and Anecdotes in the life of Junius Brutus Booth* (*The Elder*) pp. 181-2. The playbill reprinted is not, however, of *A New Way to Pay Old Debts*.

with the final exit of Mr. BOOTH, the reiterated thunders of applause with which that Gentleman's exertions were honoured,
rendering the further Progress of the Plays impossible." I feel
sure that I am skipping performances here, but the next on my
list is one at the Theatre Royal, Dublin, on March 10, 1819. I
copy the cast from the bill:

Sir Giles Overreach .... Booth
Wellborn .... Macarthy
Lord Lovell .... Thompson
Marrall .... Williams
Justice Greedy .... Johnson
Allworth .... Harvey
Lady Allworth .... Miss Whitaker
Margaret .... Miss L. Kelly

In January 1821 Booth married and, after a brief visit to France
and then the West Indies, he and his bride sailed for America. In
1825 he returned to England, but did not, as far as I know, play
Sir Giles during his London engagements. Indeed I note only
one performance of *A New Way to Pay Old Debts* in Great
Britain, that at Liverpool on October 21, when the cast on the
playbill was as follows:

Sir Giles Overreach .... Booth
Wellborn .... Bass
Lord Lovell .... Diddear
Marrall .... Rees
Justice Greedy .... Carter
Allworth .... Leaves
Lady Allworth .... Mrs. Doyne
Margaret .... Miss Kenneth

Early in 1827 Booth returned to the United States, and his story
from that point belongs to another chapter.

That Booth was a successful Sir Giles in England I do not
doubt. The critics who cavil at his performance of the rôle seem
for the most part to have based their judgments on the fact that
Booth made a fool of himself in his negotiations with the two
London theatres in 1817. On the other hand, he certainly was not
Kean's peer in the part, and in England was never regarded as
such. It was in America that he made his reputation, and it was

there that he became one of the greatest impersonators of Sir Giles Overreach in the stage-history of that country. We must inevitably consider his theatrical experience in England as merely an introduction to his greater fame in the United States.

We come now to the Sir Giles Overreach of John M. Vandenhoff. Vandenhoff, whose son, George, is perhaps better known to this country than his father, made his début at Salisbury in 1808, and shortly after played with Kean in Hughes' company at Exeter. He became very popular in the provinces, particularly at Liverpool, and was brought from there to Covent Garden where he opened as Lear on December 9, 1820. Previous to this time he had played Sir Giles in the provinces, probably at Liverpool, certainly at Dublin, November 27, 1816,[20] no doubt elsewhere though I cannot be more specific. His London début as Sir Giles came on December 14 when according to the bill the cast was as follows:

Sir Giles Overreach .... Vandenhoff
(his first appearance in that character)[21]
Wellborn .... C. Kemble
Lord Lovell .... Egerton
Marrall .... W. Farren
Justice Greedy .... Blanchard
Allworth .... Connor
Lady Allworth .... Mrs. Knight
(of the Theatre Royal, Drury Lane)
Margaret .... Miss Foote

Genest says the performance was "not repeated."[22] A writer in *The New Monthly Magazine* reviews as follows:[23] "Mr. Vandenhoff, who was disguised in Lear, *came out* in Sir Giles Overreach, and exhibited a tall figure, intelligent, but not strongly marked features, and a voice sufficiently powerful, but rather of a coarse quality. He displayed great judgment in many passages; but pitched the whole character in too low a key for the public taste,

[20] Playbill; *The Theatrical Inquisitor,* Vol. X, December 1816, p. 449 reports "prodigious applause." My general facts about John Vandenhoff are taken from Joseph Knight's article in the *DNB,* Vol. LVIII, pp. 98-9.
[21] This presumably means his first *London* appearance.
[22] Genest, Vol. IX, p. 102.
[23] *The New Monthly Magazine,* February 1, 1821, Vol. III, p. 60.

which, we cannot help thinking, the tragic harlequinade of Mr. Kean in the last scene has a little perverted."

Vandenhoff left Covent Garden in the spring of 1821, dissatisfied with the treatment he had received from the manager. From then on he was almost ubiquitous, and his performances of Sir Giles Overreach are difficult to trace; I can but give what I have. Chelli, referring to theatrical cuttings in the British Museum, notes a performance of *A New Way to Pay Old Debts* in Dublin on April 11, 1825, but does not name the Sir Giles.[24] Now on this date Vandenhoff was in Dublin but playing Rolla in *Pizarro*.[25] The clipping to which M. Chelli refers is somewhat illegibly dated the 21st and reads in part as follows:[26]

> We will not say that Mr. Vandenhoff equalled Kean in his personification of this atrocious monster, but we must in justice allow, that in most of the scenes, he displayed very powerful and effective acting. He looked the part extremely well. As an instance of his excellent delineation of this character, we may notice the scene where *Marrall* refuses to assist him in ruining Wellborn, and even unfolds the history of his wicked life; the impassioned energy with which he exclaimed, "Oh, that I had thee in my gripe, I'd tear thee joint after joint!" was loudly and deservedly applauded. The conclusion was quite overwhelming. On finding *Allworth* and *Margaret* married, he rushed, with ungovernable rage and fury depicted in his countenance, on the Parson, and demanded with a voice of thunder, "Are they married?" Then, struggling with contending passions; with disappointment, madness and despair, he sunk upon the stage, exhausted and overcome, and was carried off amidst wild applause.

At Edinburgh on March 4, 1828, Charles Kemble was the main attraction, if we may judge from the size of the capitals on the playbill, but Vandenhoff was the Sir Giles Overreach. The cast was as follows:

Sir Giles Overreach .... Vandenhoff
Wellborn .... C. Kemble
    (being his first appearance in that character in this city)
Lord Lovell ....Denham

24 Chelli, p. 66.
25 Levey and O'Rorke, p. 16.
26 Theatrical Cuttings 1820-1831, Vol. II, unnumbered p. 114. (1286. h.3.)

Marrall .... Mackay
Justice Greedy .... Mason
Allworth ....Stanley
Lady Allworth .... Mrs. Renaud
Margaret .... Miss Mason

These few performances are all that I can record in Great Britain; in 1837 Vandenhoff went to America, and we shall find him playing Sir Giles there.[27]

In his early days Vandenhoff was hampered by awkwardness; later he became a good second-rate actor, never a great success in London, almost always a favorite in the provinces, particularly in Liverpool and Edinburgh. Kean generously called him "an actor of the first consequence, and whose high talents deserve the first place,"[28] but this praise seems much too high. Coriolanus was apparently his most successful part, as might be expected from the fact that he belonged distinctly to the Kemble school. Such being the case, his Sir Giles Overreach was only moderately applauded.[29]

Heigh-ho!—to the provinces we go! At Newcastle on January 17, 1817, *"Sir Giles Overreach* by Mr. Johnson; *Wellborn,* Mr. Gordon, who failed in an attempt to perform *Goldfinch* at Drury-lane Theatre, for Munden's benefit; and *Lady Allworth,* Miss Grimani, sister-in-law to Mr. Young."[30] In 1817 the play was also presented at Sunderland, probably in February.[31] A letter in the January 1818 issue of *The Theatrical Inquisitor* announces that Bicester "has been lately enlivened by a very respectable company of comedians, the chief of whom are Messrs. Goddard, Sanson, Gordon, and Westbury, and Misses Goddard and Flynn. . . . Mr. Goddard, the manager, takes the chief tragic characters; and is an able representative of *Gambia, Inkle, Meg Merrilies,* and *Overreach.*" But alas, it is all in vain and the letter a fraud, as a correspondent points out in the next number. The company con-

---

[27] See Part II, p. 257.

[28] Kean's letter to the *Sunday Monitor,* October 3, 1819, reprinted by Hillebrand, pp. 188-9.

[29] A picture and a short criticism of Vandenhoff as Sir Giles may be found in the acting edition of *A New Way to Pay Old Debts* published without date by G. H. Davidson "with remarks biographical and critical by D.—G."

[30] *The Theatrical Inquisitor and Monthly Mirror,* February 1817, Vol. X, p. 156.

[31] *The Theatrical Inquisitor and Monthly Mirror,* March 1817, Vol. X, p. 238.

sisted of Mr. Goddard, his wife and daughter, the others being either Bicester tradesmen or fictitious. There was acting, so-called, for only a few nights, and *A New Way to Pay Old Debts* was not among the plays massacred.[32] Finally—for this paragraph—we go to Exeter where Osbaldiston, announced as from Manchester, played Sir Giles on February 10, 1819, "with the most decided success. Mr. Saltar (from the English Opera House) made his début in the part of Marral, and was much applauded. Mrs. Weston was the Lady Allworth of the evening."[33]

Osbaldiston is of course David Webster Osbaldiston, better known as a manager. Born in Manchester in 1797, he early became an actor and was something of a favorite in the provinces. Though his first London appearance was at the Haymarket, it is with the Surrey that we primarily associate him. In 1828 he was engaged by Elliston as stage-manager and leading tragedian at that theatre, of which he subsequently became lessee. He afterwards became manager of Covent Garden, Sadler's Wells, the City of London Theatre, the Surrey again, and the Victoria at which last post he died in 1850. Though he undoubtedly acted Sir Giles Overreach many times in the provinces, I can record only one more performance, at Exeter on January 11, 1827, and must confine myself to pointing out—with the help of the advertisements in the *Times*—that he played the part for the first time in London at the Surrey on April 27, 1829, with repetitions on April 28, April 30, May 4, and May 28. Wynne was the Wellborn and Mrs. Egerton played Lady Allworth. I find only two more London performances; these too are at the Surrey, the dates May 25, 1830, and May 13, 1831. Sir Giles *via* Osbaldiston seems to have been reasonably popular across the river.[34]

I must now chronicle a series of performances which are in themselves of no significance, but which are nevertheless impor-

[32] *ibid.,* January 1818, Vol. XII, pp. 61-2; February, pp. 135-6.

[33] *The Theatre, or Dramatic and Literary Mirror,* Vol. I, February 20, 1819, p. 16. Cotton, p. 46, however, says that Osbaldiston "was soon discovered . . . [to be] an imitator of Kean, and that it was only as a copier of the great actor that he showed ability."

[34] Information about Osbaldiston is scanty. His career as manager may be gathered from Baker, *passim,* and Wyndham, Vol. II, pp. 99-102, 106-9, 110-16. There is an obituary notice in *The Theatrical Journal,* January 2, 1851 (Vol. XII, pp. 6-7).

tant in that they show how widespread *A New Way to Pay Old Debts* as an acting vehicle had become. Though productions of the play in foreign countries are outside the province of this book, it will be useful to illustrate my point if I mention that *Neues Mittel seine Schulden zu bezahlen* was played in an adaptation and translation by Achim von Arnim at the Hoftheater in Berlin on January 19, 1821.[35]

But Edward Stirling, the actor and manager, tells us of a production of about this date, which, if it is not far from home in number of miles, is certainly off the beaten track in its nature. The readers of *Sketches by Boz* will recall certain "Thespian Temples" in London where stage-struck boys were fleeced of their money for the privilege of acting in costume. In such a place Stirling made his début at the age of fourteen. Shortly afterwards the incidents of which he speaks took place :[36]

The "Brown Bear" in Goodman's Fields next opened its claws to grasp my slender means. A Jew, one Ikey Solomons (lineally descended from Shylock), the landlord of the "Bear" fitted up a dirty club-room with a few paltry scenes, and a ragged green baize curtain, and illuminated the floor with half-a-dozen oil-lamps. This Ikey called a *"The-a-tar* to *hact* in," that is, if you could pay. Lord Lovell in "A New Way to Pay Old Debts" cost me two-and-sixpence, dress included. This at night, to my horror, I found to consist of my own frock-coat, russet boots, a torn scarf, and a bearskin grenadier's cap. It is said that dress makes the man, but it never made a "lord" like this. Ikey's room was filled with an uproarious assemblage : sailors and their female friends, Jews, lascars, workmen with their wives and families ; pots of beer and "goes" of gin, tobacco and pipes were in constant request, and went the round of the company to any amount, whilst Ikey Solomons' voice was always in the ascendant, crying out "give yer orders," and scolding his waiters, Moses and Aaron. I need not say our efforts on the stage could not be heard without some difficulty and under considerable disadvantage amid this universal din. Just at the critical moment when Lady Allworth, the rich widow, cries out as wicked Sir Giles Overreach draws his sword, and the audience are worked up to agony-point, Ikey bawled out in a tone more of sorrow than of anger, "Aaron, there's

[35] Goedeke, Vol. III, p. 949.
[36] Stirling, Vol. I, pp. 9-11.

that 'ere sailor, and a go of rum, a-bolting without paying. Stan 'afore the door." Not another syllable was heard; the ragged baize dropped amidst yells of laughter, and cries of "Go it, Ikey." No more Brown, Black or White Bears for my money, depend upon it, reader, after this escapade.

From court-theatre to gin-shop went *A New Way to Pay Old Debts*—and then to Edinburgh, where a low comedian, J. Russell by name, attempted to play Sir Giles on December 17, 1823, and apparently made a ludicrous exhibition of himself.[37] When we find the play at Brighton on December 1, 1827, amateurs were taking part. From Porter comes the information that on that date, "Captain Augustus Berkely (an aristocratic novice) tried his resources as Overreach . . . before a crowded house. Marall was by an amateur whose name did not transpire."[38] *A New Way to Pay Old Debts* crops up again as one of a group of plays vaguely dated 1813-1840 acted by anonymous amateurs at Cheltenham.[39] Another amateur played Sir Giles, we hope successfully, when the play was given at The College, Stonyhurst, on December 26, 1829. Canon Cruickshank has seen the book of this production and reports that "the only female character retained was Froth. Lady Alworth's place was taken by a Mr. Alworth, and the *New Way* consisted in the supposed adoption of Wellborn. Margaret does not appear on the scene. The actual text was garbled and supplemented rather freely. There is no record of the performance or of the number of performances."[40] Truly the 1820's saw *A New Way to Pay Old Debts* in various wise.

About this time Sir Giles contrived to visit two new theatres, the Royal Pavilion Theatre in Whitechapel Road, which opened in 1829, and the Garrick Theatre in Leman Street, which began a year later. At the Royal Pavilion, Charles Freer, playing the regular starring rôles, interpreted Sir Giles on February 7, 1829, to the Lady Allworth of Mrs. Wingrove. I cannot find that the performance was repeated at that theatre, but Freer played the part

---

[37] J. C. Dibdin, *Edinburgh Stage,* p. 308. The curious are also referred to the amusing but highly romantic reference in Ryley, Vol. IX, pp. 98-9, where it is told how "Mr. O'Scroggins" announced the play at Inverary!

[38] Porter, p. 56.

[39] Hannam-Clark, p. 181.

[40] Cruickshank (Edition), p. 131, n. 1.

twice in the following year at Sadler's Wells. The dates are September 30 and October 1, Wellborn by Johnson, Lady Allworth by Mrs. Wilkinson—and my acknowledgments to *The Times*. Freer was an actor of considerable versatility but of no particular ability; we shall find him popping up later in America where he became stage-manager of the Greenwich Theatre, New York.

At the inconspicuous Garrick, so called because of its proximity to the scene of that actor's début, came Edward William Elton in the spring of 1831. After opening as Richard III, he played Sir Giles Overreach, and was reviewed by the critic of *The Owl* in the number of that rare weekly published on April 16, 1831:

> We visited this little theatre, the Garrick, though far from our haunt and home, for the purpose of witnessing Mr. Elton's performance of Sir Giles Overreach. There are a variety of circumstances which render the character of Sir Giles "a mountain of difficulties," to the actor. . . . We think Mr. Elton's conception of Sir Giles infinitely superior to that of Richard. He played with greater energy and feeling than we have been accustomed to witness on a minor stage, with one or two exceptions. The point of "some widow's curse, &c," in his closing scene was very admirably given; and the transition, though somewhat rugged, was energetic. We prophecy his becoming a great favorite.

The article also mentions that Conquest, one of the managers, was the Marrall and Garthwaite the Tapwell. Elton also played Sir Giles at the New City Theatre in Milton Street—the abode of literary hacks, Grub Street so-called—on September 19, 1831. It was Buckstone's benefit, with the Wellborn by Wynne, Mrs. Knight as Lady Allworth, and the fair Margaret by Miss Bouchier. This too might, by a stretch of the imagination, be called a new theatre; it was new as a theatre at any rate, having previously been a chapel. I find also a performance of our play there on September 30 of the same year, but *The Times* gives no cast. We must not forget that Kean had prepared New City audiences for the play in at least two performances earlier in the year. A playbill shows us that Elton's Sir Giles finally graduated to the Haymarket on May 20, 1833. A portrait of Elton as Sir Giles is contained in *The Owl* in the issue of July 30, 1831. Elton gained considerable success in the east end, and afterwards accepted engagements at the larger theatres. He went down on the *Pegasus* when that ship struck a rock near Holy Island in 1843; his death caused considerable sensation, and many theatres gave benefit performances for his children. He was not an important actor but by no means deserves oblivion.[41]

One other performance, or rather my failure to find one, must be mentioned before I come again to the consideration of a particular actor's impersonation of Massinger's villain. Chelli, again referring to theatrical cuttings in the British Museum, says that *A New Way to Pay Old Debts* was the play at Brighton on May 27, 1833.[42] Now according to the historian of the Brighton stage, who appears to be reasonably accurate, the theatre was closed in 1833 from March 6 to July 29, except for the week beginning Easter Monday, April 8.[43] I cannot but think that Chelli has misread his source. Moreover I cannot find in the British Museum the clipping to which he refers.

And now we come to a man whose name, first shining in the reflected light of his father's genius, later gleamed with its own brightness, Charles Kean. If he never illuminated Shakespeare with flashes of lightning, as Coleridge said of Edmund, at least his lamp was clear and steady. Born while Edmund Kean and his wife were still provincial strollers, he received the educational advantages promised by his father's success at Drury Lane. Leaving Eton in 1827, he was offered a cadetship in the East India Company, which he agreed to accept if his father would settle on his mother, then separated from her husband, an income of four hundred pounds. This Edmund claimed he was unable to do, and Charles against his father's wishes decided to go on the stage. His name brought him entrée to Drury Lane, where he made his début as Young Norval in *Douglas* on October 1, 1827, at what was announced as eighteen years of age. This and subsequent performances were successful only from the financial point of view.

[41] Besides the sources mentioned above, I have used the article by Joseph Knight, in the *DNB* and the material on the minor theatres from Baker, pp. 404-7. I am particularly indebted to Mrs. J. D. Hall of the Harvard Theatre Collection for consulting *The Owl* in the Boston Public Library.
[42] Chelli, p. 66.
[43] Porter, p. 62.

Provincial engagements brought him no fame, nor was he accepted by his London audiences as anything more than a mediocre performer. After travelling through Holland and France in 1830, he sailed for America where for the first time his reception can be said to have been really favorable. Charles Kean's first appreciable London successes came in 1838 when he was engaged by Alfred Bunn to act at Drury Lane, and from this time on his fame grew. In August of 1850, in partnership with Robert Keeley, he leased the Princess's Theatre and appeared for the first time under his own management. At the end of the first season Keeley retired, and Charles Kean began the series of spectacular revivals for which he is best remembered. He resigned as manager in 1859. Taking a farewell at Drury Lane in 1862, he and his wife sailed around the world, reappearing in England in 1866. He made his last appearance on any stage at Liverpool in May of the following year, and after a long illness died in January 1868. Of his Shakespearean parts Hamlet and Richard III were the greatest; by far his most successful rôle was Louis XI in Boucicault's adaptation of Casimir Delavigne's play of the same name. Never inspired like his father, he was always a thoughtful and careful actor, and he has been much underrated because he happened to bear the name of a genius no one surpassed.[44]

Charles Kean made his first appearance as Sir Giles Overreach unexpectedly at the Theatre Royal, Dublin, on May 11, 1829, when his father became ill just before going on. A week later he returned to his announced part of Wellborn. He did not regularly assume the main rôle until he acted in the United States in 1830.[45] There he was successful enough in the part to keep it in his repertoire after he had returned to Great Britain in 1833. On September 12 of that year, he gave Sir Giles to the citizens of Tunbridge Wells, and in October to Dublin.[46] I cannot cite a playbill for the Dublin performance but probably the cast was the same as on January 29, 1834, when he again played the part in that city:

---

[44] This introductory paragraph is summarized from the best biography of Kean, John William Cole's *Life and Theatrical Times of Charles Kean.* Joseph Knight's article in the *DNB,* Vol. XXX, pp. 255-8, has also been used, and is the most convenient short account.

[45] Playbill; see Part II, pp. 237-42.

[46] Cole, Vol. I, p. 219; Tunbridge Wells playbill.

Sir Giles Overreach	C. Kean
Wellborn	Pritchard
Lord Lovell	Mercer
Marrall	Rees
Justice Greedy	Johnson
Allworth	Barry
Lady Allworth	Miss Cleaver
Margaret	Miss Chalmers

Very likely Kean's October audience liked his performance for in January he began his engagement with this part. Meanwhile Kean had made one of an English company "under the direction of Captain Livius" which played a short-lived engagement in Hamburg, *A New Way to Pay Old Debts* on December 12 with the cast indicated by a playbill:

Sir Giles Overreach	C. Kean
Wellborn	Vining
Lord Lovell	Gann
Marrall	Hay
Justice Greedy	Burton
Allworth	Grattan
Lady Allworth	Mrs. Burton
Margaret	Miss Graham

In the fall of 1834, we find him at Brighton, acting Sir Giles on August 20 and November 17.[47] Doubtless I am missing performances, but the next one of which I have found record was at the Theatre Royal, Liverpool, on May 28, 1835. The playbill gives us the cast:

Sir Giles Overreach	C. Kean
Wellborn	Lacy
Lord Lovell	Hamilton
Marrall	Baker
Justice Greedy	Andrews
Allworth	Durand
Lady Allworth	Mrs. Stanley
Margaret	Miss Stanley

But after mentioning a performance of *A New Way to Pay Old Debts* at Brighton on August 25, 1835, I am forced—scandalous proceeding!—to jump almost two years for a performance at

[47] Porter, pp. 63-4.

Liverpool on May 18, 1837.[48] R. M. Sillard is my authority for stating that Charles Kean played Sir Giles Overreach at the Theatre Royal, George's St., Cork, on June 19, though I certainly cannot accept his statement that this was for the first time on any stage.[49] A performance at Brighton on September 12, 1837, concludes—for me, at least—until 1842 the list of Charles Kean's provincial impersonations of the rôle under discussion.[50]

Alfred Bunn finds exultation in the fact that from January 8 to April 5, 1838, at Drury Lane, Charles Kean needed to interpret only three characters, Hamlet, Richard III, and Sir Giles Overreach.[51] Playing three times a week, Kean opened January 8 as Hamlet, acting it without interruption until Monday, February 5, when Richard III was the bill. Thereafter he played both parts until Saturday, March 3, which saw *A New Way to Pay Old Debts*. All three plays were then acted until April 5, when Kean played Shylock for his farewell.[52]

During this engagement, Kean played Sir Giles five times, all the performances coming on the Saturdays of March; the days were the 3rd, the 10th, the 17th, the 24th, and the 31st. The bills list the actors as follows:

Sir Giles Overreach	C. Kean
Wellborn	Cooper
Lord Lovell	H. Cooke
Marrall	Compton
Justice Greedy	Dowton
Allworth	Brindal
Lady Allworth	Mrs. Ternan
Margaret	Miss Poole

The Athenaeum remarks curtly:[53] "Mr. Charles Kean continues to draw crowded houses here. He has added *Sir Giles Overreach* to his short list of characters, but, in our opinion, his *Hamlet* remains his best performance. It is much clearer of imitation of his father

[48] Porter, p. 65; Liverpool playbill.
[49] Sillard, Vol. I, p. 48.
[50] Porter, p. 67.
[51] Bunn, Vol. III, pp. 26-8. Bunn states that the profits for the five performances of *A New Way to Pay Old Debts* were £1536.8s.
[52] Advertisements in *The Times*.
[53] *The Athenaeum,* March 17, 1838.

than either the *Richard* or the *Sir Giles,* and were it only for that, it would be to us much preferable,"—a review which visits the sins of the father on his son, if indeed they were sins. The *Athenaeum* was classicist and rejoiced in the fact.

But *The Times,* which I have found to be more uniformly fair than any other periodical or newspaper, is enthusiastic:

Massinger's well-known and as much admired drama, *A New Way to Pay Old Debts,* was performed on Saturday evening. . . . Mr. C. Kean on this occasion appeared, for the first time in London, as Sir Giles Overreach—that fiendish incarnation of craft and cruelty. At the outset, we pronounce his performance to be one of the most perfect in all its parts that we have seen for many years. Mr. Kean did not merely place before his auditory a strikingly effective portraiture of the leading features of the character, but he entered minutely into its finer and more subtle shades. We have seen it asserted that Mr. C. Kean lacks conception of character. . . . Now, we have attentively watched Mr. C. Kean's Hamlet and his Richard, and we could perceive no lack of conception of character. He appeared to us thoroughly to understand each situation in which the incidents of the drama placed him; he appeared rightly to estimate the value of every sentence which he had to deliver, and to give to each its due weight and importance. If this be true, and we sincerely and without prejudice think that it is, the remark applies with, if possible, increased force to Mr. C. Kean's performance of Sir Giles Overreach. We had a living picture of the tyrannical and brutal master—of the base, calculating coveter of other men's possessions—of the wretched slave to a grovelling ambition, who would even sacrifice the maiden honour of his daughter, that she might (his arm prevailing) become "right honourable"—of the fawning creature who (like our Radicals) would lick the feet of a nobleman, in the hope of effecting an alliance with a class which in his plebeian heart, he hated. . . .

In this play the chief test of the abilities of the representative of Sir Giles is in the fifth act; but there is much in the preceding acts that requires great skill and thoughtful care in the performer. . . . All these earlier scenes would, in the hands of an ordinary artist, have passed off as little more than matters of course. Not so with Mr. C. Kean. Every tittle of them was strongly marked—each point which tended to develope the depraved mind and heart of Sir Giles was given with strong effect, and the whole served as a fitting induction to the great catastrophe. In the last act Mr. C. Kean's triumph was complete. He depicted, in turns, apprehension, hope, frantic disappointment, and ultimate despair, in varied colours. Here the action is varied and strongly contrasted. Sir Giles's nephew has tricked him; the bond by which he held his relative's lands has miraculously become a sheet of blank paper. For a moment he is paralyzed,—burning wrath succeeds,—but the approach of (as he supposes) his "right honourable" daughter banishes for a moment his resentful feelings, and a paroxysm of frantic joy ensues. It vanishes almost as soon as it is created. The maiden has espoused the youth of her choice,—all Sir Giles's ambitious plans are thwarted,—and the wretched perpetrator of so many crimes, conscience-stricken, sinks on the earth, deprived of sense. Every one of these transitions was given with masterly force and fine discrimination by Mr. C. Kean. He evinced talent of the highest order in every shade and transition of the character. Whether he coaxed or threatened Marall, whether he played the fawning sycophant to Lord Lovell, or, stung with madness, defied him to mortal combat,—whether he attempted to wheedle his nephew, or, furiously exasperated gave him "the loud lie,"—in each and all of these positions Mr. C. Kean gave the most unquestionable proofs of a comprehensive and vigorous mind. He conceived boldly and correctly; and what he so conceived he executed with commensurate truth and vigour. His exit was extremely well imagined. Instead of at once sinking into the arms of the attendants, he fell forward, as if suddenly stricken by a thunderbolt; and when raised, and slowly borne away, his look was that of inanity, and his low and hysterical moanings those of a deeply suffering being. The applause throughout was very great; and at the conclusion of the play it was really enthusiastic. Mr. Kean was loudly called for, and at once came forward, and by gesture signified his gratitude to the audience. Mr. Dowton sustained the character of that first-rate gourmand very humorously. He, however, does not look the character. He is not one of those "thin-gutted squires" of whom it can be said, as the cook says of Justice Greedy,—

". . . Meat's cast away upon him,
"It never thrives."

The part of Marall was admirably played by Mr. Compton. Without effort, without straining, without grimacing, but taking all smoothly and quietly, he kept the audience in a continual roar of laughter. We shall not soon forget his look of bewilderment and bepuzzlement (as Lord Brougham would phrase it), and his grotesque action, when he finds himself, contrary to all human calculation, invited not only to dine with Lady Allworth, but to salute her. Mr. Cooper sustained the part of Wellborn judiciously. He gave the exquisitely written and most touching appeal of the broken-down spendthrift to Lady Allworth with considerable feeling. A gentleman of nobler port and bearing than Mr. H. Cooke can boast ought to impersonate Lord Lovell, the courtier and the soldier. Lady Allworth found an agreeable representative in Mrs. Ternan. The house was crowded in every part from the pit to the slips.

Indeed *The Times* becomes crusader in its efforts to right the wrongs done to Mr. Charles Kean. It stresses the point that though the critics have begrudged him admiration, his audiences have given the lie to the reportorial judgments:[54]

We witnessed Mr. C. Kean's second personation of Sir Giles Overreach on Saturday evening with very great pleasure. As his merit in the character has been impugned in some quarters, we scrutinized his performance with more than ordinary care, and we see no reason whatsoever for retracting a single iota of the praise which we bestowed on his first representation of the part. That praise was as justly due as it was freely tendered. Assuredly, if the effort had been mediocre, we should, however painful it might be, have unreservedly avowed our opinion. We consider Mr. Kean's idea of the character to be perfectly correct. He throws himself heart and soul into the part, and he produces a picture as remarkable for its unforced energy as for its true discrimination. A most crowded audience enthusiastically applauded his performance on Saturday evening. At the conclusion of the play he was loudly called for; but in consequence, we believe, of exhaustion, arising from his great exertion in the last act, a considerable time elapsed before he made his appearance. Some disapprobation was manifested, but peace and harmony were immediately restored when he presented himself, and received the hearty gratulations of the audience. In answer to the few who have cavilled at Mr. Charles Kean, and who seem disposed to create faults where in reality they do not exist, we shall merely observe, that no actor who did not possess qualifications of a very high order could, as Mr. C. Kean has done, have drawn crowded audiences for now some 30

[54] *The Times,* March 12, 1838.

nights in three different characters, each varying most essentially from the other. There must be great merit thus to attract the public. Mr. C. Kean cannot have given "powders" to the whole town to make them love him and run after him.

There is much sound logic here, and if Kean departed on April 5 without the approbations of the critics, some of whom at least damned him because he was not of the Kemble school and others because he was not his father, he certainly left behind him a manager who could smile cheerfully at the financial returns, and a public which thereafter received him with open arms.

Naturally enough Charles Kean returned to London, after provincial tours which included a Sir Giles at Manchester on May 21, 1839.[55] On Friday, June 21, *The Times* made the following announcement:

Theatre Royal, Haymarket

Last night but three of the Farewell Performances of Mr. Charles Kean previous to his departure for America. To-night he will perform (for the first time here) Sir Giles Overreach, and on Monday next (for the last time) Richard the Third. Mr. Kean's nights of performing—Monday, Wednesday, and Friday, on which evenings the free list will be suspended (the press excepted).

This Evening, *A New Way to Pay Old Debts*

Sir Giles Overreach, Mr. Charles Kean; Wellborn, Mr. Cooper; Justice Greedy, Mr. Strickland; Marrall, Mr. W. Farren; Lady Allworth, Miss Pelham; Margaret, Miss Travers.

Hamlet, Richard III, and Sir Giles Overreach again made up Kean's list of characters on this engagement at the Haymarket, which began on June 3 with Hamlet. June 21 was the date of the first performance of Sir Giles; the second came on Friday, June 28, and was announced as the concluding performance of the engagement. The next day, however, *The Times* bore the tidings that Mr. Charles Kean had been reengaged for six nights more, and *A New Way to Pay Old Debts* was again the play of the evening on Wednesday, July 10.

[55] The playbill.

An American trip followed on which, as we shall see,[56] Sir Giles Overreach remained in Kean's repertory. On his return to England he again appeared at the Haymarket, but this time he was Sir Giles on only one occasion. The performance came on Wednesday, June 24, 1840; the faithful *Times* gives us the partial cast:

Sir Giles Overreach .... C. Kean
Wellborn .... J. Webster
Marrall .... Buckstone
Justice Greedy .... Strickland
Lady Allworth .... Mrs. W. Clifford
Margaret .... Mrs. Yarnold

As far as I know, this was the last time that Charles Kean played the part in London, and except for a performance at Brighton on September 15, 1842,[57] the last time in Great Britain.

As a final estimate of Kean's Sir Giles Overreach, I shall quote a review which appeared in *The Morning Post*;[58] it seems to me to hit the mark: "But if his celebrated precursor [Edmund Kean] had never appeared before a London audience, Mr. Charles Kean's embodiment of Sir Giles Overreach last night would have caused him to be hailed as a star of no ordinary brilliance in the dramatic firmament. To enter into an analysis of a performance which has very lately been much dilated upon, would indeed be a work of supererogation. Mr. Kean's attributes for the personification of this painful conception of the poet, are extraordinary in so young a man. Last night his spirit and energy were unfailing; no point 'came tardily off.' Perhaps a fastidious observer might say that the actor's efforts to produce effect are sometimes too obvious; but this is a fault which experience will not fail to remedy completely. . . ." These remarks to my mind accurately convey the impression that Charles Kean must have made in the character. Uninspired, no genius, he nevertheless gave a careful and considered performance, intelligently conceived and thoughtfully executed. Charles Kean has been too much damned by circumstances

[56] Part II, pp. 242-3.
[57] Porter, p. 78.
[58] I quote from Cole, Vol. I, p. 302.

over which he had no control; I for one would have wished to see his Sir Giles Overreach.

The reader may or may not recall that in 1827, on July 11 to be precise, when Edmund Kean was acting Sir Giles Overreach at Leeds, a gentleman by the name of Phelps played the part of Allworth; and that we found him again at Sheffield on February 11, 1830, now graduated to Wellborn.[59] Even then Samuel Phelps was a popular young actor, and Edmund Kean himself is supposed to have prophesied that he would some day be great.[60] The prophecy was fulfilled, and Phelps became not only an actor of great versatility but a manager who dared what was almost impossible and succeeded. Born in Devonport in 1804, and educated in his native town, he was left an orphan at sixteen and made his living by newspaper work. Amateur theatricals decided him to become a professional actor, and having married in 1826, he accepted an engagement at York in the fall. He remained in Yorkshire for three years, and in 1830 became a leading man under the Butlers at Sheffield, where he was a favorite. His success increased to such an extent that by 1836 he was hailed by the critics of Exeter as a second Edmund Kean, because of his powerful delineations of Shakespearean characters.[61]

Phelps had come to Exeter in October 1836; he remained there for four months and a half, and at the conclusion of his engagement played for his benefit the character which is the subject of this book, "the house being crammed to suffocation."[62] Apparently his success was pronounced, for a week later he was announced to star at Plymouth for five nights, and Sir Giles Overreach was on the list of his parts, "all of which drew good houses, and very laudatory criticisms from all the newspapers in the three towns of Plymouth, Stonehouse, and Devonport."[63]

Phelps made his London début, as Shylock, at the Haymarket on August 28, 1837, to the Portia of Miss Huddart. Shortly after-

[59] See pp. 85-6, 88.
[60] Coleman, p. 68.
[61] Unless otherwise stated, my facts regarding the life of Samuel Phelps are taken from W. May Phelps and John Forbes-Robertson, *The Life and Life-Work of Samuel Phelps*.
[62] Phelps and Forbes-Robertson, p. 37.
[63] *ibid.*, p. 38.

wards he appeared with Macready at Covent Garden; by this time his success was assured, in spite of the fact that Macready for his own advantage gave him dwarfed parts. A regular engagement at Drury Lane followed, again with Macready, to be succeeded by summer acting at the Haymarket and in the provinces. Such was the program until 1844. Meanwhile Phelps had made his London début as Sir Giles Overreach at the Haymarket on August 1, 1842,[64] repeating the character on the 4th. The convenient *Times* gives us the cast for both dates:

Sir Giles Overreach	Phelps
Wellborn	Vining
Marrall	W. Farren
Justice Greedy	Strickland
Allworth	Wilsone
Lady Allworth	Mrs. W. Clifford
Margaret	Mrs. Yarnold
Froth	Mrs. F. Matthews

At the end of August, Phelps went again to Plymouth for a few nights; *The Devonport Independent* remarks on his performance of Sir Giles Overreach as follows:[65]

This is the first time Mr. Phelps has gratified his numerous friends in this quarter of the globe with his presence since his engagement at the Plymouth Theatre in 1837. He has now passed the trying ordeal of a London audience, and by the services of several seasons has proved himself—and the voice of criticism establishes the proof—a tragedian second to none now on the boards. His performance of the sordid, mammon-worshipping hero of Massinger's truthful play, was, in reality, a splendid piece of acting. From the moment of his entrance, in the second act, until the final exhaustion of physical and mental faculty, by the frustration of his villainous speculations, in the last act, he bore the impress of an actor gifted with real intellectual powers, and fully capable of realizing the conceptions of the author. The Sir Giles of Mr. Phelps, we do not hesitate to pronounce the most perfect the stage can now produce. What could exceed the oily,

[64] Not in July, as stated by Cruickshank (Edition), p. 127. See the advertisements in *The Times,* and Phelps and Forbes-Robertson, p. 58. Parker (*The Times Literary Supplement,* September 7, 1922, p. 569) says "first time before a London audience."

[65] Phelps and Forbes-Robertson, pp. 58-9.

smoothfaced manner with which he confided his purpose, to grind the poor man to his nefarious will, to his creature Marrall. His interview with his daughter, where he reveals that he would have her "right honourable"—aye, even at the expense of that which to a pure mind is most dear, honour—was finely executed, and the manner in which he delivered those few lines of caution to his daughter, lest her modest inadvertence "might spoil all," we shall never forget. In the last act, Mr. Phelps was electrical!—never since the days of Edmund Kean was effect produced so harrowing to mind and body as we witnessed in the convulsive throes of this demon of avarice and ambition in his struggles to obtain the mastery over his conscience. He would be forced to "Hell like to himself"; and when he lay a stiffened corse at the feet of his daughter—the child whom he would have slain in the impotence of his rage—the audience seemed relieved from the existence of a monster, and by their loud and long-continued plaudits, afforded a double compliment to the talented tragedian. At the conclusion of the play, Mr. Phelps was loudly called for, nor would the delighted auditory cease their importunities until they had again and again assured him that his efforts had proved triumphantly successful.

Even if we recall that this was written in Phelps's home-town newspaper, we cannot deny that he must have been splendid, and the constant repetition of the part in London shows what success he had with the audiences of that city. No doubt, too, he was hailed with delighted acclamation when he played the part at the Liver Theatre, Liverpool, in the autumn of 1843.[66]

Phelps now commenced the management which made him famous, a management during which he produced with the exception of *Henry VI, Troilus and Cressida, Titus Andronicus,* and *Richard II,* all of the plays included in the Shakespeare corpus, and what is more astounding, made them pay in an, at the beginning, unfashionable and, by the élite, almost forgotten theatre. Taking advantage of the removal by legislature of the privileges of the patent theatres, Phelps in May 1844 leased in partnership with Mr. and Mrs. Warner (the Miss Huddart with whom Phelps had made his London début) and Thomas Greenwood the little theatre in Islington known as Sadler's Wells. Phelps was stage manager, Greenwood acting manager, and Warner treasurer. Here

[66] Broadbent, p. 214.

SAMUEL PHELPS as SIR GILES OVERREACH, published by
A. Park, London

Phelps remained until 1862, producing brilliantly the finest plays of the English theatre.[67] His career after this date until his death in 1878, while by no means unimportant, need not occupy us, since during that period Sir Giles was not among his characters.

On May 27, 1844, Phelps made his first venture at his new theatre as Macbeth. On September 19, he played Sir Giles Overreach for the first time under his own management,[68] repeating the part on the 27th and 28th.[69] The cast was as follows:[70]

Sir Giles Overreach	Phelps
Wellborn	H. Marston
Lord Lovell	G. Bennett
Marrall	A. Younge
Justice Greedy	Forman
Allworth	Higgie
Lady Allworth	Mrs. Warner
Margaret	Miss Cooper

The play now lapsed until March 8 and 9, 1850, when Phelps produced it again.[71] A playbill of the latter date shows us four changes in the cast: Graham was now the Allworth, and H. Nye the Justice Greedy; while Lady Allworth was played by Mrs. Brougham (Mrs. Warner had retired from the management), and Margaret by Miss Edwardes. On May 26, 27, and 28, 1851, Mrs. Graham succeeded to Lady Allworth, and Miss F. Huddart to Margaret.[72]

Sometime in 1852 Phelps was at the Queen's Theatre, Dublin, for Herbert Steele saw him play Sir Giles Overreach, and wrote a review of the performance in the *Commercial Journal and Family Herald* of that city.[73] After speaking of Phelps's Richelieu, and Werner, Mr. Steele comments:

Wednesday night I saw him in Sir Giles Overreach—that Richard III of common life.[74] The character is a possible deform-

---

[67] Besides *A New Way to Pay Old Debts,* Phelps produced two other plays by Massinger, *The City Madam* and *The Fatal Dowry.*
[68] Phelps and Forbes-Robertson, p. 68.
[69] Advertisements in *The Times.*
[70] Phelps and Forbes-Robertson, p. 262, reprint the playbill.
[71] *ibid.,* p. 118, and the advertisements in *The Times.*
[72] Phelps and Forbes-Robertson, p. 121, and the advertisements in *The Times.*
[73] Phelps and Forbes-Robertson, pp. 216-19 in lieu of the paper.
[74] Compare Scott, "Sir Giles Overreach (the Richard III of middling life)"; see p. 57 above.

ity; the monster is very exceptionable, let us trust, but—it is probable. We *feel* that a man might be a Sir Giles Overreach. Vulgar in his ambition, his means towards that end approach grandeur by their subtlety and absolute beauty of adaptation. Ruthless as is his malevolence, it is not petty; fearful as is his hypocrisy, it is not mean. He has but one good quality—courage; he *does* win applause by his matchless personal bravery. You think the human devil half redeemed as you feel how reckless he is of life when revenge is his object; his blood-thirstiness becomes almost heroic in its intensity. It is a great character—a great conception—worthy of Shakespeare—true to life in every word. How the low-born soul of the man appears in the comments on his daughter's dress; he would have wished it "spangled with flowers." All through one feels the genius of Massinger—granted a Sir Giles Overreach—he could not speak other than he does. In this, as in the two others, my perfect realization of the characters comes from Phelps; the impression I had from closest study was strong enough, but the words and looks of the actor seem to *burn them in,* never to be forgotten. His anger towards the end was terrible; one felt keen pity mingled with horror; the quick changes from rage to rejoicing, and then the downfall, when there comes on that awful paralysis of soul, were thrilling; as the eye of the till then unawed wicked man wanders in wild weakness, seeing fearful visions of the hearts he had broken. Then came that final shudder, when the daughter for whom he had done all bends before his distraught gaze, and the memory comes to tear his heart and scorch his soul. I would scarcely wish to see it again; I feel almost as Byron did seeing Kean do it: the sight of wickedness so fearful, yet so painfully human, is not "good" for the thought. It fills one with a strange shudder, and brings "thoughts beyond the reaches of our souls."

I have seen Phelps in three of the most dissimilar characters, and my summary is—He is far and away the greatest artist on the stage; in fact, one might say, the only great actor now left us. One feels really grateful to a man who, with such perfect and beautiful power, can present the subtlest sensations of the soul, and the deepest passions of the heart. May he long live to convey to us the poetry of passion and the heroism of humanity!

Sadler's Wells was again the setting for *A New Way to Pay Old Debts* when Phelps revived the play in February 1854;[75] the

---

[75] Phelps and Forbes-Robertson, p. 138.

performances fell on the 25th, 26th, and 27th, with some changes in cast from previous productions :[76]

Sir Giles Overreach .... Phelps
Wellborn .... H. Marston
Lord Lovell .... Lunt
Marrall .... J. W. Ray
Justice Greedy .... Lewis Ball
Margaret .... Miss Hickson

After mentioning a performance at the Theatre Royal, Birmingham on April 28, 1855,[77] I return to London, where *The Times* advertises *A New Way to Pay Old Debts* for February 28, March 6, and March 8, 1856,[78] "characters by Messrs. Phelps, H. Marston, Ray, Lunt, and Lewis Ball; Misses Atkinson and J. Marston." The men are easily enough placed from the above list; subsequent casts will show that the Lady Allworth was Miss Atkinson, and therefore that Margaret fell to Miss J. Marston. Perhaps it was to one of these performances that A. R. Goddard referred in his letter to Phelps, dated December 3, 1857:[79] "I saw Kean *many times* in *each* of his characters, and, 'nay, do not think I flatter,' when last I saw you in Sir Giles Overreach I was transported, and my friend detected me several times saying, 'Well done, *Kean!*' Your passion scene, I may say, surpassed his; so does your Hamlet. . . . I was also acquainted with old Mr. Garner, librarian at Margate. In George III's time he was a theatrical, and had seen Garrick sixty-three times; he saw Sir Giles with me, and said Kean's was as good as Garrick's—I may safely say the same of yours." *I* may say, I hope without disrespect, that I doubt if Mr. Garner ever saw Garrick as Sir Giles.

Two more years saw productions of *A New Way to Pay Old Debts* by Phelps at Sadler's Wells. Three performances came in March 1858—the 13th, 15th, and 16th.[80] The major men-characters were by the same actors; Miss Atkinson was the Lady All-

---

[76] Advertisements in *The Times*.

[77] Cruickshank (Edition), p. 130.

[78] There were no performances in January as stated by Cruickshank (Edition), p. 128.

[79] Phelps and Forbes-Robertson, p. 402.

[80] There were no performances in November 1857 as stated by Cruickshank (Edition), p. 128.

worth, but Margaret was now by Miss C. Young. And three more came on February 23, 24, and 25, 1860,[81] for which *The Times* says only: "Wellborn—Mr. H. Marston; Lady Allworth—Miss Atkinson." After this date, I know of no performances of Sir Giles Overreach by Samuel Phelps.

Phelps was nothing if not daring. Intrepid in his managership of Sadler's Wells, he was not afraid to play a rôle which Edmund Kean had made peculiarly his own, a part which for that reason Macready always refused to act.[82] But Phelps was more than daring, for he dared intelligently. His Sadler's Wells scheme, which seemed doomed to failure, succeeded; and his Sir Giles Overreach was so well acted, in spite of Kean's colossal triumph in the rôle, that his nephew, W. May Phelps, could say:[83] "His performance of this part will never be forgotten by me. Many old play-goers have told me over and over again that it was a more powerful and terrific piece of acting than Edmund Kean's. I certainly cannot myself imagine anything could surpass it."

I am confident that Samuel Phelps's name, along with those of John Henderson, George Frederick Cooke, and Edmund Kean, should be placed upon the roster of those actors who gave especially powerful and vivid impersonations of Sir Giles Overreach.

[81] There were no performances in March 1860, as stated by Cruickshank (Edition), p. 128.

[82] Archer, p. 193. I feel sure that Brander Matthews had a slip of memory when he included Macready among the actors who played Sir Giles. See Matthews and Lieder, Appendix II, p. 1073.

[83] Phelps and Forbes-Robertson, p. 118. n.

CHAPTER VI

TO FRESH WOODS AND PASTURES NEW

IN the days of which we speak, the York circuit was always a
training-ground for the talented aspirant for theatrical honors.
Having graduated from small parts at the lesser houses, here
he could find opportunity for star rôles, and prepare himself for
London triumphs. "The delineation of the character of Sir Giles
Overreach," writes William Creswick in his *Autobiography*,[1]
"affected me so powerfully that I hoped within myself that I
should never be called upon to take it. But . . . I was solicited to
play it at Leeds, for the benefit of Mr. Crouch; and my success in
it there, as well as in Hull, made it one of my pet parts." It is
accordingly somewhat damaging for me to admit that I cannot
present a long list of performances of *A New Way to Pay Old
Debts* with Creswick as the star; my failure is perhaps partially
accounted for by his long career in the provinces and minor
theatres, and his support of other stars in the major ones.

Born in 1813, Creswick entered the theatre through an amateur
company, and after a few unimportant appearances in London,
sought experience in the provinces. He played the York circuit
from 1836 to 1839 but attracted little attention until 1846, when
he became a member of Phelps's company at Sadler's Wells. Later
we find him at the Princess's with Fanny Kemble Butler, at the
Haymarket under Benjamin Webster where he was engaged for
three years, and in 1849 at the Surrey under his own management.
He had already visited America from 1839 to 1841, and Sir Giles
was one of his parts there.[2] His London career was principally
connected with the Surrey, but he subsequently starred at the
Standard, where he became a great favorite, at Drury Lane, and
at the City of London Theatre. In 1877 he went to Australia,
where he achieved considerable popularity. Upon his return, he

---

[1] *An Autobiography: A Record of Fifty Years of the Professional Life of the
Late William Creswick.* For his life, see also C. E. Pascoe, *The Dramatic List,*
pp. 100-2; Joseph Knight in the *DNB,* Suppl., Vol. II, p. 88.
[2] See Part II, p. 260.

acted only occasionally, chiefly in Shakespearean characters. He took his farewell at Drury Lane in 1885, and died three years later.

Creswick played his first Sir Giles at Leeds in 1837; playbills point out performances by him on September 29 and October 16, the second for his benefit. I find no record of those at Hull, though the fault is doubtless mine, and jump five years to Newcastle for his Overreach on November 16, 1842, which "was enthusiastically received by his audience, and gained for him like praises from the Newcastle critics."[3] There must be many performances at the Surrey, but I note only three, on December 12 and 15, 1854, and for his farewell to management on September 27, 1862. "The house was crowded and the audience enthusiastic."[4] Curiously, Australia proves the richest mine for our records. At the Academy of Music, Melbourne, Creswick acted Sir Giles on November 17, 1877, with Lady Allworth by Mrs. G. W. B. Lewis, repeating the part five times. Six more performances began on February 9, 1878, when he was playing at the Victoria Theatre, Sydney, with Miss Mainwaring as Lady Allworth.[5] There must too have been at least one Overreach in Brisbane, for the *Courier* there asserts he is at his best in that part.[6] Beyond these occasional comments, I have no knowledge of Creswick's success or ability as Massinger's extortioner. He belonged to the old-fashioned rhetorical school, which might have fitted him somewhat for such a blood-and-thunder part as Sir Giles, but even Sir Giles would lose by too much ranting. All I can say is that Creswick, though never a first-rate actor, was always a useful and popular one.

In the spring of 1838 a young man applied to Mr. Charles Hill, the manager of the Cheltenham and Gloucester theatres, for permission to act a part, however small, with his company. Tressel in *Richard III* first fell to his lot. There is no report as to how he fared, but apparently his reception was favorable, for a few weeks later was presented "Under the patronage of Lieutenant-Colonel Pym," Massinger's *A New Way to Pay Old Debts,* the part of Sir Giles "By a Young Gentleman of this City." The performance was a success and the actor was duly engaged as a member of the

---

[3] *Autobiography.* Comment by the editor [C.O.], p. 54.
[4] *ibid.,* p. 71.
[5] Cruickshank (Edition), p. 138.
[6] *Autobiography.* Comment by the editor [C.O.], p. 110.

company. A Cheltenham playbill of April 24 dignifies the "Young Gentleman" Overreach with the name of Lee Moreton. In July of the same year Charles Hill and Lee Moreton went to Brighton to fulfil a short engagement; on the 30th, Moreton played Sir Giles Overreach to the Wellborn of Hill, with Marshall, the stage-manager, as Justice Greedy. Very likely the performance was repeated; at any rate, Porter tells us that Moreton's acting "was warmly eulogised." Though the young man was only eighteen, this eulogy is the more easily understood when we learn that Lee Moreton was none other than—of all people—Dion Boucicault!

Whether Boucicault ever played Sir Giles Overreach after this date, I do not know; it is hard to visualize his acting of the part even these few times. Conn, Shaun, Michael O'Dowd,—yes, by all means, and to Boucicault's undying fame,—but Sir Giles Overreach? Impossible—and true! Verily, Boucicault's was a varied career; an embryonic tragedian became an unparalleled actor of Irish parts and a comedian of wondrous powers; a strolling player had much to do with changing the trend of both English and American drama. Dion Boucicault as Sir Giles Overreach—I rejoice at the discovery![7]

[7] All statements regarding the early life of Boucicault must be highly tentative, and the above are no exception to the rule. The difficulty lies in the disparity of the accounts. Porter, p. 69 gives me the date of the Brighton performance. The book is compiled from newspapers and playbills and must take precedence over all stories told from memory. The events preceding that date are taken from Barton Hill's account of his father's managership, to be found in Townsend Walsh's *Career of Dion Boucicault,* pp. 15-17, where it is reprinted from "An Old Playbill" (*Appleton's Booklovers Magazine,* August 1905, pp. 235-43). A misprint may account for the fact that he has crowned Victoria a year before her time, but he has apparently confused two trips to Brighton: one in 1838, when Hill and Boucicault went to Brighton to act, and another in 1839, when Hill leased the Brighton Theatre (Porter, p. 70), neither in 1837. Barton Hill's dates therefore are not to be trusted, but his account of Boucicault's début and first performance of Sir Giles must be accepted, since it is unique. Note however that *The New York Clipper* of September 27, 1890, says that Boucicault's first part on the stage was Norfolk in *Richard III,* and so Mr. Montrose J. Moses in his *Famous Actor Families in America,* p. 117. Mr. Moses writes me that besides *The New York Clipper,* his sources were the files of T. Allston Brown and the reminiscences of Aubrey Boucicault. Boucicault himself had a slip of memory when he implied that he went to Cheltenham, Gloucester, and Brighton in 1839 for the first time, for the Hiram Stead Collection in the New York Public Library has the rare Cheltenham playbill for April 24, 1838: "Sir Giles Overreach by Lee Moreton." He apparently dictated his account to a reporter

I pause only for a moment to mention here two productions of *A New Way to Pay Old Debts,* neither of which is of any particular importance. Cruickshank records one at the King Street Theatre, Birmingham, in January 1843;[8] I am not able to throw any further light on this performance. On January 18, 1843, at the close of the Haymarket season, Mrs. Glover took a benefit as Lady Allworth; since the company had officially disbanded, she was supported "by the Members of the Histrionic Club," an amateur organization. The playbill shows the Overreach to be a Mr. Garth. The women, it appears, were the only professionals in the group. *The Times* of the following day comments curtly on the performance: "Mrs. Glover took a benefit at this theatre [the Haymarket] last night, having secured the services of the members of the Histrionic Club, who filled the male parts in the comedy of a *New Way to Pay Old Debts.* As the exertions of these gentlemen, however, lie beyond the pale of criticism, we shall merely record that they met with considerable applause. Mrs. Glover played admirably the part of Lady Allworth. . . ."

One of the best of theatrical biographies is that by W. J. Lawrence of Gustavus Vaughan Brooke, and it is Lawrence consequently who must be my chief source in the discussion of that actor. Born in Dublin on April 25, 1818, of an important Irish family, Brooke received a good education, and had not other events prevented would have entered Trinity College. But in 1832, Macready came to Dublin to fulfil a month's engagement; young Brooke, immediately upon seeing him play, became infected with stage-fever, and the next morning waited upon the actor. Though received courteously, Brooke, as was to be expected, obtained little satisfaction from the interview. A few days later he called on Calcraft, the manager of the Dublin Theatre, and asked to be allowed to play William Tell. After hearing him recite, Calcraft dismissed his visitor with a vague promise to keep him in mind for future engagements. During Easter week of 1833, Edmund Kean, who was scheduled to appear at Dublin, fell ill, and Calcraft, at his wits'

for *The New York World,* where it appeared on Sunday, May 15, 1887 (reprinted by Walsh, pp. 11-15).

[8] Cruickshank (Edition), p. 130.

end and remembering the popularity of infant Roscii, sent for Brooke.

Brooke made his début on April 9, 1833, as William Tell, and played a short engagement. The press notices, while not enthusiastic, were decidedly encouraging, and Brooke was confirmed in his desire to follow the stage as a profession. Then came the usual strolling. In the fall of 1834 he appeared at the Victoria Theatre, London, as Virginius, but his performance attracted little attention. A tour through the provinces was continued by engagements in large cities, and we find him in turn in Glasgow, Dublin, and Belfast. By this time he had acquired considerable reputation, and in December of 1841 Macready engaged him for Drury Lane, but Brooke after one look at the minor parts he would be expected to act, returned to the provinces. Manchester, Liverpool, and Cork received him *con amore,* but financial reverses followed, and Brooke was forced to tread less frequented paths. In February of 1843 he emerged from obscurity at Brighton, and later in the year at Berwick-on-Tweed, accompanied by Marie Duret, who for a number of years was under his protection and sometimes bore his name.

It is at Berwick that my history of Brooke's impersonations of Sir Giles Overreach begins;[9] Miss Duret, I suppose, was in the cast. I can find no record that he played the part again until January 30, 1845, when he was acting at the Queen's Theatre, Manchester.[10] During an engagement at the Theatre Royal, Dublin, where, with Helen Faucit, Brooke opened on October 26, 1846, Sir Giles was among the parts he played.[11] The following year, between engagements at Hull in July and September, Brooke acted in *A New Way to Pay Old Debts* at Rochdale. Lawrence tells us an anecdote of the occasion, related by J. B. Howe who played Allworth:[12] "So terrifying in its reality was the tragedian's 'death' scene that a well-known Rochdale physician, happening to be among the audience, hastened behind to give the actor his professional assistance, verily believing that simulation had merged into actuality, and

---

[9] Lawrence, p. 42.

[10] *ibid.,* p. 48. He must, however, have played Sir Giles at Aberdeen about this time. James H. Stoddart was the Marrall (*Recollections of a Player,* pp. 147-8).

[11] Lawrence, p. 55.

[12] *ibid.,* p. 69. The physician was Dr. Neild, later a dramatic critic in Australia.

culminated in a fit of apoplexy. One can realize the intensity of Brooke's acting in this scene when it is recorded that he has been known to lie prostrate for a quarter of an hour after the falling of the curtain—utterly dominated and overcome by the Frankenstein of his own creating."

Brooke now accepted an offer to play at the Olympic Theatre in London, and began an engagement which was perhaps the greatest triumph of his career. He opened on January 3, 1848, as Othello, and played the part twenty-four times in succession to thunderous applause from both his audience and the metropolitan critics. On January 31, he changed the bill for his second play, *A New Way to Pay Old Debts*. It was cast as follows:[13]

Sir Giles Overreach	Brooke
Wellborn	H. Holl
Lord Lovell	Archer
Marrall	W. Davidge
Justice Greedy	Conquest
Allworth	Morton
Lady Allworth	Mrs. Brougham
Margaret	Miss Hill

Lester Wallack states[14] that although Brooke's Sir Giles Overreach "was as consistently fine a piece of acting as his *Othello,* perhaps more perfect, it did not seem to strike the people by any means so forcibly." This is true perhaps if we count performances, for Brooke played Sir Giles only nine times that season, as against twenty-seven for Othello, but certainly the critics give the opposite impression.[15] The *Sun* of the following day, for example, says that his acting "more than justified the most ardent hopes which had been formed by all admirers of the drama from his impersonation of Othello. No such actor has appeared on the boards since Edmund Kean; and Mr. Brooke's performance of Sir Giles did not fall far short of that of Edmund Kean, in this his greatest character. The third act was a masterpiece of wheedling and villainy; and

[13] The playbill announces Brooke's "First Appearance in London in that Character."

[14] Wallack, p. 43.

[15] According to *The Times,* the performances came on January 31; February 1, 3, 5, 7, 8, 10, 12, and 15. Lawrence (p. 85) says Brooke played the part eleven times, but I cannot find the other two.

—*From* The Illustrated London News, *February 5, 1848*

Brooke as Sir Giles Overreach at the Olympic Theatre

in the scene with his daughter, the 'kiss close' was given with immense effect. It is the closing scene of the play, however, which is Mr. Brooke's great triumph. Here we have a succession of violent contrasts, of bright light and dark shadows, and it was in setting off these contrasts—in bringing out these lights and shadows, that Mr. Brooke showed himself so admirable. The madness of the triumph of the scoundrel at the success of all his schemes for securing to his daughter the hand of the popular Lord Lovell, and to himself the fortune of the Lady Allworth, was admirably given, and contrasted finely with the agony of despair at finding the deed securing to him the Allworth property a mere blank, and the mad fury of rage with which he rushes at his daughter, changing suddenly into the paralysis of death, when he says, 'Some undone widow sits upon my arm and takes away its strength.' In this scene he was quite equal to Edmund Kean. Mr. G. V. Brooke is far and away the greatest actor of the day."

This is high praise—*very* high praise! *The Morning Advertiser* of February 1 is probably nearer the truth: "He [Brooke] is stated in the bills of the day as 'being universally acknowledged to be the greatest living tragedian,' and certainly if his representation of other characters be equal to his Sir Giles Over-reach last night —if not the 'greatest living tragedian,' he is equal to any that now tread the stage. Nothing could be more exquisite than his conception of the wicked, ambitious villain who spared no exertions to accomplish his purpose, and laughed at all moral and religious obligations in the pursuit of it, and the manner in which he portrayed his feelings and passions proved him to be gifted with genius of the first order."

John Coleman, the actor and manager, has given currency to a story which completeness urges me to reproduce here. After mentioning truthfully enough the excesses in which Brooke was indulging, he continues:[16]

> Sometimes he sought relief from these ignoble occupations in rowing and boating. One day he rowed up the river from Earl's Wharf Pier to Putney and back; a jovial dinner and skittles and other diversions followed, then it became necessary to "put on a spurt" to get back in time for the performance. It was his first

[16] Coleman, *Players and Playwrights,* Vol. II, pp. 228-9.

appearance in town as Sir Giles Over-reach; there had been no
Sir Giles in London since Kean's day, and it was characteristic of
the man that Brooke treated so fiery an ordeal so lightly. When he
arrived at the theatre it was long past the time of commencement;
the audience (a densely crowded one) were already impatient; it
was three-quarters of an hour late when the curtain rose, but the
delay was condoned, and he was received with unusual enthusiasm.
He wore a new dress that night; the heat was overpowering, and
he was in a bath of perspiration, arising principally from the hasty
pull down the river. At the end of the first act he desired his
dresser to strip off his singlet; the new canvas lining of the dress
was damp; a chill struck to his lungs; by the time he reached his
great scene in the fifth act he was totally inaudible, and his failure
was as complete in Sir Giles as his triumph had been assured in
Othello. Instead of resting and nursing himself, he tried to fight
off his malady with drink; but he got worse and worse, collapsed
utterly and left the theatre.

Now it is hardly necessary for me to point out that this anecdote is
ridiculous, since Lawrence has already done so.[17] If Brooke had
been late for the performance, the papers would have taken pains
to mention it; if he had been inaudible in the last act, he could
hardly have obtained the triumph which the *Sun* discusses in detail.
And if he had collapsed utterly from a chill to the lungs, he certainly would not have repeated the part on the following night.
Coleman's narrative is typical of the loose theatrical memoir which
makes the scholar's task so difficult.

On August 12, 1848, Brooke performed Sir Giles Overreach at
Brighton. The inevitable Marie Duret was with him, and C. Fisher,
and J. Howard contributed to his support.[18] A playbill shows a
presentation at Edinburgh on November 28. *The Times* advertises
a performance at the Marylebone Theatre on May 8, 1850, with
Wellborn by Bolton and Lady Allworth by Miss Richardson. The
next season found Brooke again at the Olympic, but his dissipations were already beginning to tell on him, and he was by no
means as popular as he had been. Performances of *A New Way to
Pay Old Debts* came on January 2, 3, 4, 7, 9, and 10, with the
following cast:[19]

17 Lawrence, p. 87.
18 Porter, p. 85.
19 Playbills, and the advertisements in *The Times*.

Sir Giles Overreach	Brooke
Wellborn (1st time)	Leigh Murray
Lord Lovell	Diddear
Marrall	W. Farren
Justice Greedy	Compton
Allworth	W. Farren, Jun.
Lady Allworth	Mrs. Leigh Murray
Margaret	Miss Adams

Lawrence writes[20] that on January 2 Brooke played "with such terrific force in the final scene as to conjure up visions to at least one imaginative spectator of 'some incarnate demon, blasted and paralysed at the moment of triumph by the avenging lightning of Providence.'" That summer an Edinburgh audience deemed him unapproachable in the rôle.[21] In November, having accepted an offer from Hall Wilton, one of P. T. Barnum's agents, Brooke sailed for America, where he remained until June 1853. Needless to say, Sir Giles Overreach was included in his repertoire for the American tour.[22]

Upon his reappearance in England, Brooke opened at Birmingham, and then returned to his beloved Ireland. On August 26, 1853, he played Sir Giles Overreach for his benefit at Cork.[23] A successful Drury Lane engagement followed, with *A New Way to Pay Old Debts* the play on September 12, 14, 17, and October 1 with Brooke "supported by Messrs. Davenport, G. Bennett, Younge, Belton, Leslie, Edgar &c; Mesdames Anderton, Vickery, Leslie &c."[24] The Davenport was of course E. L. Davenport of whom much is to be said later; a review in *The London Weekly Times* of September 18 informs us that he played Wellborn. Only once more do I find that Brooke played Sir Giles Overreach before he again left England—at Bingley Hall, Birmingham, on July 24, 1854, the opening night of his engagement there.[25] At Birmingham, Brooke met George Coppin, who induced him to sign articles

---

[20] Lawrence, p. 113.

[21] *ibid.*, p. 115.

[22] For Brooke's American performances of Sir Giles Overreach, see Part II, pp. 267-71.

[23] Lawrence, p. 129.

[24] Advertisements in *The Times* for dates cited; the list is from the issue of September 12.

[25] Cruickshank (Edition), p. 130; Lawrence, p. 144.

by which he was to act in Australia and New Zealand. Brooke sailed on the steamship *Pacific* on November 25, not to return to England until 1861.

Brooke landed at Melbourne on February 22, 1855, and four days later made his Australian début as Othello at the Queen's Theatre. Here he acted until March 23, playing Sir Giles Overreach on March 17.[26] I have not seen a playbill of the occasion, but no doubt Fanny Cathcart, who accompanied Brooke, was the Lady Allworth; Mrs. Charles Young, later Mrs. Hermann Vezin, I suspect, was the Margaret, and Richard Younge, since he played the part later, may have presented Marrall. Brooke was the first great actor that Australia had seen, and he was looked upon as the fosterer of the theatre there. In spite of his occasional excesses the man was idolized and the actor overwhelmed with plaudits. Under these circumstances departure became difficult. It became doubly difficult when Brooke must needs burn his fingers with theatrical management, by which he lost all the money his popularity had procured for him. When he sailed for Liverpool in 1861, he was not only in debt, but in consequence had lapsed into the deplorable habits of dissipation from which his self-respect and his popularity as an affluent and successful actor had so far kept him. Before he sailed, however, he had played Sir Giles at least twice more. On June 9, 1858, he wrote from Hobarton, Tasmania:[27] "The Governor patronized me a few weeks ago at Launceston . . . and I have this morning received a note from him requesting me to play Sir Giles Overreach on Wednesday next." I think that there can be little doubt that Brooke complied and played in *A New Way to Pay Old Debts* for the Governor on June 16. The last Australian performance that I can chronicle came at the Theatre Royal, Melbourne, on April 22, 1861, when Brooke began his series of farewell appearances. Lawrence tells us that "he met with a very flattering reception, and was recalled after the second and fourth acts, and again at the conclusion of the performance."[28]

After engagements at Dublin and Drury Lane, the first prosperous, the second a financial failure, Brooke went to Brighton,

[26] Cruickshank (Edition), p. 138; Lawrence, p. 161.
[27] Lawrence, p. 189.
[28] *ibid.*, p. 207.

where he played Sir Giles on December 4, 1861. Younge was the Marrall, Steele the Lord Lovell, and Miss Bowering the Lady Allworth.[29] On December 24, 1861, Brooke opened at Belfast with *A New Way to Pay Old Debts;* Younge and Avonia Jones were in the cast. The hobgoblin of pecuniary embarrassment again followed Brooke, for the receipts were only £12.8s.[30] On March 19, 1862, a playbill shows his Sir Giles raging at the Queen's Theatre and Opera House, Edinburgh. In May, in the heat of a prosperous engagement at Birmingham, when no less a person than Bancroft played Allworth to his Sir Giles,[31] Brooke was arrested for failure to pay his debts and lodged in Warwick Gaol. That difficulty removed, he played the part again at the City of London Theatre, on October 20, 1862, where in spite of the fact that on certain nights it was evident that he had imbibed too freely, his campaign was tolerably successful.[32] Brooke's future was now, however, a past, and his fall rapid. When he played Sir Giles at the Clemens Street Theatre in Leamington in May of 1863, the receipts—unbelievable as it may seem—were 17s 6d.![33] When he acted the part at Belfast on January 12, 1864, however, he showed much of his early power; "he was honoured with a call at the close of the trying climax, and on appearing before the curtain apologised to the audience for first picking up the sword which had fallen near the footlights from the maniac's hand. 'It is,' he said, 'a reminiscence of Edmund Kean. With it he played the part in the tragedy you have just seen.' "[34] Perhaps this was the Damascus blade that Byron had given Kean, and which had by some means fallen into Brooke's hands.[35] Cruickshank chronicles a performance at Aberdeen for this year.[36] For his penultimate engagement at the Queen's Theatre, Dublin, Brooke opened as Sir Giles on November 20, 1865, and though other performances were marred by intoxication, this one was received enthusiastically.[37] *Saunder's News Letter* com-

[29] Porter, p. 125; I correct Porter's misprints.
[30] Lawrence, p. 222.
[31] *ibid.,* p. 227.
[32] *ibid.,* p. 232.
[33] *ibid.,* p. 238.
[34] *ibid.,* p. 245.
[35] See Hawkins, Vol. I, p. 392; Lawrence, p. 54.
[36] Cruickshank (Edition), p. 132.
[37] Lawrence, p. 258, quotes the review.

mented on the performance as follows: "The genius of this great actor eminently fits him for the part, and he has made it one of his most important characters. Mr. Brooke portrayed the ambitious, unscrupulous, passionate knight last evening in a manner that elicited the warmest marks of approval by the auditory. The upper part of the house was crammed to excess, and the pit was fairly filled, but the boxes, owing probably to the inclemency of the weather, were but sparsely attended."

On December 18, 1865, Brooke gave at Belfast what proved to be his last performance of Sir Giles Overreach.[38] He now determined to return to Australia, there to recoup his fortunes. Under the incognito of Mr. Vaughan, he sailed on the *London* on December 28, with the premonition that something was wrong. He was right; the *London* sank on January 11, and Brooke, though invited to try his chances in the cutter which contained the only survivors, went down with the ship.

Brooke in his prime must have been a magnificent Sir Giles. Overcoming a youthful tendency to play tricks with his extraordinary voice, he was by the time of his first Olympic engagement the equal in some parts of any actor living. Othello seems to have been his most splendid standard rôle, but his Sir Giles cannot have been very far behind. Brooke was a curious combination; taking Vandenhoff as his model, he followed also the quite different style of Cooke[39] and Kean in this part. An unintellectual actor, he was almost always an intelligent one, but he relied chiefly upon the genius which allowed him immediately to grasp the character which he was to impersonate, and a memory which unfortunately made study unnecessary. I cannot close this section without quoting H. Barton Baker, who saw him in many parts, and who can tell us the impression which Brooke created as Sir Giles Overreach:[40] "Whatever might have been Brooke's faults, there was no Othello between his and Salvini's. His Sir Giles Overreach was a remarkable piece of acting. I have never seen anything more startling upon the stage than his last act, especially that point where, in the full tempest of his fury, he was rushing sword in hand upon

---

[38] Lawrence, p. 262.
[39] See for example Porter, p. 125.
[40] Baker, p. 267.

his creature Marrall—the sudden stop, as one struck by palsy, the horror of the fact, the gripping of the wrist that refused to perform his will, and the muttered cry: 'Some undone widow sits upon my arm!' Even the actors engaged in the scene were appalled by the terrible realism and almost forgot their parts." And we shall see later that in America, Brooke's last act of *A New Way to Pay Old Debts* was hailed as one of the finest exhibitions of histrionic power in the history of the theatre.

At the Royal Victoria Theatre on September 2, 1844, J. Hudson Kirby, a young London-born American actor, opened his engagement by playing Sir Giles Overreach. Louisa Lyons was associated with him, but the Lady Allworth was Mrs. W. West.[41] As far as I know, this was the only time that Kirby played the part in England, though E. L. Blanchard notes in his diary:[42] "House crammed; Kirby well received." In general the higher drama was above this actor's powers, but he had made a great reputation in the United States in melodrama, particularly in a piece called *The Carpenter of Rouen.* So famous were his death-scenes that "Wake me up when Kirby dies" became the slogan of his audiences in New York City. Though he never became a first-rate actor, he later repeated his success in melodrama at various minor London theatres.[43]

The performances of another actor may be as briefly chronicled. An advertisement in *The Times* of April 18, 1845, announces the "Triumphant Success of Mr. Graham" at the City of London Theatre, and contributes the information that the first play of the evening is to be *A New Way to Pay Old Debts* with that actor in the leading part. At the Marylebone Theatre three years later, Graham played Sir Giles on January 31, February 1, and February 2, with Lady Allworth by Mrs. Warner.[44] John Graham[45] was at

[41] Advertisement in *The Times.*

[42] Scott and Howard, Vol. I, p. 35.

[43] Short notes on J. Hudson Kirby may be found in Phelps, p. 221; Ireland, Vol. II, p. 244; Brown, Vol. I, p. 301; and Appleton's *Cyclopaedia of American Biography, s.v.*

[44] Advertisements in *The Times.*

[45] John Graham has been confused by Lawrence (p. 52) with Robert E. Graham, who was in America at this time; I know of no such person as P. M. Graham, as cited by Cruickshank (Edition, p. 127). His real name was G. Munro. See his obituary in *The Theatrical Journal,* Vol. 24, No. 1245, October 21, 1863, and *The Theatrical Times* of November 27, 1847, for a portrait.

this time leading man to Mrs. Warner, who after leaving Phelps at Sadler's Wells took over the management of the Marylebone. Graham was a pleasant actor who excelled by reason of his fine elocution; he had been with Phelps and was later to appear at the Princess's Theatre and at Drury Lane, where he enacted minor parts with considerable distinction. Doubtless he played Sir Giles on this occasion partially because Mrs. Warner wished to repeat her characterization of Lady Allworth; it is to be noted, however, that the performances came in opposition to those of Brooke at the Olympic.

A New Way to Pay Old Debts was on parade at the Belfast Theatre Royal according to *The Theatrical Times* of October 24, 1846. The Sir Giles is not given but the date seems to be later than October 9 when Mr. James Bennett, who afterwards appears in Boston as a Sir Giles, took his benefit. We shall leave Sir Giles temporarily a ghost.

A more famous actor, John R. Scott, who since he is an American will be discussed later at length,[46] opened his engagement at the Princess's Theatre on November 4, 1846, with Sir Giles Overreach. *The Times* gives the cast as follows:

Sir Giles Overreach	Scott
Wellborn	J. Vining
Lord Lovell	Ryder
Marrall	Compton
Justice Greedy	Granby
Allworth	Roxby
Lady Allworth	Miss Harrington
Margaret	Mrs. Stirling

The performance was evidently a success, for the play was repeated on November 6, 26, and 30. For the last two dates, Fisher succeeded Roxby as Allworth, and Mrs. H. Hughes took over Lady Allworth.[47]

Two issues of *The Theatrical Times* comment upon this production of *A New Way to Pay Old Debts*. Of Sir Giles Overreach the number of November 14 comments in part as follows:

[46] See Part II, pp. 244-8.
[47] Advertisements in *The Times*.

The various phases of this extraordinary creation were given with great originality and impressive vigour by Mr. Scott. He might have been considered inefficient in the earlier parts of the play, but he amply atoned for this reservation of power, in the third act. His vehemence of rage, the intense struggle of the passions, and his scene of death, were triumphs of art. The performance taken altogether may be pronounced as an eminently successful one :—the actor possesses every requisite for his profession,—a powerful voice, expressive countenance, and a good figure ; and his metropolitan essay has secured to him the fame already bestowed in the provinces and his native country.

And on December 2—my long-suffering readers will no doubt thank me for various omissions :[48]

"Sir Giles Overreach" is a very powerful character, but it requires an actor of no ordinary intellect to bring out all its strong lights. Mr. Scott is a steady and judicious performer, perfectly versed in the business of the stage. He is not remarkable for great originality; but he has sense and vigor, and is less melo-dramatic than the generality of his countrymen. We think he is not at all inferior to Edwin Forrest and Charles Kean ; and perhaps in some parts, which he has not yet attempted—such as "Shylock" and a few others, he might more than equal them. At all events he is a great addition to the stage, and we trust he will remain among us for sometime. We cannot help alluding once more to Compton's "Marrall" and Mrs. Stirling's "Margaret." The former bids fair to rival Farren, and we do not think the *"Cock Salmon"* would surpass him in this part. The feminine delicacy, the winning grace, the ease, the nature, and the polish of charming Mrs. Stirling in "Margaret," are worthy of the best days of the drama. We like sometimes to cast off our critical glasses, and be children again in the enjoyment of the mimic scene; and it is impossible to *be* a critic when this actress is before one. She is entirely English in her style, and yet we think she must have studied in the French school of art—she is so entirely free from mannerism and affectation. . . . But we must not linger over the recollection of her faultless impersonation.

Nor, much as we may wish to, can we, for though I should not like to have missed this comment, this book is after all about Sir Giles.

[48] Allen, p. 95, quotes portions of this review, but misdates it.

The Theatrical Times continues to serve us in the next two items, admittedly minor. The issue of November 28 comments briefly on the success of Mr. G. Owen at the Ulverstone Theatre Royal among whose parts "this week is Sir Giles Overreach, which was most ably supported by the efficient company." I omit the bouquets thrown at the manager; Mr. Owen we shall not meet again in this chronicle.

At the Theatre Royal, Woolwich, however, there was strange business. The same periodical in the issue of December 19 remarked that "a most extraordinary scene was presented to the Woolwich public. *A New Way to Pay Old Debts* was announced when Mr. Warren, for reasons of his own, would not perform 'Justice Greedy,' and Mr. Hambleton to the astonishment of both the audience and the actors actually played the part, and his own part 'Marrall.' To judge by the applause and laughter, the audience did not regret the 'double.' Mr. Rivers was good in 'Sir Giles,' Miss Neale grossly imperfect in 'Margaret'; Mrs. Coates correct as usual, the other performers call for no particular notice." The punctuation and spelling of *The Theatrical Times* do, however, so to avoid a whole row of [*sics*], I have taken the liberty of making a few changes, none so violent as doubling Marrall and Greedy.

The next actor on my list of the impersonators of Sir Giles Overreach is Barry Sullivan. Thomas Sullivan—he did not take the name Barry until his English début—was born in Birmingham in 1821, and brought up in Bristol whither his parents had moved in 1824. Left an orphan at eight years of age, he was sent by his grandfather to school, where he remained until he was fourteen, when he was apprenticed to a Bristol attorney. Having seen Macready, he determined to become an actor, and joined a straggling theatrical company in 1837. Finding his way to Cork, he made his début there in the same year as Jack Eustace in *Love in a Village*. His appearance was successful and he became a member of the stock company at the Theatre Royal. Sullivan was connected with various Cork theatres until late in 1841 when he appeared in Edinburgh. Engagements in Glasgow and Aberdeen followed, where he played with Brooke and gained considerable popularity, finally becoming the regular leading man. He made his English début to empty benches as Hamlet at Wakefield in 1847. The next year he was at Manchester, and as far as I can find out, it was in this city that he first played Sir Giles Overreach.[49]

It was sometime in March that Barry Sullivan played Massinger's extortioner in Manchester;[50] the impersonation was repeated in the latter part of November.[51] In December of 1849, Sullivan leased the Theatre Royal, Bolton, and managed it for this and the following month. On the 17th of December, *A New Way to Pay Old Debts* was on the bill, and, unless I misinterpret my source, it remained on the bill for a week, and was repeated during the following month.[52] The Royal Amphitheatre, Liverpool, saw Sullivan's Sir Giles Overreach on May 19, 1851.[53]

Barry Sullivan's decision to play leads in the provinces rather than secondary parts in London is responsible for a gap of nine years in my chronicle, for I can find no evidence that he acted Sir Giles again in Great Britain[54] until he appeared at the Standard Theatre, London, in the latter part of 1860. Sillard includes *A New Way to Pay Old Debts* among the plays which Sullivan acted in November and December of that year.[55] Three years later Melbourne, Australia, was the scene of a performance on July 18, 1863, with Sir Giles by Barry Sullivan and Lady Allworth by Mrs. R. Heir.[56] Again, I can trace nothing for a number of years —indeed nothing until 1874. *The Times* of February 2 of that year contains the following announcement: "Barry Sullivan as Richard III, Lear, Hamlet, Richelieu, Claude Melnotte, and Sir Giles Overreach, at Her Majesty's Theatre, Aberdeen, during this week." This, I gather, gives us a performance on Saturday, February 7.

Except for American performances later to be mentioned, this concludes my list; it is of course incomplete, made so by the scar-

[49] The source of my information on Barry Sullivan is Robert M. Sillard, *Barry Sullivan and His Contemporaries.*
[50] Sillard, Vol. I, p. 177.
[51] *ibid.*, Vol. I, p. 186.
[52] *ibid.*, Vol. I, p. 206.
[53] Broadbent, p. 230.
[54] He played the part in the United States in 1859; see Part II, p. 347.
[55] Sillard, Vol. II, pp. 35-6. I cannot check his evidence without the playbills; *The Times* contains no announcement of the play, but the Standard did not advertise regularly.
[56] Cruickshank (Edition), p. 138.

city and inaccessibility of provincial records, but I can take no more time for Barry Sullivan. I can find not a single English review of Sullivan as Sir Giles, but relying as he did on vigorous action and forceful declamation, he must have made a success of the rôle. Sullivan was a popular actor of the old school, and except for a tendency to rant deserved the favor in which he was held.[57]

In the same year in which I have placed Barry Sullivan's first performance of Sir Giles Overreach, Tom Mead made his début on the London stage in that part. This was at the Victoria Theatre on November 8, 1848. Mead proved to be a capable performer of considerable promise, and he thenceforth became a fixture of the London theatres. After a term at the Surrey, he was in 1852 engaged by E. T. Smith for Drury Lane, where he acted many important characters. He appeared subsequently at the St. James's, the New Grecian Theatre, Sadler's Wells, the Princess's, the Queen's, and then at the Lyceum, where he performed in the various Shakespearean revivals under the supervision of Henry Irving. He probably played Sir Giles many times in the provinces; a playbill notes a performance at the Queen's Theatre and Opera House, Edinburgh, on March 1, 1856 and the part was still in his repertoire in October 1870, when it was given "by desire" at the Theatre Royal, Dundee.[58]

McKean Buchanan was an American actor who had played Sir Giles Overreach in the United States before he came to England. I leave discussion therefore until later, except such as throws light on his reception in Great Britain. *The Times* of Monday, May 24, 1852, contains the following announcement; I will be pardoned, I hope, for reducing the capitals: "First appearance in England of the celebrated American tragedian, Mr. Buchanan; also the reappearance of Miss E. Lewis, from the Broadway Theatre, New York.—Mr. E. T. Smith informs his friends and the public that he has engaged these celebrated artists for four

---

[57] It is perhaps hardly necessary to mention Bernard Shaw's vivid estimate of Barry Sullivan in the Preface to *Ellen Terry and Bernard Shaw, A Correspondence*. He cites a performance of *A New Way to Pay Old Debts* coupled with Tom Taylor's *Joan of Arc* at the Theatre Royal, Dublin, sometime before his "Hegira to London in 1876." Though Shaw does not say so, I am tempted to believe that Sullivan was the Sir Giles Overreach on this occasion.

[58] Boyd, p. 64. Pascoe, pp. 240-1, lists Wellborn as one of Mead's parts at Drury Lane; to whose Sir Giles?

nights. The extraordinary sensation caused throughout the United States by the performance of Mr. Buchanan, Mr. Smith trusts will also be appreciated by a generous English audience on his appearance this evening, Monday, and Wednesday, May 24 and 26 in the play of A New Way to Pay Old Debts: Sir Giles Overreach, Mr. Buchanan." Thus heralded, Buchanan made his London début at the Marylebone Theatre, and was received with appropriate applause.

On May 25, *The Morning Advertiser* says, among other things: "The management chose Sir Giles Overreach for Mr. Buchanan's début, and in doing so exhibited much judgment, for they applied to him the severest test that can be imagined. Mr. Buchanan passed through the ordeal, and achieved a triumph, of which he and his countrymen may well be proud. The new actor is endowed with a majestic appearance, and possesses *physique* of no ordinary kind. The first three acts presented little or no opportunities for the actor to display his abilities, but in the fourth and fifth he made ample amends. In the scene where he draws forth the deeds and discovers the fraud that has been practiced upon him, he was truly energetic. On the discovery of his daughter's marriage, and the sequent frustration of his plans he was fearfully impressive. The ebullition of fury which closes the catastrophe approached the awful. At the termination of the play he was called before the curtain to receive the ovation of a crowded and delighted auditory."

Reynolds' Newspaper of May 30 was likewise impressed: "In the earlier portion of the play, his *brusque* manner was certainly new to us, and rather startled the audience from its propriety; but in the end he reconciled us when he exhibited the extent to which he allowed his passion to carry him. His last scene was terrifically grand." And the *Dispatch* of the same date calls Buchanan "an actor of much merit, possessing good physical qualifications, and rendering, with intelligence, the forcible passages which abound in Massinger's play." Buchanan's engagement at the Marylebone was in every way successful, perhaps more so than one might have expected. It seems unnecessary to quote further from the reviews.[59] I pause to note only the fact that the critics uniformly stress McKean Buchanan's *physical* qualifications for the rôle.

I come now to an actor the story of whose impersonations of Sir Giles Overreach is difficult to tell. There is no biography of Hermann Vezin, and only the sketchiest sort of biographical notes are available.[60] Vezin was born in Philadelphia and was educated at the University of Pennsylvania, where he took two degrees. In 1850 he went to England, and there, partially influenced by Charles Kean, abandoned his idea of becoming a lawyer, and entered the dramatic profession. After various provincial engagements, he accepted a place under Kean at the Princess's, where he remained until 1853. Provincial tours now lasted four years, and it was during this period that he first began to play the leading part in *A New Way to Pay Old Debts*. After a trip to America, he returned to England in 1859, and undertook the management of the Surrey Theatre for six weeks, opening on June 13 as Macbeth.[61] Vezin was now recognized as an actor of considerable importance, and henceforth he appeared regularly in various London theatres, notably Sadler's Wells under Phelps, the Princess's Theatre with Fechter, the Lyceum under Edmund Falconer, and the Gaiety with Phelps, Mathews, and J. L. Toole.

Cruickshank chronicles a performance of *A New Way to Pay Old Debts* with Vezin as Sir Giles, at the Crystal Palace in 1874, on which occasion Bella Pateman was the Lady Allworth.[62] Late in 1874 some of the old comedies were revived for morning performances at the Crystal Palace under the direction of Charles Wyndham. It is perhaps to one of these that Canon Cruickshank refers; I confess, however, that I can find neither playbills nor advertisements to verify his statement. Moreover, if Vezin *did* play Sir Giles in 1874, Bella Pateman could not have been the Lady All-

[59] See also, however, *The Illustrated London News* of May 28, *The Era* of May 30, *The Theatrical Journal* of May 26, *The London Weekly Paper* of May 29, and *The Weekly Times* of May 30.

[60] The two most convenient accounts are those by John Parker in the *DNB* (2nd Suppl., *s.v.*) and by Pascoe in *The Dramatic List*. Unless otherwise noted my facts are from these sources.

[61] An obituary in *The Times* of June 14, 1910, states that he played Sir Giles during this engagement. This is incorrect; at least there are no advertisements for *A New Way to Pay Old Debts*.

[62] Cruickshank (Edition), p. 128.

worth, since she was acting with great success in the United States at that time, and indeed did not make her first appearance in London until two years later.[63]

I am inclined to doubt that Vezin played Sir Giles in London before his appearance in that character at the St. James's Theatre on April 14, 1877.[64] On that date *The Times* announced the play with a cast which I copy from the playbill:

Sir Giles Overreach	Vezin
Wellborn	Clayton
Lord Lovell	Markby
Marrall	Flockton
Justice Greedy	Clifford Cooper
Allworth	Charles Cooper
Lady Allworth	Miss Le Thierre
Margaret	Miss Pattison

So successful was Vezin's impersonation of Sir Giles Overreach that the play ran twelve consecutive nights.[65]

On this production Joseph Knight in *The Athenaeum* expressed himself as follows:[66] "Mr. Vezin's performance of *Sir Giles* is eminently thoughtful and capable. It does not reach grandeur, but it abounds in fine and intellectual touches. We fail to see the splendid vitality that triumphs over all obstacles and revels in the sense of power, but we see the resolute bad man, implacable in animosity and defiant in wrong doing. The finest point is that in which the actor seeks to approach his daughter, whom he purposes to slay for her disobedience. This was finely conceived and finely executed. The whole performance is worthy of Mr. Vezin's reputation."

If Hermann Vezin played Sir Giles in London again I do not know it; doubtless however it was a favorite of his provincial tours. Cruickshank mentions a performance at the Grand Theatre, Glasgow on February 17 (?), 1880 with Lady Allworth by Miss

[63] See Pascoe, p. 255; the memoir on Miss Pateman in *The Theatre,* London, February 1, 1879 (Vol. II, New Series, pp. 12-13); Brown, Vol. III, pp. 101-3; and the advertisement in *The Times,* London, of October 28, 1876.

[64] Not *August* 14, as stated by Cruickshank (Edition), p. 128. As will appear, Cruickshank's "eleven consecutive nights" is incomplete.

[65] April 14, 16, 17, 18, 19, 20, 21, 23, 24, 25, 26, 27, skipping only Sundays.

[66] *The Athenaeum,* April 21, 1877, pp. 523-4; or Knight, *Theatrical Notes,* pp. 178-82.

C. Daubeney,[67] and another at Southport on January 20, 1893.[68] I can cite no other dates. Vezin's interpretation of the rôle, as far as I can discover from his general histrionic qualities, must have been able and intelligent rather than very moving. Always a distinguished elocutionist, Vezin was lacking in the warmer qualities which make for magnetism between the actor and his audience. But he was always a fine and capable actor, and if he could play Sir Giles Overreach in London for twelve successive nights without the physical expression so associated with the part, the more credit to him!

I pass over with slight reference performances of *A New Way to Pay Old Debts* at the Macready Concert Hall, Birmingham, vaguely dated by Cruickshank 1857-1861,[69] to consider another American actor, J. B. Roberts. He had played Sir Giles before coming to England, and belongs primarily to the history of the American stage.[70] Roberts selected Massinger's extortioner as the character in which to make his London début. He acted Sir Giles Overreach at Drury Lane on September 21 and 22, 1857.[71] A bill gives us the cast:

Sir Giles Overreach .... Roberts
Wellborn .... Belton
Lord Lovell .... Stuart
Marrall ....A. Younge
Justice Greedy .... Tilbury
Allworth .... R. H. Lingham
Lady Allworth .... Mrs. Vickery
Margaret (first app.) .... Miss Portman

E. L. Blanchard saw the second of these performances, and found Roberts "good."[72] The review in *The Times* of September 22, I conceive to be a fair estimate of his interpretation of the rôle:

> Last night this house was opened for a short season that Mr. Roberts, an American tragedian, new to this country, might have a fitting opportunity of displaying such talents as he might be sup-

[67] Cruickshank (Edition), p. 132. The question-mark is his.
[68] *ibid.*, p. 131.
[69] *ibid.*, p. 131.
[70] See Part II, pp. 273-7.
[71] Advertisements in *The Times*.
[72] Scott and Howard, Vol. I, p. 180.

posed to possess. For his first part he selected Sir Giles Overreach in the *New Way to Pay Old Debts,* by which selection he exposed himself to no slight ordeal. By the dint of much spirit and a great deal of judgment he passed through the ordeal with credit.

His earlier scenes did not promise much. His words were with difficulty audible, and a tame rendering of one of the most stormy of characters might not unreasonably have been anticipated. Still the careful correctness of his reading and the ease of his manner showed that he had taken no vulgar view of the gigantic usurer, and when it is recollected how much Sir Giles has to do in the fifth act, he will always be pardoned for reserving his moral and physical energies as much as possible in the first two. In the interview with Lord Lovell, when he offers to reward at any expense of purse or conscience the bounty that would ennoble his daughter and make her "right honourable," he began to show a degree of force which, contrasted with his beginnings, was not a little remarkable, while he judiciously blended a tuft-hunting respect for the "lord" with the evident surgings of gratified ambition. The applause that followed this scene was spontaneous and genuine. Here was evidently an actor who had thought over the peculiarities he had to portray, and who had resolved to execute his conceptions to the best of his ability.

The great passionate act with which the piece concludes, and which by the dint of accumulated mishaps elevates a bad man into a hero who can command the sympathy of his spectators, was most conscientiously rendered. That physical force that can carry along an audience like the action of a whirlwind was certainly not to be found in Mr. Roberts; but while his foaming mouth bore witness to his own sense of rage, his management of the situation throughout showed that he was perfectly alive to all the points of passion. So obviously was he master of the business of the scene that perhaps his head was a little too conspicuous above the torrent of his heart, but this very peculiarity checked the perpetration of much unmeaning rant. On the other hand, Mr. Roberts certainly made the most of the groans that follow the collapse of the defeated sinner, and showed that if his last *exit* is to be deemed a death, he died very hard indeed. At the fall of the curtain, he had the honour of a separate call, and we may say that the guerdon was fairly merited.

But four years later a much greater American actor made his début in England, when Edwin Booth began his engagement at

the Haymarket under J. B. Buckstone as Shylock on the last day
of September, 1861. After playing this part three times, he acted
Sir Giles Overreach on October 7, 9, 11, and 14, concluding his
stay at the Haymarket with Richelieu.[73] The cast for *A New Way
to Pay Old Debts* according to the playbill was as follows:

Sir Giles Overreach	Booth
Wellborn	W. Farren
Lord Lovell	Howe
Marrall	Compton
Justice Greedy	Chippendale
Allworth	E. Villiers
Lady Allworth	Mrs. Wilkins
Margaret	Miss M. Oliver

Since Booth will be treated largely in another section,[74] I need
say little about him here, but it must be remarked that he was received without much enthusiasm. Of course he was at this time still
a young man and had by no means reached the height of his
powers, and this partially accounts for the fact that his engagement
can hardly be reckoned a success. The public, it is true, treated him
with every respect, though it did not crowd to see him, but the
critics were inclined to be cold, pointing out that he was "promising" and by amending his errors might in time become "great."[75]
Of his three characters Richelieu alone was looked upon with unalloyed favor, and it is to be regretted that Buckstone did not let
him open with this part in accordance with the tragedian's wishes.[76]

Such being the case, we must not expect to find rhapsodic criticism of Booth's Sir Giles Overreach. I append here the review
from *The Athenaeum,* which sums up the opinion of the
majority:[77]

[73] Advertisement in *The Times* for dates cited. Cruickshank (Edition), pp.
128, 129 n. 13, and Baker, p. 235, state wrongly that Sir Giles was Booth's first
part in London. Lockridge, pp. 101-3, dates Booth's parts at the Haymarket inaccurately.

[74] See Part II, pp. 311-45.

[75] "The latest revival of the play . . . took place at the Haymarket, in October,
1861, during the short engagement of Edwin Booth, and is remembered less on
account of the impersonation of Sir Giles Overreach by that rather tumid
tragedian, than because of Mr. Compton's masterly performance of Marrall."
(Joseph Knight in *The Athenaeum,* April 21, 1877.)

[76] Winter, *Booth,* pp. 24-5.

[77] *The Athenaeum,* October 12, 1861, p. 485.

Haymarket.—Mr. Booth made a second appeal to the public on Monday, and in the character of *Sir Giles Overreach* confirmed the good opinion of him that we had formed from his performance of *Shylock*. Perhaps the part of Sir Giles is a more arduous character than that of the unrelenting Jew. There is more violence to be displayed, more difficulty to be dared, more effect to be produced. It is, in a word, an exceptional part, and requires energies which the actor may not be called upon to exert in any other. As an ordeal, therefore, it is a severe one. The actor who passes safely through it may be regarded as having credentials beyond dispute. Mr. Booth in the great scenes and speeches was greatest; but he reserved himself for these with remarkable care. He appeared to be conscious of a want of sustaining power, and therefore, cautiously subdued the ordinary course of the action and dialogue, which gave an abrupt suddenness to the tragic portions. Mr. Booth is a good elocutionist, and the American intonation seldom intrudes; when it does, it is in those level passages where the conversational tone prevails. He is not skilful in making sarcastic points, and passes over many little phrases which, in themselves, are fertile of suggestion, of which other actors generally take advantage, but which he would appear purposely to suppress: probably this arises from a desire to appear original; a not unusual error, but still an error. Good acting does not consist either of omitting to do what is ordinarily done, or of doing what has never been done before, but in doing well what ought to be done at all. There is no need to avoid conventional points where conventional points are right. In the search for new points there is always peril. Selection is necessary, and in the attempt to give extra emphasis there is danger of loading the text with an overweight of demonstration. Mr. Booth has taste, and will improve on these hints. His person and features are good, and his voice pleasing. He is yet young, and has in him capacity for a good actor, perhaps for a great one. The support rendered to him, on this occasion, by his fellow actors was very small. The drama had not received due rehearsal, and the text was languidly and incorrectly delivered. Some of the characters were improperly allocated. Miss Oliver was incapable of speaking the part of *Margaret,* and her blank verse was unintelligible. Mrs. Wilkins, as the *Lady Allworth,* was magnificently dressed, but was evidently in doubt as to the deportment proper to be observed, and hesitated in her delivery of the text. Both these ladies, in fact, were out of their element. Mr. Chippendale, as *Justice Greedy,* and Mr. Compton, as *Marrall,* made some compensation for these defects. Really, when a work of Elizabethan art is revived at the West End, it ought to be efficiently rendered. Either ignore it altogether, or treat it well when recognized. Many of the audience came not only to see the new actor, but the play; and these surely merit consideration.

Whether Edwin Booth played in *A New Way to Pay Old Debts* at Liverpool, his next stop, I do not know, but from there he proceeded to Manchester, where we again find him as Sir Giles Overreach sometime in November. This time another great name appears in the cast, for the Wellborn was Henry Irving, then a member of the stock company in that city. Lloyd was the Marrall, and Thompson, Justice Greedy.[78] After his Manchester engagement, Booth, feeling the force of anti-Yankee sentiment during the American Civil War, took a trip to Paris, and then sailed for New York to resume his profession in the United States.

Since Irving's name has now appeared in this chronicle, I may be pardoned a paragraph on his connection with *A New Way to Pay Old Debts*. The late Canon Cruickshank, in his edition of the play, states that Irving played Sir Giles in Manchester in 1860.[79] To the best of my knowledge Irving *never* played Sir Giles Overreach; that he may have *intended* to do so is suggested by the following letter from the Dean of Winchester, quoted by Cruickshank: "Unless my memory deceives me, he [Irving] told us, in one of his charming speeches at the end of a Lyceum season, that he intended to revive the play in his next season, but he never did." On the other hand, that Irving was tremendously interested in the part is not open to question. H. Chance Newton (Carados of *The Referee*) records how he and Irving used to discuss the subject:[80]

> Irving and I were wont to discuss many a time and oft two of Massinger's plays. One was *The City Madam,* the other was *A New Way to Pay Old Debts,* with their respective terrific and terribly exacting leading characters, Luke and Sir Giles Overreach.

[78] Winter, *Booth*, pp. 25-6.
[79] Cruickshank (Edition), p. 131, citing Stoker, p. 55. Stoker makes no reference to Irving in this part on this or any other page; on pp. 86-7 he remarks that Irving played Wellborn to the Sir Giles of Edwin Booth in November 1861.
[80] *Cues and Curtain Calls*, p. 40.

Phelps had played these two characters before I was born, and never after, but Irving had seen Phelps as Sir Giles, if not as Luke. I had, however, seen several later players of Sir Giles.

So obsessed was Irving, especially with the part of the tyrannical monster, Overreach (which is based on that famous, or rather infamous, Star Chamber extortionist villain, Sir Giles Mompesson), that he had read and re-read everything he could lay his hands on concerning Edmund Kean's Overreach.

Many a lunch time, or supper time, at the Garrick Club have Irving and I sat beneath Kean's portrait as Sir Giles (which he had given the club) while he held forth on what he (and I) had read of the Great Little Edmund's evidently electric outburst. Undoubtedly of all the actors of the past whom he had never seen, *the* Kean was Irving's idol.

Of those he *had* seen he always declared that Phelps was the greatest of all.

Except for a passing reference to a performance of *A New Way to Pay Old Debts* at Brighton on December 7, 1867, by the stock company under the direction of Henry Nye Chart,[81] I can ignore the next ten years, for I find no other production of the play until it was presented at the Gaiety, London, when that theatre was under the management of the ill-fated Walter Montgomery. The performance came on August 16, 1871, with the manager as Sir Giles, and was not repeated.[82] Montgomery, though he had been born in America and had played Sir Giles Overreach there, really belonged to the English stage. He made his début at the Princess's Theatre, London, in 1863, and was thereafter connected with various houses in England and Australia. Always a promising actor he rarely showed complete fulfilment, and though his impersonations were earnest and intelligent studies, they somehow failed to be illuminating interpretations. Montgomery committed suicide, under peculiar and unusual circumstances, several weeks after his only performance of Sir Giles in London.[83]

---

[81] Porter, p. 151. *A New Way to Pay Old Debts* is called a stock play.

[82] Advertisement in *The Times* for date cited. Parker (*Who's Who in the Theatre,* p. 1751, and *Times Literary Supplement,* September 7, 1922, p. 569) and Cruickshank (Edition, p. 128) give the date wrongly as August 12, when the play was *As You Like It*. Parker also is in error in spelling the name Montgommery, evidenced by autograph letters in my possession. For an American performance, see Part II, pp. 353-4.

[83] Brown, Vol. I, p. 209; Phelps, pp. 385-86, 393-4.

At this point *A New Way to Pay Old Debts* undergoes trans-formation. We have found it for many years a stock play, one of the regular starring vehicles for important actors, a popular success in London and the provinces. Now *tout ça change*. It would be a mistake to think that the change came for any one reason, but broadly speaking what pushed the play into antiquarian revivalism was a tendency in the direction of realism, not a realism necessarily as we know it today, but one happily discernible as we compare it with an older traditionalism. It would be equally a mistake to say that this change came suddenly, though I cannot stop to show the development in such detail as would demonstrate how gradually it occurred. For long years England had been held in the grip of an unfortunate and often unmeaning adoration of William Shake-speare. What more natural, if he were our greatest dramatist, than that playwrights should imitate him, actors should make their styles, however much they varied among themselves, adaptable to the presentation of his plays? Only when entertainments and parts differed so widely from the master's that comparison became im-possible, in pantomime, in melodrama, in burlesque, did one dare to be otherwise. Thus the typical dramatists were on the one hand, Sheridan Knowles and Bulwer Lytton, on the other Boucicault, descending after an initial attempt to revive the comedy of man-ners, into adaptation from the French. Dialogue, often in blank verse, was rhetorically stilted and fluently verbose; plots, cut to pattern, intricate, abnormal; characters automata without the sem-blance of truth, all acted the same way, artificial and high flown. By the 1880's, however, there had come a strange but healthy metamorphosis. "Nursed on rose-pink and cradled on properties," Tom Robertson had appeared on the dramatic horizon with plays which attempted to show simple people taking part in commonplace events and talking an ordinary and life-like language. In a word, the cup-and-saucer comedy had been born, and its novelty stimu-lated a taste for home products. Out of Planché had developed W. S. Gilbert, with his fantastic and charmingly mocking comedies, and then, in collaboration with Sullivan, the Savoy operas. Robertson gave way in his turn to Pinero and Jones, and heralded by William Archer there were signs of the coming of Ib-sen. The change in acting, noticeable before Robertson, was fostered by his success. It lies not in the players who are discussed in this book, but in a different line of succession: Vestris and Charles Mathews, E. A. Sothern, the Bancrofts, John Hare, Madge Kendal, Forbes-Robertson, Mrs. John Wood, Charles Wyndham, all of whom strove in their separate ways to be natural. Indeed one sees already the stock company giving way, actors with specialized abilities, engagements for individual characters. Dangerous as this summary is—as all summaries are—it should be plain that in the new school, Sir Giles Overreach could not be a pupil. He was not, as we say, the type. Consequently we shall find *A New Way to Pay Old Debts* no longer in the theatres whose names have been sprinkled throughout our chapters, but characteristically in institutions of learning, in dramatic societies, or still newer repertory theatres, where it seems no longer an active part of the dramatic life of the present, but an old play, revived because it *is* old, or because though outmoded, it still had something to say which *might* be valuable, a precious stone in an antique setting mirroring the glories that were.

The succeeding productions of *A New Way to Pay Old Debts* all are characteristic of the change. Three performances of the play were given at St. Peter's School, York, in December 1884, with Sir Giles by P. E. Lord, Justice Greedy by R. Crosthwaite, and Wellborn by H. W. Rhodes.[84] The Marlowe Dramatic Society produced Massinger's drama at Cambridge on March 9, 1912.[85]

The Birmingham Repertory Theatre in its third season revived the play for seven performances, beginning October 24, 1914. The producer was John Drinkwater, the Sir Giles Frank Moore, the Allworth John Dunn-Yarker, and the Lady Allworth Margaret Chatwin. The setting consisted only of a successful arrangement of draperies.[86] Mr. Nugent Monck produced *A New Way to Pay Old Debts* for six performances in November 1921, at the Maddermarket Theatre, Norwich, which he had reconstructed as an Elizabethan playhouse earlier in the year.[87]

[84] Cruickshank (Edition), p. 131.
[85] Child, "Revivals of English Dramatic Works, 1901-1918, 1926," *RES*, April 1927, Vol. III, No. 10, p. 177.
[86] Bache Matthews, pp. 58, 208, 222, 231; Cruickshank (Edition), p. 131.
[87] Cruickshank (Edition), p. 131. For a description of this theatre and its program, see the article by Andrew Stephenson in *Theatre Arts*, Vol. VII, pp. 203 *ff*.

The last professional presentation of *A New Way to Pay Old Debts* in England began on November 20, 1922, when it was produced by Mr. Robert Atkins and played by the Shakespearean Company at the "Old Vic." The program advertises evening performances for November 20, 22, 24, 27, 29, December 1, and December 10; matinees on November 23, 30, and December 2.[88] The cast was as follows:

Sir Giles Overreach .... Robert Atkins
Frank Wellborn .... Douglas Burbidge
Lord Lovell .... Rupert Harvey
Marrall .... John Garside
Greedy .... D. Hay Petrie
Tom Allworth .... Alan Watts
Lady Allworth .... Althea Glasby
Margaret .... Nancy Harker

Various reviews will give us the best idea of the success of the revival. *The Times* says, for example, on November 21:

> Massinger's play, *A New Way to Pay Old Debts,* which was given first,[89] provides Mr. Robert Atkins a fine opportunity as Sir Giles Overreach, and proves how steadily Mr. Douglas Burbidge, who plays Wellborn, is gathering strength. Both these performances, particularly Mr. Atkins's scene of madness, deserve the immense enthusiasm with which the Old Vic received them, and Mr. Alan Watts, as Tom Allworth, gave the best work we have yet had from him. The play, which has a joyful artificiality and a pleasant rhyme to its carefully balanced story, is a welcome revival.

Gigadibs in *The Guardian* remarks that the *whole house* rose at Robert Atkins's performance of Sir Giles Overreach; the review, however, is hardly worth quoting.[90] W. J. Turner, the dramatic critic of *The Spectator,* is enthusiastic:[91]

---

[88] Cruickshank (Edition), p. 128, however, says twelve performances; my dates and cast are from the program in the Harvard Theatre Collection. For the entire cast and accounts of its members, see Parker, *Who's Who in the Theatre, s.v.*

[89] *Britain's Daughter* by Gordon Bottomly was presented on the same evening.

[90] *The Guardian,* London, November 24, 1922, Vol. 77, p. 897.

[91] *The Spectator,* November 25, 1922, p. 764.

The performance of the "Old Vic" was a good one. Mr. Robert Atkins as Sir Giles Overreach was greeted with tremendous enthusiasm at the fall of the curtain; he deserved his reception, for although he lacked the last particle of fire which would have given complete spontaneity to his Sir Giles, it was altogether a quite exceptional piece of acting which ought to draw crowded houses to the "Old Vic." Mr. D. Hay Petrie was perfect as Justice Greedy. I should not be surprised to learn that hundreds go to the "Old Vic" just to see Mr. Petrie. Mr. John Garside's Marrall was by far the best thing that capable actor has yet done. The women were good; and there is no doubt that *A New Way to Pay Old Debts* is one of the two or three shows in London worth seeing.

And though he criticizes the performance as not quite satisfactory, Francis Birrell in *The New Statesman* concludes, "Altogether a very good show, having lost little of its vivacity in the course of three centuries,"[92] a statement decidedly significant.

Two more productions deserve paragraphs, before we start Sir Giles on his travels over-seas. *A New Way to Pay Old Debts* was presented by the Merton Floats at Merton College, Oxford, for five performances, December 3 to 5 inclusive, 1930. The production was in the hands of Sir Nigel Playfair, whose son played Sir Giles, and Mr. Wilfred Fletcher; their program note reads as follows: "The fame of the play rests on its interpretation and not upon the literary commentators, who, indeed, spoke little of its merits till that fame had been achieved. It is as a tribute to Edmund Kean that the present producers have endeavored to show, however inadequately, something of his 'lightning' methods and have even suggested the influence of Regency fashion in the carrying out of the Elizabethan costume. The grouping in the last act reproduces that in the famous picture of Kean as Sir Giles Overreach in the Garrick Club in London." A special prologue was written for the occasion by Mr. A. P. Herbert, and the Magdalen Orchestra played Mr. Alfred Reynolds's incidental music, as well as Haydn, Mozart, and Purcell between the acts. Men's parts were played by students, women's by professionals imported for the occasion, somewhat, I gather, to the ruin of the financial success of the play. The cast of principals was as follows:

[92] *New Statesman,* Vol. XX, pp. 267-8.

Sir Giles Overreach .... Giles Playfair
Wellborn .... E. K. Willing-Denton
Lord Lovell .... M. F. Easton
Justice Greedy .... F. E. Whitbourn
Marrall .... W. G. Devlin
Allworth .... J. H. Barber
Lady Allworth .... Joan Buckmaster
Margaret .... Hermione Baddeley

The reviewer in *The Times* of December 5 after an introductory paragraph on the passing of the Kemble school of acting with Kean's Sir Giles Overreach, continues: "Sir Nigel Playfair and Mr. Wilfred Fletcher have had the happy idea of staging *A New Way to Pay Old Debts* in a manner that recalls the Regency rather than the early Stuarts. . . . But the production of Massinger's play at Merton College last night by the Merton Floats did not go far enough in this direction for the audience to pass judgment. The proscenium, indeed, suggested private theatricals at Carlton House and the plumes and high waists of the ladies in the last act were delightful. But, otherwise, the playing was frankly seventeenth century, except for the unnecessary pauses after every episode. A programme note says that the grouping in the last act reproduces the Garrick Club picture of Kean's performance. It was certainly a very effective grouping and suggests that such pictures are less fanciful than is usually assumed." The reviewer commends Miss Buckmaster as Lady Allworth, Mr. Mills as Tapwell and Mr. Giles Playfair's "very able Overreach." It were fitting if we could close our English section with the production of Massinger's greatest play at his own college in the manner of the greatest representative of Sir Giles, Edmund Kean, but the end is not yet.[93]

The last presentations of *A New Way to Pay Old Debts* in England were given by the Literary Society of Birkbeck College, University of London, at the Birkbeck College Theatre on the evenings of the 9th and 10th of December, 1932. The production was under the direction of Professor J. H. Lobban and his assistant,

[93] For a program and information about this presentation, I am indebted to my colleague, Mr. Walter B. C. Watkins, then secretary of the presenting organization and manager of the production. Other press notices will be found in *The Morning Post*, December 3 and 4; *The News Chronicle*, December 4; *The Sunday Times*, December 7; *The Oxford Mail*, December 3 and 4; and *The Era*, January 1.

Miss Marjorie Daunt. The play was presented simply in a manner approximating the Elizabethan, with music, and costumes against a black velvet curtain, and without any front curtain. Free use was made of a small inner stage at the back. The only properties were a few stools. The anonymity of the players is a tradition of the Literary Society, but all the parts were taken by students. The theatre, which seats seven hundred, was well filled for both performances of the play. *The Daily Telegraph* noted that "the performance was commendably free from affectation, and the anonymous cast acquitted itself of a difficult task with considerable success."[94]

To Americans who were present, however, the most striking part of the performance must have been Professor Lobban's wise and witty prologue, spoken by Mr. F. I. Venables:

> 'Tis easy to perceive why fame should crown
> This play when first 'twas launched upon the town,
> And why delighted groundlings flocked to see
> The baffled miser in his misery.
> Tears have been shed (that was our Shakespeare's way)
> For lonely Shylock as he stood at bay,
> But no such tribute of a sigh is due
> The soulless villain whom to-night you view.
> He stands unmasked, a bully, thief and snob,
> Ready to crush the poor, the orphan rob,
> Cruelly indifferent to a daughter's fate,
> Slave of three passions, greed and pride and hate.
> Nor think our author's zeal the truth outran;
> The groundlings cheered—because they knew the man.
> They had seen Sir Giles, at Parliament's command,
> Dragged at the horse's tail along the Strand,[95]
> And flung their caps i' the air with joy to see
> A swindling statesman reap his infamy,
> Judging aright no sentence too severe
> For one who raised the price of coal and beer.

[94] I am indebted for the above information to my colleague, Professor T. M. Parrott, who saw the production, and to Professor Lobban and Mr. G. F. Troup Horne of Birkbeck College who kindly sent long and interesting letters. The prologue is quoted with Professor Lobban's permission.

[95] I have found no evidence that the ceremony of degradation was ever performed.

The fame of Giles some critics leads astray
Who dub our comedy a one-man play—
A theory that quickly proves untrue
To all who will not only read but view.
Our play's a crowded and a varied scene,
Its humour rich, its insight true and keen.
The slimy notary, with his scurvy trick,
Whose exit's hastened with a parting kick,
The obsequious parson, and the bullying host,
The porcine justice in his food engrossed,
The kindly prodigal, and, best of all,
The ageless humours of the servants' hall—
All these, when fiction gained upon the stage,
You'll meet once more on Fielding's joyous page.

Now that the sun no longer seems to set
On pale Britannia's lengthening roll of debt,
You well may hope to draw from such a play
Some useful hints on problems of the day—
As how to shun the downfall of the axe,
Or 'scape the bludgeon of the income-tax,
Or how to bear with Christian disconcertion
The joyless creed of forcible "conversion."
While horrors quite like these had not yet come
In Charles's day, and so our author's dumb,
Yet Massinger, from long financial sorrow,
Would surely say to all who fain would borrow:—
Whether his name be Moses, Giles, or Sam,
An Uncle's charity may prove a sham;
His method 's one, though under various types,
(It may be "Three Gold Balls" or "Stars and Stripes")
And small 's the difference to the dispossessed
Whether his gold go West or Middle-West.

Though we shall find Sir Giles many times in the United States, this is, I think, the only time he ever became star-spangled to those who were looking for a new way to pay old debts.

Thus ends, as far as Great Britain is concerned, what can only be considered as a remarkable stage-history. Many Elizabethan and early Stuart plays were revived in the Restoration, continued to hold the boards hesitantly through the eighteenth century, lapsed in the nineteenth, and then were revived as antiquarian pieces in the twentieth for occasional performances. But here we have an example of a play which the Restoration and the early eighteenth century slighted, but which from Garrick to the present day has never really left the English theatre. Almost every great name in the history of English acting has at some time or other been connected with the play. But *A New Way to Pay Old Debts* outstrips all non-Shakespearean competitors in that it did not remain the property alone of that country which saw its birth. As we shall shortly see, it became as popular in the United States as it did in Great Britain.

PART II

A NEW WAY TO PAY OLD DEBTS
IN AMERICA

CHAPTER VII

LEAVE YOUR HOME BEHIND

L ONG as has been the history of Sir Giles, there is still much to tell of him, for the rascal, not content to prosecute his nefarious schemes in the country of his birth, sailed to the United States at the end of the eighteenth century, grew and flourished there with the same dogged persistence which had characterized his career in Great Britain. If ever a man lived a double life, he did, though in this case the lives are both representative of one personality and strikingly alike in their actions and effects. There is no Dr. Jekyl on the one hand, able, scientific, respected, and Mr. Hyde on the other, vicious, selfish, and criminal. Sir Giles changed neither his name nor his character, but repeated in America in the most brazen fashion the pursuits of the cruel extortioner in Great Britain.

When the Old American Company, directed by Hallam and Henry, opened its New York season at the John Street Theatre, in October 1791, there was absent from the roster the name of Thomas Wignell, one of the principal performers. Dissatisfied with the treatment he had received from his managers, Wignell had associated himself with Alexander Reinagle, a musician already connected with the theatre, and together they had planned a rival organization which was to have its headquarters in a new theatre in Philadelphia. While the theatre was being built, Wignell went to England in search of promising material for his new company, and returned in 1793 with a group which far surpassed in ability that of his rivals in New York City. Unfortunately yellow fever was then ravaging Philadelphia and it was not until February of the following year that he was able to commence his first season as manager at the newly erected Chestnut Street Theatre.

Among the recruits whom Wignell had brought back from abroad was an actor by the name of James Chalmers. He turns up first in a neat sketch by the incorrigible Tate Wilkinson who engaged him for his York season of 1779-1780 and afterwards for Hull, Edinburgh, and York for the seasons of 1780 and 1781. Tate thought him "one of the best Harlequins I ever recollect (Woodward excepted) and was thought so by the different audiences that he has tripped before, at London, Dublin, Edinburgh, York, &c. That gentleman has great merit in several parts peculiar to Mr. Lewis, who seems to have struck his stage mind ever since seeing that gentleman perform at Edinburgh and York, in the year 1780. Mr. Chalmers certainly has not his features at command, like his limbs, but he has spirit, utility, neatness, and merit in several particular characters. The punctuality of his payments, and a strict observance of his word, with several good points, do honour to him as a man. I say no more than a strict truth, when I pronounce Mr. Chalmers deserving such eulogium. On the other hand, he is not the Tamest of comedians; but soon, porcupine like, sets up his quills, and levels his darts. A love of lace, spangles, and satin, is not more predominant in any actor, than in Mr. Chalmers."[1]

Chalmers made his London début at Covent Garden on October 8, 1783, as Tom in *The Conscious Lovers*. As a light comedian he was successful without being important. He made a hit, however, the following year in a piece got up especially to display his agility as a harlequin and pantomimist: *Harlequin Rambler, or The Convent in an Uproar,* September 20, 1784. Thereafter he was at Dublin for a season and then at Weymouth for several years. Wignell finally engaged him for the lead in genteel comedy and for secondary rôles in tragedy, and he seems to have been satisfactory in both, though preferred in the former. When in the fall of 1794, James Fennell left his tragic rôles in the theatre to engage in the manufacture of salt—a project which soon lost its savor— Chalmers fell heir to most of his parts for the season of 1794-1795. The following year Chalmers left the Philadelphia company and though he occasionally came back to it, we find him successively in Charleston, New York, and Boston. He subsequently returned to England, where he died in 1806.

[1] Wilkinson, *The Wandering Patentee,* Vol. II, pp. 90-1, 96-7. Other material on Chalmers will be found in Seilhamer, Vol. III, index *s.v.*; Odell, Vols. I, II, index *s.v.*; Durang; Willis, index *s.v.*; Clapp, p. 39; Wemyss, *Chronology s.v.*; Brown, *American Stage,* p. 66, etc.

It was James Chalmers who first reincarnated Sir Giles Over-reach in the United States.[2] At the end of Wignell's second season at the Chestnut Street Theatre, Billy Bates, the low comedian of the company, took a benefit. The plays for the evening, May 11, 1795, were O'Keefe's *A Beggar on Horseback* with Bates as Corney, and *A New Way to Pay Old Debts,* Bates playing Justice Greedy. I copy from Seilhamer the entire cast :[3]

Sir Giles Overreach .... Chalmers
Lord Lovel .... Moreton
Justice Greedy .... Bates
Tapwell .... Wignell
Amble .... Blissett
Wantwell .... Warrell
Welborn .... Whitlock
Allworth .... Cleveland
Marall .... Harwood
Order .... Warrell, Jr.
Furnace .... Francis
Lady Allworth .... Mrs. Shaw
Margaretta .... Mrs. Marshall
Froth .... Mrs. Rowson

Since we do not know how *A New Way to Pay Old Debts* fared on this occasion—it was not repeated—we may turn at once to the question why it was produced at all. Who was responsible for bringing over and getting acted this not yet very popular play? Wignell? I doubt it; the manager did not usually choose the plays in which his actors were to take benefits. Bates, then? More likely

[2] Unless, as Professor Thomas Clark Pollock has conjectured, *The Credulous Steward, or, A New Way to Get Money,* presented by the American Company at the Southwark Theatre in Philadelphia on July 11 and July 23, 1788, was *A New Way to Pay Old Debts* in disguise. Because of the law against theatres, Hallam and Henry were forced to resort to all sorts of expedients to produce plays. Names were changed and the Southwark was called an opera house for the presentation of "concerts" or "spectacula vitae." See Pollock, *The Phila-delphia Theatre,* pp. 141-2, and *The Pennsylvania Packet, and Daily Advertiser* for appropriate dates. If Pollock is right, I suspect that only parts of the play were given; on the other hand there is no evidence except this that Hallam and Henry ever presented *A New Way to Pay Old Debts.*

[3] Seilhamer, Vol. III, pp. 175, 180, 183; Pollock, p. 251. In this case, the origi-nal spelling is retained.

of course, but how is one to account for the *series* of Massinger plays at this time? A week after *A New Way to Pay Old Debts,* Chalmers himself took a benefit and the part he acted was Paris in a condensed version of *The Roman Actor,* called *A Defense of the Stage,* which no doubt consisted of the celebrated scene of the Curia, already used for the same purpose by Kemble.[4] And then to cap the climax on June 19 came Mrs. Rowson's *The Female Patriot,* an adaptation of Massinger's *The Bondman* (by the lady, note, who played Froth in *A New Way to Pay Old Debts*), Pysander by Mr. Chalmers. Does the reader begin to suspect, as I do, that it was Chalmers who started this Massinger cycle? A word with Billy Bates, a hint to Suzanna Rowson, the easy permission of Mr. Wignell—he had nothing to lose at these benefits— and the thing was done and Mr. Chalmers had three fat parts, all new to America. Does not that suspicion become almost a certainty when we remember that Chalmers had acted at York with Kemble when the latter had played the same scenes from *The Roman Actor,* and that he also played Amble, or perhaps Marrall, when Kemble made his début in Sir Giles Overreach at Edinburgh on July 30, 1781? Moreover John Henderson was playing Sir Giles at Covent Garden the very season that James Chalmers was a member of the company. What is more likely than that this actor, fresh from abroad where except in the provinces he had played small parts, suddenly elevated by the grace of James Fennell to the rank of first tragedian, should wish to play the same rôles in which he had seen his betters star abroad? I cannot, therefore, but feel that it was Chalmers who was responsible for introducing *A New Way to Pay Old Debts* to America; and the first to introduce Sir Giles.

Another benefit was the occasion of the next performance of *A New Way to Pay Old Debts*; this time the part of Sir Giles was chosen by an actor whose name is much better known to

[4] Seilhamer, Vol. III, pp. 175, 184, 186. The cast as given by Seilhamer names only the parts of Paris, Aretinus, Aesopus, and Latinus, the characters who would appear in Act I, scenes i and iii.

students of the theatre, John Hodgkinson.[5] Hodgkinson was born in Manchester sometime in the 1760's, and after a somewhat adventurous boyhood, ran away from home and made his professional début at Bristol when only fourteen years of age. Deficient in education, he made up for this lack by a memory which was extraordinary, and an energy which was unbounded, and before long he was engaged by the eccentric James Whitely to act on his midland circuit. He is next traceable in the northern line of theatres of which Munden was co-manager, and where for one summer he had the advantage of the tutelage of Mrs. Siddons in tragic parts. Comedy and opera he had already made his own; as a matter of fact, it was Hodgkinson's voice and his fiddle which brought him entrée to the stage. Having acquired considerable fame, he again became attached to the Bath and Bristol theatres, and was about to make his London début, when Henry came over to England in search of talent for New York City. Anxious to rid himself of various entangling alliances into which his natural gallantry had led him, and having fallen seriously in love with Miss Brett, afterwards his wife, Hodgkinson found it advantageous to accept Henry's offer to act in America, painted as a land of golden dramatic opportunity. Consequently he and various members of the Brett family sailed from England on the 28th of June, 1792, and landed in New York City early in the following September.

Hallam and Henry's company was at that time acting in Philadelphia, and there Hodgkinson made his American début as Belcour to considerable applause. His astonishing range of characterization soon brought him great success, and when he made his first appearance in New York on January 28, 1793, as Vapid in *The Dramatist,* a critic in *The New-York Journal* for February 2, hailed him as "at *least* equal to any person who has hitherto tried the American Sock." It would be useless for me to sketch John Hodgkinson's career as an actor and manager in New York, Bos-

---

[5] The following sketch of Hodgkinson's career is taken from [S. C. Carpenter], "Sketch of the life of the late Mr. Hodgkinson," *The Mirror of Taste and Dramatic Censor,* Philadelphia, Vols. I and II, 1810, *passim*; William Dunlap: *History of The American Theatre,* pp. 95-100; Odell, Vols. I and II, *passim.* For Hodgkinson in New York, see his own *Narrative of his Connection with the Old American Company,* New York, 1797.

ton, and Charleston. Unfortunately his tireless energy often brewed trouble both for himself and for others, but it was only on rare occasions that he was unpopular with his audience, and when he died of yellow fever in 1805 he was sincerely regretted. Hodgkinson's histrionic versatility was extraordinary; during one engagement in South Carolina in 1803, he is said to have acted eighty different parts; though best in low comedy, he was almost equally good in high comedy and tragedy, and though occasionally he stumbled upon a part which proved a failure, more often he made it his own. Rarely as brilliant as his only real rival, Cooper, he was more steady, besides being able, unlike Cooper, to step from one genre to another with perfect ease. Consequently he became one of the two finest actors on the American stage before the arrival of Cooke.

Hodgkinson's only performance of Sir Giles Overreach came when he played in *A New Way to Pay Old Debts* for his own benefit on May 15, 1801, at the conclusion of a season at the Park Theatre, under Dunlap, with whom he had formerly been co-manager. The major cast was as follows:[6]

Sir Giles Overreach	Hodgkinson
Wellborn	Hallam
Lord Lovell	Tyler
Marrall	Martin
Justice Greedy	Jefferson
Allworth	Fox
Lady Allworth	Mrs. Melmoth
Margaret	Mrs. Hodgkinson

As far as I can ascertain, Hodgkinson never played the part again, and I therefore cannot but agree with Ireland and Odell that his ambition had o'erleapt itself, and that in spite of his versatility, he was not a success as Massinger's extortioner. Nothing more need or can be said, except that here we have again ample proof that not every good actor, even though the part be in his line, can necessarily play Sir Giles Overreach.

[6] Odell, Vol. I, pp. 113-14; Ireland, Vol. I, p. 199; the Greedy is Joseph Jefferson, the first, grandfather of *Rip Van Winkle* Jefferson.

Both Philadelphia and New York City had now seen a Sir Giles, but neither of them had really seen the character vivified by a great actor. Sir Giles had arrived but had made little impression; he was soon to stand forth clear and strong in the impersonation of the first great English actor to visit America, George Frederick Cooke. I have already said something of the life of this dissipated but gifted man, and I stop only for the reminder that in the fall of 1810 Cooper induced him to try to piece together his shattered fortunes by a trip to America. Just how the inducement was brought about it is hardly my province to discuss; the whole matter has been treated by Dunlap, and his account still stands, though a great deal has been and perhaps should be said on the other side—of the Atlantic!

The news that Cooke had engaged to come to America created no small excitement in New York City, as well as a good deal of disbelief. But doubts were banished when Cooke arrived on the 16th of November and prepared for his engagement at the Park Theatre. Twenty-two hundred people paid the then prodigious sum of eighteen hundred and twenty dollars to see his Richard III on Wednesday, the 21st, and went home enthusiastic. Though the receipts did not continue quite at this high level, his succeeding parts were all welcomed with fervor, even his second Richard III on the 24th when, alas, he was too drunk to speak louder than a whisper. Meanwhile there were two performances of Sir Giles Overreach, the 12th and 17th of December, 1810, on which we must focus for a moment. The cast was as follows:[7]

Sir Giles Overreach	Cooke
Wellborn	Simpson
Lord Lovell	Stanley
Marrall	Doige
Justice Greedy	Bray
Allworth	Robertson
Lady Allworth	Mrs. Stanley
Margaret	Mrs. Mason

[7] Odell, Vol. II, p. 361; Ireland, Vol. I, p. 275.

Reviews of these two performances seem to be wholly lacking, so we must content ourselves with the remarks of Cooke's friend, biographer, and daily guardian from temptation, William Dunlap:[8]

> The next performance [December 12, 1810] was *A New Way to Pay Old Debts,* a play which, notwithstanding Mr. Cooke's wonderful performance in Sir Giles Overreach, did not please in New-York. The character of Sir Giles shocks by his atrocity, and even his punishment, though we rejoice in it, strikes us with horror. The acting of Mr. Cooke at this terrible point, can never be forgotten. His attempt to draw his sword, and the sudden arrest of his arm, palsied and stiffened, and rendered powerless, as if by the stroke of Heaven's avenging thunder—the expression of his countenance at this moment, and his sinking convulsed, and then lifeless, into the arms of his servants, were so frightfully impressive, and true to nature, as to leave an image never to be erased.
>
> One night, in this situation, by some accident, the attendants were not ready to receive him, when he fell back, expecting to be caught in their arms as usual; but instead of losing, the effect was heightened by the omission; for he fell so perfectly dead to appearance, and was carried off so much like a corpse, as only to increase the horror of the scene. The receipts were this night nine hundred and sixty-three dollars.

Dunlap must be right about the unpopularity of the play, for the receipts for the performance of December 17 dwindled to seven hundred and ninety-eight dollars.[9] There is something strange about this: here was the first great Sir Giles that New York had had an opportunity to see, and New York found the character so horrible that it failed to enjoy the play. That night Cooke gave way to his old enemy and when he appeared for his benefit on the 19th, so intoxicated that his mind was utterly bewildered, "the audience which had assembled to admire, turned away with disgust." Though reasonably successful in his next four and concluding performances in New York City, Cooke single-handed had stopped the Cooke furor, and the admiration of the actor was forever dimmed by the revelation of the man.

[8] Dunlap, Vol. II, pp. 190-1.
[9] *ibid.,* Vol. II, p. 194.

Cooke now left for Boston where he acted from the 3rd to the 25th of January, 1811, but for some reason or other, perhaps because of its indifferent success in New York, Sir Giles Overreach was not included among his performances. Cooke's history here repeated itself maddeningly—the same enthusiasm, the same intoxication. Back in New York, when he returned there, receipts dwindled, Cooke drank himself to serious illness, and Sir Giles was still omitted from his repertoire.

Cooke now journeyed to Philadelphia and here at last he played Sir Giles Overreach again, on April 6, 1811, "very finely," comments Dunlap.[10] The Chestnut Street audience paid ten hundred and thirty dollars to see the performance, more it is to be noted than was received at the Park.[11] Washington Irving saw Cooke play Macbeth during this engagement and pronounced him much better than he had been in New York:[12] "The old boy absolutely outdid himself. . . . The more I see of Cooke the more I admire his style of acting—he is very unequal, from his irregular habits and nervous affections—for when he is in proper mood, there is a truth and of course a simplicity in his performances that throw all rant, stage trick and stage effect completely in the background. Were he to remain here a sufficient time for the public to perceive and dwell upon his merits and the true playing, he would produce a new taste in acting. One of his best performances may be compared to a masterpiece of ancient statuary; where you have the human figure destitute of idle ornament. . . . Such a production requires the eye of taste & knowledge to perceive its general excellencies; whereas a vulgar spectator will turn from it to be enraptured with some bungling workmanship, loaded with finery & drapery, and all the garish ornaments in which unskillfulness takes refuge." Poor Cooke, he had little time left to reform the taste in acting, or to reform himself either. It is not without interest that this performance, in which Irving took so much

---

[10] *ibid.*, Vol. II, p. 293.
[11] Wood, p. 133; James, p. 87.
[12] In a letter to Henry Brevoort; see Odell, Vol. II, p. 360.

artistic delight, brought in less money than any of the ten previous Philadelphia performances.[13]

We need not trace Cooke's performances in detail from this point. New York and Baltimore engagements followed—as well as a marriage—but *A New Way to Pay Old Debts* was not performed. It reappears, however, during Cooke's second engagement at Philadelphia, on November 23—receipts six hundred and forty-six dollars,[14] with one exception the lowest so far during the engagement. Sir Giles evidently was no favorite in Philadelphia either, despite the crowds on his first appearance and Durang's statement that when Cooke was himself in parts suited to him— and Sir Giles is listed—"he soared above all competitors on eagle wings."[15]

In January 1812, Cooke was at Boston, playing Massinger's extortioner on both the 22nd and 28th.[16] The receipts were comparatively low: on the 22nd, four hundred and seventeen dollars, sixty-two and one-half cents; on the 28th, four hundred and fifty-one dollars, fifty cents, partially to be explained by Cooke's inebriation on the 10th; it was, however, a much smaller theatre and the repetition seems significant, the increase even more so.[17] Part of Boston at least seems to have taken to Sir Giles Overreach. At any rate the *Repertory and General Advertiser* of Friday, January 24, is complimentary: "Mr. Cooke performed the character of Sir Giles Overreach on Wednesday for the first time in Boston and displayed powers of conception and execution superiour to any other actor that has appeared in this Theatre. To particularize the many beauties of this inimitable performance would exceed our limits, suffice it to say, that it fully equalled his best personations of Shylock and Richard. . . ." *The New England Palladium* of the previous day gives us the cast for this auspicious occasion:[18]

---

[13] Wood, p. 133.

[14] Dunlap, Vol. II, p. 353; Wood, p. 154; James, p. 98, ($646.06).

[15] Durang, Chap. XLVI.

[16] Harvard Boston list.

[17] Dunlap, Vol. II, pp. 357-8. The explanation of the half cent is contained in the following list of prices given by Clapp, p. 134: "boxes $1; green boxes, 75 cents; pit, 50 cents; gallery 37½ cents."

[18] The number of January 24 calls Cooke's Sir Giles "The *ne plus ultra* of fine acting."

Sir Giles Overreach .... Cooke
Wellborn .... Duff
Lord Lovell .... Vaughan
Marrall .... Drake
Justice Greedy .... Entwistle
Allworth .... Robertson
Lady Allworth .... Mrs. Powell
Margaret .... Mrs. Doige

Dickenson succeeded Entwistle for the performance of the 28th;
Clapp says Cooke's disease of drinking had proved contagious;[19]
though he specifies no dates, we may have found the reason for
the substitution.

After some desultory playing in New York, Cooke once again
joined the Boston company though this time they played at Providence where Cooke opened on July 13, 1812, as Shylock, with
his usual characters following. His last performance during this
engagement was his last performance on the stage, and fittingly
enough, it was Sir Giles Overreach that he acted on that occasion.
The date was Friday, July 31, and the cast presumably much
the same as that at Boston given above. The house was full though
the total receipts came only to two hundred and eighty-five dollars.[20] Various historians give us the thankful news that Cooke
was himself as well as Sir Giles, and the effect of his interpretation is testified by the following account:[21]

S. S. Southworth, the veteran journalist, has recorded the following incident, which occurred at this time. One of the most
honoured citizens of the town was Thomas Lloyd Halsey, a man

[19] Clapp, p. 127.
[20] Dunlap, Vol. II, pp. 366-7. The facts about this performance have been
curiously muddled and I risk a lengthy footnote to point out the danger. Canon
Cruickshank for example (Edition), p. 132 gives the date of Cooke's farewell
as July 31, 1811, thus making his ghost give the two performances he records
on January 22, 28, 1812, in Boston. The error has been copied from T. A. Brown,
Vol. I, p. 14. Both Doran (now corrected by Lowe), Vol. III, p. 235, and Ireland,
Vol. I, p. 275 wrongly place this performance in Boston. While I am on the subject, Parker is also wrong when he says Cooke played Sir Giles in *November*
1810 at the Park (*TLS*, September 7, 1922, p. 569).
[21] Blake, pp. 122-3. This whole chapter as well as the rest of Blake's book is
reproduced *verbatim* in George O. Willard's *History of the Providence Stage*.
Willard makes acknowledgment to Blake in the Preface, but apparently feels
no scruples about putting his own name alone on the title-page, and the reader
unconsciously gives Willard credit when half of the book is really Blake's.

of large fortune, of irascible temperament, and great fondness for theatrical entertainments. . . . On the night when Cooke was playing *Sir Giles Overreach*—at that point where he is overwhelmed by the production of the forged parchment—Mr. Halsey became so excited that he involuntarily rose from his seat, and ejaculated in the presence of a crowded audience, "Throttle the damned infamous villain!" to the amazement and horror of the whole assembly.

This outburst of such an impulsive person as Mr. Halsey is to be regarded as strong testimony to the genius of the matchless Cooke, whose personations of the malignant passions have never been equalled. . . .

Cooke went out in a blaze of glory making his impersonation so lifelike that reality and illusion became entangled. He had been a great Sir Giles. Dr. Francis counted Cooke's impersonation "not so terrifically impressive as that of Kean,"[22] but Dunlap confidently pronounced Cooke's "the greatest . . . that the western world has seen."[23] American audiences were not, as has appeared, quite prepared for such a performance, not appreciative of the simple and natural technique so admired by Washington Irving, not finding much relish in the malignancy of Massinger's horrible villain, not a little apprehensive of this blurring of reality and illusion. They had, however, now seen how powerfully the part could be rendered, had been in a way prepared for the presentations of Sir Giles which were soon to come, when they could abandon their former distaste and call for him again and again.

Among these presentations I do not include two by an unimportant actor named Bibby—his first name escapes research. He played *A New Way to Pay Old Debts* for his benefit at the Boston Theatre on November 11, 1816, and likewise for his benefit at the Park Theatre, New York, on the 22nd of the month.[24] Bibby deserves distinction only as being the first American to play Sir Giles Overreach. He made "his first appearance on any stage" in New York in February of the previous year as "a young Gentleman of this City" and surprised his audiences by the fidelity with

[22] Francis, *Old New York*, p. 206.
[23] *History of the American Theatre*, p. 384.
[24] Harvard Boston list; cast is given in *Boston Clippings 1816-1820*, Harvard Theatre Collection; Odell, Vol. II, p. 466. On Bibby himself, see Odell, Vol. II, pp. 439, 450, 466; also Ireland, Vol. I, p. 308; and Genest, Vol. VIII, pp. 550, 552.

which he aped Cooke. He had some success and even made a London début at Covent Garden in April 1816, but thereafter returned to this country, married wealth, and became a lawyer. I do not know or greatly care about his Sir Giles, no matter how brightly he shone with the reflected glory of Cooke.

Quite otherwise is it with Robert Campbell Maywood, an actor whose talents for some reason or other never received their just reward. Born in Edinburgh in 1790, he acted in the provinces with Kean, of whose style he became an example. A success in Glasgow, he was finally brought to Drury Lane and made a satisfactory appearance there as Shylock on September 25, 1817. Shortly afterwards, however, he tried parts which were not suited to him, and the obvious comparison with Kean, to his own disadvantage, brought him to America. Beginning as a successful star, he the next year was merely a member of the company at the Park. He later transferred to Philadelphia; and was manager of the Chestnut Street Theatre for eight years, and connected with it until 1843. His career as an actor after that date was sporadic and unsuccessful both here and abroad, and he died, deranged, penniless, and in pitiful circumstances in 1856, deserted by a worthless stepdaughter then living in extravagant wealth in a villa on Lake Como. She had become a successful continental dancer largely through the advantages given her by her stepfather. A melancholy tale, but we need not at present look so far ahead.

Maywood made his New York début on January 4, 1819, as Richard III, following this two nights later with Sir Giles Overreach. The Park cast was as follows:[25]

Sir Giles Overreach	Maywood
Wellborn	Simpson
Lord Lovell	Robertson
Marrall	Barnes
Justice Greedy	Kilner
Allworth	Moreland
Lady Allworth	Miss Leesugg
Margaret	Miss Johnson

[25] Maywood's copy of *A New Way to Pay Old Debts* is among the prompt books in the Harvard Collection (Oxberry's ed., London, 1818). The New York cast is written in; material on Maywood's life above is from Ireland, Vol. I, pp. 350-2; Odell, Vol. II, pp. 526-8; Hawkins, Vol. II, pp. 4 *ff*.

Maywood's easy, natural acting made a hit, and the *Columbian* of January 29 concludes by saying: "In short, from what we have witnessed of Mr. Maywood's talents, we are of opinion that his style of acting is an acquisition to the American stage—and it is sincerely hoped that it may be instrumental in eradicating a school of performance which is insulting to common sense." Just that for the old school of rant and rhetoric!

In February, Maywood went to star in Philadelphia, appearing in *A New Way to Pay Old Debts* on the 5th, "not acted these six years," says the playbill. Had someone played Sir Giles there later than Cooke in November of 1811, or is this merely the often inaccurate statement of the bill writer?

Sir Giles Overreach .... Maywood
Wellborn .... H. Wallack
Lord Lovell .... Hughes
Marrall .... Herbert
Justice Greedy .... Jefferson
Allworth .... T. Jefferson
Lady Allworth .... Mrs. Lefolle
Margaret .... Mrs. Darley

Do not confuse Henry Wallack with his more famous brother, nor young Tom Jefferson with his grandfather, some years deceased. Wood counts the receipts for the performance as two hundred and forty-nine dollars,[26] a small house compared with what Cooper and Wallack usually drew, but Maywood was not yet well known. Some enthusiast, however, became poetic; I quote from an unidentified newspaper clipping in the Harvard Theatre Collection:

TO ROBERT CAMPBELL MAYWOOD, ESQ.
OF THE THEATRE ROYAL DRURY LANE, LONDON.
On witnessing his splendid exertions in the tragic walks
of the Drama—Philadelphia, March, 1819.

Farewell the ranting school,—the measured tone
Ever to nature, now to Taste unknown!
Farewell, ye ten feet syllables, that travel
To the strain'd ear, like broad wheel carts on gravel,
Lazy and long, bombastically full,
Sublimely mad, or impotently dull!

[26] Wood, p. 229; James, p. 274 ($249.50 in spite of "fine" weather).

Hail! MAYWOOD, hail!—whose skill opposing art,
Through nature's coil, strikes boldly on the heart. . . .
The wealthy villain, *Massinger* gave down
From times of earliest guilt to warn our own,
Portrayed by thee, casts of its hyperbole,
And lives the being of the Poet's soul!

After which effusion, further comment is unnecessary. Would there were some poet for the Boston performance of February 22.[27]

Five years pass before we see Maywood again, no longer star but with the stock company at the Park and according to the *Mirror* of April 24, 1824, being pushed aside for much less able actors: "We are sorry to learn that our old friend and favourite Maywood, intends leaving our stage." On the same date he played Sir Giles Overreach, his last at the Park.[28] When he returned from abroad, he appeared at the Chatham Garden, this time definitely as a star. He never again became mere stock actor. Such being the case it is fitting to find him acting Sir Giles on November 3, 1825.[29] A year later he played the part again, at the Lafayette Theatre, October 19.[30] Maywood's last appearance as Sir Giles was unexpected. On January 4, 1830, Booth was to have played the part at the Chestnut Street Theatre, Philadelphia, with the following cast:[31]

Sir Giles Overreach .... Booth
Wellborn .... Wemyss
Lord Lovell .... Rowbotham
Marrall .... Foot
Justice Greedy .... Jefferson
Lady Allworth .... Mrs. Wood
Margaret .... Miss Rowbotham

On the Harvard bill for this date, however, is a note in contemporary longhand: "Mr. Booth taken in a crazy fit"; his name is crossed out and Maywood's substituted. Farewell, Maywood, you

---

[27] Harvard Boston list and *Boston Clippings 1816-1820*.
[28] Odell, Vol. III, p. 106.
[29] *ibid.*, Vol. III, p. 205.
[30] *ibid.*, Vol. III, p. 275.
[31] Allworth is not on the bill.

deserved better fortune as an actor! Of your Sir Giles we know precious little but applaud in retrospect!

Canada saw what I suspect was its first Overreach early in 1819. In that year W. H. Dykes leased the Montreal Theatre and opened it on January 14 with *Othello,* the title-rôle acted by Frederick Brown. The latter, who was accompanied by his wife, the sister of Mrs. Charles Kemble, played a round of characters among which was Sir Giles. Brown, born in England and a favorite in Liverpool, had been engaged by Dickson of Boston and came to the Federal Street Theatre in 1816. His career is not easy to trace. In 1819 he was in New York, in 1824 stage-manager at Charleston, in 1826 lessee of the Theatre Royal, Montreal, where he supported Kean, in 1830 with James E. Murdoch in the South. He died in miserable circumstances in North Carolina in 1838. Small in stature, gentlemanly, affable, he was a conventional actor of the Kemble school. His Sir Giles remains a dim and shadowy figure, important only for its precedence in the place where it was represented.[32]

I come now to chronicle the visits to America of that greatest Sir Giles, Edmund Kean. It is not altogether a happy story. Foolish as Kean was at various times, he never deserved the storm of intemperate abuse that was heaped on him in the United States. The actions of the citizens of New York, Boston, and Philadelphia, particularly upon his second visit, may be understood but they cannot be condoned. We had with us an extraordinary actor and we sent him away both times after scenes in which one finds mingled hypocrisy, cant, and moral hysterics.

Fortunately none of this was at first in evidence. The enthusiasm that greeted Kean's performances at the Anthony Street Theatre, New York, in November and December of 1820 was unprecedented in this country. When he opened on November 29 in *Richard III,* the crowds both inside and outside the theatre were immense. Though there were a few instances of foolish and carping criticism, the newspapers the next day proclaimed him the greatest actor they had ever seen. Both crowds and criticism swelled his praise during the whole engagement. When Kean left

[32] Graham, *Histrionic Montreal,* p. 36. This sketch of Brown is taken from Charles Durang's account in the same book.

for Philadelphia at the end of December, the citizens of New York testified their admiration by giving him a dinner. All so far was as it should have been.

Kean played Sir Giles twice during this stay at the Anthony Street Theatre—the Park, you will remember, had burned—on the 8th and 11th of December, the latter for his benefit:[33]

```
Sir Giles Overreach ............................... Kean
Wellborn ....................................... Simpson
Lord Lovell .................................... Woodhull
Marrall ......................................... Barnes
Justice Greedy .................................. Kilner
Allworth ...................................... Moreland
Lady Allworth .............................. Miss Denny
Margaret .................................. Miss Johnson
```

"Garrick's" remarks in the *Evening Post* will serve as an index to the criticism. He prefers Kean's Sir Giles to any part previously played. "The part is particularly adapted to his style . . . his peculiarities are no blemish here, he even turns his faults and deficiencies to account; for the absence of personal dignity, of clear and melodious tones and of smooth and measured declamation, is in truth not wanted in the personification of this odious character. . . . The final exhibition of mingled fury, disappointment, and agony of conscience, goading him to madness, formed a grand and terrible picture. It was indeed most awful to listen to the hoarse war [?] of his voice, and to look on the daring eye, and convulsed features, and writhen lip of this insane victim of passion." I cannot refrain from following Odell further in quoting the letter of Edward Simpson, the manager, to a friend in Dublin, written on the 7th. This letter is invaluable in its first-hand impression.[34] "Kean is with us & playing to great business; he averages about $1000 a Night—the people don't know exactly what to make of him—his strange manner surprises them but his style gains converts every night. . . . We find him extremely agreeable in The Theatre & are agreeably disappointed in finding him in manner and conduct exactly the reverse of what we expected." With which benediction we proceed to Philadelphia.

[33] Odell, Vol. II, pp. 587-8; the cast from clipping, Harvard Theatre Collection.
[34] Harvard Theatre Collection; Odell, Vol. II, pp. 587-8.

Beginning on the 8th of January, 1821, Kean played for sixteen nights at the Walnut Street Theatre, awaking fervent admiration. Reviewers who had persuaded themselves that no one could be better than Cooke, condemned his Richard on the first night, but completely capitulated on the second when he played Othello. *A New Way to Pay Old Debts* was presented for Kean's first benefit on the 19th of January and according to Wood's figures drew the amazing amount of thirteen hundred and seventy-nine dollars.[35] A playbill contributes the cast:

Sir Giles Overreach	Kean
Wellborn	Wood
Lord Lovell	Wheatley
Marrall	Herbert
Justice Greedy	Jefferson
Allworth	Darley
Watchall	J. Jefferson[36]
Lady Allworth	Mrs. Williams
Margaret	Mrs. Darley

The Literary Gazette commenting on the large audience makes the curious statement that during the first four acts "an uncommon apathy appeared to reign, considering the ordinary proneness to clapping, and the kindly mood which prevail whenever an actor of much celebrity is treading the boards." Possibly this was the calm before the storm of the Fifth Act or merely the hush of approbation, "the profound and expressive silence during the play, that would hardly admit of an interruption of plaudits."[37] At any rate other papers were feverishly enthusiastic and commented on the admiration of the audience; indeed the custom of calling out performers for a final curtain call began in Philadelphia during this Kean engagement.[38] Wood gives two comments on Kean's Sir Giles which will be apt here:[39]

A gentleman known throughout this country for eminence in the profession of law, but whose sensibilities to literature, music, and

---

[35] Wood, p. 256; James, p. 321. (The weather was "fair.")

[36] Joe Jefferson II. Winter, *Jefferson*, p. 137, also lists Tapwell as one of his parts.

[37] This is from a review of Kean's Shylock (December 2, 1820) in the *New York Evening Post*.

[38] Wood, pp. 260-1.

[39] *ibid.*, p. 264. The lines I reproduce as Wood gives them.

EDMUND KEAN as SIR GILES OVERREACH, from the painting by
George Clint, A.R.A., engraved by T. Lupton, published
by Milburn Kenneth, 1833

the arts are not less well known in the city where he resides, in the retired dignity of advancing life, not long since paid the following high tribute to Kean's excellence as Sir Giles Overreach. He had been discussing in conversation the merits of other actors of former times with equal justice and delicacy, but added, "No impression I ever received from a play, or an actor, approached the effect produced by Kean as Sir Giles, in the scene where, after a powerless attempt on his daughter's life, in the mad rage at her stolen marriage, which defeats the ambitious views of his whole life, he exclaims

> "I'm feeble—some undone widow
> Sits upon my arm, and takes away
> The use on't; and my sword—
> Glued to the scabbard with wronged
> Orphans' tears, will not be drawn."

Cooper delighted to expatiate on the surprising variety and force of genius exhibited by Kean in this character. He was indeed, as Kemble quaintly observes, "terribly in earnest."

The news that Kean was to appear in Boston caused as much excitement as did later the arrival of Jenny Lind. Tickets were sold at auction and the premiums given by the managers to various charitable institutions. The usual Richard opened the proceedings on the 12th of February, 1821. Kean was engaged for nine nights, reengaged for six, and then begged to stay longer. Unfortunately there were other engagements. Sir Giles Overreach trod the stage on February 23 and March 2; I copy the cast from a somewhat mutilated prompt-book in the New York Public Library:[40]

Sir Giles Overreach .... Kean
Wellborn .... Duff
Lord Lovell .... Pelby
Marrall .... Brown
Justice Greedy .... Bray
Allworth .... Perkins
Lady Allworth .... Mrs. Pelby
Margaret .... Mrs. Drummond

[40] No title-page. (NCO p.v. 349. No. 5.) The cast is written in, and the book may have been used for this revival.

Kean's next engagement was in New York, where he again played Overreach on the boards of the Anthony Street Theatre on April 3, 1821.[41] Triumphant again, he proceeded to Philadelphia, commencing his second engagement there on the 9th; *A New Way to Pay Old Debts* was not played. On the 18th comes an ominous note. Kean's performance of Jaffier was thought eccentric, and the audience expressed its disapproval; Kean very foolishly retorted; an incipient riot was brought to a close by putting out the lights. Fortunately it was Kean's last night of playing there.[42] The company with Kean as star opened the next week in Baltimore; Kean played brilliantly, and there was no disorder. *A New Way to Pay Old Debts* was his fourth play here, April 28; it brought in six hundred and ninety-six dollars, which was a good house.[43] It was the last time he played Sir Giles on his first visit to this country. Trouble was brewing.

Early in May, Kean wrote to the Boston manager, signifying his intention of playing there at the end of the month. Dickson replied, strongly advising him to do no such thing. The season was really over, a good many people out of town, and the theatre not patronized by those who remained. Confident in his powers to draw, Kean disregarded all this and opened in Boston on the 23rd of May in *Lear*; the house was fair. For *Venice Preserved*, the next night, it was slim. On the 25th, when Kean appeared to play Richard III, he was astonished to find only a few scattered spectators. Kean, much mortified, lost his head, refused to act, and then was too proud to change his mind. Meanwhile the house was filling up. When informed by the manager that Kean refused to appear, the audience expressed dissatisfaction, but a substitution was made and the play went on. Kean left early the next morning for New York.

Kean had been foolish and discourteous and deserved a rebuke; instead he was showered with abuse and hostility. The public de-

---

[41] Advertisement in the *New York Evening Post.*

[42] Durang, Chap. LXXI.

[43] James, p. 329 ("fine"—$696.75—the first performance of the play in Baltimore).

cided to be insulted, and the newspapers became virulent in re-crimination. Clapp quotes characteristic bits:[44]

ONE CENT REWARD

Run away . . . a stage-player, calling himself KEAN. He may be easily recognized by his misshapen trunk, his coxcomical cockney manners, and his bladder actions. His face is as white as his own froth, and his eyes are as dark as indigo. . . .

PETER PUBLIC

THE TWO MURDERS

When Cain the first foul murderer, as we're told,
His righteous brother slew in days of old,
God drove him forth and damned him with a stain,
That all might know the guilty reach again.

But modern Kean—that vagrant cockney wight
Who murders sense and nature every night,
Forestalls *his* doom, *runs* off—crack-pated elf,
Proves *fool* as well as knave, and *damns* himself.

Kean's apologies and explanations were of no avail; somewhat bewildered by American acrimony, he sailed for England, expressing to the last his admiration and respect for the public, and not without having erected at his own expense a monument to George Frederick Cooke in St. Paul's Churchyard.[45]

When Kean reappeared in America in 1825, his so-called insult to the American people was carefully played up in the cheap newspapers. He was not to think that Americans ever forgot injuries. More grevious still, the Cox scandal had blown its dirty way across the Atlantic; distorted and greatly exaggerated, it added to the feeling against him. *The New-York Mirror* of November 12, announcing Kean's first appearance, remarks gravely: "We hope there will not be a single *lady* present." The result was that on November 14 when he tried to act Richard III at the new Park, there was a disgraceful riot. The noise was bedlam, objects were thrown on the stage—Kean himself was struck with an orange—and the curtain dropped.

[44] Clapp, pp. 187-8.
[45] In February 1822 Tyrone Power wrote to William Wood at Philadelphia proposing an engagement in both tragedy and comedy; among the characters which he suggested was Sir Giles Overreach. As a matter of fact Power did not come over until 1833 and by that time of course was acting his Irish parts.

Fortunately the riot overreached itself. Most of the audience saw its folly, and when Kean published an apology and promised to conduct himself in exemplary fashion, succeeding performances in New York went off with but slight or no opposition, though women studiously avoided the theatre, judging not lest they be not judged. *A New Way to Pay Old Debts* was acted on November 21.[46] The engagement over, Kean proceeded directly to Albany, where at the South Pearl Street Theatre he was greeted with much applause. During this highly successful engagement he acted with Edwin Forrest, "a young man," as he said later, "who will rise to great eminence." On the 12th of December, Kean acted Sir Giles Overreach;[47] Forrest, playing second to him, probably acted Wellborn—would I knew definitely!

Encouraged by the diminution of hostility, the Boston Theatre now engaged Kean. But Boston was not New York and by no means Albany. On the 21st of December 1825, when he appeared as Richard, another disgraceful scene took place, this time much worse than any previous. Apologies were useless. Kean was not allowed to speak and was pelted from the stage; the mob, incited by the lower element, became excited, and the riot act was read twice to no avail. Conflict, terror, feverish attempts to escape from the mêlée. The theatre was damaged to the extent of eight hundred dollars, while Kean fled through an alley and with the help of some friends escaped the town. Those who will may read in detail a shabby page in the annals of the American theatre.[48]

In January Kean was playing at the Chestnut Street Theatre in Philadelphia. Some opposition was manifest—Wemyss and Wood differ as to how much[49]—but disorder was apparently suppressed and the engagement proceeded. *A New Way to Pay Old Debts* on the 25th brought in seven hundred and twenty dollars.[50] Back at the Park in February, Sir Giles on the 9th was followed eventually by a repetition of the character the 19th of May.[51] In between

46 Odell, Vol. III, p. 181.
47 Phelps, pp. 94-5.
48 Clapp, pp. 230-7.
49 Wemyss, pp. 98-9; Wood, pp. 309-10.
50 Hillebrand, p. 266; Wood, p. 310.
51 Odell, Vol. III, pp. 190, 195; advertisements in *The New-York American*.

Sir Giles visited Charleston for appearances on March 17 and 27.[52] Baltimore saw fit to follow Boston, and rioted when Kean appeared there early in June. Aided and abetted by Wemyss, he fled an angry mob and proceeded secretly to Philadelphia by steamboat. In the summer season at Philadelphia, Sir Giles was Kean's character on the 16th of June.[53]

During the remainder of summer, Kean rested for a while and then went to Canada. His first Canadian Sir Giles was given at Montreal on August 7, the second at Quebec on September 18.[54] During part of the latter engagement Indians were present whose profound admiration Kean reciprocated to the extent of becoming a member of their tribe and assuming the name Alanienouidet, upon whom Dr. Francis was invited to call when he reached New York, much to his astonishment and, after recognition, delight. So far as I know Kean's last performance of Sir Giles Overreach on this continent was the one mentioned above. His mental suffering had been followed by physical exhaustion, and rest was essential. Moreover his friend Stephen Price had taken over Drury Lane from the now bankrupt Elliston, and a return to England seemed much more advisable than his planned engagement with Caldwell at New Orleans. In December he made his last appearance in America and sailed away, after a period of storm and stress which he was never to forget.

Kean's acting on his second visit seems to have been, however, as effective as on his first. So Dr. Francis anyway, who ought to know: "His Sir Giles in New York abated not of the vehemence and terror that characterized it as I had witnessed it at Old Drury in London, in 1816. The sarcastic parts of this great drama yielded the richest opportunities for the display of his acting powers, and of an utterance most natural as the outpouring of a consummate villain."[55]

[52] Hillebrand's notes.

[53] Durang, Second Series, Chap. XXXI; Hillebrand, p. 270.

[54] Hawkins, Vol. II, p. 262; Hillebrand, pp. 272, 274. The Montreal *Herald* did not like Kean's Overreach, largely because it did not like the "inconsistencies and absurdities" of the play; at Quebec, Kean was supported by Mr. and Mrs. Barnes of the Park company.

[55] Francis, p. 229.

Kean can be said, I think, to have established Sir Giles in this country, to have been the first to make him feel at home here. I do not mean of course in any way to take from the achievements of the previous impersonators. Chalmers and Hodgkinson, Cooke, Bibby and Maywood all made friendly overtures, made evident something of the power of the man. But Chalmers and Hodgkinson presented Sir Giles only once; Bibby was too unimportant to be of much service; Maywood was more or less inadequate. Cooke of course had much more influence but apparently did not with all his ability succeed in making Sir Giles popular in America. With Kean, however, came the realization that Americans now had within their midst a character who could not be pushed away with the epithet "horrible," who, whether they would or no, was a moving force and must be recognized. They could despise the wretch, but they could no longer deny that he was a living being.

Something of this feeling is communicated in the essay from which I shall quote in conclusion, an essay which is certainly no masterpiece of writing but which pays tribute both to Edmund Kean and Sir Giles Overreach, and does so with understanding and appreciation. It was written by Isaac Harby, teacher, editor, and sometime dramatist of Charleston, South Carolina, and it forms a fitting conclusion to this section of Sir Giles's life:[56]

KEAN'S SIR GILES OVERREACH

Mr. Kean's performance of *Sir Giles Overreach,* has excited, as it deserved, universal admiration. It is one of those parts which, constructed upon the excellent design of the middle comedy, is never so far removed from common life as to lift the actor upon tragic stilts; nor so very familiar with our every day objects, as to lose ought of freshness or of vigour. A hard-hearted, worldly-minded and tyrannic villain, whose opinion of human nature is so

[56] *A Selection from the Miscellaneous Writings of the late Isaac Harby, Esq.,* arranged and published by Henry L. Pinckney and Abraham Moise, for the benefit of his family . . ., Charleston, 1829, pp. 280-3. I have corrected obvious misprints. See also the sensitive and discriminating essay on Kean's acting in America by Dana (*Poems and Prose Writings,* pp. 420-37); he particularly commends Kean's "domestic acting" in Act IV, scene i: "His manner at meeting Lovell, and through the conversation with him, the way in which he turns his chair, and leans upon it, were all as easy and natural as they could have been in real life, had Sir Giles been actually existing, and engaged, at that moment, in conversation in Lovell's room."

base, that he hesitates not to avow to those of nobler natures than himself, the very plans and structure of his rogueries, and even plumes himself upon the utter want of feeling, honesty or humanity. Such a character, it has been urged, to be consistent, should like Iago, at last —

> "Assume a virtue if he have it not."

But Massinger has given Sir Giles a strong spice of folly in one grand point: The devil, *Ambition*, prompts him to commit the most barbarous deeds, and to justify the means by the end. To the honourable triumphs of virtue he is insensible, he has no perceptive organs for any such ideas. The sentiment of the Poet—

> "Who noble ends by noble means obtains,
> Or, failing, smiles in exile; or in chains;
> Like good Aurelius let him reign, or bleed
> Like Socrates—that man is great indeed."

This sentiment, *Sir Giles* would snap his fingers at. But while the imp Ambition, lifts him above the ordinary and better feelings of man, another daemon, Vanity, frustrates all his schemes. *Vanity* betrays him into the exposure of his own character, and his glib tongue and self-sufficiency, and want of virtue, all united, are unable to contend against the principles of his daughter and the courage of her lover. He is outwitted by his tools, outcozened by his attorney, and lays the mesh that entraps him and his hopes. The character unfolds a striking *moral,* and the dramatist has woven the threads of it with such nice skill, that while *Sir Giles'* self-love prompts him to submit his daughter's "virgin modesty" to the rudest exposure, the same self-love would make him risk his life to revenge any insult that might be cast upon her. . . .

If we were asked what was the predominating feature in Mr. Kean's performance of this singular character, we should answer what few indeed have pronounced as the *characteristic* of his acting, but which (with one exception) we venture to say marked his performance throughout, viz: CHASTENESS—A clear, decided, almost rigid chasteness, marked the four first acts of the play. A discriminating conception of the author, and a still and steady expression of each thought and sentence. Had the fifth act been entirely omitted, we should pronounce Mr. Kean a great actor, from only the preceding scenes. 'Tis not in the glow of feeling, and the full tilt of passion, where the author partakes with the actor in the exciting causes of applause;—but 'tis in the busy and characteristic dialogue, in which the author is at the mercy of the actor, that we are to see the latter's triumphs in his art. The looks, the tones, the very postures of the worldly-minded father, gave emphasis and power to the whole, and the discrimination Mr. Kean displayed in his interview with Wellborn [Lord Lovell?], when he discloses Sir Giles' secret nature, were as worthy admiration, as the highest exhibition of passion in any succeeding scene.

We have said that chasteness was predominant throughout this fine piece of acting with but *one* exception. That exception, however, is problematical. To cooler and calmer spirits, the violence of the disappointed father, when displayed by *rending his clothes,* would appear as "tearing passion to tatters, to very rags"—not, indeed, to "split the *ears* of the groundlings," but to astonish their *eyes.* Less temperate spirits are, however, carried along in the tide of passion—and do not *feel* the outrage against propriety, until they are told of it. This is indeed a triumph of the *Ars Dramatica* —that an action which would have damned a score of players, was innocuous as to effect, in as great a scene as we have ever witnessed on the stage. The experiment is, however, dangerous. *Les extremes se touchent.* "From the sublime to the ridiculous is but a step." Napoleon has said it.

The discovery of the *blank* bond was another triumph of the art. The look of astonishment and horror, the incredulity of the sense of sight, struggling for a moment, then yielding to the appalling truth, the flash of conviction, which consumed rather than enlightened the brain, were all powerfully, beautifully expressed. The serpent which the sorcerer was about to uncage, had lost its poison—it lay inanimate and dead before him, and he stood like the son of Agenor, who gazes on the slain monster, and suddenly hears the preternatural voice:

> "Ille diu pavidus, *pariter cum mente colorem*
> *Perdiderat*; gelidoque, comae terrore rigebant."

CHAPTER VIII

FULL SUNLIGHT

THERE is no more trite and no more curiously truthful saying than the maxim that history repeats itself. The doctrine applies equally well to stage-history. In Great Britian *A New Way to Pay Old Debts* developed from revival to revival, from actor to actor, until Sir Giles Overreach burst forth in full magnificence in the person of Edmund Kean, who spread his characterization throughout the theatrical length and breadth of the land until the figure of the extortioner was famous and undying. In America the phenomenon proved similar. Cooke and Kean were over here too short a time to give Sir Giles a national reputation. That honor in this country goes to Junius Brutus Booth, who, from New York to San Francisco, from Boston to New Orleans, impersonated Massinger's villain for thirty years. If the most famous Sir Giles in Great Britain, judging both by geographical area and the ability of the actor's impersonations, was undoubtedly Edmund Kean, his counterpart in the United States, equally undoubtedly, was Junius Brutus Booth.

I have dealt at some length with Booth in England, and all that will be necessary here will be a brief recapitulation. Born in London in 1796, he made his début in 1813, and his first important success in 1816 when he substituted for Kean in Sir Giles Overreach. Subsequently he appeared in London at both the major theatres, gained some success, but was unfortunate in his negotiations with the managers and in his rivalry with Kean, with the result that he alienated both the public and the newspaper reviewers and never enjoyed the success his ability promised.

Booth came to the United States in 1821 in the schooner *Two Brothers,* which landed at Norfolk, Virginia, on the 30th of June, and his first engagement in America was under the management of Charles Gilfert at the Richmond Theatre. The characters of course can almost be guessed: Richard III on the 6th of July and then Lear, Sir Edward Mortimer, and Bertram. Other Southern engagements during the summer were followed at last by his first appearance at the Park Theatre, New York, on October 5 as the inevitable Richard. His New York engagement was a success though by no means an extraordinary one. Critics disagreed: some were warm in praise, others lukewarm; others still pointed out his resemblance to Kean, and to Kean's trick of walking through the level parts of the play in order to give more emphasis to the impassioned scenes.[1] His receipts at Baltimore were by no means extraordinary; and there was here the same violent enthusiasm on the one hand, and the same undervaluation on the other, but "with all his follies and attempts at singularity, this really fine actor was an object of interest to all who can appreciate genius and study."[2] Another southern tour followed, during which Booth decided to give up acting to become a lighthouse-keeper and actually made arrangements for the Cape Hatteras light. This is not the first strange action of Booth—nor the last; whether or not this is an example, there is no doubt that there was a strain of insanity in the man which occasionally found emergence. Needless to say, Booth was persuaded to continue his career on the stage.

It was on this southern tour that I find the first evidence of Booth's Sir Giles in America. A clipping in the Harvard Theatre Collection, dated Charleston, December 7, 1821, reads: "Mr. Booth continues to attract crowed houses. His success with the audience, in 'Sir Giles Overreach' on Wednesday evening [the 5th] was complete; indeed, the whole play (more particularly *Marall* by Mr. *Brown*) was performed with great spirit and effect." It is difficult to follow Sir Giles on this tour, and I cannot trace him specifically elsewhere until Booth's first engagement at New Orleans; he opened there on January 11, 1822, and Ludlow says Sir Giles was one of his parts.[3]

In May 1822 Booth made his début in Boston where, perhaps because of the hostility to Kean with whom he was so often compared, he was more vigorously and more unanimously applauded than heretofore. Booth's Sir Giles Overreach made *his* Boston début during this engagement, on the 10th, with marked success. The newspapers seem not to have reviewed the performance, so we

[1] Odell, Vol. III, pp. 10-13.
[2] Wood, p. 273.
[3] Ludlow, pp. 229-30.

shall have to wait until we get to New York for first-hand information. May I comment here that there are without doubt a great many performances of *A New Way to Pay Old Debts* with Booth as Overreach not here recorded? The history of Booth in America lies in playbills and newspapers which are scattered far and wide. There is no life of him which even pretends to record his multifarious performances. To find where he was at such and such a time, or at what time he was at such and such a place is a perplexing task and not always capable of resolution. Let him who differs try his hand.

In the summer of 1822 Booth bought the farm near Baltimore about which Mrs. Clarke is so descriptive. Here, she says, was "his constant resort when free from the excitement of his profession." It is not surprising therefore to find him playing Sir Giles at Baltimore on October 30; in spite of "fair" weather, the receipts were only two hundred and seven dollars.[4] On February 17, 1823, Booth made his first appearance at the new Chestnut Street Theatre in Philadelphia, having driven there perhaps in his carryall, drawn by "Captain" and "Peacock." *A New Way to Pay Old Debts* was the play on February 21. The weather was "dull" and the receipts three hundred dollars and twenty-five cents.[5] A playbill fortunately contributes the cast:

Sir Giles Overreach	Booth
Wellborn	H. Wallack
Lord Lovell	Wheatley
Marrall	Burke
Justice Greedy	Jefferson
Allworth	Darley
Watchall	J. Jefferson
Lady Allworth	Mrs. Jefferson
Margaret	Mrs. H. Wallack

What would the Philadelphia company be without the Jeffersons and Wallacks? The receipts for this engagement were low, however, much less than either Cooper or Mathews drew. Booth apparently had not yet come into his own. Sir Giles went to Washington for a performance on July 26.[6]

4 James, p. 371.
5 *ibid.*, p. 382.
6 *ibid.*, p. 395.

In September 1823, Booth was again at the Park, where he presented Sir Giles for the first time in New York on the 12th. *The Albion* makes the odious comparison with Kean:[7] "Of this performance we hardly know how to speak. The truth is, that it is dangerous for any actor to attempt the character where Kean is known in it; his mighty powers embodied in it so much genius, and delineated it with such a masterly hand, that we fear all his successors exhibit too broadly the difference between an original and a copyist." Indeed the papers say over and over again: this is not Kean, but evidently a man of genius. Kean was apparently too close in remembrance for Booth yet to be a favorite. Much as Booth admired Kean, however, he thought the comparison unjust:[8] "I will yield Othello to him but neither Richard nor Sir Giles." On the above occasion the cast on the playbill was as follows:

Sir Giles Overreach .... Booth
Wellborn .... Clarke
Lord Lovell .... Woodhull
Marrall .... Watkinson
Justice Greedy .... Kent
Allworth .... Richings
Lady Allworth .... Mrs. Stevenson
Margaret .... Miss Johnson

Booth also played Sir Giles at the Chestnut Theatre, Philadelphia, on December 20, 1823, with the cast as of February 21 except Lady Allworth by Mrs. Anderson.

When Booth returned to the Park as Sir Giles on March 26, 1824, we find at last the first revealing criticism, and the picture it conveys is enthusiastically painted. I quote from *The New-York Mirror* of April 3, which, after commenting unfavorably on his Richard, proceeds as follows:

> The other evening we went to see his *Sir Giles Overreach*, and without exaggeration, we were actually astonished. The part was sustained with masterly genius; and when Sir Giles was borne out, and even after the first glow of our feelings had departed, we felt

[7] Odell, Vol. III, pp. 89-90; *Albion* of September 13.
[8] Winter, *Shadows of the Stage* (First Series), p. 75. The remark is general and does not refer to the above performance or criticism. As to the source of the statement, I suspect Winter got it from Edwin Booth.

no hesitation in saying that we never saw better acting. We have felt some exquisitely tender tone of Kean's voice go straight to the heart—we have wept over the pathos of Conway, and warmly admired the classic elegance of his style, and the nobleness of his princely figure—we have started at the impressive vehemence of Cooper's anger—but we solemnly declare, that no acting ever made more impression on us—more completely wrought up our feelings, and made our blood curdle with horror, than the *Sir Giles Overreach* of Mr. Booth.

There was spirit throughout the piece, though at the beginning we saw not the strong genius that could so effectually "call his slumbering passion into play."

Mr. Booth is not taller than Mr. Kean—his figure, as far as we could judge of it in his dramatic dress, is good, and his face is almost the handsomest we ever saw ; a clear, unclouded forehead—eye-brows regularly arched—a Grecian nose—lips well formed, and calculated to express the feelings—large dark eyes, rich with the finest expression, combined in Mr. Booth's face, present a countenance formed to display the most delicate shades of passion.

His advice to his daughter, when he is urging her to espouse the wealthy lord, whom she has never seen, and become "Right Honourable," was given with excellent conception; and the cold-blooded and brutal command of heartless ambition, "Be not coy; and if perchance he wish to kiss you—*kiss close*," never came from any lip more fraught with expression, and pregnant with meaning.

The performance of the scene of his harsh dialogue with his daughter, where he listens to her fear "that after all her husband will forsake her," was admirable; and the proud answer to her suggestion, "Forsake thee!—Do I wear a sword for fashion? or is this arm shrunk up," &c., was spoken with an impatient fury, blended with consciousness of power, as well as will, to resent such an insult. The transitions too of his manner from high altercation with his daughter, to deep obeisance and servility to the lord, were very fine: and the manner of his pronouncing the word "re-mem-ber" to the trembling girl—the altering of his voice—the different appearance of his lip, from the easy and apparently affectionate smile, to the threatening position of anxious care—but most of all the change of his eye, which before rested with pleasure on his noble guest—but upon his departure, fixed on his daughter such an expressive stare—the large dark eye dilating its determined gaze upon her with so much language in the look, that the spirit of the timid girl seemed scathed by its lightning into hopeless inaction.

But all this is nothing to the last scene; the scene where the intrigues of the ambitious hypocrite return upon his own head, and drive him to madness. When he enters, after having caught a whisper of the report that his daughter had united herself to a private gentleman, and thus blasted all his glorious hopes of becoming "Right Honourable," his demeanor was fine. Every feeling of diffidence—every consideration of the audience, or the stage—every idea that would interrupt the torrent of his passion, seemed to have been long ago swept away—fury breathed in every word—deep hatred and vengeance flashed from his eye— every step and motion were but subservient to his burning anger —insults were heaped upon him—he heard the scoffs of his nephew—the jeers of the wife, and he seemed often to pause in his delirious restlessness, look around like a baited lion upon his enemies—to measure, with fiery eye, the distance between—and to choose which one he should first tear in pieces. The theatre rung with the plaudits of a fashionable audience, at these successive flashes of genius; but a deeper homage was paid to the succeeding.

The daughter enters with her husband—the holy man avers that they are married—*Sir Giles* finds every avenue to future greatness shut against him—the deed presents but a page of useless blank paper—his proud and angry spirit writhes under the lash of his nephew's satire—one single hope sheds a faint gleam upon him; one single way by which he may preserve his stolen wealth, and thus the power of revenge; it lies with his steward—he draws him forward, and trembling with feverish anxiety, condescends to sue in the most servile terms to his domestic to lend his testimony and rescue him from despair. Hope, for a moment, beams from his eyes, and the deep and heavy current of his passion, for an instant, ceases to flow; 'tis but for an instant—his servant repulses him with scoffs, and contempt, and exultation in his sorrow: then comes the increased fury—then bursts forth the whole extent of his anger—he turns to bathe his hands in blood— he strives to slay his daughter—he is mad with the desire to grasp the throat of his valet, and tear him to atoms—his voice becomes choked with rage until his exhausted strength gives way, and he faints; he is raised up, and as he revives, the death-sweat stands in drops upon his pale face—the colour came and went, and left it of an ashy and death-like paleness; one would have supposed

JUNIUS BRUTUS BOOTH as SIR GILES OVERREACH,
from a water-color by W. Heath

repentance and returning affection, was the cause of his stretching forth his arms towards his trembling daughter—she accordingly approached to embrace him in his dying moments—but, as she drew near, with a hellish intent to cool his burning vengeance in her blood, he clutches at her throat; there was something so fiend-like—so diabolical in the motion, and Mr. Booth grasped at her with a spring so like some hungry tiger springing on his prey, that approbation lost its speech—the hand that was stretched forth to place the laurel on the brow of genius, dropped it in amazement, and shrunk terrified away; the convulsive start of many of the audience, and the emotion that frightened the blood from almost every cheek, were the symptoms that pervaded the house, until the corpse of the demon was borne off amidst loud and long acclamations.

For this extended article we are indebted to George P. Morris, who with Samuel Woodworth edited *The New-York Mirror,* and only my readers perhaps can realize how important it is in its detailed depiction of the stage-business used and in the elaboration with which Booth is described in the part. In our enumeration of names and dates and our search for first-hand testimony it is not often that we find this early a gem so precious. Moreover, it is immensely valuable in our history of the development of Booth in that, as Odell points out, it is "about the first really cordial and unalloyed approval . . . of the since so celebrated father of Edwin Booth." We hope that this critical enthusiasm drew a large audience for Mr. Booth when he repeated the character at the Park on May 28, 1824.[9] Meanwhile he had played Sir Giles at the Arch Street Theatre, Philadelphia, on April 7 for the benefit of Burke, who played Marrall. The bill shows the rest as follows:

Wellborn	Wemyss
Lord Lovell	Wheatley
Justice Greedy	Jefferson
Allworth	Darley
Lady Allworth	Mrs. Battersby
Margaret	Mrs. Wallack

About a year later Booth made his début at the South Pearl Street Theatre, Albany, then managed by Charles Gilfert under whom he had first acted in this country. Sir Giles Overreach was

[9] Odell, Vol. III, pp. 105, 108; Ireland, Vol. I, p. 429.

his character on May 23, 1825, a part says Phelps,[10] the source of my statement, in which "he was unrivalled for near a quarter of a century." Soon after he returned to England for a Drury Lane engagement, followed by a provincial and foreign tour. Booth's daughter says he returned from England in 1827, but the date is wrong for he played in *A New Way to Pay Old Debts* at the Chatham Garden Theatre in New York, now rival of the Park, on November 6, 1826, for his benefit.[11] Moreover, he was playing Sir Giles on Christmas Day of the same year at the South Pearl Street Theatre in Albany.[12]

Henry Placide's copy of *A New Way to Pay Old Debts* in the Harvard Theatre Collection[13] lists a production at Philadelphia in 1827. This, I strongly suspect, was in late January or February of that year at the Chestnut Street Theatre, but I cannot be more precise. Anyhow the cast is a Chestnut Street cast:

Sir Giles Overreach	Booth
Wellborn	Wemyss
Lord Lovell	Wheatley
Marrall	Cowell
Justice Greedy	Jefferson
Allworth	Forrest
Taylor	Jefferson, Jr.
Lady Allworth	Mrs. Anderson
Margaret	Mrs. Hilson

A fine list even if the Forrest is not Edwin. Will my readers recognize Miss Johnson transformed into Mrs. Hilson, whose portrait in the character of Margaret forms the frontispiece to this edition? If my guess is correct, there were two performances here, for a playbill of February 14, 1827, enumerates the same players, except that Mrs. Darley was the Margaret.

There was no performance of *A New Way to Pay Old Debts* at the Park in March of 1827 as recorded by Mrs. Clarke; she

---

10 *Players of a Century*, pp. 70, 73.

11 *Elder and Younger Booth*, p. 74; Odell, Vol. III, p. 280.

12 Phelps, p. 106.

13 Lopez and Wemyss (eds.), Philadelphia, 1827. There is also a prompt-copy of this edition in the New York Public Library, signed successively H. Murdock, James Stark, George Becks (1885).

has confused the year with 1824.[14] Where Booth really was I
know not; in September he was in Philadelphia, in November in
Nashville, early in 1828 at the Camp Street Theatre in New Orleans, temporarily a stage-manager under Caldwell.

On the evening of January 18, Booth played Sir Giles, and
Harvard comes to the rescue with a rare playbill, though the cast
itself is not particularly rare. Note Sol Smith, however, as
Furnace:

Sir Giles Overreach	Booth
Wellborn	Anderson
Lord Lovell	Jones
Marrall	Gray
Justice Greedy	Russell
Allworth	Lear
Furnace	S. Smith
Lady Allworth	Mrs. Hartwig
Margaret	Mrs. Rowe

It is not without considerable interest that on the 19th of February Booth, an astounding linguist, acted Oreste in Racine's *An-
dromaque* in French at the Théâtre D'Orléans, to the rapture of
his audience.[15] Engagements at Natchez, St. Louis, Nashville,
and Cincinnati followed. Indeed it was not until June of 1828 that
he was again at the Park. The 21st and 24th were Sir Giles's
dates, Mrs. Hill as Lady Allworth, and the recurrent Mrs. Hilson as Margaret.[16]

On September 23, Booth again played Sir Giles in Boston, the
first since the spring of 1822. This time, however, he was not at
Federal Street, but at the new Tremont Theatre of which he had
taken the stage-managership.[17] A Harvard clipping obliges with
a partial cast:

[14] *Elder and Younger Booth,* p. 75. She has erred through a misleading passage
in James T. Vail's anonymous book, *The Actor,* p. 74. This book, by the way, is
not to be trusted; it is grossly inaccurate. Since Mrs. Clarke's books are tragi-
cally incomplete, the life of J. B. Booth is yet to be written.

[15] Ludlow, pp. 229-30, says the performance was in English (*The Distressed
Mother*) in 1822, but Mrs. Clarke, p. 77, prints the playbill.

[16] Odell, Vol. III, pp. 323-4.

[17] Clapp, p. 263; Harvard Boston list.

Sir Giles Overreach .... Booth
Wellborn .... Archer
Marrall .... Cowell
Justice Greedy .... Jones
Lady Allworth .... Miss Hamilton
Margaret .... Mrs. Cowell

And another clipping—from the *Courier*—obligingly reviews:

On Tuesday evening, Mr. Booth made his second appearance—
[his first was as the inevitable Richard]—in the part of Sir Giles
Overreach. It is almost unnecessary to say, that he "played his
part"; his correct reading, his knowledge of stage effect, and his
whole qualifications for an actor were never displayed with more
judgement than upon this occasion. He was the character he
represented; the avaricious, hard-hearted and cruel Sir Giles,
with but one deity—Plutus, and one earthly desire towards which
all his words and deeds tended, to make his daughter "right-
honourable." During the quarrel with Wellborn, and when he
fancied his triumph was complete over his rebellious nephew,
his face spoke a volume; rage and revenge were joined with a
sneer, which the devil himself might have envied, and before which
the stoutest heart might have quailed with good reason. But when
he discovered the deed to be nothing but a blank scroll of parchment, when he endeavored to wheedle the villainous Marall to
swear for his old master, we almost pitied the old man's sufferings; the broken-hearted tone of his voice, and the inward agony
shown in the writhings of his whole frame, would have disarmed
any judges but those by whom he was surrounded. With the
exception of some little rant which Mr. Booth was hurried into
by the excess of his feelings, the remainder of this scene could
not have been played more in conformity with our conceptions
of the part. When he discovered the failure of all his schemes,
the loss of his nephew's lands, the double-dealing of his servant,
and worse than all the rest, his last hope blasted in the deceit
practised by his daughter,—and that she was not "honourable"—
the change of the old man from rage to idiocy, the violent struggles
of the maniac, and his dropping senseless in the arms of his attendants—all proclaimed the triumph of his feelings over his reason;
the miser and the father, the villain, and the old man, all the
leading passions of his nature as shown in the last scene of the
play, were sufficient to establish the fame of Mr. Booth as a
great actor—that is, one who follows nature.

And by this time, note, not nature as interpreted by Kean. No wonder that the advertisement of October 28 remarks: "At the general request of the public to witness MR. BOOTH's performance of *Sir Giles Overreach,* before his departure for the South, the Play of *A New Way to Pay Old Debts,* will be repeated for positively the last time, this evening."[18] The cast of major parts was the same as on September 23 except Justice Greedy by Mr. Clarke.

Was New York the South or just on the way? At any rate, Booth was Overreach at the Bowery Theatre, the second one (the first having been burnt to the ground in May), on November 3,[19] perhaps to help out the not too successful Gilfert, who was now manager there. To answer my own question, Booth *did* go farther south, as scattered New Orleans bills at Harvard show— doubtless his usual southern and Mississippi circuit. He did not leave the Camp Street Theatre until May, and when we next catch a glimpse of him, *via* a playbill, he is back at the Tremont in Boston, Sir Giles on June 26, 1829. I lose him again until September 25, when Sir Giles greeted the audience at the Walnut Street Theatre, Philadelphia. We have not seen this cast before:[20]

Sir Giles Overreach	Booth (bt.)
Wellborn	Langton
Lord Lovell	Porter
Marrall	W. Chapman
Justice Greedy	Jefferson
Allworth	Ball
Lady Allworth	Mrs. Greene
Margaret	Miss Chapman

On the 25th of the next month, Sir Giles at the Tremont again,[21] the last I find for the year 1829. One wonders whether to stop and tell anecdotes or hurry over this compilation of names and dates; suffice it to say that during the engagement Booth went temporarily insane.[22] During the early months of 1830 Booth was mostly in Philadelphia, first at the Chestnut Street Theatre, later at the

[18] Not the 26th as given by Cruickshank (Edition), p. 135.
[19] Odell, Vol. III, p. 406.
[20] Playbill.
[21] Harvard Boston list.
[22] Clapp, pp. 276-9.

Walnut Street. At the first Booth was to have played Massinger on January 4, but, as already noted, he was "taken in a crazy fit," and Maywood substituted. At the second I find the next Sir Giles on my list—blame Booth, not me—June 1. The cast has changed somewhat since the previous season, so completeness urges me to copy the playbill, even if Boredom shrieks "No!":

Sir Giles Overreach .... Booth
Wellborn .... Flynn
Lord Lovell .... Chapman
Marrall .... W. Chapman
Justice Greedy .... Sefton
Allworth .... Porter
Lady Allworth .... Miss Chapman
Margaret .... Mrs. Flynn

Early in September Booth was playing at the Bowery in opposition to Charles Kean, who was making his début at the Park. Booth's Sir Giles on the 2nd, for example, came the night before Kean's, bringing up invidious comparisons.

April 15, 1831, the Tremont Theatre, Boston, Sir Giles Overreach by Booth, was followed by an engagement at the Bowery where *A New Way to Pay Old Debts* was the play on May 7; parts of the play were repeated on June 27 for the benefit of Cooper, whose attraction was now waning.[23] During the summer and fall Booth seems to have acted in Philadelphia, Annapolis, and Baltimore, part of the time exhibiting mental aberration and strange humor, if tales be true. He is taken to task by the critic of the *Mirror* for his Sir Giles at the Bowery on August 27:

> . . . Mr. Booth's performance of Sir Giles Overreach was a spiritless affair; noisy where it should have been subdued—tame where it should have been passionate—until the last act, wherein he several times flashed with a fine talent, which redeemed his character for the evening. It is these sudden bursts of excellence that help Mr. Booth through his part. He shuffles along most of it with unpardonable carelessness. He appears quite satisfied with a few touches sprinkled over his personation, and rather more numerous towards the conclusion. He resembles an artist who finishes a face here, and an arm there—and leaves all the groups

23 Playbills, and Odell, Vol. III, pp. 524, 526.

and landscape in the background, rudely sketched. The whole
scene with the lord—"and though I do contemn report"—and the
emphatic "kiss close," were entirely without weight. Nothing
could be finer than his entrance after having challenged his foe,
and indeed numerous passages in the whole scene. . . .

After reading the whole review, in the latter part of which the
critic is satiric about old Cooper, we can impute something to
carping fault-finding, though there is no doubt, I think, that
Booth underplayed the early parts of the drama; this is no new
tale. Odell gives Booth's support for this performance "now quite
ordinary"—Phillips, Stevenson, George Jones, Mrs. Stevenson,
Miss Waring.[24] After a performance at the Walnut Street Theatre, Philadelphia, on September 30, to two hundred and thirty
dollars, we conclude the year at the Tremont with Sir Giles stalk-
ing the boards on the 12th and 17th of December.[25]

The United States Gazette shows that Booth appeared in three
presentations of *A New Way to Pay Old Debts* in Philadelphia
in 1832.[26] The first of these came on March 21 at the Chestnut
Street Theatre; the other two on April 26 and June 29 at the Walnut Street Theatre. Philadelphia, for this season at least, took to Sir
Giles better than New York. There was only one performance in
the latter city, on November 21 at that house of melodrama, the
Bowery.[27] However, on the 12th of January, 1833, the Bowery
company—Booth seems to have had an extended contract with
Hamblin—traded houses for one night with the Italian singers
at the Richmond Hill Theatre, and Sir Giles stormed his way
through *A New Way to Pay Old Debts* at the little west-side
house for the first time.[28]

I despair of following Booth's wanderings through 1834, nor
is it for our purpose entirely necessary. Philadelphia, New York,
and Boston are fortunately not so difficult. In the first city,
Booth's Sir Giles was at the Walnut Street Theatre on April 9;
the receipts were two hundred and fifty dollars.[29] We return from

[24] Odell, Vol. III, pp. 561-2.
[25] James, p. 493; Harvard Boston list.
[26] James, pp. 513, 515, 519, does not name the star.
[27] Odell, Vol. III, p. 633.
[28] *ibid.*, Vol. III, p. 646.
[29] James, p. 598.

there to the now familiar Bowery, where the character was of
course repeated and in which the *Mirror* of May 3 now admits
Booth "is unapproached by any living actor."[30] A stand at the
Tremont, Boston, Overreach on October 23, concludes the year
as far as we are concerned.[31]

Vail says that Booth was in Louisville in March 1835 and that
Sir Giles was one of his characters there,[32] but inasmuch as that
author treats dates with downright abandon, the reference is
suspect from the beginning, especially since Booth seems to have
been in Philadelphia a good part of the spring. His Sir Giles
appeared at the Chestnut Street Theatre there on June 29 for the
benefit of Miss E. Riddle who presented Margaret. Others in the
cast, according to the bill, were:

Wellborn .... Wood
Lord Lovell .... Walstein
Marrall .... Burton
Justice Greedy .... Faulkner
Lady Allworth .... Mrs. Maywood

All in all, what with Wood and Burton, some interesting names!
In July Booth was playing the part again at the Bowery, July 11,
after an interval repeated on the 5th of November:[33]

Sir Giles Overreach .... Booth
Wellborn .... Pickering
Lord Lovell .... Woodhull
Marrall .... Flynn
Justice Greedy .... Gates
Allworth .... Jackson
Lady Allworth .... Mrs. Herring
Margaret .... Miss Woodhull

Meanwhile there had been a performance at the Walnut Street
Theatre on August 24.[34]

---

[30] Odell, Vol. III, p. 684.
[31] Harvard Boston list.
[32] Vail, p. 124.
[33] Odell, Vol. IV, pp. 36, 49, and playbill.
[34] Wilson, p. 140.

Odell says Booth acted Iago on November 9;[35] as a matter of fact the performance was never given. The bill of November 14 is headed by the following—I reduce *some* capitals—:

Mr. Booth's APOLOGY to the New-York Public!!
TO THE PUBLIC!!!

Allow me to apologise, for the non-fulfilment of my engagement with Mr. Hamblin to appear before you on Monday Evening last, at the Bowery Theatre. The excuse I have to offer, is, a serious visitation, affecting and enfeebling my nerves, and a long deprivation of sleep, acting on a body debilitated by previous illness, and a mind disordered by domestic affliction, occasioning a partial derangement. Should I again be permitted to appear before you, it will be an additional indulgence, which a most sensitive heart will ever acknowledge and appreciate, but should I have forfeited all charity and forgiveness, by that sad and unconscious act, I must abide by the fatal result—yet if I am again restored to public favor, and to the kind friendship of Mr. Hamblin, whose forgiveness for my apparent wanton conduct, I most sincerely crave, and which I have ever experienced, I trust that my future course will be such as will atone for past digressions—but if on my appearance, I find by your reception that I have offended beyond forgiveness, I will immediately withdraw from that stage, where I have ever been treated, both by the Public and the Manager, with kindness and liberality.

J. B. BOOTH
NOTICE

In consequence of Mr. Booth having written the above apology to the Public, and having been solicited by a number of citizens, requesting me to allow him an opportunity of ascertaining whether his fault has been forgiven, I have been induced to forego the resolution I expressed on Monday last, from the stage, and to announce him for the character of

Sir Giles Overreach

this (Saturday) Evening, not however holding myself responsible any further, than at all times to return the price of admission, should This Gentleman be absent from any cause whatever.

THOMAS S. HAMBLIN

[35] Odell, Vol. IV, p. 74.

I cannot believe that Booth wrote the grovelling apology printed above; Vail as a matter of fact says it was by Booth's old friend and associate, stage-manager Flynn. It seems that on the afternoon of the 9th, Hamblin gave a dinner party at which Booth drank rather freely, though apparently he was none the worse for wear. Upon their adjournment to the theatre, Booth proceeded to make up Hamblin as Othello, forgetting that he himself was to play Iago. Reminded of the fact, he took Flynn aside, told him that he had better get another Iago, and disappeared through the stage-door. An apology from the stage was necessary, and Flynn explained graphically how Booth was pursued to the Battery where he "suddenly disappeared, and it is feared, drowned himself." As a result about three hundred dollars left the theatre, though the most part of the audience stayed to hear the substitute. After the performance, Flynn went in search of Booth and found him mounted on a table at a public house, haranguing a hundred and fifty people about the wants and distresses of the inhabitants of Texas and endeavoring to obtain volunteers to emigrate thither.

According to Vail, when Booth appeared as Sir Giles on the 14th, instead of being hissed off the stage as was anticipated, "he never received a more cordial reception, the audience reiterating cheer upon cheer, until the applause became almost deafening." Booth's love for the Bowery audience was apparently returned in kind, and the king could do no wrong. How much this strange story has taken rise in Vail's imagination, I shall not attempt to explain, but it accounts, somewhat luridly, for the facts stated in the playbill. The cast at any rate we can be sure of; it was identical with that of November 5.[36]

November 26 and 28, 1835, seem to have been notable occasions at the Walnut Street Theatre in Philadelphia. Booth and Jim Crow Rice both appeared, the first as Sir Giles Overreach, the latter in a piece called *Oh! Hush!*. Wemyss reports the receipts for the second night as eight hundred and seventy-five dollars, which certainly was nothing to complain about.[37] On the

[36] Vail, pp. 106-11.
[37] Wilson, p. 145; Wemyss, p. 264, who misprints 1836; in November 1836, Booth was abroad.

12th of January 1836, Booth commenced at the same theatre a farewell engagement prior to a visit to England, "And a brilliant one it was—Hamlet, Sir Giles Overreach, Sir Edward Mortimer, Pescara, Octavian, Othello, and Richard III. This last was played twice to eight hundred dollar houses and repeated by request. Such is the hold this wonderful man possesses over the minds of his audience, and such was the estimation of his talents during this engagement."[38]

Booth's next appearance as Sir Giles was at the somewhat equestrian Lion Theatre in Boston, which had sprung into being in January 1836, a house of a somewhat checkered history. Booth opened a short engagement there, May 16, with the leading character of *A New Way to Pay Old Debts*. It was a poor company and the partial cast dug from the *Daily Advertiser* is almost unnecessary; it shows Blaike as Wellborn, J. S. Jones as Marrall, Crane as Allworth, and Mrs. Anderson as Margaret. A performance ten days later, however, at another Lion Theatre, this time in Providence, is worth considering. Booth was the Sir Giles of course, Mrs. Anderson the Margaret, David Ingersoll the Wellborn, and George F. Browne, not yet of Browne's Chop House, the Tapwell. A gentleman by the name of Mr. Dee played the small part of Parson Willdo; the actor of that character will some day be a famous Sir Giles himself, but not under the assumed name of Dee, in reality only the initial of his real name, Edward Loomis Davenport.[39] How curiously *A New Way to Pay Old Debts* ties up with Providence, Rhode Island, and becomes consequential: the last performance of Cooke, the first of Davenport. And at Davenport's début, the Sir Giles was Booth who had made his first success in the same play. The distance between Providence and Philip Massinger is not so great, though the dramatist never heard of the city. Who would have said they had anything to do with each other?

At about this period of his life, Booth's mental aberrations began to increase in frequency and singularity, but they seem not to have interfered with his power as an actor to the last; indeed Mrs. Clarke comments on the proximity of genius and insanity. Mad or

[38] Wemyss, p. 265.
[39] See below, p. 281.

sane, Booth continued to play Sir Giles with devastating power. On
the 21st of September, 1836, a bill shows that he played the part
on the new stage of the National Theatre, Boston, the Warren re-
built. A performance at the little Franklin Theatre, New York, on
October 13, Froth by Miss E. Anderson, finishes the year for us.[40]
What a penchant Booth seems to have had for new theatres!
Shortly thereafter Booth sailed for Europe, and we have an interim
for breath.

Back in this country again, Booth returned to his favorite
Bowery Theatre where Sir Giles Overreach was impersonated on
August 30, 1837. Hield was Wellborn, Matthews played Lovell,
and Lady Allworth was represented by Mrs. Hield.[41] The critic in
the October number of the *Knickerbocker Magazine* never saw the
representation of Sir Giles excelled. It "was *masterly,* beyond any
previous effort of the actor. The interest was so intense, during the
last scene, that a play-bill, falling from some 'rapt god' in the gallery eddied *audibly* down into the pit, amid the 'shuddering stillness'
which the great power of the artist had created, even in a theatre
never remarkable for silence. It was emphatically the triumph of
mind over matter." The Hields unfortunately did not fare so well.
Mr. Hield especially "was beneath criticism. He evidently never
studied the character," and depended on "rant and fustian. Surely
this course, on the part of one in whose *professional* countenance
inanity seems to contend with disgrace, and whose gestures and
actions are not unlike those of a galvanized baboon, is very unwise.
Mrs. Hield has great energy of action, but unfortunately the
unpardonable fault of emulating her husband in over-doing everything. The features of her expressive but plain face, owing to this
cause, seem to be marked by a secret forty-horse power." If such
was Booth's support, and such his effect, the adjective "masterly"
cannot be gainsaid. C. R. Thorne we hope was better than Hield
when he acted Wellborn to Booth's Sir Giles at the Olympic on
November 27—another new theatre, note, invaded by Massinger's
villain, one would think out of place in this "veritable little drawing-room, quite the handsomest playhouse in America."[42]

[40] Odell, Vol. IV, p. 152.
[41] *ibid.,* Vol. IV, p. 231.
[42] *ibid.,* Vol. IV, pp. 246, 250.

After an engagement at the National Theatre, Washington, with Sir Giles on January 18, 1838,—I thank a Harvard clipping —Booth returned to New York, arrived there on the 18th of February to play again at the Bowery, but was astonished to find no theatre. The scene of many of his histrionic triumphs had burnt to the ground earlier in the day. Booth consequently shifted over to J. W. Wallack's management at the National Theatre, where Massinger's play was acted on the 22nd.[43] This theatre, late the Italian Opera House, was conducted with careful attention to detail, and became a serious rival to the Park. I have no doubt that the production of *A New Way to Pay Old Debts* left no openings for carping critics.

Our next paragraph must chronicle three strangely diverse things, Booth's attempted suicide, the breaking of his nose, and a performance of *A New Way to Pay Old Debts* at Charleston, not one of the regular havens of the play. On the voyage down, Booth seemed depressed, talked of Conway who had taken his life by intentional drowning, committed various strange and eccentric extravagances. As they neared Charleston, Booth came hurriedly on deck, said that he had a message for Conway, and jumped overboard. When rescued with some difficulty, he seemed to be entirely sane and remarked to Tom Flynn who was in the boat, "I say, Tom, look out! You're a heavy man,—be steady; if the boat upsets, we'll all be drowned." So Mrs. Clarke, at any rate, though of the nose incident she is skeptical of the story as Vail tells it. It seems that after arriving in Charleston Booth and Flynn repaired to the New Theatre, and acted Sir Giles and Marrall to a crowded house, whence they returned to the hotel. During the night, Booth, again under a spell of temporary derangement, attacked Flynn and during the scuffle had his nose broken, a terrible disaster for Booth as actor since it permanently marred his noble profile and for a while at least rendered toneless the subtle music of his voice.[44]

Just when the events chronicled in the preceding paragraph happened I do not know. All Booth's biographers are maddening about dates; time apparently did not exist for them. I suspect, however, that it was after August 29, 1838, when Booth played Sir

[43] Odell, Vol. IV, p. 223.
[44] *Elder and Younger Booth*, p. 97; Vail, pp. 142-3.

Giles at the Olympic,[45] and before his next visit to New York,
which he seems to have avoided in 1839, perhaps afraid of his reception with some of his old power gone.[46] In fact in 1839 Booth
seems to have stuck, when he was acting, pretty closely to the
southern circuit. I find two Sir Giles's, both in New Orleans: the
first at the St. Charles Theatre on February 6,[47] the second at the
Camp Street Theatre on March 22.

It is a year later when I find Booth in New York again, this time
at the Chatham, the New Chatham now under the management of
Charles R. Thorne, who perhaps repeated his Wellborn to Booth's
Sir Giles on March 25, 1840.[48] On April 15 and 21, Sir Giles
walked the boards of the National Theatre, Boston:[49]

Sir Giles Overreach .... Booth
Wellborn .... Jones
Lord Lovell .... Marshall
Marrall .... Hunt
Justice Greedy .... Spear
Allworth .... Leman
Lady Allworth .... Mrs. Cantor
Margaret .... Mrs. Cramer

Both Walter Leman and George G. Spear also played Sir Giles at
one time or another, so that there are really three in the above cast.
Back at the Chatham again, Booth repeated the part on July 9
and November 2.[50] *The Spirit of the Times* of July 11 remarks
that "the only great houses are the nights when Booth plays."
Booth seems to have borne no grudge against Flynn for his broken
nose; at any rate he played Sir Giles for Flynn's benefit at the Arch

[45] Odell, Vol. IV, p. 254.
[46] It is only fair to say, however, that a clipping in the Harvard Theatre Collection dates the nose incident in 1837, whereas Mrs. Clarke (p. 97) and Vail (pp.
141-3) put it subsequent to the burning of the Bowery, and the latter "at the
termination of this engagement at the National Theatre." In view of the scarcity
and disparity of the evidence, it seems to me profitless to waste further time at
an attempt to be more precise. Moreover, much as the incident affected Booth's
career as actor, the exact date makes no particular difference. He who wishes
may go to the trouble of searching the Charleston newspapers.
[47] I am indebted to Miss Lucile Gafford, who has been working on the stage-
history of New Orleans, for this and other references.
[48] Odell, Vol. IV, p. 385.
[49] Harvard Boston list, and playbill.
[50] Odell, Vol. IV, pp. 390, 482.

Street Theatre, Philadelphia, on December 16. The cast is from a bill:

Sir Giles Overreach	Booth
Wellborn	Crane
Lord Lovell	Mills
Marrall	Lewis
Justice Greedy	Collins
Allworth	Vanstavoren
Lady Allworth	Mrs. Cantor
Margaret	Mrs. Preston

Booth's single performance of *A New Way to Pay Old Debts* in the following year was again at the Chatham, on July 8, Booth and Massinger mingling with melodrama and Jim Crow Rice.[51]

"During the last ten years of his life the elder Booth," says Mrs. Clarke,[52] "passed a considerable portion of his time in the midst of his family, occasionally making professional tours with a careless disregard of fame, which may be accounted for by the depressing consciousness of the accident which had marked his face and voice." Poor Booth was going downhill then, Cyrano-like in the consciousness of his nose? Personally I find little so far to back the statement, and certainly no relaxation in the playing of Massinger's extortionate villain. In 1843, as a matter of fact, I find nine performances of *A New Way to Pay Old Debts,* six in 1850, five in the last year of his life—and heaven alone knows how many I have failed to chronicle. Let us go back, however, with this warning, to 1842 where I can record five.[53] Two were in Philadelphia: at the Walnut Street Theatre on April 4, at the Chestnut Street on November 15. Two were in New York; another Bowery has now reared its structure from waves serener far, and there to the Margaret of the old Bowery favorite, Mrs. Flynn—how conscious he must have been of his nose on that occasion—Booth acted Sir Giles on August 16; at the Chatham on September 20, he was supported by the playing of Proctor as Wellborn and Mrs. Hautonville as Margaret. The last performance was on December 7 in Pittsburgh.

51 Odell, Vol. IV, p. 492.
52 *Elder and Younger Booth,* p. 98.
53 Wilson, pp. 262, 273; Odell, Vol. IV, pp. 559, 637; Fletcher, pp. 84-5, 380.

1843 was, as I have said, a big year for Sir Giles: he appeared at the Walnut Street Theatre in Philadelphia on January 12,[54] and then returned to the Park where he had not stormed (*via* Booth, that is) for some fifteen years; April 11 is the date, and a bill contributes the cast:

Sir Giles Overreach	Booth
Wellborn	Barry
Lord Lovell	Lovell
Marrall	Fisher
Justice Greedy	Placide
Allworth	Andrews
Lady Allworth	Mrs. Barry
Margaret	Miss Buloid

Regarding the whole engagement, the *Knickerbocker Magazine* can hardly be kept within bounds: ". . . If a deep insight into character; if a moulding not only of the outer expression, but of the very soul and spirit of the man into the object to be personated, impelled and fashioned by the force and impulse of genius, can give claim to the possession of the requisites of an actor, then has Mr. BOOTH a full and acknowledged title. We do not wish to be enthusiastic, but to speak the words of soberness and moderation, when we say, that since the days of KEAN we have seen no actor who so completely embodied the meaning of his author, who so fairly set before the mind the character he attempted to portray, as has Mr. BOOTH in all the personations which he has exhibited to the Park audiences; and without entering into any criticism of his performances, we will say generally, that they are of such a character that we believe it to be in the power of this man absolutely to resuscitate the drama in this country. . . . "

Such being the case, Booth departed to resuscitate the drama at the Bowery by dint of Shakespeare and Massinger; *A New Way to Pay Old Debts* was presented on April 29 with Booth's daughter-in-law—Miss DeBar until she married Junius, Jr.—as Margaret.[55] He then left the Bowery to take care of itself and travelled

[54] Wilson, p. 276.
[55] Odell, Vol. IV, p. 632.

to Boston to present Sir Giles on May 9 at the Tremont. Some of the cast are old friends, some new to the bill:

Sir Giles Overreach	Booth
Wellborn	W. H. Smith
Lord Lovell	Ayling
Marrall	Chapman
Justice Greedy	Gilbert
Allworth	Howard
Lady Allworth	Mrs. W. R. Blake
Margaret	Mrs. Cramer

Note John Gilbert there as Justice Greedy; it was Mrs. Blake's first Lady Allworth. We return then to the Park for three performances, May 25, June 17, and November 17 and note from the various bills that Shaw has now taken over Andrews' rôle of Allworth and for the June performance that Mrs. H. Hunt succeeds Miss Buloid; Mrs. Hunt was to become Mrs. John Drew, Sr. In November, there are more changes: Chippendale becomes Greedy, Wheatley becomes Wellborn, and Andrews is back as Allworth. The Arch Street Theatre, Philadelphia, saw Booth's Sir Giles on September 7.[56] Can the reader stand one more playbill cast for the year?—they are full of meaning to the lover of the theatre's past— that for the performance of *A New Way to Pay Old Debts* at the National Theatre in Boston, December 14:

Sir Giles Overreach	Booth
Wellborn	Howard
Lord Lovell	Hamilton
Marrall	Chapman
Justice Greedy	Gilbert
Allworth	Fenno
Lady Allworth	Mrs. Cramer
Margaret	Mrs. Abbott

On the first of January, 1844, Booth made a single appearance at the fast fading Park to play *A New Way to Pay Old Debts*; the cast is familiar, though we note Tom Barry as Wellborn again instead of Wheatley. On the 17th, Sir Giles was at the Walnut Street Theatre, Philadelphia.[57] After another performance at the Park on

---

[56] Wilson, p. 284.
[57] *ibid.*, p. 292.

March 12,[58] we take again the now apparently inevitable and certainly tiresome trip to Boston, where at the National Theatre Booth appeared as Sir Giles on April 10 with the bill showing the same support as of December 14, 1843. Would that this routine could be varied a bit and that Booth had made his engagements with an eye to the future stage-historian! He did not, however, and I cannot help the trip back to the Park for the Sir Giles of April 16, nor the return journey to the National—this is almost commuting—for *A New Way to Pay Old Debts* on May 15 and 23.[59] Pittsburgh on September 25 is at least a change.[60] We breathe a sigh of relief too for a performance at Palmo's Opera House, whence Italian opera had fled, on April 21, 1845, and a cheer of joy for the knowledge that the companion-piece presented Hervio Nano in *Bibbo, or, the Patagonian Ape!*,[61]—but it is merely a pleasant interlude between two performances at the Walnut Street on April 2 and May 23,[62] and another trip to Boston (or two) where according to the Harvard Boston list Sir Giles again frightened the audiences of the National Theatre on May 6 and October 7. Shortly thereafter Booth again took his southern tour, opening at the St. Charles Theatre, New Orleans, on November 18, 1845, and playing Sir Giles Overreach on his third night. Following the Ludlow and Smith circuit, he proceeded to Mobile to repeat the part on December 6; "Mr. Webb played *Wellborn,* Mr. Skerrett *Marall,* Mr. Marks *Justice Greedy,* Mrs. Stuart *Margaret Overreach,* Mrs. Russell *Lady Allworth.*"[63] For this relief much thanks!

1846 gives us a brighter outlook, however, for though inevitably we go back and forth between Boston and New York, it is fortunately to different theatres. After the familiar Walnut Street on February 20,[64] it is now the Chatham in New York which houses *A New Way to Pay Old Debts* again, the date March 2,[65] Marshall and Mrs. Nichols lending chief support. Pittsburgh saw Sir Giles

[58] Odell, Vol. V, pp. 12, 13, and playbills.
[59] *ibid.,* Vol. V, p. 14, and Harvard Boston list.
[60] Fletcher, pp. 384, 564.
[61] Odell, Vol. V, p. 135.
[62] Wilson, pp. 313, 316.
[63] Ludlow, pp. 619-20, 636.
[64] Wilson, p. 330.
[65] Odell, Vol. V, p. 200.

on May 26.[66] During the summer, Booth again went south and west for an engagement at St. Louis which opened on June 22 with—is it possible?—*The Iron Chest*. During the play Sir Edward Mortimer became somewhat eccentric, coming to life twice after his death upon the stage in order to take bows, and then lying quietly down again. Ludlow was furious to have an actor take such liberties in his theatre, but was persuaded to let the engagement proceed, "and so, missing one night, Mr. Booth reappeared on Wednesday, June 24, as *Sir Giles Overreach,* in 'New Way to Pay Old Debts,' finishing his regular number of nights, and never playing better at any time within my observation."[67] It is with something like cheer that we return to the Bowery for the play on November 19, though the receipts were only one hundred and fifty-eight dollars and twelve cents. This from *Report of Receipts Bowery Theatre (1845-1847)* in the Harvard Theatre Collection, which also explains the cause : "dull hazy Weather with the appearance of a Rain Storm; at night raining tremendously." How uncertain was the manager's lot in those days,—not the star's, for Booth had one hundred dollars a night regardless. When at long last we take the necessary trip to Boston again, we find ourselves at the newly opened Howard Athenaeum under James H. Hackett and Co.; on November 24, from the bill:

Sir Giles Overreach	Booth
Wellborn	Ayling
Lord Lovell	Bradshaw
Marrall	Warren
Justice Greedy	Chippendale
Allworth	Phillips
Lady Allworth	Mrs. Maywood
Margaret	Miss Maywood

This Marrall is William Warren, who had just made his Boston début as Sir Lucius O'Trigger and was to become the delight of the audiences at the Boston Museum.

Booth played Sir Giles at least four times in 1847, with single performances at four different theatres in Philadelphia, New York, and Boston. *A New Way to Pay Old Debts* was the bill at

[66] Fletcher, pp. 389, 565.
[67] Ludlow, pp. 644-5.

the Walnut Street Theatre on April 19,[68] at the Bowery during an engagement which commenced on May 24,[69] at the Howard Athenaeum on September 9 with Lyne making his first appearance as Lord Lovell,[70] and finally back in Philadelphia, though this time at the Arch Street, on November 22.[71]

Sir Giles returned to the Park for a performance on March 2, 1848, which, for a wonder, Odell fails to note. *The Spirit of the Times* of March 4 comments on the poor attendance and "the disastrous turn of fortune this establishment has felt," and explains that it is "because the stock company is very indifferent," and the managerial policy mistaken. One feels for Simpson though there is little doubt that the statements were true. The glory of old Drury, built up largely through his efforts, was almost gone, and Simpson retired in June after thirty-eight years as stage and acting manager, to die of grief the following month. Of Booth, the paper continues:

> We have no hesitation to pronounce him, as we have done heretofore, the very best actor of the present day. It is true, that his voice is impaired; that he is physically inferior to his former days but his acting, where great energy is not required, and his reading, are the most faultless exhibitions now given in the histrionic art. . . . His performance of Sir Giles Overreach, in the play a "New Way to Pay Old Debts," on Thursday, was like his previous personations, a powerful, nay wonderful embodiment of a great conception. Booth has always been unrivalled in this character, and cannot perform it too often either to gratify public taste, or increase the measure of his own glory. There are many originalities in the acting of Booth, that close copyists and imitators have never been able to acquire, and in these he displays more genius than can be collected from a glorious commingling of all the actors we have seen. We presume that all our readers have seen Mr. Booth, but if they would look upon him as an Atlas of the drama, they should visit the Park during his present engagement, where, with scarcely any support from the company, he works his own glory and sustains the author's reputation.

[68] Wilson, p. 356.
[69] Odell, Vol. V, p. 274.
[70] The playbill.
[71] Wilson, p. 368.

On March 17, 1848, Booth appeared as Sir Giles Overreach at the Chatham Theatre, New York, sharing honors with Augustus A. Addams who impersonated William Tell.[72] Addams was for some years the rival of Forrest for the title of *the American* tragedian; though he apparently had as much natural ability as Forrest, he lacked both his application and strength of character, and, though we need not the lesson, what does his name mean now? An unsuccessful rival's lot is not a happy one, particularly when he takes to drink. But though I am, the reader is not interested in Addams and this book is after all about Sir Giles. We go to Boston —monotonous words!—but there is a surprise in store, for we find Booth not at his old familiar haunts, but at the Boston Theatre in Federal Street, where, I think, he had not acted Sir Giles since his first appearance there in 1822. *A New Way to Pay Old Debts* was acted on March 28—so the Harvard Boston list—but unfortunately I can find no playbill. After a performance on August 10 at the Arch Street Theatre, Philadelphia,[73] we move to the Albany Museum, expensively enlarged and now in its palmy days; Booth began an engagement there on the 14th of August, during which he played Sir Giles, but Phelps is not more precise.[74] He does say precisely, however, that Booth "was accompanied at this time, by his son Edwin—the present eminent tragedian—then a mere strippling, but who kept as close an eye on his father as possible. While acting, [*sic*] the boy sat in a box watching him and reading the play after him, line by line, and when off the scene, was on hand and ready to dress him for the next." Apparently a close eye was necessary if, as Phelps says, Booth helped fight the great Albany fire of 1848 which destroyed one-thirtieth of the city. There are also other stories, but one does not know whether to believe them. The year concludes with a performance at Pittsburgh on December 9, in which "scarce a symptom of decline is visible."[75]

In the fall of 1846 was opened on Tremont Street the famous playhouse called the Boston Museum which was to house for almost fifty years one of the finest stock companies that this

[72] Odell, Vol. V, p. 362.
[73] Wilson, p. 383.
[74] Phelps, p. 253.
[75] Fletcher, pp. 157, 403. The quotation is from the *Journal* of December 11.

country has ever known, a company with which all the famous stars of the American theatre were proud to perform. We shall find in the course of this history that one of its most consistently successful plays was Massinger's *A New Way to Pay Old Debts.* Junius Brutus Booth first presented the play on August 24, 1849, and repeated the performance on September 14.[76] Both performances were for the benefit of Mr. Booth, though this was hardly a new way to pay debts. The cast was as follows:

Sir Giles Overreach .... Booth
Wellborn .... W. H. Smith
Lord Lovell .... Whitman
Marrall .... Warren
Justice Greedy .... Curtis
Allworth .... J. A. Smith
Lady Allworth .... Mrs. Judah
Margaret .... Miss L. Gann

Elsewhere this year Booth played Sir Giles in Pittsburgh on April 5 and December 7, and at the Chestnut Street Theatre in Philadelphia on October 5.[77]

For 1850, I report a Sir Giles at Connor's Theatre (the rechristened Arch Street) on May 17,—credit to a playbill. Back at the Boston Museum, "Massinger's great play" was repeated on August 12 and 29, the cast as above. Booth's Sir Giles at the National Theatre (late Chatham), New York, on September 25 just missed the possible assistance of young Edwin who made his New York bow two days later in *The Iron Chest.*[78] I wish I could find a bill of this performance. I suspect strongly that the Marrall on the occasion was Mr. Rip Van Winkle Jefferson. In his *Autobiography* Jefferson says he played Marrall to Booth's Sir Giles (certainly by implication) at the Chatham Theatre—it was now called The National—"when but twenty-two years of age." As a matter of fact Jefferson was under twenty-two at this particular time, but since he left the National in November of this year, I do

[76] Playbills, and Harvard Boston list; Cruickshank (Edition), p. 136, records performances of Sir Giles by Booth at the Museum on December 18, 19, 1848; the Sir Giles on these dates was J. W. Thoman, to be treated later.

[77] Fletcher, pp. 169, 405, 409; Wilson, p. 403.

[78] Odell, Vol. VI, p. 34. Edwin Booth had made his first appearance on the stage at the Boston Museum on September 10th.

not see how his reference can apply to any other performance. But let Jefferson tell his story:[79]

When but twenty-two years of age I was cast for Marrall in "A New Way to Pay Old Debts," the elder Booth playing *Sir Giles Overreach*. There can be no doubt about the fact that I was entirely unfit for so important a part; it is a very difficult one, and to give it effect requires that an actor should be in his prime, both as to his age and his talent. A mere boy, with but little physical or dramatic strength, coming upon the stage to rehearse so important a character, must have been rather a shock, and somewhat of a disappointment, to the great actor whom he was to support. But Mr. Booth wisely made the best of a bad bargain, and, instead of annihilating me with a look, took much pains to teach me the business of the part. Surely this was better than disapproval or petulance; for as it was I acquitted myself respectably, whereas it is most likely that I should have done the reverse had I met with discouraging treatment.

The elder Booth's acting of *Sir Giles* was indeed something to be remembered. During the last scene he beats *Marrall,* who hides for protection behind *Lord Lovell*. Booth's face, when he found he could not reach his victim, had the look of an uncaged tiger. His eyes flashed and seemed to snap with fire; his nostrils dilated; his cheeks appeared to quiver; his half-opened mouth, with its thin lips pressed tightly against the white teeth, made a picture of anger fearful to look upon. At the point where he is about to draw his sword his arm shakes, his right hand refuses to do its office, and, stricken with paralysis, he stands the embodiment of despair; then come his terrible words of anguish and self-reproach:

> Some undone widow sits upon my arm,
> . . . my sword,
> Glued to my scabbard, with wronged orphans' tears.

His whole frame, shaken with convulsions, seems to collapse, his head sinks upon his breast, his jaw drops, and the cruel man is dead. There was no applause the night I speak of; the acting was so intense and so natural that the mimic scene seemed really to have happened.

[79] *The Autobiography of Joseph Jefferson,* pp. 129-30.

Delightful this account—how delightful only those can know who have read through with me this terrifying list of names, dates, and commonplace comments. I must, however, to be truthful, cast a little gloom by quoting also from *The Spirit of the Times* of September 28: "Mr. Booth appears to be in good condition, and as full of energy and poetic fire as ever. We can perceive no lack of spirit, and no falling off of the extraordinary ability for which he has been and is justly celebrated. We much regret, however, that he has not been engaged at a theatre where he would receive some support from the characters of the play . . . it is exceedingly unpleasant to be a spectator of such an occurrence as we were on Wednesday. Mr. Booth was miserably sustained, and we marvel that he could brook such disrespect." In the light of Jefferson's comment, I do not enjoy this quotation in the least, poetry being so much greater than truth. One cannot help wondering how Booth continued to put over his characterization where his support was clumsy and incompetent. In an interview with Thomas R. Gould, printed as a dialogue in Gould's *The Tragedian,* Booth answers the question himself:[80]

> Guest—I saw your "Sir Giles" last evening. How do you manage to carry the scene so smoothly, with such weak support?
> Actor—By close attention to the business of the stage.
> Guest—But you seemed to lose yourself in your impersonation.
> Actor—Else how could I identify character?
> Guest—And can you keep up these two diverse processes of thought at the same time?
> Actor—Nothing easier—after the machinery is oiled.

The next appearance of Booth as Sir Giles is a melancholy one; it took place at the Brooklyn Museum on December 2, 1850. The houses at this engagement were poor, and Booth himself "ill and disabled." On the 3rd, indeed, Booth was unable to act Iago, though he had recovered by the 9th sufficiently to play Richard. So small were the receipts, however, that he made the 10th his (and Edwin's) last night; "it was not," says Harrison,[81] "worth the great actor's exertions to continue." The cast was in part as follows:

[80] Gould, p. 184.
[81] Harrison, *History,* p. 7; Odell, Vol. VI, p. 102.

Sir Giles Overreach .... Booth
Lord Lovell .... Linden
Marrall .... Kent
Justice Greedy .... King
Allworth .... Lovell
Margaret .... Mrs. Lovell

We conclude the year on December 26 at the Boston Museum with the familiar cast already printed.[82]

Be patient, reader, for there are only two more years to chronicle, and I can promise you some variety, especially in the second. The first has the usual jumps from Philadelphia to New York to Boston. In the first city, Sir Giles has a new habitation, Barnum's Museum, on March 4, 1851.[83] At the National, New York, *A New Way to Pay Old Debts* was the play on the 2nd of April; it was on this week's engagement that Edwin substituted for his father in *Richard III,* his first real part and his first success.[84] *The Spirit of the Times* on April 5 praises the elder Booth but scores the company. On the 11th of August, he was supported at the same theatre by Mrs. Nichols as Margaret.[85] There then follow three performances of Massinger at the Boston Museum, August 25, September 10, October 29. We note on the bills two changes in this surprisingly uniform company. Davies has become the Lord Lovell, and Mrs. Wolf Fries has superseded Miss Gann as Miss Overreach. We may say good-bye to Boston now; it had seen Sir Giles by Booth for the last time.

Booth's Sir Giles bade farewell to Philadelphia at the Chestnut Street Theatre on January 20, 1852, to New York at the National on February 4, and to the East at the Holliday Street Theatre in Baltimore on June 4.[86] In June Booth and Edwin, at the solicitation of the younger Junius, who had come home to visit the family, left for California, a trip from which the older Booth never returned. He opened at the Jenny Lind Theatre in San Francisco, and attracted crowded audiences for his engagement of two weeks. The Harvard Theatre Collection has a clipping of an article by

---

[82] Cruickshank (Edition), p. 136, wrongly says the 28th; I have checked the playbills.
[83] Wilson, p. 434.
[84] Odell, Vol. VI, p. 43.
[85] *ibid.,* Vol. VI, p. 46.
[86] Wilson, p. 456; Odell, Vol. VI, p. 143; Baltimore playbill.

William Winter which describes the western activities of both the Booths.[87] From that it appears that the elder played Sir Giles Overreach on July 31, his second appearance there. I leave the reader to guess what was the first, though Winter does not say. "On Friday October 1, 1852, the elder Booth sailed from San Francisco, aboard the steamer *Independence,* on his return journey to the East. He crossed the isthmus, from Panama, and sailed from Colon to New Orleans, where he acted six times, at the St. Charles Theatre. . . . " The St. Charles was then under the management of Sol. Smith and he records[88] Booth's "last professional appearances on earth! The characters he personated were 1. *Richard;* 2. *Sir Giles Overreach;* 3. *Pescara;* 4. *Shylock;* 5. *Bertram;* 6. (Benefit and last appearance), *Sir Edward Mortimer.*" To the last, notice, Richard, and then Sir Giles, his masterpieces of histrionic art. Harvard has the Richard playbill, and it announces Sir Giles for the following night, Monday, November 15, 1852. "I was acquainted," continues Sol. Smith, "with Junius Brutus Booth for about a quarter of a century. When I first knew him (in 1827) he was a truly great actor, and continued so to be until he fell into bad company in New Orleans, and took to hard drink. Then he became undependable, and, 'putting an antic disposition on,' made many believe that he was crazy. *I* never believed him to be a crazy man except when he was excited by liquor, and that was pretty often—nearly all the time, in fact.[89] I have seen him act *Richard* many times as no other man could or can act it. . . . His *Sir Giles Overreach* (in the last scene) was terrific!"

Last scene of all: exhausted by his performances in New Orleans and anxious to join again his family in Baltimore, Booth took passage for Cincinnati on a river boat, became fatally ill, and died on board November 30. "It was with deep regret and sorrow," wrote Ludlow to Mrs. Booth,[90] "that we read here a telegraphic paragraph . . . announcing the decease of your late worthy husband. It was the more startling because the least expected. During

---

[87] *The New York Tribune Illustrated Supplement,* August 24, 1902, p. 12; and see later *s.v.,* Edwin Booth.

[88] *Theatrical Management in the West and South for Thirty Years,* pp. 229-30.

[89] An opinion with which Edwin Booth in a manly and spirited article (contributed to Matthews and Hutton, Vol. III, pp. 102-3) violently disagrees.

[90] *Elder and Younger Booth,* pp. 108-9.

his engagement with us in the St. Charles Theatre it was generally remarked how well he looked and how well he performed. For myself, who remember him since his first week's performance in the United States, and have been well acquainted with his professional career, I was agreeably astonished at the vigor evinced by him during the six nights he performed with us, and the conclusion of his engagement seemed a cause of regret to the public generally." When Booth's admirer, Rufus Choate, lover of Shakespeare and Shakespeare on the stage, heard of Booth's death, he exclaimed sorrowfully, "Then there are no more actors!" Thus passed Junius Brutus Booth, Sir Giles extraordinary. Rest, rest, perturbed spirit!

Numerous and definitive have been the first-hand opinions of Booth which I have already quoted on particular performances, but there are others which must not be omitted if we are to taste, many years after, the flavor of his Sir Giles. Booth like all great actors was never at a loss on the stage. His command of the situation is evidenced by a paragraph in Jefferson's *Autobiography*[91] which has to do with the very play under discussion, though I cannot identify the performance in question: "Mr. Barton Hill relates to me an incident that occurred during Mr. Booth's performance of . . . *Sir Giles Overreach*. Mr. Hill was acting *Lord Lovell,* and in the scene where the crafty *Sir Giles* is endeavoring to court the favor of his lordship, a large, ostrich feather, which formed one of the plumes in *Lovell's* hat, became by some accident detached, and fell in the center of the stage. A conspicuous object like this, had it been allowed to remain where it fell, would have marred the effect of the scene. Booth seeing the mishap, came quickly forward, and, raising the feather from the floor, presented it with becoming humility to its owner. This admirable point not only removed the obstacle but heightened the effect of the situation. Here was a display not merely of presence of mind, but of good taste. . . . " Jefferson is also responsible for a revealing statement made to William Winter:[92] "The greatest tragic actor I have ever seen was Junius Booth. He was not the equal of Macready as an intellectual artist, but his spirit was extraordinary and overwhelming. When he acted Sir Giles you never thought of looking

[91] pp. 130-1.
[92] Printed as a footnote to *Shadows of the Stage*, Second Series, p. 37.

at his gestures and motions; it was what was inside of the man
that you saw. His face, in the last act, used to twitch: he was like
a caged wild beast."

Thomas R. Gould, the American sculptor—he did the bust of
Junius Brutus Booth which later stood in Booth's Theatre—has
left us an interesting little book about the elder Booth called *The
Tragedian.* Like his sculptures, it is over-flattering, which is a pity;
but also minute in its analysis, which is a blessing. He has given
us in his short chapter on Sir Giles Overreach an extraordinarily
vivid full-length of Booth in the part:[93]

. . . His "Sir Giles Overreach," in Massinger's play, "A New
Way to pay Old Debts," stands in our memory as a representation of singular solid force. . . . When he speaks of having, as
servants to his daughter Margaret—

>   "The ladies of errant knights decayed,"

he adds,—
>   "There having ever been
> More than a feud, a *strange antipathy*
> Between us and true gentry,"

Booth infused into those two italicized words the aspiring
and implacable hatred of the rich and overbearing commoner.
His gesture, like his speech, escaped the confinement of rules.
It was the natural language of imaginative passion; or the "com-
plement extern" of fine perceptions. In the scene where Sir Giles
urges Marrall to work the ruin of Wellborn, and says—

>   "Persuade him that 'tis better steal than beg,"

he gave the word "steal" with the fingers of his right hand down-
ward, and as in act of taking: "than beg," palm up, as in act of
solicitation—and both movements with rapid ease.

The scene with Margaret, where he tries to induce her to
receive, or if need be, catch, the attentions of Lord Lovell was a
masterpiece. . . . Margaret protests—

>   "If to obey you I forget my honor,
>   He must and will forsake me."
>   *Sir Giles,* "How! Forsake Thee!
>   Do I wear a sword for fashion; or is this arm
>   Shrunk up or withered? Does there live a man,
>   Of that large list I have encountered with,
>   Can truly say, I e'er gave inch of ground,
>   Not purchased by his blood, that did oppose me?"

[93] pp. 153 *ff.*

These lines were so full and bristling with shining points of the actor's art, that we shall attempt an analysis of Mr. Booth's victorious method of rendering them. He uttered "forsake thee!" with a shriek of astonishment.

> "Do I wear a sword for fashion?"

beginning low, and as on a rising wave of passion, the last word blown disdainful, like the foam from its crest. In saying it, he clutched the scabbard with his left hand, and struck the sword-hilt with his right.

> "Or is this arm
> Shrunk up or withered?"

He grasped his outstretched right arm with the fingers of the left hand, and gave the phrase in throated and roughened tones of scorn. The words of the continuing lines were "rammed with life," and full of the solid temper of Sir Giles, down to the word "blood"; when his voice dropped suddenly to its subterranean chamber, and he uttered the phrase "that did oppose me," in a cool depth of tone, which seemed to assure the doom of all antagonists.

Wellborn, cheated and hated of Sir Giles, is presented to him by Lady Allworth, with the remark, "If I am welcome, bid him so." The manner in which Booth stood, with his back turned, betraying an inward strife by subtle motions of head, hands, and features, until, mastering repugnance by policy, he turned suddenly with affected heartiness and grasped the youth's hand, "My nephew!"—was a most felicitous touch. To Lord Lovel's question if he is not moved by the imprecations of those he has wronged, Sir Giles replies—

> "Yes, as rocks are
> When foaming billows split themselves against
> Their flinty ribs; or as the moon is moved
> When wolves, with hunger pined, howl at her
> brightness."

The change of voice from the howling pack to the silver clearness of the moon, in the words, "at her brightness," made the listener feel the assumption of unapproachable serenity. The whole speech was a magnificent example of self-assertion. . . . When Booth, on a certain occasion, as Sir Giles, challenged Lord Lovel, and ran (*not shuffled*) out, but finding he was not followed, came

directly back, stood just within the scene, and uttered these words
in his deepest voice,

"Are you pale?"—

he took his stature from the mind: his figure seemed to dilate
with the least expansion of his will; and actually to overstate in
physical dimension, the bulky and brawny Scotchman who played
Lord Lovel.

Edwin Booth says in the article on his father to which I have
already referred that Sir Giles was one of the characterizations
which remained most distinct in his memory, and admits that for
many years he had to be most watchful in order to avoid making
a close copy when he played the part. Speaking of the last scene, he
agrees with Gould on the extraordinary effect which Booth was
able to obtain in the challenge business. "Take, for example, his
mad challenge to *Lord Lovel* when as *Sir Giles* he dashed like
lightning from the scene and as quietly returned to ask with livid
lips and chilling voice, "Are you pale?" at which not only the pit,
as in Kean's case, rose at him, but the whole audience frequently
started to its feet in amazement and with cheers. The effect was
electrical—indescribable! To produce such a scene as he gave it, is
simply impossible, and all attempts to do so by his many imitators
were ridiculous." And Henry Dickinson Stone in his *Theatrical
Reminiscences*[94] shows that Kean was not alone in his ability to
make even the actors with whom he was playing blur the line between reality and illusion: "We saw the stock actors lose their
presence of mind in Sir Giles Overreach, in 'New Way to Pay Old
Debts' and actually start to follow the prostrate form of the elder
Booth, as he was borne, in the last scene, fainting and dying, from
the stage, while the audience arose, and pale with terror, leaned
forward with painful interest to see the end of what, for the
moment, appeared a *real* catastrophe!"

To quote well is some virtue, and much quotation in a book of
this kind is more revealing than any comment which I with my
second-hand information could make. It is my function, in attempting to solidify in the sculpture of memory how Booth spent his
hour upon the stage, how lifelike, how real was his characterization, and what its effect upon those who saw him, only to explain

[94] p. 10.

and to interpret. In closing, therefore, the chapter on this amazing and eccentric genius, I cannot do better than to resist the temptation to present my own opinions and in their place give the words of the son who inherited his ability, who, as an actor himself, must necessarily speak with more illumination than is possible for the layman; who, as the child and friend and personal witness of his father, can speak with ultimate authority. His words, when we make allowance for the bias of intimate admiration, will tell us what we wish to know :[95] "To see my father act, when in the acting mood, was *not* 'like reading Shakspere by flashes of lightning' which could give but fitful glimpses of the author's meaning; but the full sunlight of his genius shone on every character that he portrayed, and so illumined the obscurities of the text that Shakspereans wondered with delight at his lucid interpretations of passages which to them had previously been unintelligible. At his best he soared higher into the realm of Art sublime than any of his successors have reached; and to those who saw him then it was not credible that any of his predecessors could have surpassed him."

[95] Matthews and Hutton, Vol. III, p. 100.

CHAPTER IX

SCATTER THE LEAVES

A S a result of the presentations and excursions of Cooke, Kean, and Booth, most particularly of the last, Sir Giles Overreach was now very much at home in these United States. It followed too that whereas formerly he had been looked on with some suspicion, he was now, villainous as he was, received rapturously into the theatrical arms of many cities and many companies. An established figure, he had now made *A New Way to Pay Old Debts* a play well known in America, and one which all stock companies of any importance, if they expected to support stars, had to learn, lines, business and all. In turn Sir Giles was presented by most of the popular stars, as well as by a host of lesser satellites who found Massinger's play a vehicle for their exuberant but undisciplined abilities, knowing full well that one must be a very poor actor indeed not to make something out of the big scenes. This chapter therefore must chronicle not only the presentations of certain histrionic lions, but a whole series of rats and mice and such small deer, which we will occasionally find very amusing, occasionally very dull; all, however, contributing to the tableau of the nineteenth century theatre in America and to Sir Giles's place in the picture.

The first actor to be discussed is very much of a lion, though his connection with *A New Way to Pay Old Debts* on the stage was not apparently of long duration. I refer to the man thought of as preeminently *the American* tragedian, Edwin Forrest. So well known an actor hardly needs more than the briefest of biographical notices, especially since, though we should like to linger, we must very shortly pass to other figures who, not so important as actors, identified themselves more particularly with Sir Giles Overreach.

Born in Philadelphia in 1806, Forrest made his real début in that city in 1820. So successful were his appearances at the Walnut Street Theatre that he broke the bands which chained him to a trade and went west, young man, for his period of training and experience. We have found him, that period over, in Charles Gilfert's company at Albany where he played subordinate rôles to Edmund Kean when the star visited that city. In 1826 he made his début at the Park Theatre on June 23 for the benefit of Woodhull, as Othello. Praised by the critics, he was engaged by Gilfert to appear at the new Bowery Theatre where he became a favorite and was played as trump card against Macready at the Park. From this time on, his success was assured and his ability recognized. His later career need not detain us, not even his quarrels with Macready nor his notorious divorce. He did something towards fostering American drama by offering prizes for plays, to which of course he claimed exclusive rights, and he endeared himself forever to the profession by founding the Edwin Forrest Home, a retreat for aged and indigent actors. Yet he died in 1872, bitterly disappointed, a tragic figure as well as a great tragedian. He created many characters, but his own character destroyed him; he was a great actor, but not a great man. Let Lawrence Barrett describe his acting for us: "*Coriolanus* died with him, the last of all the Romans. He was greatest, however, in such parts as *Virginius, William Tell,* and *Spartacus.* Here his mannerisms of gait and utterance were less noticeable than in his Shakesperean characters, or were overlooked in the rugged massiveness of the creation. *Hamlet, Richard* and *Macbeth* were out of his temperament, and added nothing to his fame; but *Richelieu* is said to have been one of his noblest and most impressive performances. He was in all things marked and distinctive. His obtrusive personality often destroyed the harmony of the portrait he was painting, but in his inspired moments, which were many, his touches were sublime. He passed over quiet scenes with little elaboration, and dwelt strongly upon the grand features of the characters he represented. His *Lear,* in the great scenes, rose to a majestic height, but fell in places almost to mediocrity. His art was unequal to his natural gifts. He was totally unlike his great contemporary and rival, Macready, whose attention to detail gave to every performance the harmony of perfect work."[1]

[1] I quote from Matthews and Hutton, Vol. IV, pp. 45-6. There are a number of biographies of Forrest, all curiously unsatisfactory: James Rees (Colley Cibber), *The Life of Edwin Forrest,* Philadelphia, [1874]; W. R. Alger, *Life of Edwin Forrest,* 2 vols., Philadelphia, 1877; Lawrence Barrett, *Edwin Forrest,* Boston, 1881; Gabriel Harrison, *Edwin Forrest, the Actor and the Man,* Brook-

Alger says that up to Forrest's visit to Europe in 1834 his favorite and most successful characters were Rolla, Tell, Damon, Brutus, Virginius, Spartacus, and Metamora. "Jaffier, Octavian, Sir Edward Mortimer, Sir Giles Overreach, Iago, and other kindred parts, which he often acted with distinguished ability and acceptance, he liked less and less, and gradually dropped them altogether." Harrison admits that Sir Giles was one of Forrest's less successful parts.[2] From both these statements one would infer that the part had been played a number of times, and yet I can find record of only one authentic performance. Cruickshank, it is true, lists a performance at the Boston Theatre on November 8, 1854, but the play on that night was *Richelieu*. I have seen the playbills for Forrest's whole engagement at Boston lasting from November 8 to 24 and there is nowhere any reference to *A New Way to Pay Old Debts*. Cruickshank seems to have copied an error in Tompkins and Kilby's *History of the Boston Theatre, 1854-1901*, or else he has been misled by Couldock's performance of Sir Giles at the Boston Museum on the date he cites.[3]

There is no doubt, however, of the performance of *A New Way to Pay Old Debts* at the Bowery Theatre on April 18, 1828, Sir Giles by Forrest, Margaret by "A Young Lady," meaning an amateur.[4] Odell gives this, but no more, and we must supplement by quoting from a review in *The New-York Mirror* of April 26— I omit a long discussion of Sir Giles's character:

> . . . Forrest, in assuming this arduous and repulsive character— a line very materially different from any he had previously appeared in—excited doubts and fears in the minds of some of his warmest friends as to the issue. It is needless to say that it was triumphant.
>
> The Sir Giles Overreach of Mr. Forrest is marked with physical defects—for, like a true critic, we must enumerate defects first—of a kind that are perceptible to every eye, and yet which

lyn, 1889; and more recently, Montrose J. Moses, *The Fabulous Forrest,* Boston, 1929. In many ways the most trenchant study of Forrest's character is that by William Winter in *Brief Chronicles,* Vol. I, p. 94-Vol. II, p. 126; much of this in revised form went into the article on Forrest in *Shadows of the Stage,* Second Series.

[2] Alger, Vol. I, p. 258; Harrison, p. 63.

[3] Cruickshank (Edition), p. 137; Tompkins and Kilby, pp. 24-5.

[4] Odell, Vol. III, p. 340.

no observer can wish removed. His port is too commanding and stately, his form too symmetrically moulded, his brow too open and expansive—and there is too much *candour*, too much nobleness in his whole bearing, to consist exactly with the idea which every reader of Massinger's play must form of its hero, whose body, and whose air are expected to comport with the contractedness and sinuosity of his mind. With Mr. Forrest's conception of this, as with the rest of his parts, but little fault can be found; and the execution, when it is considered that but a very short time had been afforded for study since he first resolved to attempt it, gives likewise small space for critical comment. There was not, we thought, sufficient testiness of manner in some of the scenes; and now and then we detected a drawling of the words, as if the text had not been distinctly impressed upon his memory, which it is probable was the case. In the dressing of the part too, there was the usual fault in relation to age, it being no doubt extremely difficult to conceal altogether the juvenility of his open and handsome countenance. Yet these are trivial blemishes, which scarcely deserve critical mention; and we should not notice them, could we find as many of a more important nature as it is necessary to enumerate, in order to sustain the reputation of a critic.

There are two or three bad *practices* to which Mr. Forrest is accustoming himself, and which it may therefore be well to point out, that, by being made aware of them, he may prevent their growing into *habits*. The first is in his walk, in which we now often notice a *roll* "that was not there before." Another is a way he has acquired of sawing with his body, during unimpassioned declamation; and the third, and last is, a frequent twitching at his girdle, in by-play, as a mode of expressing impatience, or rising anger, or some rough mood of mind. These are all trifles. . . .

It is useless to protract remarks on the performance of Sir Giles Overreach, which was good throughout—we speak in reference to Forrest—not to those who committed ruthless murder— and which, in the fifth act, gave an opportunity for some of as fine acting as we ever witnessed. There are opportunities of making more *points,* as a certain way of prominently showing particular beauties is technically called; but as the rough draft of a first study, as the embodying of a first conception, we do not believe that Sir Giles was ever better performed. The attitude, expression, manner, tone and emphasis, when the blank parchment . . . met, like a basilisk, his astonished eye, were forcible and appropriate in an uncommon degree. The burst of anger that falls on his varlet, when he finds that he is in the plot against him, well deserved the rounds of applause that followed it. The challenge to Lord Lovell, too, was admirably given. But the concluding paroxysm of exasperated, foiled, and reckless courage, and blind distraction, was uttered and acted with an electrical effect—it was an astounding and triumphant exhibition of physical and intellectual energy, which may have been equalled, but has never been excelled by any actor, in any similar passage. The whole of the last speech was so pronounced as to yield great additional lustre to Mr. Forrest's fame. For several minutes after Sir Giles was removed from the stage, the applause was maintained, with unanimous accord, and with deafening energy; thus evincing the general and deep impression which this wonderful actor's genius and energy never fail, properly excited, to create.

Mr. Archer sustained the character of Wellborn in a masterly manner; Mr. Roberts and Mr. Faulkner, as Marall and Greedy, were unusually happy; and Mrs. Young as Lady Allworth, never appeared to greater advantage. . . ."

The reader will perceive at once how unbalanced is this criticism and how contradictory its evidence. The reviewer spends a large part of his time mentioning Mr. Forrest's faults, some of which seem considerably more than "trifles," and then says they are of no importance. He gives the impression that the play was murdered by minor characters and yet praises everyone he mentions. He thinks Forrest's Sir Giles was fine "as the embodying of a first conception" and then goes on to say that the end of the last scene has never been excelled by any actor and that the applause was deafening. It is therefore difficult to obtain anything like a clear view of the picture. And yet certain things are evident that were not evident before. The part was plainly enough out of Forrest's line of "the heroic," and as played was effective only at certain times. Moreover this was probably the first time that Forrest had played the part, which is not without importance, since I was about to hazard the suggestion that Forrest might have played the part in his earlier wandering in the West. Lastly, Forrest's Sir Giles, whether because he felt it out of his line or because the audience did not take to it, was not repeated in New York—nor, as far as I know, elsewhere—and may quite well have been abandoned, as Alger says, though I suspect it was done quite definitely and not gradually at all. And with this we take leave of the Sir Giles of Edwin Forrest.

It is a little difficult for us now to realize how attractive our ancestors found the numerous infant Roscii, but there seems to be no doubt that Master Joseph Burke was an extraordinary child, both as actor and as musician. He was born in Dublin and made his début on the boards in May 1824 in that city when only five years of age. He afterwards appeared successfully in various provincial cities and finally in London at the Haymarket and the Surrey. At the latter, on his farewell evening, he played eighteen different characters, uttered from memory at least three thousand lines, dressed no fewer than twenty times, played a difficult overture on the violin, an accompaniment on the violoncello, and a prelude on the pianoforte, not to mention in conclusion an address to the audience. Not content with that, he came to America where he made his début at the Park on November 2, 1830, and played nine nights to an average of twelve hundred dollars a night. His success elsewhere was equally extraordinary. After retiring from the stage, he became a brilliant violinist, assisting at the concerts of Jenny Lind and conducting her orchestra.[5]

Why all this matter? Because this Joseph Burke, according to Ireland, actually played Sir Giles Overreach so well that "none sneered at the absurdity of a child's assuming such parts." When or where this phenomenon took place I have not been able to discover; besides Burke travelled all over the United States as a child actor, and it is not at all remarkable that I have not been able to find specific reference to his Sir Giles. I shudder a little to think of the performance, but art or no art, it must have been something worth seeing. This is not the last of the children to attempt the character, either; we shall find shortly—*mirabile dictu*—Sir Giles being acted by an extremely young lady!

If Edmund Kean had little for which to thank America, his son Charles had a great deal. Previous to his first trip to the United States in 1830, Charles Kean had really had nothing which could be called success. An indifferent actor when he first walked the boards, it was only after a period of training and hard work that he made for himself an enviable position and became an actor of

---

[5] Ireland, Vol. I, pp. 641-2; Harvard clipping.

distinguished ability. In the English section of this book, I have already shown what damage was done to Kean's reputation by the inevitable comparison with his father and by his own lack of the qualities of inspiration and genius which had made Edmund famous. The result was that in 1830 Charles was a profoundly discouraged young man : "The indulgence usually extended to novices was denied to me. I was not permitted to cherish the hope that time and study could ever enable me to correct the faults of youthful inexperience. The very resemblance I bore to my late father was urged against me as an offense, and condemned as being 'strange and unnatural.' Sick at heart, I left home and sought the shores of America. To the generous inhabitants of that far land I am indebted for the first ray of success that illuminated my clouded career."[6]

The success of Charles Kean in America is perhaps not immediately discernible for the odious comparison with the genius of his father crossed the water with him. He made his American début at the Park Theatre, New York, on September 1, 1830, as, of course, Richard III, and Booth playing the same part at the Bowery drew much better criticisms. His second rôle, on the 3rd, was Sir Giles Overreach, anticipated the night before by Booth at the Bowery— the reader will remember that the Park and the Bowery were in heated conflict for supremacy and monopoly. The reviews for the second rôle are more encouraging. The *American* of September 6 said "there was a want of discrimination in the plaudits . . . bestowed . . . where the striking resemblance between his acting and that of his father was most apparent." There was some talk of "mimicry" and "caricature." However, "of his great merit as a tragedian . . . there can hardly be a doubt. . . . His conception of the part was just, and in many respects complete." Edmund Kean "is constantly brought to mind . . . the husky yet varied intonations of the voice are similar; they possess the same command over the features and the frame; and have in common the most expressive eye that ever portrayed the workings of the mind upon the stage." There is no question that Charles Kean is "a most promising actor."

[6] From a later address quoted by Charles Kean's biographer, Cole, Vol. I, p. 180.

CHARLES KEAN as SIR GILES OVERREACH, from a lithograph
by R. J. Hamerton, published by Welch & Gwynne

The New-York Mirror of September 11 is both sensible and encouraging:

> . . . It is now no longer a question whether he shall be placed in the first class of actors, even resting his reputation upon the two parts already personated. The bold points of this terrific play were developed by our new acquaintance with skill and power, and we were highly gratified in witnessing the confirmation of his success on Wednesday night by a new audience. Mr. C. Kean may be now considered safe so far, and it only remains to determine the precise degree of his excellence. We see no *veto* which can be pushed in his face, to forbid him from modelling himself upon his father's bust . . . considering that Mr. C. Kean is not yet of age, his *judgement,* the quality to be least looked for in a very young man, is very wonderful. Indeed we almost regret that before "the gristle of youth is quite hardened into the bone of manhood," he should be able to draw upon his physical resources for such tremendous bursts of passion as they can hardly yet furnish; and we attribute the evident fatigue in the last act to that cause. In confirmation of the opinion given above, we adduce the relenting of paternal affection which occasionally softened the delivery of his harsh and brutal instructions to his daughter; and we noticed the tones of the voice to shape themselves to this with great flexibility. When the crisis in the third act [*nota*], so trying to the powers of an actor personating Sir Giles, arrived, no fault could be found either with conception or execution; the first shock over of the blank deed, the faculties gradually rally themselves to look for a cause; the suspicions hastily thrown upon Wellborn, the fierce and commanding, and subsequently imploring and abject manner towards Marall, the ultimate fits of ungovernable passion, the final paroxysm, the hysteric laugh, the groan, the syncope—all these were unexceptionable in point of judgement, although the degree of positive power in comparison with his father might be disputed. It remains only to say, that the most efficient assistance was given by the corps generally in all the under parts; a strong conviction of which we do not the less entertain because we do not particularize names.

I must particularize, however, and the cast was as follows—I quote from Odell, supplemented by a playbill of September 16, when Kean repeated the part for his benefit:[7]

[7] Odell, Vol. III, p. 482.

Sir Giles Overreach .... C. Kean
Wellborn .... Barry
Lord Lovell .... Woodhull
Marrall .... Barnes
Justice Greedy .... Placide
Allworth .... Richings
Lady Allworth .... Mrs. Wallack
Margaret .... Mrs. Blake

Though Kean's Othello was pronounced uneven, his other characters, Hamlet and Romeo in particular, were decided successes,
and when he left New York, his eye must have brightened and his
step quickened as he thought of his encouraging reception. Cole is
quite useless in tracing Kean in America, so I shall have to piece
out his engagements from memoirs and playbills. He seems to
have gone from New York to the Arch Street Theatre, Philadelphia, where he opened on the 23rd of September as Richard III,
and disappointed Wemyss who had come to see him act.[8] May we
postulate a performance of Sir Giles there on the 25th? It is a
reasonable guess, but I can find no playbills and shall not go to
Philadelphia to make sure. Let us return then to the Park to see
Kean's Overreach on November 17, the cast as before,[9] and then
go to Boston for the performance at the Tremont Theatre on
November 24 with the cast the same, I suspect, as of December 6
when the play was repeated. A Harvard clipping gives only partially the support, with Marrall by Finn, Wellborn by Smith,
Margaret by Mrs. Smith, and Lady Allworth by Mrs. Stone. We
close the year 1830 with another Park performance on the 14th of
December, the stability of the Park company rendering the printing of the playbill unnecessary.

I cannot trace in detail the Kean-Overreach tour which followed. It is clear that Sir Giles was not popular at the Chestnut
Street Theatre, Philadelphia, on January 13, 1831, for the house
was only eighty dollars.[10] And then I lose sight of the pair until
Ludlow mentions that following an engagement at the Camp Street
Theatre, New Orleans—where I strongly suspect Sir Giles was
present—Charles Kean played under his management at Natchez,

---

[8] Wemyss, pp. 185-6.
[9] Odell, Vol. III, p. 490, and playbill.
[10] James, p. 465.

where Sir Giles was quite definitely present, sometime in the spring
—I know not the precise date.[11] Kean's performance of the part,
however, did not in Ludlow's estimation "approach in excellence
that of the elder Booth," though he thinks his Reuben Glenroy the
best he has ever seen, "and when he left Natchez, his bearing had
been of such a nature that he left upon the minds of a high-toned
and educated class of people, such as then dwelt in and around
Natchez, the impression of a gentleman and a scholar." It is a long
jump now to Montreal but we must make it in one sentence. Sir
Giles coincided with Kean's first appearance there on August 25,
1831, reappearing on October 8.[12] Following this, we are back
from the wilds, when Kean presented Overreach again at the Park
on the 2nd of September, and at the Tremont Theatre, Boston, on
the 7th.[13] We may skip the return to Montreal already chronicled,
and go from here to Albany, Sir Giles on November 14, Kean's
opening night. "Not being properly advertised, he did not attract
largely," says Phelps.[14] Perhaps he was better advertised in Philadelphia, where *A New Way to Pay Old Debts* was the play at the
Chestnut Street Theatre on the 24th; the receipts at any rate increased to one hundred and forty dollars.[15]

A prompt-book in the New York Public Library marked "as
played by . . . C. Kean at Walnut St., Phila." makes us hunt for
a performance there, and we find it on May 16, 1832.[16] We leap
over vacuity again to November 15 at the Tremont in Boston, on
which occasion—so a Harvard clipping—Woodhull was Lovell,
Smith Wellborn, Andrews Marrall, Mrs. Smith Margaret, and
Mrs. Hughes Lady Allworth. Back at the Park with Booth again in
opposition at the Bowery, the receipts were poor, less than three
hundred dollars an average night, but Sir Giles was unperturbed
and fumed as ever on December 31 and in part—only the fifth Act
was presented?—for his benefit on January 14.[17] I do not know
the cast though John Kemble Mason was chief support and may

[11] Ludlow, pp. 376-7.
[12] Graham, p. 59.
[13] Odell, Vol. III, p. 544; Harvard Boston list.
[14] Phelps, p. 156.
[15] James, p. 501.
[16] *ibid.*, p. 516, supplemented by the *United States Gazette*. The prompt-book
is Oxberry's edition, Boston, 1822.
[17] Odell, Vol. III, pp. 614-15.

have been Wellborn. In spite of Kean's failure to attract money, the *Mirror* of January 12 sincerely regrets to observe it is his farewell engagement before leaving for Europe. "This gifted and accomplished performer has won justly and worn modestly, a high reputation." With which benediction, we may say "bon voyage" and "come again."

Charles Kean did "come again" but it was not until 1839, and his Sir Giles by that date was not so often exhibited. I note only five performances, and call attention to the fact that when he made his third visit in 1845, though he remained several years, Overreach seems to have been dropped as completely in this country as in England, where I note his last performance in 1842. As Kean developed his own individual qualities, and they were quite different, as we have seen, from his father's, he apparently grew away from the exuberant Sir Giles to quieter parts more fitting his careful and intelligent acting. To proceed, however, with the catalogue, Kean's first Sir Giles on his second visit seems to have been at the National Theatre, New York, September 10, 1839.[18] He was now a much improved actor and had, we have noted, triumphed at Drury Lane and over Macready's management at Covent Garden. *The New-York Mirror* of September 21 remarks in part: "In . . . Sir Giles Overreach, Mr. Kean developed new powers, and gave additional indications of that high histrionic genius which he has matured by assiduous practice and study. The tempestuous scenes in the last act . . . were rendered with extraordinary effect. The manner in which he sprang across the stage with every limb quivering, when he gives the lie to Wellborn, was a most thrilling piece of acting. Indeed the whole scene was inimitably fine. . . ."

At the Chestnut Street Theatre, Philadelphia, Kean was Sir Giles on October 2 and 4 with the cast on the playbills as follows:

Sir Giles Overreach . . . . C. Kean
Wellborn . . . . Wood
Lord Lovell . . . . Harrington
Marrall . . . . Johnson
Justice Greedy . . . . Faulkner
Allworth . . . . Lindsay
Lady Allworth . . . . Mrs. Thayer
Margaret . . . . Miss Fisher

18 Odell, Vol. IV, p. 336.

and the small part of Parson Welldo [*sic*] by E. L. Davenport, now supporting his second Sir Giles and no doubt acquiring valuable training, by comparing Booth and Charles Kean, for the creation of his own. At the Tremont in Boston, Kean "performed Sir Giles Overreach very well"—says a Harvard clipping—on November 12, with a support not unknown to us but authenticated by a playbill:

Sir Giles Overreach	C. Kean
Wellborn	W. H. Smith
Lord Lovell	Ayling
Marrall	Andrews
Justice Greedy	Gilbert
Allworth	Muzzy
Lady Allworth	Mrs. Muzzy
Margaret	Mrs. Anderson

Kean's last performance of Overreach in America—I include the saving "so far as I know"—was at the Bowery Theatre, New York, on December 20, 1839, and again a bill comes to the rescue with the cast:

Sir Giles Overreach	C. Kean
Wellborn	Howard
Lord Lovell	Proctor
Marrall	Blakely
Justice Greedy	Gates
Allworth	Foster
Lady Allworth	Mrs. Hield
Margaret	Miss Proctor

The subject of the Keans in America has presented a curious contradiction: genius Edmund stampeded out; Charles, able but no genius, welcomed, encouraged, and applauded. They are now both gone and we shall see them no more in this book.

I am not much interested in the performance of *A New Way to Pay Old Debts* at the Chestnut Street Theatre, Philadelphia, on May 12, 1831; nor, I gather, was the public, since the receipts were only eighty-four dollars and fifty cents for Mrs. Moreland's benefit.[19] This was a summer season under the temporary and chaotic management of Lamb and Coyle. The Sir Giles was William

19 James, p. 481.

Isherwood, and that he never repeated the part is significant. Isherwood was a mediocre and undistinguished stock-company actor who later was engaged at the Park; his line was old men, not Overreach's.

Nor need we waste much time on a performance of *A New Way to Pay Old Debts* at the Bowery Theatre on September 24, 1831, Sir Giles Overreach by Mr. J. H. Barton from the Edinburgh Theatre.[20] Barton was an English actor who had attracted some attention in the provinces. After starring engagements in this country he became stage-manager for James H. Caldwell in New Orleans and Mobile. Ludlow says he was "a sensible and classic actor, and very particular in his stage business . . . a *gentleman* in every respect, and enthusiastically fond of his profession." He is perhaps chiefly remembered by stage-historians as the subject of an amusing anecdote by Sol. Smith, according to which he was not satisfied with the realism with which he was attacked by supers in *William Tell* and was consequently dealt with quite effectually during the next performance. Barton probably played Sir Giles several times on the southern circuit, but I note only that a letter from Caldwell in the Harvard Theatre Collection, dated September 15, 1832, Cincinnati, says that Barton will open on the 20th and will subsequently play Sir Giles. This letter is directed to Ludlow at Louisville and refers to performances in that city, which Ludlow is to arrange. More of Barton's Sir Giles I know not—nor greatly care.

The case is somewhat different, however, with John R. Scott, an actor of the Forrest school but by no means a servile imitator. Scott had natural ability enough to become an actor of the first rank, and there is plenty of testimony as to the power of his playing and the esteem in which he was held by his contemporaries. Unfortunately he dissipated his fine talent by acting broadly characterized melodrama which blunted his powers of creation, and by a lack of application to the more serious parts he sometimes played. The result was that, though an actor of real talent, his name is now remembered only by the professed stage-historian. Born in Philadelphia in 1808, Scott disappointed his father's wish that he become a

[20] Odell, Vol. III, p. 564. On Barton, see Ireland, Vol. I, pp. 646-7; Ludlow, p. 449; Sol. Smith, p. 117.

merchant, joined an amateur Thespian club, and finally made his professional début at the Park in New York, playing Malcolm to the elder Booth's Macbeth, July 2, 1828; on which occasion, according to his own statement, he acted wretchedly. Shortly after, he became a member of the Tremont company in Boston where upon his first appearance he made such a mess of his two lines that he was immediately lowered to the class of "super" and did not for three months have an opportunity to speak again on the stage. He made good, however, thereafter and rapidly developed into an extremely popular tragedian. He acted with most of the reigning stars, toured the country playing anything and everything, and was always a favorite at the popular theatres. So extensive was his playing and so inadequate are the accounts of his career, that, like Booth, he is extremely difficult to trace. His engagement at the Princess's Theatre, London, in November of 1846 has already been noted. During his later years his habits militated against his success and mutilated his fine presence. He died of apoplexy in 1856.[21]

Scott played Sir Giles Overreach intermittently for over twenty years and many more times than my scanty records show. Apparently the first performance was at the Park on December 4, 1832, for the benefit of Yankee Hill; Mr. Scott—says the playbill—"of the Philadelphia Theatre . . . has politely volunteered his services":

Sir Giles Overreach	Scott
Wellborn	Barry
Lord Lovell	Clarke
Marrall	Wilkinson
Justice Greedy	Placide
Allworth	Richings
Lady Allworth	Mrs. Wallack
Margaret	Mrs. Sharpe

The *Mirror* of December 8 speaks of Mr. Scott as "a very clever young American"—no more. The Harvard Boston list shows this

---

[21] The material on Scott in the usual reference books is sparse; but see Ireland, Vol. I, p. 552, and T. A. Brown (*American Stage*), p. 327. More satisfactory accounts, however, are the newspaper obituaries (of which the best is by James Rees (Colley Cibber) in the Philadelphia *Mercury*) filed in the Harvard Theatre Collection.

actor's next *New Way* at the Tremont, Boston, March 5, 1833. A
Baltimore bill contributes a cast for a performance at the Front
Street Theatre on January 8, 1834:

Sir Giles Overreach .... Scott
Wellborn .... B. Blaike
Lord Lovell .... Ray
Marrall .... Wills
Justice Greedy .... S. P. Jones
Allworth .... Garner
Lady Allworth .... Mrs. McKenzie
Margaret .... Mrs. Willis

Scott is, however, more in his natural habitat at the Bowery Theatre, where Sir Giles Overreach was very much alive on August
13, 1834.[22] Back in Boston in 1835, this time at the Warren, Scott
acted Overreach on August 17.[23] The following year he was at the
Franklin playing in *A New Way to Pay Old Debts* on March 12
and June 14 with J. M. Brown as Marrall, Thayer as Wellborn,
John Sefton as Greedy, and Miss Fisher as Margaret.[24] It is a long
way from New York to St. Louis—it was longer in those days—
but we must take it in our stride. Scott was at the New Theatre
there in June 1838 and acted Overreach. So at least Ludlow,
though Carson shows room for reasonable doubt.[25] When I find
the Scott-Sir Giles combination again, it is back East, for a bill
shows the cast for a performance at the Holliday Street Theatre,
Baltimore, on September 19:

Sir Giles Overreach .... Scott
Wellborn .... Wood
Lord Lovell .... Lyne
Marrall .... Stanley
Justice Greedy .... Riddle
Allworth .... Hautonville
Lady Allworth .... Mrs. Hughes
Margaret .... Miss McBride

Apparently Scott did not mind travel: Miss Lucile Gafford tells
me that he played in *A New Way to Pay Old Debts* at the St.

---

22 Odell, Vol. IV, p. 25.
23 Harvard Boston list.
24 Odell, Vol. IV, pp. 99, 101.
25 Ludlow, p. 503; Carson, p. 249.

Charles Theatre, New Orleans, on January 7, 1839. On September 11, 1839, he opened the New Chatham Theatre, New York City, with his portrayal of Sir Giles. In this "New and Splendid Establishment"—I quote from the bill—Flynn's company gave Scott the following support:

Sir Giles Overreach .... Scott
Wellborn .... Harrison
Lord Lovell .... Buttingham[26]
Marrall .... Barnes
Justice Greedy .... Jones
Allworth .... Russell
Lady Allworth .... Mrs. Bannister
Margaret .... Mrs. Flynn

A bill shows John R. Scott at the Chestnut Street Theatre, Philadelphia on December 12—note the Allworth:

Sir Giles Overreach .... Scott
Wellborn .... Wood
Lord Lovell .... Harrington
Marrall .... Johnson
Justice Greedy .... Faulkner
Allworth .... Davenport
Lady Allworth .... Mrs. Thayer
Margaret .... Miss Fisher

The next collaboration between Scott and Massinger is again at the Chatham, in an engagement which began on March 29, 1842; *A New Way to Pay Old Debts* on the 31st.[27] Let two years and a half pass, and we are at the Bowery late in October or early in November 1844, with Sir Giles very much at home in his old haunt.[28] We skip England now, having already covered it, and bring Scott back to New York for *A New Way to Pay Old Debts* at the St. Charles Theatre (late White's Varieties), March 16, 1853, repeated on the 24th.[29] Scott, it is plain, is getting more and more "popular." We close Scott's career as Sir Giles at the Chatham on August 2, 1854, and for the first time cite Brown, Odell not having

[26] Not Henry E. Stevens, as Odell (Vol. IV, p. 376) and Ireland (Vol. II, p. 321) say, unless there was a substitution.
[27] Odell, Vol. IV, p. 567.
[28] *ibid.*, Vol. V, p. 107.
[29] Odell, Vol. VI, p. 246.

recorded the performance.[30] The reader will note that I have found practically no references to Scott as Sir Giles in the way of first-hand criticisms or reviews. Scott was a popular phenomenon, so common that it appeared unnecessary to comment on his appearances. The newspapers mention the "ever popular tragedian," "successful Scott," "welcome him back," etc., but are to blame in not telling us how he acted the part. Obituaries mention it as one of his best, but give no details. It is curious: Scott is one of the mysteries of histrionic history—praised, admired, accepted as a matter of course, but commented on very little. We must go to London in 1846 for anything really enlightening. Scott was a good actor, almost great, but he has practically passed into oblivion.

I am not stirred at all by D. D. McKinney; nor by his performance of Sir Giles Overreach for his own benefit at the Park Theatre on March 25, 1834. He had not the calibre for a Park actor, though he starred there for a space before returning to his Bowery audience.[31] Ireland says with proper cultivation he would have been a very creditable actor. He left the Bowery later in 1834, dismissed because of his connection with the riot which drove stage-manager George P. Farren from that theatre, and is principally heard from after that date—if indeed he is heard from at all —as manager in Buffalo, Columbus, and briefly at the Olympic Theatre, New York. D. D. McKinney need trouble us no further.

The next actor to play Sir Giles was Charles H. Eaton, whose untimely death in 1843 when he was not yet thirty brought to a sudden close a career that showed signs of being really distinguished. Born in Boston in 1813 of comfortably well-off parents, Eaton received a good education, and showed at the same time a decided bent for the stage by joining an amateur theatrical society where he soon towered over his fellows. He made his professional début at the Warren Theatre on January 15, 1833, in *The Stranger*, and critics who came to jeer remained to cheer. Wisely enough, Eaton put himself through a rigid course of training before he joined the theatre in earnest and did not act again until at the request of numerous citizens he appeared with the Kembles when they played in Boston in September. From this time on,

[30] Brown, Vol. II, p. 17.
[31] Odell, Vol. III, p. 688; Ireland, Vol. I, p. 660.

Eaton's success in Boston, and indeed elsewhere, was assured, and he became a star of the first magnitude. Various tours carried his success west and southwest where he was favorably compared with Booth. His brilliant career hardly started, he returned to the Exchange Hotel in Pittsburgh after playing at the Pittsburgh Theatre one night in May 1843, and, seized with dizziness, the result of an exhausting performance of *William Tell,* he fell down the well of a spiral staircase. He died of a fractured skull a few days later, mourned by all who knew him and all who admired his able acting. His style was his own. "With all the physical essentials of face, form, voice, and natural grace, he was enabled, thus richly endowed, to convey fully and forcibly, his minutely accurate and scholarly conceptions. His performances all bore an intellectual impress. As a reader of Shakespeare, he was unsurpassed."[32]

Eaton made his first appearance as Sir Giles Overreach at the Tremont Theatre in his native city on May 8, 1834; a Harvard clipping contributes to our information by telling us that the Lord Lovell was Williamson and the Wellborn that favorite stock actor, W. H. Smith. The Margaret of the occasion obtains a local habitation and a name when a Harvard clipping of June 12, announcing the play for that night, gives Miss Clarke as the impersonator; this was her first appearance in Boston in seven years, and it was for the benefit of Mrs. Barnes. Eaton made his New York début at the Park on July 8, 1834, four days later presenting his interpretation of extortion, but the heat apparently so discouraged the reviewers that they did not attend.[33] On September 23, at the Tremont, however, according to a Boston clipping in the Harvard collection, his performance was "masterly." In 1835 there were engagements in Philadelphia (Walnut Street) and Baltimore (both Holliday and Front Streets), and what happened there I can only guess, except for a performance of *A New Way to Pay Old Debts* at the first on June 3.[34]

[32] Clapp, p. 313, who on pp. 306-13 gives much the best account of Eaton and whose information is first-hand. Charges of intoxication and deliberate eccentricity against Eaton—see for example the gossip of Joe Cowell, p. 679—seem to be utterly false. (Cowell, *Thirty Years Passed Among the Players,* New York, 1844.)

[33] Odell, Vol. III, p. 673.

[34] Clapp, p. 310; Wilson, p. 137.

In the spring of the next year, *A New Way to Pay Old Debts*
had an adventure to delight the heart of the stage-historian after
a previous paragraph of desiccation. It floated out on the water of
the Ohio River and was presented on the show-boat of the famous
Chapman family about whom Sol. Smith and Ludlow tell such tall
and interesting anecdotes.[35] *This* tale belongs to Eaton, and the
reader will perceive how well he relates it. I need only say that it
is one of a series of letters which appeared in the *Cincinnati Daily
News*. The letter is dated Cincinnati, May 1836, though I take it
from *The Spirit of the Times* for November 3, 1838. Eaton's
words follow:

> Played two engagements for Mr. Potter, at the Third street
> Theatre, and one for the Chapman family, on the Ohio river, at
> their *Floating Theatre*. This last engagement fully tested my
> powers of gravitation. The Floating Theatre speaks much for the
> ingenuity and enterprise of Mr. Chapman. It was constructed
> somewhat in the manner of our smallest steamboats, save that the
> engine was placed directly under the pit, or (as the bills of the day
> announced it) the parquette. The front of the theatre was very
> conveniently arranged, and several rooms were neatly made in
> the stage, for the accommodation of Mr. Chapman and his amiable
> family. The steam-engine attached to the boat, obviated a most
> important difficulty which was attendant upon their previous
> exertions. A temporary affair had been erected by Mr. Chapman,
> a year or two ago, in which he gave theatrical entertainments at
> all of the principal towns on the Mississippi. This would have
> been all very well, if, like the boy in coasting, he might have re-
> turned to repeat the trip. But as it was impossible to ascend the
> river without steam, there was a veto placed upon the boat the
> moment it reached New Orleans, and they were compelled to sell
> it for firewood.
>
> But the steam-engine (thanks to the immortal Fulton!) entirely
> removed this check to the treasury. I played Richard III. on the
> first night; James Crow Rice, or more classically speaking, Daddy
> Rice, played in one of his farces—having been engaged by Mr.
> Chapman to play with me for four nights. The performances
> went off with much eclat. The second night was to be played "A
> New Way to pay Old Debts," and "Oh Hush." On this occasion
> "the public were most respectfully informed, that the theatre

[35] Sol. Smith, p. 89; Ludlow, pp. 567-70.

would float down some two or three hundred yards, in order that those ladies and gentlemen who were unaccustomed to *wading,* might be accommodated." We had a fine house, or as we then termed it, *"an excellent boat."* Every one who has visited Cincinnati is aware of the noise and confusion which the continual plying of the boats up and down the river, makes. This evening it appeared to me to be worse than ever. During the first four acts, the boat rolled first on one side then the other, and the text of Massinger was most rudely mangled by the escape-valves of the neighboring boats. Here is a specimen. *Marrall*—"Sir, for what cause do you use me thus?" *Sir Giles*—"Cause, slave, why I am angry." (Here a boat came up to the wharf next to the theatre, there being no other vacant spot. The engineer's bell rang, away went the steam, with a tremendous noise, which completely drowned my voice.) *Sir Giles*—"Wer't in a church, by heaven and hell I'd do it." (Here a black fellow thrust his head behind the scenes, mistaking, as I suppose, in the hurry and confusion, that we had just arrived, and asked me "if I *had any baggage?*" but when he saw my theatrical dress, the poor fellow was completely thunder-struck; he retreated by the door through which he came, and was pushed by the door-keeper with such force as to precipitate him into the river. Fortunately for him, the water was not deep where he fell, and he crawled up to the wharf half dead with fright. Porters, boatmen, coachmen, &c. &c., were hurrying over our deck to get upon the next boat, which made her roll with increased force—when some in front cried out, "Gentlemen, trim the boat, she'll capsize." *Sir Giles*—"Oh that I had thee in my gripe, I'd tear thee, joint after joint." "It's no use, stranger," exclaimed the same voice, "you can't play while the boat zigzags in this fashion;—come over this side, gentlemen." Obedient to his summons, two thirds of the audience rushed to the other side of the boat, which made the matter still worse, for the weight was so unequally divided, that she gave one lurch and sent me, "with all my blushing honors thick upon me," head-first off the wing; as the boat inclined to the other side. I returned to the stage with the prompter, whose face was blacked to play with Rice in the after-piece. And such a picture!! I thought at the time —Oh. Hogarth, where art thou. Lord Lovell was on his hands and knees, vainly attempting to rise as the black prompter came tumbling over him. The audience mistook the prompter for Rice, and called for Jim Crow, while others told me to go on with my part. I tried to go on with the scene, but looked in vain for

Marrall—when to the astonishment of all he came to the front of the stage and told the audience *"that the cables had given way, and that we were moving rapidly down the river."* One wild and deafening yell was the response. They all rushed upon the deck, and as I was about to leave the stage, Daddy Rice came to me with his face half blacked, and a piece of burnt cork in his hand, and he laughed so violently that he actually fell on the stage. He said he was glad of it, for it was impossible to sing the beautiful music of Oh! Hush "when de debilish steamboats were lumbering round the theatre." I went on deck, and found Wellborn had thrown a rope to a boat which we were passing, which had effectually stopped us. As soon as the audience were seated, the farce of Oh Hush proceeded, in which Rice sang extemporaneously to the audience, but Rice told me afterwards that they had laughed so much during the first piece, that he stood no chance.

After this gorgeous event, it is shameful to have to return to the Bowery Theatre, New York, where on the 3rd of August, 1836, Eaton presented the fifth Act of *A New Way to Pay Old Debts* with Mrs. Watts as Margaret; Ingersoll, Pickering, Woodhull, Hamblin, Barton and Miss Waring played other scenes from other plays, making a somewhat disjointed evening.[36] A playbill relieves at least the monotony of the look of this page by giving us the cast when Eaton played Sir Giles at the National Theatre, Boston, September 1, 1836:

Sir Giles Overreach	Eaton
Wellborn	W. H. Smith
Lord Lovell	Lyne
Marrall	Jones
Justice Greedy	Spear
Allworth	Crane
Lady Allworth	Mrs. Sheridan
Margaret	Mrs. W. H. Smith

In January 1837 Eaton was back at the Bowery, acting Overreach on the 12th.[37] On February 20 he began an engagement at the South Pearl Street Theatre, Albany, and *A New Way to Pay Old Debts* was one of the plays in which he starred.[38] In April, how-

[36] Odell, Vol. IV, p. 85.
[37] *ibid.*, Vol. IV, p. 162.
[38] Phelps, p. 207.

ever, he was in New York again, though at a different theatre, the Franklin; the play in question on the 29th.[39] At the Lion Theatre, Boston, on August 21, only the fifth Act was presented, and I care not at all what made up the rest of the program.[40] Eaton now went touring in the West, and his Sir Giles there—if there—I shall let someone else trace, having had no success. His extortioner returned East by October 4, 1841, when he was exhibited at the Arch Street Theatre in Philadelphia, repeated there the following April 29, and at the Walnut Street on May 28; Pittsburgh, meanwhile, had seen it on April 4.[41] He made his reappearance in Boston—not his "first appearance for seven years," as the playbill announces; it was only five—on October 24, 1842, in Payne's play *Brutus, A New Way to Pay Old Debts* following on the next evening[42] with a familiar Tremont cast:

Sir Giles Overreach	Eaton
Wellborn	C. Howard
Lord Lovell	Ayling
Marrall	Chapman
Justice Greedy	Gilbert
Allworth	G. Howard
Lady Allworth	Mrs. J. Greene
Margaret	Mrs. H. Cramer

Eaton's last appearance as Sir Giles Overreach was at the Chatham Theatre, New York on March 15, 1843, for his own benefit, only part of the play being given.[43] Within two months, death cut short the career of a man whose name deserves to be remembered.

Charles Kemble Mason, nephew of Charles Kemble and brother of the more popular John Kemble Mason, made his first appearance in this country in 1834. In that year, indeed, he played Sir Giles Overreach at the Park, December 13.[44] He is chiefly interesting to us, however, as providing an entrance to the theatre on the frontier, specifically St. Louis, where Sir Giles was very much at

---

[39] Odell, Vol. IV, p. 158.
[40] Harvard Boston list.
[41] Wilson, pp. 251, 264, 266; Fletcher, pp. 377, 562.
[42] Cruickshank (Edition), p. 136, erroneously says *A New Way to Pay Old Debts* was presented on both the 24th and 25th.
[43] Odell, Vol. IV, p. 643.
[44] *ibid.*, Vol. IV, p. 12.

home. At the salt-house theatre (between Olive and Locust Streets) on August 10, 1835, I note an evening of "dramatic mélange" which included parts of *Julius Caesar, Richard III, The Hunchback,* and *Napoleon,* besides the last act of *A New Way to Pay Old Debts.* "Notwithstanding the supposed strength of the bill," remarks manager Ludlow, "the theatre was not over-crowded."[45] Apparently Mason's Sir Giles was not a drawing card; —and it continued not to be, when the play was presented at the new St. Louis Theatre on May 1, 1839. With Thomas F. Lennox as Wellborn, Mat Field as Marrall, Green as Justice Greedy, Mrs. McLean as Margaret, and Mrs. Henry as Lady Allworth, the receipts were only a hundred and nineteen dollars, and Sol. Smith was moved to exasperation. "I tell you," he writes to Ludlow, "the people don't care a d—n for anything less than *Tree, Forrest, & Celeste!*" A few days later, on May 4, Mason had his benefit, and the mélange of the evening consisted of acts from *Macbeth, The Wife, A New Way to Pay Old Debts, Napoleon,* and, according to Sol. Smith, *Hamlet.* However, the house was so small that Mason, after going through with *Macbeth,* refused to continue, and departed St. Louis forever. Shades of Edmund Kean—but there was no riot here! To tell truth, it was a little hard on Mason, who was a capable actor and who later played with Charlotte Cushman, Wallack, and Edwin Booth—was in fact the Ghost during Booth's long run of *Hamlet* at the Winter Garden in 1864-1865.[46]

On September 14, 1835, Matthew C. Field wrote from St. Louis to Sol. Smith: "I think the impression here regarding Sir Giles goes to Jo rather than Mason."[47] "Jo" was Matthew's brother, Joseph M. Field, the father of Kate Field and an actor who looms large in any history of the theatre on the frontier. An Englishman born in Dublin, he came to America as a child of two, and made his St. Louis début in 1830 at the age of twenty. His first recorded Sir Giles was exhibited at the old salt-house theatre on July 20, 1835, on the occasion of a farewell benefit, which Ludlow says was "remunerative to Mr. Field":[48]

[45] Ludlow, p. 437.
[46] Unless otherwise stated, the material on Mason in St. Louis is from Carson, pp. 276-8.
[47] Carson, p. 153.
[48] Ludlow, p. 436.

Sir Giles Overreach	Field
Wellborn	Ludlow
Lord Lovell	M. C. Field
Marrall	Watson
Justice Greedy	Sol. Smith
Allworth	Thompson
Lady Allworth	Mrs. Ludlow
Margaret	Mrs. Watson

Ludlow, indeed, sees fit to warn his readers not to be surprised to find Field essaying so difficult a rôle "but this . . . gentleman was just about that time beginning to think he was equal to any part in the round of the Drama. He afterwards settled down to what he really was clever in—eccentric comedy." Some of this pride is reflected in a letter Field wrote to Sol. Smith in the fall from Washington: "I played Sir Giles in Balte., Booth's own town—plenty of applause, and I am told they speak well of it here too."[49] Not yet having become an eccentric comedian, Field after a Sir Giles at the St. Charles Theatre, New Orleans on June 11, repeated the part in St. Louis on June 28, 1836, with the cast, I imagine, much the same as before. At any rate, Sol. Smith played Greedy, for Ludlow says wickedly: "In this character Mr. Smith was quite at home; he looked the part admirably." Since Ludlow has just been stigmatizing his partner, this appears to be a left-handed compliment to "a man six feet and an inch in height, and at the same time constructed pretty much after the style of a hop-pole."[50] On July 31, 1837, Field played Overreach at the New St. Louis Theatre with brother Mat as Wellborn, Vincent de Camp as Justice Greedy (Sol. Smith being absent and ill with brain-fever—nay, even reported dead in August!), Thomas Placide as Marrall, and Field's wife-to-be, Eliza Riddle as Margaret.[51] Certain features of the performance annoyed "Asmodeus" in the *Missouri Republican* two days later: "Again was the performance of Monday evening marred by the 'gagging' of one or two protégés of the managers. Asmodeus entered the theatre with the purpose of forming an opinion of Field's 'Sir Giles Overreach'; but it was impossible. As

[49] Carson, pp. 148-9.
[50] Ludlow, pp. 452-3, 456: New Orleans performance through the kindness of Miss Lucile Gafford.
[51] Carson, p. 195, who supplies the quotation.

well might he attempt to criticize the performance of a Paganini, when accompanied by the music of a hand organ." I do not know but I suspect that Joseph M. Field impersonated Overreach when *A New Way to Pay Old Debts* was revived for one performance in the fall of 1838; at least it was his part and he was a member of the company.[52] There is no doubt, however, about his Sir Giles at the Walnut Street Theatre, Philadelphia, on April 26, 1839.[53] Field might have become a really good actor, if he had had the time for it, but he became more distinguished as a newspaper editor and writer of essays and plays. He built and managed the Varieties Theatre in St. Louis, and was manager of the Mobile Theatre when he died.[54]

Walter M. Leman was a call-boy at the Tremont Theatre, Boston, when it began its first season in the fall of 1827; he was the last of the old Tremont company to die. The first part of his career is inevitably associated with Boston, the last equally inevitably with the West Coast. Those who remember him as "the good old man" of many plays may find it somewhat difficult to believe that, at least twice, he enacted Sir Giles Overreach. A stock actor, he naturally enough played the part only at his own benefits. The "first time" was at the Tremont Theatre, April 12, 1837, with Mrs. Muzzy as Lady Allworth and Miss McBride as Margaret; the second performance I note was at the National, same city, on June 21, 1839, when Lady Allworth was played by Mrs. Pelby and Margaret by Mrs. Anderson.[55] Four years before his death in 1890, he published a book of anecdotes and reminiscences, *Memories of an Old Actor,* an interesting comment on the theatre of the nineteenth century in America, even if it tells us in all modesty less about himself than we should like to know.

[52] Carson, p. 262. Meanwhile the play had been presented at the New St. Louis Theatre on January 18, 1838, during the unfortunate winter season when Ludlow and Smith took over a stranded rival company in Mobile and sent it to St. Louis under the leadership of Matthew Field. The cold was deadly, and the company also. The play drew only $62.50. Carson, pp. 224-5, does not name the Sir Giles; he was probably Thomas Lyne, a dimly twinkling "star" who took most of the big parts.

[53] Wilson, p. 206.

[54] Ireland, Vol. I, p. 631.

[55] Harvard Boston list, and clippings.

We shall mercifully skip a performance of *A New Way to Pay Old Debts* at the Franklin Theatre on April 14, 1837, Sir Giles Overreach by Mr. Barry—even Odell calls him "one Barry"—to return again to a gentleman already noticed in the first section of this book, John M. Vandenhoff, who made his American début at the National Theatre, New York, on September 11, 1837, "the first really distinguished English actor who had not first appeared at the Park."[56] He played out the season in this country and then returned to England; though he visited this country later, Sir Giles Overreach seems not to have been with him. On his first visit, however, Vandenhoff enacted Sir Giles four times. His first appearances were at the National, November 20 and 29, his third at the Tremont, Boston, on March 6, 1838, and his last back at the National on March 27.[57] The cast for the Boston performance of March 6,[58] which a Harvard newspaper clipping calls "masterly," was as follows—I quote from the bill:

Sir Giles Overreach	Vandenhoff
Wellborn	Murdock
Lord Lovell	Gilbert
Marrall	Andrews
Justice Greedy	Johnson
Allworth	Muzzy
Lady Allworth	Mrs. Muzzy
Margaret	Mrs. G. Barrett

Vandenhoff's engagements in this country were decidedly successful though he appealed mostly in parts better suited to his style, such as Hamlet, Cato, and Coriolanus. Since his Sir Giles Overreach has already been discussed, I see no point in discussing it again. Vandenhoff was a fine actor, but not a very distinguished Overreach. His later career in London and the provinces need not interest us here; significantly, he seems to have dropped Sir Giles after his first American trip.[59]

[56] Odell, Vol. IV, pp. 157, 213.

[57] *ibid.*, Vol. IV, pp. 218, 220, 224.

[58] Not the 5th, as Cruickshank gives (Edition), p. 135.

[59] The picture in Coad-Mims, p. 113, is of John Vandenhoff as Sir Giles, not George Vandenhoff. See the *Catalogue of Engraved British Portraits . . . in the British Museum* (by F. O'Donoghue, Vol. IV, p. 329, *s.v.* J. M. Vandenhoff, no. 2).

From Vandenhoff we descend to a series of minor actors who in
their day may have been popular and useful but who have not come
down to us with that éclat which makes them memorable. Our next
Sir Giles is Nathaniel H. Bannister who played the part at the
Franklin Theatre, New York, on April 30, 1838, with his wife as
Lady Allworth and T. S. Cline, always popular at the minor theatres, as Allworth. Bannister's wife was late Mrs. Stone, widow of
the author of *Metamora*. She seems to have preferred dramatists
as husbands, for Bannister is better known as playwright than as
actor, especially in the East. As actor he appeared first in Baltimore, the city of his birth, at the age of sixteen, with the usual
young aspirant's part of Young Norval in *Douglas*. In New York
he was generally at the Bowery or the Chatham but had no great
success, though he was a favorite in the Western theatres. As playwright, he composed almost a hundred trifles of no enduring value,
the most successful called *Putnam;* he also performed the prodigious feats of adapting *Timon of Athens* and *Titus Andronicus*
to the modern stage. I cannot find that he played Sir Giles again,
though he may have done so in the more open spaces; at any rate
we shall not follow him further.[60]

Not long back, I promised you a young lady as Sir Giles Overreach; if you have not already escaped, it is not my fault. The child
wonder was Jean M. Davenport, who after a previous success at
the National made a triumphant entry into—of all places—the
Park Theatre in July 1838, and with her mother's assistance acted
such rôles as Young Norval, Shylock, and Richard III. For her
benefit on August 1, she played Sir Peter Teazle to her mother's
Lady Teazle—how the proud lady must have stooped!—five parts
in a new piece called *Paul Pry in Petticoats,* and in the last act of
A New Way to Pay Old Debts, Sir Giles Overreach. About this
chaotic hodgepodge and this eleven year old Sir Giles, I write with
more sorrow than amusement. The bill notes that this was the first
time Miss Davenport played Overreach, and I hope it was the last:

Sir Giles Overreach	Miss Davenport
Wellborn	Richings
Lord Lovell	Gann
Marrall	Fisher

[60] Odell, Vol. IV, p. 312; Ireland, Vol. II, p. 205; Wemyss: *Chronology, s.v.*

Allworth .... Wheatley
Lady Allworth .... Mrs. Richardson
Margaret .... Mrs. Pritchard

Her childish days over, Miss Davenport became a good actress and played successfully, though intermittently, for many years. In 1860 she married Colonel Frederick W. Lander, who as General Lander of the Union Army was wounded in battle and died in March 1862. She seems to have been a clever child, and a charming and cultured lady, but I should prefer not to meet her as the terrifying Sir Giles. It was more the public's fault than hers. She is said to have been the original from whom Dickens drew Ninetta Crummles, "the infant phenomenon."[61]

Charles Freer we have met before, in London at the Royal Pavilion and Sadler's Wells. He developed no more in this country than in England, hopping back and forth between extravagant melodrama and tragedy, popular at minor theatres without ever achieving distinction. Alas, he finally committed suicide in London in 1858, unable to secure further employment. His first consecutive engagement in New York began at the Olympic on May 27, 1839, with Sir Giles Overreach his fourth part.[62] I do not know that he acted the rôle again in this country. Another single *New Way* may be as briefly recorded; this was at the Franklin on July 28, 1840, for the benefit of Watson who on that occasion presented himself as Overreach.[63] Odell does not dignify this gentleman by a first name, but he was, I suspect, the Charles Watson mentioned in Wemyss's *Chronology*; if so, he made his début under Wemyss at the Chestnut Street Theatre in Philadelphia in 1829 and was "a most excellent representative of Old Men." Too many "old men" played Sir Giles!

I cannot help including these minor Sir Giles's, little as many of them deserve inclusion; these little grains of sand go to make up the theatrical landscape of *A New Way to Pay Old Debts,* and it is not without significance that so many performers choose the play for their benefits and are then never heard of again in this chronicle. So popular was the play, and so convenient for the stock

---

[61] Ireland, Vol. II, pp. 227-8; Odell, Vol. IV, p. 210.
[62] Odell, Vol. IV, p. 315.
[63] *ibid.,* Vol. IV, p. 399.

company, that it seems to have been one of the inevitable benefit
choices. So it seemed at least to William Creswick who acted Sir
Giles at the Tremont Theatre, Boston, on February 8, 1841. The
bill gives familiar names as support:

    Sir Giles Overreach .... Creswick
    Wellborn .... Leman
    Lord Lovell .... Ayling
    Marrall .... Andrews
    Justice Greedy .... Gilbert
    Allworth .... Muzzy
    Lady Allworth .... Mrs. Muzzy
    Margaret .... Mrs. H. Cramer

Creswick, however, must not be included among the grains of
sand. He had, as we have seen, an important career in London and
Australia, and got into the *Dictionary of National Biography*.

The benefits pile up! George G. Spear ("Old Spudge") played
Sir Giles in the last act of *A New Way to Pay Old Debts* for his
benefit at the Tremont only a little over two months later, June 16,
1841, the main part of the evening being devoted to *William Tell,*
the cast as before except Marrall by Benson—this from the bill.
The best account of Spear, to my knowledge, is the obituary in
The Boston Herald of July 11, 1887, three days after his death,
and I note briefly, that he played "old men"—what, again?—, had
a long and successful career, largely in Boston, and had the good
fortune to spend his last years in the Forrest Home. A fine man
and an able comedian, admired and beloved. He was on the stage
of Ford's Theatre in Washington, as Binney the Butler in *Our
American Cousin,* when Wilkes Booth leaped upon it after shoot-
ing President Lincoln.

J. Hudson Kirby seems to have confined his performances of
Sir Giles Overreach to one in London, already chronicled, and one
in New York, that at the Bowery Theatre, inevitably associated
with Kirby's name, on July 5, 1842. Only the two last acts were
played for the benefit—did you not guess a benefit?—of Waldron.[64]
No doubt, in accord with the slogan, "Wake me up when Kirby
dies," his death scene was terrific—and *very* melodramatic. I have
said something of Kirby earlier in this book. Though born in

[64] Odell, Vol. IV, p. 557.

London, he is chiefly associated with the American stage where his "piled-up agonies" made him popular at the minor theatres in New York. Wemyss in his *Chronology* says he first played in this country under his management in 1837 at the Walnut Street Theatre, Philadelphia, "went to Pittsburgh, and was entrusted with a part of three lengths, became so frightened, that he went on board a boat after rehearsal, and started down the Ohio," all of which did not prevent his later becoming a howling success—I use the adjective advisedly. He died in London in 1848 after becoming popular at the Surrey Theatre.

Charles Mestayer benefited from a production of *A New Way to Pay Old Debts* at the Chatham, New York, on the 25th of February, 1843. Odell does not mention the Sir Giles of the occasion, but the *Herald* reveals that it was Mestayer, himself. Mestayer was apparently a comedian for the newspaper emphasizes that the part will be played "seriously."[65]

The next Sir Giles on my list—Reader, think up for me a new way to start an old paragraph—is William M. Fleming, who, though completely forgotten now by everyone except the professed stage-historian, had a career as actor and manager which might almost be called distinguished. He was born in Connecticut in 1827 and as a boy worked in a printing office. Amateur theatricals finally brought him to the professional stage, and in 1840, March 31, to the Chestnut Street Theatre in Philadelphia as Shylock, a character which was followed on April 10 by Sir Giles Overreach.[66] Though he appeared in New York as early as 1843—much earlier according to clippings not backed by the weight of Odell— I cannot find that he played Overreach there until his performance at the Chatham Theatre between March 11 and 18, 1847.[67] What a haven, by the way, the Chatham seems to have been for *A New Way to Pay Old Debts,* at least its more melodramatic aspects! And then we skip nine years before I find another Sir Giles by Fleming, on June 24, 1856, at Burton's Chambers Street Theatre, Palmo's Opera House "undergone a thorough renovation," and

[65] *ibid.,* Vol. IV, p. 642; *The New York Herald.*
[66] Wilson, p. 222.
[67] Odell, Vol. V, p. 283.

now famous for its manager, its company, and its productions. A bill preserves the cast:

Sir Giles Overreach .... Fleming
Wellborn .... Prior
Lord Lovell .... Edwin Adams
Marrall .... Fuller
Justice Greedy .... George Holland
Allworth .... Dunn
Lady Allworth .... Mrs. Lesdernier
Margaret .... Mrs. Fleming

I shall be forgiven for pointing out the importance of the Justice Greedy and the Lord Lovell by the addition of first names usually omitted in my casts. Whatever Fleming's Sir Giles—and generalizing clippings in the Harvard Theatre Collection especially commend it—this must have been a fine performance. Fleming's later career, besides his success as an actor, was a series of managerships in Albany, Boston, New York, Savannah, Macon, and the Southern circuit generally. Through the influence of Horace Greeley, he was appointed paymaster on General W. T. Sherman's staff and at the close of the war was a brevet colonel. With all his ability and all his reputation, he remains for me, after considerable study, a vague and shadowy figure, and his Sir Giles Overreach equally nebulous.

Three of the Booths played Sir Giles, two of them famously. The third, Junius Brutus Booth, Jr., was an actor of only ordinary gifts, though a manager of undoubted ability. He was born in Charleston in 1821 and spent his boyhood mainly on the Booth farm near Baltimore. He made his first appearance on the stage as Tressel in *Richard III* at Pittsburgh in 1834. After journeying for a number of years with his father, he became a leading member of Hamblin's company at the Bowery Theatre, New York, which he left in order to act for C. R. Thorne at the Boston Theatre in Federal Street and for Pelby at the National. Catching the California fever, he went west in the early 'fifties and gained there perhaps his greatest success as actor and manager. Upon his return to the East, he became lessee and manager of the Boston Theatre, and for a short while succeeded his brother Edwin as manager of Booth's Theatre. After various starring tours, he became the proprietor of the Masconomo House in Manchester, Massachusetts, where he died in 1883.

Booth, Jr.'s Sir Giles was a pigmy beside the Titans of his father and brother, and needs little comment here. The first time that I know he played the character was for his benefit—of course! —on March 31, 1847, at the Bowery Theatre, New York.[68] It may have been a reasonably happy event, for the bills announcing the play with Booth as Sir Giles for the Boston Theatre (Federal Street) on August 17 of the same year say, "as performed by him at the Bowery Theatre, New York, with the most distinguished success." Or was this mere advertising?

Sir Giles Overreach . . . . .J. B. Booth, Jr.
Wellborn (first app.) . . . . Sullivan
Lord Lovell . . . . McFarland
Marrall . . . . Johnson
Justice Greedy . . . . Spear
Allworth . . . . Watkins
Lady Allworth . . . . Mrs. Cramer
Margaret . . . . Mrs. Mestayer

And Junius Brutus Booth, Jr., as Sir Giles, may, for all I care, fade into the dim light of theatrical history.[69]

Henry Lynne (Leach) from the Liverpool and Manchester theatres played Sir Giles, the favorite of Bowery audiences, at that theatre on May 22, 1848, with Mrs. Abbott as Margaret and Dyott as Wellborn.[70] There is an account of him in *The Spirit of the Times* of August 5, 1854, where the curious may read. Lynne stayed in this country until his death, playing the minor Eastern and Western theatres, I gather sometimes venturing into the seats of the mighty without ever being very comfortable there. Postmortem accounts are always flattering, so we may take with some salt the praise in the paper cited above, but "some of his portrayals of characters, selected from the highest range of the drama, will long be recollected by those who witnessed them, by the deep thought, close study, and understanding appreciation which they

[68] Odell, Vol. V, p. 273.

[69] It was the senior Booth who played Sir Giles at the Boston Theatre on March 28, 1848; Cruickshank in error gives the performance to his son (Edition), p. 136.

[70] Odell, Vol. V, p. 352.

manifested." Among these, curiously enough, is listed Sir Giles Overreach, which would seem to indicate more familiarity with the rôle than I have been able to discover.

Charles Dibden Pitt was also a success as an English provincial actor before coming to this country. Ludlow says he "was a very clever general actor, but not great in any line. His best specimens of acting were in characters of the melodramatic line; his Shakespearean characters were only mediocre. There was a great sameness in his personations; he could never divest himself of himself —he was always Mr. Pitt."[71] He first appeared in this country in 1847 and stayed about four years before returning to Great Britain to take part in management at Manchester. I find his Sir Giles at the Arch Street Theatre, Philadelphia, on January 21, 1848, and at Pittsburgh on March 20 and July 10.[72] During an engagement at the St. Charles Theatre, New Orleans, which began on December 9, 1848, Pitt played Overreach on the 13th. Ludlow and Smith's bill gives the cast:

Sir Giles Overreach	Pitt
Wellborn	Morton
Lord Lovell	Dougherty
Marrall	Fuller
Justice Greedy	Watson
Allworth	Wright
Lady Allworth	Mrs. R. Russell
Margaret	Miss Stuart

If Pitt played Sir Giles in New Orleans, heaven knows how many other places saw his performance, but in New York I find *via* Odell only one, that at the Brooklyn Museum late in September 1850, with Lynne as chief support.[73]

About the time that Pitt was Sir Giles in New Orleans, Jacob W. Thoman was another self at the Boston Museum, December 18, 1848. It was Thoman's benefit, the first time he played the part, and according to the bill the "First time in this Establishment." Though I am a bit suspicious, the play, according to J. B. Clapp's Harvard Boston list, was repeated the following night. If so, Thoman must

---

[71] Ludlow, pp. 680-1.
[72] Wilson, p. 371; Fletcher, pp. 398, 401, 567, 568.
[73] Odell, Vol. VI, p. 100; on September 18?

have made something of an impression, for the procedure was not at all usual.[74] The cast was as follows:

Sir Giles Overreach .... Thoman
Wellborn .... W. H. Smith
Lord Lovell .... Whitman
Marrall .... W. Warren
Justice Greedy .... Curtis
Allworth .... J. A. Smith
Lady Allworth .... Mrs. Judah
Margaret .... Miss L. Gann

Thoman was a Philadelphian who was destined for the ministry but became actor instead. He made his début in 1834 at the age of eighteen at the Chestnut Street Theatre; he is best remembered as a member of the Boston Museum company and later as manager of the American Theatre in San Francisco. He was a clever and versatile but not distinguished actor, and I note his Sir Giles only to pass on to a new production.[75]

This was, I believe, the first amateur production of *A New Way to Pay Old Debts* in this country, but by no means, as we shall see when the time comes, the last. At the Histrionic Temple, "the well-known Amateur Theatre in Nayades Street," the play was presented on May 14, 1849, for the entertainment of subscribers to the Louisiana Histrionic Association. Gaisford's curious little book on the drama in New Orleans is the source of this interesting information but gives no cast.[76] I am sorry; I should like to have the name of this amateur Sir Giles. There were of course many Thespian societies in the cities of America active earlier than this, and it is odd that *A New Way to Pay Old Debts* should be selected only at the mid-century. Such seems to be the case, however; within a few years amateurs, we shall find, present the play in New York for the first time there. One does not know whether this is a phenomenon to be explained or due merely to unsatisfactory earlier records.

The history of Charles W. Couldock is almost a history of nineteenth century acting. When he died, in 1898, he was eighty-three

---

[74] Cruickshank gives the performance to Booth (Edition), p. 136.
[75] Material from an article by J. B. Clapp in the *Boston Transcript* of January 30, 1916.
[76] Gaisford, p. 44.

years old, over sixty of which had been dedicated to the profession. Born in England he obtained the usual training in amateur and provincial companies and played with Fanny Vining, Charles Kean, Mathews, Mme. Vestris, Macready, and Charlotte Cushman. He came to the United States in 1849 with the last named and toured the country with her. Since then he has been a well known figure here, and deserves to remain so. He was a capable and versatile actor, and a much admired man.[77]

It was inevitable that an actor of the type of Couldock, playing stock and leads, trouping and touring, should play Sir Giles Overreach in *A New Way to Pay Old Debts*. It was a piece too widely known, too satisfactory for all sorts of purposes, to be omitted from the repertoire of any actor who could play it satisfactorily. I have no doubt that Couldock acted Sir Giles many times and with varied experience; I know of only a few performances, but it is significant how many years separate them. How many hypothetical performances must we place between them? The reader may well imagine. The first I find is at the Walnut Street Theatre, Philadelphia, on May 23, 1851, with Margaret by Miss Kinlock for the benefit of Dr. Cunnington, the musical director. The bill shows the rest of the cast:

Wellborn .... Dyott
Lord Lovell .... McMillan
Marrall .... Chapman
Justice Greedy .... A'Becket
Allworth .... Kames
Lady Allworth .... Mme. Ponisi

It is two years before we find Sir Giles in Pittsburgh on May 16, 1853.[78] The next two performances are only a week apart; at the Boston Museum on November 1 and 8, 1854:

Sir Giles Overreach .... Couldock
Wellborn (1st time) .... Keach
Lord Lovell .... Davies
Marrall .... Warren

[77] The Harvard Theatre Collection has a fine batch of clippings about Couldock.
[78] Fletcher, pp. 432, 575.

Justice Greedy .... W. H. Smith
Allworth .... Bascom
Lady Allworth .... Mrs. Vincent
Margaret .... Mrs. Rainforth

But six years go by before the next bill I have found; at the
Bowery Theatre, June 27, 1860:

Sir Giles Overreach .... Couldock
Wellborn .... Lingham
Lord Lovell .... Taylor
Marrall .... Hill
Justice Greedy .... Pearson
Allworth .... Stewart
Lady Allworth .... Miss Singleton
Margaret .... Miss Couldock

Harry Pearson and Eliza Couldock had their names in capitals
along with the Sir Giles of the evening. And now twelve years go
by, and we brush away time with one stroke, almost to the present,
for the performance I am about to mention was rescued from
oblivion by the extraordinary memory of William Seymour, actor,
stage-director, and charming conversationalist. He remembered
playing one of the small parts in *A New Way to Pay Old Debts* in
J. W. Lanergan's stock company at the Academy of Music, St.
John, New Brunswick, in June or July of 1872. Couldock was the
Sir Giles and Louis Aldrich the Wellborn. Lanergan had played
Valentine in Roberts's version of *Faust*; Roberts first acted with the
elder Booth. Lanergan's company played Sir Giles in 1872, and a
member of its cast lived until 1933 to tell about it. A century swept
away in two sentences, intimately connected. What a piece of work
is a man!

Fortunately we come now to an actor to whom we can fairly
give considerable space. Gustavus Vaughan Brooke, his life, and
his performances of Sir Giles have been treated earlier, and no
further estimate of the ability of his impersonation is really
needed. He played the part a number of times in this country, how
many I have not been able to discover. The terrors of stage-history
are partially revealed by the statement made by Brooke's accurate
biographer that between the 6th of September, 1852, and June 14,
1853, Brooke played Sir Giles Overreach fourteen times, more

than the total number of performances I have been able to find for his whole American sojourn.[79] The reader must therefore supply in his imagination performances in the cities to which I can give but scant attention. But is it not possible, someone will say, to find these other performances? Granting that it were worth while to devote time to visiting the cities in question, turning over all newspapers that carried theatrical advertising and reviews, scanning playbills collected and situated in various parts of this country and abroad, perfectly possible—or at least very probable. But does the reader have any conception of what this would mean for, say, Kean or Booth? It would mean tracing year by year, almost day by day the life of every actor treated. We should end up without doubt with some very interesting information, and with some very sparse white hair. And I question seriously whether we should have succeeded any better, though more thoroughly and pedantically, in reaching the goal desired: to show how widespread was the popularity of *A New Way to Pay Old Debts,* how it was interpreted by actors, why it stirred people to such enthusiasm, and incidentally how very fascinating is the history of the stage and theatre and how revealing of the times and customs. No, reader, you must hunt for these other performances yourself, if you *will* have them.

Gustavus Vaughan Brooke made his first appearance in this country on December 15, 1851, as Othello at the Broadway Theatre, New York. Sir Giles Overreach followed on the 16th, 18th, and 25th, the last of which goes unnoticed by Odell, but is presented conclusively by a bill as a "splendid dramatic festival":[80]

Sir Giles Overreach .... Brooke
Wellborn .... Fenno
Lord Lovell .... Pope
Marrall .... Davidge
Justice Greedy .... Whiting
Allworth .... Reynolds
Lady Allworth .... Mrs. Abbott
Margaret .... Miss Crocker

In line I suppose with the Christmas spirit, "a portion of the third circle has been appropriated for the accommodation of respectable

---

[79] On Brooke in America, see Lawrence, pp. 118-28.
[80] Odell, Vol. VI, p. 115, and playbill.

Colored Persons." Brooke's New York engagement, partly due to the efforts of his friend, Edwin Forrest, was a distinct success personally and financially, though the critics, not realizing how fast Brooke had been going down hill, were somewhat at a loss to account for his great reputation. *The Albion* of December 20 did not entirely approve of Othello: "Since writing the above, we have seen Mr. Brooke in *Sir Giles Overreach,* but do not find him rise higher in our estimation. . . . He is a good actor spoiled by mannerism and trickery . . . certainly not a great one. . . . In the last act he was decidedly good . . . his death scene though elaborated exceedingly fine." His habit of voice-changing, thus creating notable transitions in common dialogue, the reviewer particularly scored. The critic in *The Spirit of the Times* of December 20 also notices this trick and deplores it but after seeing his Sir Giles Overreach remarks: "We are convinced that he is a gentleman of excellent taste, of learning, and of a high order of histrionic ability. His action is graceful, his enunciation generally very distinct, and his declamation more 'trippingly on the tongue' than in most actors. When he makes a point the audience feel it, and he makes it effective, physically and intellectually, by suiting the action to the word. We mean by this that his attitudes, though studied and extremely artistic, are nevertheless, often well designed and natural."

From New York, Brooke went to Philadelphia, opening at the Walnut Street Theatre on January 5, 1852 as Sir Giles Overreach, repeated on the 7th.[81] With the warning to make all due allowances for the advertisement, I note that the playbill of January 8 calls it "a signal triumph." From Philadelphia, *we* go to Boston, though Brooke continued south as we learn from the National Theatre, Boston, playbill of February 23. It announces that the "Eminent English Tragedian, Mr. G. V. Brooke . . . who having met the most brilliant success at New York, Philadelphia, Washington, Baltimore, and Richmond, will make his First Appearance in Boston in his celebrated character of Sir Giles Overreach"—the capitals I have as usual reduced:

[81] Wilson, p. 455.

Sir Giles Overreach .... Brooke
Wellborn .... Leman
Lord Lovell .... Monroe
Marrall .... Spear
Justice Greedy .... Williams
Allworth .... Sandford
Lady Allworth .... Mrs. Tyrrell
Margaret ....Mrs. Prior

Walter Leman, who, notice, was the Wellborn on this occasion, gives in his *Memories*[82] a valuable description of Brooke: "He opened in 'Sir Giles Overreach,' and made a most marked impression. There was an intensity, a fire of energy in his representations that took captive the auditor, whether he would or no; and he was always so essentially in earnest that he inspired those who acted with him with the same feeling. The magnetism of an earnest actor is more likely to develop what is worthy of development in the histrionic Neophite, than the chilly, arms-length manner and spirit which says, 'stand at a distance; be a nonentity; do nothing.' The Macready theory was the very reverse of the Booth school; the one said 'I'll do all the acting,' the other said, 'Act up to me.' Brooke was a disciple of the Booth school." The part was repeated at the Walnut Street Theatre, Philadelphia, on March 30.[83] Lawrence remarks of the series of engagements[84] that, though all were financial successes, "none save the Boston critics went into strophes of enthusiasm over his superb physical endowments, or expatiated at length on the Rembrandt-like skill with which he relieved the tones of his rich and sonorous voice by facile transitions from high to low notes."

The first tour over, Brooke was now in funds, and he foolishly leased the always disastrous Astor Place Opera House on May 2, 1852, and played Sir Giles there on the 12th with Mrs. Charles Hale making her American début as Margaret.[85] The Astor Place Opera House soon proved unsatisfactory, and Brooke had the misfortune to quarrel with Hamblin at the Bowery. Things went from bad to worse, and soon he was deeply involved in debt. The hot

[82] Leman, p. 120.
[83] Wilson, p. 459.
[84] Lawrence, p. 121.
[85] Odell, Vol. VI, p. 160.

weather made his performances at Niblo's and Brougham's Lyceum in June completely unsuccessful, and there was nothing for it but to rest for the summer.

Fortunately in August, Brooke, who was a child where money was concerned, secured the services of Hall Wilton as his manager and was shortly prosperous again. Phelps notes a performance of Sir Giles at the Albany Museum late in September,[86] but this is only one stop on a tour which included Philadelphia, Buffalo, Cincinnati, St. Louis and other cities, and the reader must supply performances for himself. In December, Brooke was back in Boston, again at the National, playing Sir Giles on the 10th—so the Harvard Boston list. During the early months of 1853 it is difficult to follow him, but he played Sir Giles in Pittsburgh on January 7.[87] He was in Boston for his farewell benefit on May 27 when he was presented with a magnificent service of silver plate—Boston was strong in its opinions—and in Philadelphia early in June, Overreach at the Walnut Street on the 2nd,[88] to make his last appearance in America. During this last tour (starting September 9) Brooke averaged about forty-five pounds a night for approximately one hundred eighty performances, fourteen of which, as I have already noted, were as Sir Giles. He sailed for England with much praise for the country "where every man, whether English or Irish, receives the best reward for his labours." These are Brooke's own words.

After Brooke, a great Sir Giles though on the decline and the last great Sir Giles to come to us from England, we return to the dead level of competent mediocrity. McKean Buchanan, almost always attractive in the West, never made much of a to-do in the East, though Easterners may remember him from an anecdote in Mark Twain's *Roughing It*. Originally a cotton broker in New Orleans, he made his New York début at Burton's Theatre on July 16, 1849, as "a distinguished amateur from the South." Phelps says[89] that "he was a bad imitation of Forrest" and that the one thing he could really play to perfection was draw poker, which, in the light of his successful career all over this country, England,

[86] Phelps, p. 267.
[87] Fletcher, pp. 429, 574.
[88] Wilson, p. 485.
[89] Phelps, pp. 262-3.

and Australia, is probably too harsh a judgment. We have seen that London newspapers gave him due praise when he acted there in 1852. It was earlier in that year, January 5, that Buchanan played Sir Giles in Pittsburgh;[90] the part was repeated on February 12 at the Howard Athenaeum in Boston with a cast revealed by a bill:

Sir Giles Overreach	Buchanan
Wellborn	Meeker
Lord Lovell	Ayling
Marrall	H. Lewis
Justice Greedy	Brand
Allworth	Hamblin
Lady Allworth	Mrs. Cramer
Margaret	Mrs. M. Jones

The Harvard Boston list does not show any further Boston Sir Giles by Buchanan. Odell, however, notes two performances in New York, March 17 and June 28, 1858,[91] for both of which I have seen bills. The first announces that "the distinguished American Tragedian" will play Sir Giles, and that the secondary attraction, Miss Alice Grey, will appear as Meg Overreach, but I had better give the cast entire:

Sir Giles Overreach	Buchanan
Wellborn	Fenno
Lord Lovell	Fitzgerald
Marrall	Sefton
Justice Greedy	Lingard
Allworth	Ferdon
Lady Allworth	Mrs. H. Jorden
Margaret	Miss Grey

The second bill proclaims that Buchanan "will appear in his great character of Sir Giles Overreach . . . received on his former engagement with the greatest favor." The lesser lights, though they achieve capitals, are R. Johnston as Wellborn and Mrs. A. Parker as Lady Allworth. Otherwise the cast was as before with the exception of Miss Silvia—who is Silvia?—as Meg Overreach. The

90 Fletcher, pp. 422, 573.
91 Odell, Vol. VII, pp. 44, 46.

Sefton who played Marrall was J. O., not John. We need linger no longer on McKean Buchanan.

Numerous amateur organizations were playing in New York in 1851-1852, but we need signal out only The Union Amateur Dramatic Club which on April 7, 1852, acted among other things *A New Way to Pay Old Debts* at the Gothic Hall, 316 Broadway. Why, by the way, has nothing been written about these nineteenth century amateur dramatic organizations? There were many in New York, Boston, and Philadelphia, and no doubt elsewhere, and out of them developed such actors as Forrest and Scott and C. H. Eaton.

James B. Roberts had a long and interesting career. Born on September 27, 1818, at Newcastle, Delaware, and making his début by playing Richmond to the elder Booth at the Walnut Street Theatre in 1836, he lived until September 14, 1901, to be the oldest American actor. After his début he wisely studied elocution under Lemuel G. White, Forrest's teacher, for two years before appearing again. His next ten years were taken up by gaining experience in stock companies mostly in the West. His first appearance in New York was at the Chatham Theatre, where he starred for a short engagement beginning on February 22, 1847. Numerous tours followed but Roberts was now fairly well known and his name appears frequently in theatrical annals. In 1856 he toured Great Britain where we have found him playing Sir Giles in London. Returning to America he wrote and produced the first version of *Faust* to be played in America, he himself acting Mephistopheles. Roberts continued to star in this and the more customary repertory until 1876 when, except for very brief engagements, he practically retired from the stage. For many years he was instructor in elocution at the Theological Seminary of Saint Charles Borromeo in Philadelphia. Beloved of many, he belonged to many organizations, Shakespearean and Thespian. In many ways he was an extraordinary man; yet such is the brevity of memory that he is now almost unknown.[92]

When Roberts first played Sir Giles Overreach I do not know; the first performance I can record took place in Pittsburgh on

[92] The best material on J. B. Roberts is in *The New York Dramatic Mirror,* November 11, 1899; September 28, 1901.

April 8, 1852; it was repeated on October 18.[93] The Howard
Athenaeum in Boston saw it on February 22 and 24, and March 7,
1854. The bills announcing Roberts's engagement call this his first
visit to Boston. The cast for February 22 was as follows:

Sir Giles Overreach	Roberts
Wellborn	Hanley
Lord Lovell	Warwick
Marrall	Hunt
Justice Greedy	Williams
Allworth	Loveday
Lady Allworth	Miss Cutler
Margaret	Mrs. Nichols

On the other two dates the English actress, Miss Fanny Morant,
played Margaret. The following announcement at the bottom of
the program is, I hope, without any special significance: "$25 Re-
ward will be paid by the Manager for such information as will lead
to the detection of any person or persons throwing articles from the
Gallery of this Theatre." A clipping from the Harvard Theatre
Collection is illuminating with regard to Roberts's success:

> This actor has just completed a three weeks' engagement in this
> city, under auspices not flattering or conducive to that popularity
> which a few claim for this new aspirant for histrionic laurels. He
> came here a stranger, and it is but justice to remark, that there are
> those whose opinions are entitled to respect, who rank him high
> in the calendar of actors, and predict for him a brilliant future.
> We sincerely trust that their hopes may be realized. We are not
> inclined to pronounce a man a giant, because he has a large nose,
> nor do we think that one or two scenes well acted, entitle an
> actor to the applause which only a Booth or a Vandenhoff may
> merit. The last scene in "New Way to Pay Old Debts," acted by
> Mr. Roberts, as *Sir Giles Overreach,* is a most effective bit of
> acting, and denotes careful training, for it is purely mechanical.
> It is great, nevertheless, and as a death scene, it is powerful. But
> it indicates neither genius or talent, for constant application will
> enable a man to die well, and by constant application also, the
> vaulter learns to throw his fifty consecutive somersets . . . we
> wish him success in his career, for he appears neither puffed up

[93] Fletcher, pp. 424, 427, 573, 574.

with vanity, nor fool enough to believe one half the praise that has been bestowed upon him here.

I find Roberts's next Sir Giles at the City Museum, Philadelphia, on November 5, 1855, for which another Harvard clipping contributes the cast:

Sir Giles Overreach .... Roberts
Wellborn .... Baker
Lord Lovell .... Byrne
Marrall .... Johnston
Justice Greedy .... Worrell
Allworth .... Lingham
Lady Allworth .... Miss Wells
Margaret .... Mrs. Baker

We have already met Mrs. Baker under the name of Alexina Fisher. Still another Harvard clipping quotes from the Philadelphia *Dispatch*:

> Mr. Roberts is one of the most promising among American actors. By care, reflection, study and practice, he has obtained an eminence in the profession which entitles him to a position in the first class. Careful, deeply versed in the idiosyncrasies of the characters he undertakes, he combines with intellectual perception, capacity to delineate the lights and shades of passion with warmth, faithfulness and impression. Identification with the part he assumes is one of his peculiar merits. Intensity, and that thorough sympathy with the action which absorbs all ideas of self, is peculiar to his personations. This capacity of assimilation is necessary to every great dramatic artist, and Mr. Roberts possesses it in a remarkable degree. His *Sir Giles Overreach* is consequently a great piece of acting. He carries the feelings of his audience with him throughout. The finale to the fifth act is rendered thrilling by his vivid portraiture of anger, malice and avarice, all foiled at the moment of anticipated triumph. . . .

Roberts's popularity in Boston is revealed by a return trip, when he played Sir Giles at the National Theatre on March 24 and 26 of the next year:

Sir Giles Overreach .... Roberts
Wellborn .... Rays
Lord Lovell .... Parsons
Marrall .... Burke

Justice Greedy .... Allen
Allworth .... Edwards
Lady Allworth .... Mrs. Archbold
Margaret .... Miss Emmons

One Boston newspaper became rhapsodic—why will people omit identification marks from clippings? "His rendering of the character of Sir Giles Overreach must be considered a masterly performance. There are portions—we would particularize the scene where the old miser urges his daughter to unwelcome nuptials—in which this young tragedian surpasses the best efforts of Booth, when 'Richard was himself.' " *This* I very strongly doubt. What was Pittsburgh's reaction to his Sir Giles, I wonder, on May 1?[94]

When Roberts returned from his trip to England, Sir Giles was still among the characters he enacted. The first performance I note is at Burton's Theatre (Tripler Hall), New York, on September 15, 1858, with the cast on the bill as follows:

Sir Giles Overreach .... Roberts
Wellborn .... Briggs
Lord Lovell .... Canoll
Marrall .... Smith
Justice Greedy .... Moore
Allworth .... MacRae
Lady Allworth .... Mrs. A. Parker
Margaret .... Miss Miller

Commenting on the engagement Odell[95] says: "Though a careful actor, Roberts never inflamed the East River." Perhaps not; he seems, however, to have inflamed the critic of the *Tribune*: "We have seen no such *Sir Giles Overreach* since the time of the elder Booth, and, indeed, we imagine that Mr. Roberts has some merits to which older actors were strangers. We mean particularly in his ability to speak rationally. Without being positively graceful, he is easy; without a commanding stature, he commands universal attention." I hope he received it in Pittsburgh on October 7.[96]

At the National Theatre, New York, on March 17, 1859, Roberts was again Sir Giles. The bill shows:

[94] Fletcher, pp. 450, 579.
[95] Odell, Vol. VII, p. 113.
[96] Fletcher, pp. 469, 583.

Sir Giles Overreach .... Roberts
Wellborn .... Prior
Lord Lovell .... Nunan
Marrall .... Jordan
Justice Greedy .... Weaver
Allworth .... Everitt
Lady Allworth .... Miss Crampton
Margaret .... Mrs. Jones

Charlotte Crampton, the "little Siddons" of the West, representative of Richard III and Mazeppa, must have taken Lady Allworth in her stride; as in life, she played many parts. We finish with Roberts by citing three performances, two of which were at the Walnut Street Theatre, Philadelphia, April 4, 1859, and January 31, 1860; for the first, the bill reads:

Sir Giles Overreach .... Roberts
Wellborn .... Perry
Lord Lovell .... Dubois
Marrall .... Rogers
Justice Greedy .... Thayer
Allworth ....Bascomb
Lady Allworth .... Mrs. Perry
Margaret .... Mrs. Leonard

For the second performance the cast was the same except Shewell as Wellborn, Bowers as Marrall, and Miss Anna Cowell as Margaret. To the best of my knowledge, his Sir Giles made a last stand at Pittsburgh on May 15.[97] I wonder did part of Sir Giles reappear when Roberts played Hertzog in *The Black Crook*?

The last time we saw James Bennett was dimly at Belfast in 1846; he now turns up as Overreach at the Boston Theatre on September 25 and 27, 1854, his fourth and fifth appearances:[98]

Sir Giles Overreach .... Bennett
Wellborn .... Pauncefort
Lord Lovell .... Daly
Marrall .... Gilbert

[97] *ibid.*, pp. 484, 586.
[98] The playbills; Cruickshank wrongly says the 22nd (Edition), p. 137.

Justice Greedy .... Wood
Allworth .... Cowell
Lady Allworth .... Miss Biddles
Margaret .... Miss Taylor

and Froth by Mrs. Dixon from Sadler's Wells. The Boston Theatre had, as will be plain, no ordinary stock company. Sir Giles was not perhaps so well supported at Montreal on August 15, 1855,[99] but he was in better company at the Boston Museum on May 20 and 30, 1856, when the playbills show the following taking part :[100]

Sir Giles Overreach .... Bennett
Wellborn .... Keach
Lord Lovell .... Davies
Marrall .... Warren
Justice Greedy .... Smith
Allworth .... Bascom
Lady Allworth .... Mrs. Vincent
Margaret .... Mrs. Rainforth

Of James Bennett not much is easily discovered. He was a provincial actor before coming to America; in 1859 he was at the Lyceum Theatre, London; in 1871 he appeared at Niblo's Garden, New York, and then returned to the provinces abroad; he died in 1885. Colonel Brown in his vague, broad way says he was a failure in this country on both visits; for the first, Harvard clippings contradict.[101]

We have seen in this chapter Sir Giles Overreach *en voyage*. He has now travelled much of the country, though there is much that his black heart cannot understand. He is sought after in many circles and consequently is to be found in the most unexpected quarters, appearing suddenly and disappearing as suddenly. Sometimes he has been invisible, and we have gathered his presence only from mysterious hints; sometimes there have been no hints, and he may have been near us without our knowledge. He has as many personalities as he has places of residence. Some of them are clear, some blurred by time and mediocrity, some not worth hunting.

[99] Graham, p. 115.

[100] Cruickshank (Edition), p. 137, gives Bennett a Sir Giles at the Museum on June 22, 1857; according to the Harvard Boston list, "Mr. Charles Jackson of Boston volunteers."

[101] Adams, *Dictionary, s.v.*; Brown, Vol. I, p. 210.

Who cares what Sir Giles was like when he took the name of Barry? How much more interesting when he was Eaton or Roberts; how revealing, how fascinating when he was Kean or the elder Booth! His career was nothing if not checkered. Though that section of it just discussed has been at times prosaic, it is significant and could not be omitted. Shortly, however, two great personalities emerge to take their places beside earlier histrionic Titans, personalities which really dominate the Sir Giles who lived in the third quarter of the nineteenth century in America. This last chapter is a history of dispersion, the next of local habitation and of two names, Edward L. Davenport and Edwin Booth.

CHAPTER X

BOTH ALIKE IN DIGNITY

T HE names of Edward Loomis Davenport and Edwin Booth may be fairly bracketed as the leading stars of the third quarter of the nineteenth century in America. Contemporary accounts call them both great actors, hardly dare say which is greater; yet it is one of the mysteries, perhaps one of the caprices, of theatrical history, that the name of Edwin Booth has meaning and import to the intelligent, whether theatrically inclined or not, while Davenport's has little significance except to the profession or the stage-historian. Part of this phenomenon may perhaps be explained by the statement that Davenport was often the critic's, rather than the people's, actor even in his own time, and though reviewers united in his praises, he was allowed to dissipate his fine talents in minor theatres and ephemeral pieces. Moreover Davenport's very versatility counted against him: a man who was excellent in so many different rôles became memorable in none; no particular characters were associated with his name, and the outline became confused and blurred. The public, once this was the case, no longer flocked to see him; the managers were dubious about engaging him. Davenport was really born too late; he belonged to the age of Junius Brutus Booth, when acting meant acting in anything and everything, not to the age of Edwin, where versatility gave way to a limited but concentrated proficiency. Edwin Booth's name means—shall we say?— Hamlet; Davenport's unfortunately an oblivion quite undeserved.

At the beginning of Davenport's career, however, we need not fear this spectre. Davenport was born on November 15, 1815, the son of a Boston inn-keeper. His schooling does not much concern us except we note that it was respectable and that even during it he was a member of a juvenile stock company, indeed its leading man. He became successively connected with a wholesale dry-goods house, the confectionary business, his elder brother's hotel in Lynn, and his father's Exchange Coffee House, Edwin Forrest's headquarters when he was in Boston. Meanwhile he had become a member of the Siddonian Dramatic Club, and determined if possible to adopt acting as a profession. Through the influence of a member of the stock company at the Tremont Theatre, he was finally engaged to support the elder Booth on a brief excursion to Providence, and it was here, at the Lion Theatre, that he made his professional début, under the assumed name of Dee, on May 26, 1836, as Parson Willdo, in *A New Way to Pay Old Debts*.[1] All roads, seemingly, lead to Massinger.[2]

A week after his Providence engagement, Davenport boldly appeared at New Bedford in the exacting part of Young Norval, and such was his success that he became a member of the company at the Tremont Theatre in Boston and after a season there was engaged for the Walnut Street Theatre, Philadelphia, where he had the good fortune to receive the praise of Edwin Forrest. But this is a sketch, not a biography, and succeeding years must be briefly summarized. In New York, Davenport added to his reputation, appearing at Niblo's and the Bowery, old and new, as a regular stock actor and finally as leading player. In Albany in 1846 he was a success from the first and Phelps, the historian of the stage of that city, comments:[3] "The American stage has had few, if any, better general actors. Versatile to a remarkable degree, refined, polished and classical, yet capable of most powerful acting, while he may have been excelled in single characters, he was the peer of any when tragedy and comedy are both considered." In 1846 he was engaged by Mrs. Mowatt as her leading man and with her he toured the country: "His high moral character, his unassuming and gentleman-like manners, his wonderful versatility and indisputable talents, caused him to be selected as the person who was to travel with us during my second year on the stage. Upon this selection, every

[1] Edgett, pp. 8-9; Willard, p. 27, corrects Blake, p. 220, who says Davenport's part was Marrall; Hornblow, Vol. II, p. 134, and Phelps, p. 238, wrongly give the part as Wellborn. None of the above give the exact date (or the part of Margaret), gleaned from the *Providence Journal*, examined for me by Miss Edith Blanchard of the Brown University Library. For cast, see under Booth, p. 211 above.

[2] The facts of Davenport's life and career, unless otherwise noted, are taken from Mr. E. F. Edgett's *Edward Loomis Davenport*, Publications of the Dunlap Society, New Series, No. 14, New York, 1901. I have been given the benefit of the reminiscences of Davenport's son-in-law, the veteran actor and stage-manager, Mr. William Seymour.

[3] Phelps, p. 238.

succeeding month and year gave us new cause for congratulation. The prominent position he has since won upon the English Stage, and the honors he has received from fastidious English audiences, are the just reward of intrinsic but most *unostentatious* merit."[4] Alas, it is a sad comment that *unostentatious* merit is so easily forgotten. The references to English audiences refer of course to Mrs. Mowatt's English tour begun in 1847; it was six years before his return to America. The month before he left for England, Edwin Forrest, who did not do this sort of thing freely, wrote Davenport: "I have not words to express the gratification and pleasure I felt in witnessing your masterly performance."[5]

Of Davenport in England little need be said. His American success was duplicated; his versatility newly demonstrated by parts so diverse as Claude Melnotte, Othello and Iago, Adam Trueman in *Fashion,* Romeo, and William in *Black-Eyed Susan,* the latter including songs and a hornpipe. After the return of Mrs. Mowatt to America, Davenport played with Macready and Brooke, to both of whom he was favorably compared. With Brooke, as already noted in the English section of this book, he again appeared in *A New Way to Pay Old Debts,* Drury Lane, September and October 1853; Parson Willdo had now graduated to Wellborn.[6] One other item cannot be omitted from Davenport's English experiences. In 1849 he married Miss Fanny Vining, who returned with him to America in 1854, and who founded with him a remarkable stage-family, of whom the best known was another Fanny Davenport, imperishably connected with the presentaton of Sardou in America.

Davenport's return to America was something like a triumph; New York and his native city, Boston, were especially enthusiastic. Of most interest to us, however, is his appearance at the Walnut Street Theatre, Philadelphia, on April 19, 1855, as Sir Giles Overreach, his first recorded performance of this rôle. The playbill, to be sure, prefaces the cast with the somewhat startling announcement that Sir Giles is "A Character in which he became so Famous in Europe, Having acted it in all the principal Cities of England, Ireland, and Scotland." Now it is of course possible that Davenport

---

[4] Mowatt, *Autobiography,* p. 253.

[5] Edgett, p. 20.

[6] Through Allworth, which he played to Scott's Sir Giles at the Chestnut Street Theatre, Philadelphia on December 12, 1839.

had played Overreach abroad, though I have no account of it, but the implication that Davenport's Sir Giles was a familiar character all over the British Isles must be put down to an enthusiastic but inaccurate press agent. The American public would of course not know whether the statement were true or not; if it could be led to think so, more would undoubtedly be present at the performance; this is nothing more or less than an extravagant "blurb." The cast on this occasion was as follows:

Sir Giles Overreach	Davenport
Wellborn	Perry
Lord Lovell	Young
Marrall	Chapman
Justice Greedy	A'Becket
Allworth	Eytinge
Lady Allworth	Mrs. Muzzy
Margaret	Mrs. Duffield

The following month Davenport was at the Broadway Theatre, New York, presenting Sir Giles Overreach on the 26th.[7] The next issue of the *New York Daily Times* says that "the house was densely crowded by a delighted audience. At the close of the play, Mr. Davenport was again called before the curtain, and in response to a general demand for a speech said: Ladies and Gentlemen: In answer to your call, I can only express to you my gratitude for the great Kindness you have evinced on every occasion on which I have appeared before you. [Applause.] And for the very flattering manner in which you have been pleased to receive my efforts to-night to represent a character which required all the genius and talent of one of the greatest among actors to do it justice, (I refer to Junius Brutus Booth.) [Enthusiastic applause.] I am particularly thankful. When I consented to appear as *Sir Giles Overreach,* I knew nothing of how I should succeed. It was to me a comparatively new character, but like Yankees generally I concluded to try it. [Applause.] Your kindness tonight gives me courage and invites me to persevere and by courage and perseverance, I trust at some future day to be able to render the character in such a manner as to be more worthy of your applause. [Cheers.]" Alas, for the

[7] Edgett, p. 61; Odell, Vol. VI, p. 347; advertisements in the *New York Daily Times.*

accuracy of the man who wrote the Philadelphia program! The account closes with the extraordinary, and, I fear, dubious statement that "Mr. Davenport, had he chosen, might have said, while speaking, what but few, if any, other actors could say of the play in which he had just appeared, namely: that he has played every male character in it, from the *Parson* up to *Sir Giles Overreach*." Edgett says Fanny Vining was the Margaret of the occasion; if so, there was a substitution, as will appear from the cast below, culled from a playbill:

Sir Giles Overreach .... Davenport
Wellborn .... Leffingwell
Lord Lovell .... Hanchett
Marrall ....Davidge
Justice Greedy .... Whiting
Allworth .... Lanergan
Lady Allworth .... Mrs. Abbott
Margaret .... Mrs. Nagle

Sir Giles *via* Davenport "first time in this city" awoke no extraordinary furor though he was well received.

After a summer tour, Davenport returned again to open the new theatrical season at the Broadway Theatre on September 17, 1855. *A New Way to Pay Old Debts* was presented three days later with enough changes to make it necessary again to present the cast on the bill:

Sir Giles Overreach .... Davenport
Wellborn .... C. Fisher
Lord Lovell .... Lanergan
Marrall .... Chapman
Justice Greedy .... Whiting
Allworth .... Eytinge
Lady Allworth .... Mrs. Buckland
Margaret .... Mme. Ponisi

And now, strangely enough, I do not find that Davenport played Sir Giles for seven years. The fault is doubtless mine, but I cannot follow Davenport through his various tours. On the other hand, Odell lists no other performances of the part by Davenport in his sixth and seventh volumes which cover the seasons up to and including 1864-1865. This lapse is curious, all the more so perhaps

E. L. DAVENPORT as SIR GILES OVERREACH, from a photograph by
Suddards & Fennemore of an engraving by H. A. Thomas,
published by T. H. Morrell

because Edwin Booth was now playing the part. Indeed, we must content ourselves with only one performance before 1865, at the Walnut Street Theatre, Philadelphia, on December 18, 1862:[8]

Sir Giles Overreach .... Davenport
Welborn .... Tilton
Lord Lovell .... Young
Marrall .... Hemple
Justice Greedy .... Thayer
Allworth .... Bascomb
Lady Allworth .... Miss Wood
Margaret .... Miss Johnson

In 1865, Davenport's Sir Giles burst out anew in full vigor, yet characteristically aroused no extraordinary enthusiasm in spite of more than usual repetition. Following a somewhat unsuccessful period as manager of the Howard Athenaeum, Davenport began a series of engagements in partnership with James W. Wallack, Jr., at Wallack's Theatre, New York; *A New Way to Pay Old Debts* was presented in November of 1865, performances falling on the 11th, 13th, 15th, 17th, and 20th with a cast which I copy from bills:

Sir Giles Overreach .... Davenport
Wellborn .... Charles Fisher
Lord Lovell .... Norton
Marrall .... Holston
Justice Greedy .... John Gilbert
Allworth .... Ringgold
Furnace .... George Holland
Lady Allworth .... Miss Fanny Morant
Margaret .... Miss Ione Burke

In spite of this apparently impressive cast, the *New York Tribune* of November 13 says that the play was "not remarkably well acted," and criticizes the production from the point of view of historical accuracy. The play drew, however, "a crowded audience"

[8] The playbill; John Drew in his *My Years on the Stage*, pp. 23-6, refers to a performance at the Walnut Street Theatre of Sir Giles by Davenport which must have taken place about this time and may be the one I have recorded. He was very much impressed and numbers Davenport, Forrest, and Edwin Booth as the greatest actors of the day; if this was the performance, however, Drew was only nine years old at the time.

and was "well received." "Mr. Davenport's Sir Giles is an artistic personation of character, and is especially powerful in the closing scenes of the drama. Mr. Gilbert's Justice Greedy is correct and full of humor. The best performance of all, however, is Mr. Holston's Marrall, which perfectly embodies all that is contemptible in meanness and cunning and duplicity. Mr. Fisher is quite at home whether in Wellborn's rags or Wellborn's laces, and Mr. Holland is, as ever, scrupulously faithful to the demands of art in the insignificant part of Furnace. The acting in the other parts calls for no remark." Does not the reader, as I do, draw the conclusion that the play was somewhat better acted than the earlier generalization implies? We had best couple these remarks with the comment in the *Times* on the 20th at the close of Mr. Davenport's engagement: "His best performance was *Sir Giles Overreach,* which he made noteworthy for elaborate study and finished execution. . . . Mr. Davenport's picture was more refined than that of Mr. Booth [the elder], and lacked in some degree the magnetic power of that erratic genius, but it was, all in all, a noble performance." This is not exactly ecstatic but it is at least impressive.

Now why this series of Sir Giles's after what appears to be, with rare exceptions, a lapse of years? Fortunately, Mr. Davenport himself explains:[9] "I was playing at Wallack's and talking over with the younger Wallack the characters in which I should appear. He objected to one after another, mainly on the ground that they were his father's rôles, till finally I exclaimed: 'There's that devilish *Sir Giles!*' 'Ah, that's just the thing,' he replied. I played it and it has been one of my favorite parts ever since." On this last he is more specific. He admits that Othello was his favorite rôle, but also that he had 'a kindly liking for that miserable *Sir Giles Overreach—Sir Giles* has not a single virtue.' 'Why then play him?' 'Because of his tremendous power and passion.' "

The performances at Wallack's established Davenport's Sir Giles, and when he performed at Mrs. John Wood's Olympic Theatre in January of the following year, the part was repeated "in accordance with a Universal Desire." Some of the cast are worth noting:[10]

[9] Edgett, pp. 115-16.
[10] The playbills give the dates as the 25th, 26th, and 27th.

Sir Giles Overreach	Davenport
Wellborn	Studley
Lord Lovell	Blaisdell
Marrall	J. H. Stoddart
Justice Greedy	James Lewis
Allworth	Garrison
Lady Allworth	Mrs. G. H. Gilbert
Margaret	Miss Kate Newton

The New York dailies do not review these performances; and I have no information about Davenport's Sir Giles at the Academy of Music, Providence, on the 26th of April.[11]

We return to Wallack's for performances on November 1, 6, 9 and 20, December 26, 1867, and April 18, 1868:[12]

Sir Giles Overreach	Davenport
Wellborn	Ringgold
Lord Lovell	Rockwell
Marrall	J. H. Stoddart
Justice Greedy	John Gilbert
Allworth	Polk
Lady Allworth	Fanny Morant
Margaret	Clara Jennings

and a gentleman in a subordinate part by the name of E. Milton, to which later will be added his last name, Holland.[13] Marrall was, moreover, J. H. Stoddart's first performance at Wallack's though not his first Marrall for Davenport's Sir Giles. Speaking of the incident in his *Recollections of a Player*,[14] he calls Davenport's performance "masterly." "When a youngster in Aberdeen I had played *Marall* with Gustavus V. Brooke, and his performance made a great impression on me; but Mr. Davenport's impersonation, I think was equally great with that of Brooke." I print part of the review from *The New York Herald,* not because I entirely like it or think it entirely fair, but because it strikes an ominous note which one cannot neglect: ". . . Although the play is obsolete in tone, character, language, and almost in sentiment, yet the

---

[11] Willard, p. 176.

[12] The playbills; not, however, on October 28 as given by Cruickshank (Edition), p. 134.

[13] Moses, *Famous Actor Families*, pp. 275-6; Clapp-Edgett, Part I, p. 159. The newspaper advertisements give the part of Order to G. Milton.

[14] pp. 147-8.

very strong cast with which it is presented . . . gives it a new
vitality. Mr. Davenport's personation of Sir Giles is sufficiently
familiar to our citizens as a piece of acting in the good old-fashioned taste, without any of the fire with which genius has at times
illuminated the part, yet carefully studied and wrought out on the
actor's idea. All the honors of last night, however, were taken by
Mr. Stoddart. . . . "

> What, all my pretty chickens and their dam
> At one fell swoop?

A New Way to Pay Old Debts of a sudden obsolete and Davenport old-fashioned and without fire? Fortunately a dated but
otherwise unidentified clipping in the Harvard Theatre Collection
gives a different impression. Of Davenport it says, "his representation of Sir Giles Overreach is neither a copy, a substitute, or an
imitation, but a delineation to which he has been led by the only
safe and reliable guides—reflection, study, and practice. It was well
appreciated by a numerous, attentive, and critical audience.
Throughout the whole performance, but especially in the final scene
of the fifth act where the interest of the play is concentrated, there
was a vigor, a freshness, an individuality which discriminated it
from every other, and afforded a good illustration of its scope for
a different yet original conception, which has given the drama such
deserved preeminence among the imitative arts. . . . "

Some of this vigor, freshness, and individuality is made vivid to
us in the notes in a book of the play in the Harvard Theatre Collection describing Davenport in the last scene. Since they are partially illegible, I paraphrase rather than quote:[15]

> All through the "undone window" speech he indicates by his ac-
> tion that his mouth is filling with blood, which he tries to spit out
> without stopping the words. He passes his hand unconsciously
> across his lips to clean away the foam [Mr. Davenport's son-in-
> law, Mr. Seymour, has told me that Davenport used powder here
> to give the effect of frothing at the mouth]. At the end of the
> speech he rushes madly forward and falls full-length flat on his
> face. Two of the servants raise him up and bear him back senseless

[15] Ts 2455.300. This play-book was the property of John Moore, stage-manager and Marrall when Edwin Booth played Sir Giles at Burton's on August
31, 1857. Moore was later at Wallack's and the New Fifth Avenue Theatre.

towards L.H. He partially recovers, looks at the two men in bewilderment, tries to separate their two hands which they had passed under him to raise him. He speaks half inaudibly between his teeth, "Let me go, let me go," sees Margaret, looks at her viciously for a moment; assuming a kindly tone, "Margaret, Margaret," he beckons to her. By the time she has almost crossed to him, he tries to get at her but is prevented by the men, who do not let go their hold. Raging, and foaming, "Curse, curse," he chokes and falls forward senseless in their arms.

It seems no wonder that, as Mr. Seymour has told me, May Davenport, who later in our chronicle we shall find playing Margaret, was often terrified during the acting of this scene.

In the spring of 1868 Mr. and Mrs. Davenport left the East for California, and we find Sir Giles at the Metropolitan Theatre, San Francisco, on the 12th and 13th of June. I take the cast from a bill:

Sir Giles Overreach .... Davenport
Wellborn .... Edwards
Lord Lovell .... Harrison
Marrall .... Barry
Justice Greedy .... Hawk
Allworth .... Bates
Lady Allworth .... Mrs. Annie Jackson
Margaret .... Mrs. F. Bates

Davenport's San Franciso engagement, if we judge from the newspaper criticism, was not exactly a success, "chiefly," says Mr. Edgett,[16] "because he lacked the physical power and animal magnetism which the restless Californians were accustomed to consider the sole attributes of effective acting." *A New Way to Pay Old Debts,* however, was the play most heartily received.

Back East, I find Davenport's Sir Giles at the Walnut Street Theatre, Philadelphia, not altogether happy in competition with the popular Lotta, who was drawing most of theatrical Philadelphia to the Arch Street Theatre. The dates are October 22 and November 14, 1868, with the cast—from the playbills as usual— as follows:

[16] p. 92.

Sir Giles Overreach .... Davenport
Wellborn .... Walcott
Lord Lovell .... Chester
Marrall .... Fawcett
Justice Greedy .... Bailey
Allworth .... Taylor
Lady Allworth .... Mrs. Chester
Margaret .... Miss Graham

I find no record of *A New Way to Pay Old Debts* during the New England tour which followed.

In August of 1869, Davenport became a member of Augustin Daly's stock company for its first season at the Fifth Avenue Theatre, New York, where for a while his name heads the list on the bills. *A New Way to Pay Old Debts* was of course inevitable, and Davenport's Sir Giles was, in the words of Laurence Hutton[17] "unquestionably the finest piece of acting this house has seen"—no small praise in so distinguished a company. The impersonation was given on November 23 and November 27, 1869, and January 5, 1870, the last for Davenport's benefit.[18] I copy a bill for the important cast:

Sir Giles Overreach .... Davenport
Wellborn .... Clarke
Lord Lovell .... Evans
Marrall .... Davidge
Justice Greedy .... James Lewis
Allworth .... Egbert
Lady Allworth .... Mrs. G. H. Gilbert
Margaret .... A young lady of this city
(her first appearance)

On the second bill the "young lady" is called Miss Teresa; she was Miss Theresa Sherk who "had been heard in this city as a reader, at Steinway Hall."[19] She seems to have made no success as an actress, however, for on the third bill Miss Emilie Kiehl [Keuhle], a regular member of the company, became the Margaret.

[17] Hutton, *Plays and Players,* p. 86, reprinted from "Recollections of the Stage," by a Young Veteran, No. III, *The New York Evening Mail,* January 20, 1873.
[18] Not November 22 as given by Cruickshank (Edition), p. 134.
[19] Brown, Vol. II, p. 407; Odell, Vol. VIII, pp. 518, 577.

Over Davenport's presentation of Sir Giles with Daly's company, the *New York Daily Tribune* of November 24, 1869, waxes both eloquent and enthusiastic; it is perhaps the first review which really makes vivid Davenport's conception and personation, and which ranks it where it deserved.

A good performance of "A New Way to Pay Old Debts" was given, last night, at the Fifth Avenue Theatre. This tragical drama was revived for the purpose of presenting Mr. Edwin L. Davenport [*sic*] in the character of *Sir Giles Overreach*. The part is one in which this great artist is able to do himself justice. Not that it calls out the sweetness of his temperament and the fine breadth and dignity of his mind. But it arouses the power of his emotional nature, fires his imagination, and calls into play his finished skill in delineating character, and his extraordinary physical force. He acted, last night, with uncommon fire, and with a careful attention to minute detail—that yet seemed born of inspiration—which showed a master mind in natural and powerful action. At this late date there is no need to recognize Mr. Davenport's complete identification with this character—the wild energy, the terrible purpose, the utter heartlessness and selfishness, the incarnate spirit of worldly ambition, that he blends into a finished work of art. He is quite alone in the part; and saying this we say all. It is worth while, though, to direct the attention of the student of acting to the entire absence of theatrical trickery in this performance. There are no picturesque "flaws and starts" in it—imposters to true acting, which should present individuality, within the scope of nature, and there stop. We were likewise particularly impressed, last evening, with the superb mark [*sic*] of the face that Mr. Davenport presented. The iron nature of *Sir Giles,*—the horrible strife of his wretched existence,—was expressed to the life, in every lineament of his countenance. With the audience his success was complete. He was three times called before the curtain. . . .

Davenport, however, was not entirely happy with Daly's company. With all his versatility, there was one kind of play in which he felt out of place and that was Tom Robertson and similar drama. He was too grand and too eloquent a figure to be able to subdue himself satisfactorily within the bounds of what must have seemed to him trifling realism. And yet it was this type of play that Daly was often presenting. As a result Davenport left the company when the season was half over to return to more robust trouping.[20] Edward A. Dithmar in his *Memories of Daly's Theatres*[21] lists Davenport's parts at the Fifth Avenue, ending with Sir Giles Overreach: "This last-named part was one inseparably associated with his fame. The picture he presented as the protagonist in this play of Massinger, of sordid avarice and malignant spite was incomparably vivid and impressive. No other actor, after the elder Booth, could play *Sir Giles* as well as he, and I doubt if he ever played it better than he did at the little theatre on West Twenty-fourth Street. . . . On the whole, I think Davenport was rather too large a figure for Mr. Daly's pretty little stage. His was the broad manner of tragedy and the higher kind of romantic drama. But his presence as a member of the company undoubtedly helped the theatre in the beginning." There is evidence a-plenty here that times were changing, and with them the taste for the older acting, but it is a little sad to find Davenport uncomfortably taking himself off, and not a little revealing of the subsequent wane in his popularity.

He who will may follow Davenport's possible Sir Giles's in the subsequent touring through Washington, Pittsburgh, Brooklyn, Boston, Philadelphia and elsewhere, but I shall wait for some localization. It is to be found in the assumption by Davenport of the managership of the Chestnut Street Theatre, Philadelphia on October 12, 1870. Here he presented *A New Way to Pay Old Debts* on February 24, April 3, and June 2, 1871. Playbills give us the casts for the first two performances:

Sir Giles Overreach	Davenport
Wellborn	C. R. Thorne, Jr.
Lord Lovell	Metkiff
Marrall	Lennox
Justice Greedy	Phillips
Allworth	Egberts
Lady Allworth	Mrs. E. L. Davenport
Margaret	Miss Lily Vining Davenport

Three Davenports concentrated is one way to pay old debts! For the performance of June 2, I note, however, that the Lady All-

[20] He played Sir Giles at Mrs. Conway's Brooklyn Theatre, late in June 1870 (Odell, Vol. VIII, p. 665).
[21] Edgett, pp. 98 *ff.*

worth was Miss Mary Maddern, aunt of Mrs. Fiske. And to be unimportant but complete, Coles took over Marrall and Redifer, Allworth.

Between the last two performances in Philadelphia, Davenport presented his Sir Giles again in New York, at Niblo's Garden on the 1st and 3rd of May. The programs speak of it as "his matchless impersonation":

Sir Giles Overreach	Davenport
Wellborn	C. R. Thorne, Jr.
Lord Lovell	Shewell
Marrall	Morton
Justice Greedy	Jack
Allworth	Howard
Lady Allworth	Mrs. M. A. Farren
Margaret	Miss Louisa Hawthorne

Mrs. Mary Ann Farren (Mrs. George Farren) was one of the projectors and a popular member of the Davenport-Wallack-Farren touring combination. Some idea of the general even excellence of Davenport may be gathered from an unidentified clipping in the Harvard Theatre Collection, dated May 7, 1871: "Mr. Davenport, it may be remembered tempers the extravagant passion of *Sir Giles,* making the part less repulsive than is customary with many actors, though he does not fail to show the old villain up in a true light, and his acting is always effective. It is not alone in those scenes where one is accustomed to look for extraordinary display that Mr. Davenport shines conspicuously, but throughout the play his acting, even and kept under good control, shows him a thorough artist even in uninteresting situations. He was applauded with real enthusiasm, and at the end of the last act was called before the curtain and was obliged to respond to the demands of the audience with a speech."

Perhaps a more interesting comment is offered, however, by the *Tribune,* which I give almost entire. May I take the liberty of asking the reader to note, to the discomfiture of the author, that Davenport has recently played Sir Giles in Philadelphia "twenty-nine times in almost uninterrupted succession"? This would be at the Chestnut Street Theatre, of course, where I have noted only two antedating the Niblo's Garden performance. This is significant in more ways than one. While I am on the subject, it may be well to say that I have in my possession a travelling bill of Davenport's on which it is stated that Davenport has played Sir Giles more than five hundred times! I shall be lucky if I record a tenth of that number. In extenuation, I hasten to add that I shall have recorded perhaps ten times more than anyone else. But to the review :

Edwin L. Davenport [*sic*] played, last night, at Niblo's Garden, appearing as *Sir Giles Overreach* in the painful but powerful drama of "A New Way to Pay Old Debts." The theatre was completely filled, and lively popular enthusiasm gave animated interest to the occasion. Mr. Davenport was cordially welcomed. His *Sir Giles* has often been seen in New York before, and always with admiration. He acted the part, last night, with all the old artistic correctness, and with even more than the old fire. It is an exacting and harrowing character, and, except that it affords abundant occasion for explosive energy, it is an ungrateful one for the artist. *Sir Giles* wins no sympathy. He is altogether hateful. But he is a tower of strength, in his dreadful selfishness and malignity, and it is by power that he conquers. We speak of trite truths in speaking of these matters. The part is one of the oldest in which great actors have won distinction. Mr. Davenport has made a special study of it, and is the best representative of it on the modern stage. Other artists that we have seen make more start-ling physical demonstrations, at certain points; but no actor, in our time, has given us the probable, natural, coherent *Sir Giles* that Mr. Davenport embodies. Lately, in Philadelphia, he played this part twenty-nine times in almost uninterrupted succession to crowded houses. The success is natural. Last night's performance riveted the attention of the large audience, and evoked frequent and hearty manifestations of enthusiastic admiration. Possibly an assemblage of Americans must need sympathize with a man who embodies worldly success. No assemblage, at any rate, could fail to admire a work of art so vital with intellectual and physical fire, and so perfectly natural in form. . . .

It is a digressive but important comment on both Davenport and the theatre of his time that in between the two performances at Niblo's, the play was *As You Like It,* with Charles R. Thorne, Jr., as Orlando, Davenport as the melancholy Jacques, and—oh, un-necessary realism—the pugilist, Jem Mace, as Charles, the wrestler!

Boston too saw a series of Sir Giles's before the last recorded in Philadelphia,—all at the Globe Theatre in May of 1871,—the 8th, 9th, 12th, 13th (matinee), 22nd, and 23rd, an impressive succession:[22]

Sir Giles Overreach	Davenport
Wellborn	Daly
Lord Lovell	Rand
Marrall	LeMoyne
Justice Greedy	Griffiths
Allworth	Stedman
Lady Allworth	Mrs. Melinda Jones
Margaret	Mrs. T. M. Hunter

Davenport was always popular as a native son, but this alone will not explain the number of times Sir Giles was represented, for Walter Montgomery and Edwin Booth played him in the same year. Apparently aristocratic Boston had no scruples about welcoming the villainous Overreach. *Noblesse oblige?* At any rate, Sir Giles after six days' labor, rested—at Roxbury for the summer.

I have no record that Davenport presented *A New Way to Pay Old Debts* during his second season as manager at the Chestnut Street Theatre, Philadelphia, but in the third Sir Giles emerges again for three appearances on the 3rd, 5th, and 9th of November, 1872. Mr. Edgett says that on the 9th, Mr. Davenport " 'made his first appearance of the season,' playing *Sir Giles Overreach* to a large audience," but playbills give the two anterior dates with the cast as follows:[23]

Sir Giles Overreach	Davenport
Wellborn	Fitzpatrick
Lord Lovell	Vanhorn
Marrall	Vincent
Justice Greedy	Phillips
Allworth	Norris
Lady Allworth	Mrs. E. L. Davenport
Margaret	Miss Lily Vining Davenport

[22] These dates from the Harvard Boston list, the casts from scattered bills. Davenport did not play Sir Giles at the Boston Museum on the 18th as recorded by Cruickshank (Edition), p. 137; the performer was Walter Montgomery.
[23] Edgett, p. 103.

In December of 1872 died one of Davenport's most persistent admirers, Edwin Forrest, and Davenport was appointed a member of a committee to draft an appropriate resolution in his memory. A statement made by James Rees, one of Forrest's biographers, will not be amiss here:[24] "Now that the actor master of the art is gone, who will rule the stage and sustain its classic characters? Not Edwin Booth; he has not the physical or mental capacity. . . . There is one man, and the only man who, if he knew his own worth as we know and appreciate it, whose name should now become the synonym of Edwin Forrest, and that man is E. L. Davenport, the best living actor on the stage." That this was the opinion of Forrest himself, rather than that of his biographer, is made plain by confirmation from Alger:[25] "Forrest assigned an exalted artistic rank to the very varied dramatic impersonations of Mr. E. L. Davenport, every one of whose rôles is marked by firm drawing, distinct light and shade, fine consistency, and finish. His *Sir Giles Overreach* was hardly surpassed by Kean or Booth, and has not been approached by anybody else. His quick, alert, springy tread full of fire and rapidity, the whole man in every step, fixed the attention and made everyone feel that there was a terrific concentration of energy, an insane possession of the nerve centers, portending something frightful soon to come. An old playgoer, on witnessing this impersonation, wrote the following impromptu:

> While viewing each remembered scene, before my gaze appears
> Each famed depictor of *Sir Giles* for almost forty years;
> The elder Kean and mighty Booth have each held hearts in thrall,
> But without overreaching truth, you overreach them all.

And in conversation with James Oakes, Forrest remarked shortly before his death, "Well, Oakes, they may say what they please, although Davenport and I haven't spoken for years, he is the best actor on the American stage."[26]

After such lavish encomiums, it is distressing to find Davenport, having retired, with a loss, as manager of the Chestnut Street Theatre, playing Sir Giles at Wood's Museum in New York. Davenport himself could not explain his lack of popularity in the

[24] Rees, quoted by Edgett, p. 104.
[25] Alger, Vol. II, pp. 540-1.
[26] Edgett, p. 105.

regular theatres. In August of 1874, he wrote his friend Morrell, the publisher:[27] "Of course it would be far better for any legitimate actor to be in a regular theatre; but am certain no other theatre company would have taken more pains (of the scenery and appointments I say nothing). If I were indeed *'the ablest representative of the Legitimate Drama living,'* I fancy some manager who charges more would want me, but No. They all turn a deaf ear to applications, and the general reply is *'a devilish good actor, but don't draw.'* My dear fellow, we are obliged to take 75 cents when we can't get a dollar, and if the manager who opens his doors at 75 can afford to receive and pay the star better than the $1 fellows, why then that settles it. Excuse my profanity, but I do think it a d——d shame that I am thus *compelled* to be banished from the regular theatres, but I will play in New York willy-nilly as often as I can. . . . I *do* play in N.Y. this fall, and when you see it announced you'll know it. Niblo's wanted me, but I was afraid of it. Daly offered me two weeks at two different parts of the season, to get up *Sir Giles* and *Shylock* for me, but I do not think it would be policy for me to let my name down again in N.Y., and I had better reign in H— than serve in H——n."

However ominous and persistent this note, there is no lack of Sir Giles during 1874. The first performance at Wood's Museum served as a prelude, for it fell on December 23 of the previous year. A playbill gives us the cast:

Sir Giles Overreach .... Davenport
Wellborn .... Keene
Lord Lovell .... Meeker
Marrall .... Mestayer
Justice Greedy .... Edwards
Allworth .... Morris
Lady Allworth .... Mrs. E. L. Davenport
Margaret .... Miss Gussie DeForrest

A New England, then a Southern, tour preceded Davenport's next appearance as Sir Giles at Wood's Museum,—for his benefit on April 17, 1874—"in which character he stands pre-eminent, and [to drive the point home] with no living equal."[28] The cast was as

[27] *ibid.,* pp. 110-11.
[28] Playbill and newspaper advertisements. Brown, Vol. II, p. 537 and Cruickshank (Edition), p. 134, give the 16th, when the play was *Oliver Twist.*

above, and may have remained so for the performances on September 30 and October 1.[29] Five days later, Davenport played Sir Giles at the Opera House, Albany, repeating it on the 7th.[30] On November 9 Sir Giles moved to Mrs. F. B. Conway's Brooklyn Theatre; a bill supplies the cast:

Sir Giles Overreach .... Davenport
Wellborn .... Kennedy
Lord Lovell .... Hastings
Marrall .... Lennox
Justice Greedy .... Bokee
Allworth .... McDowell
Lady Allworth .... Mrs. Farren
Margaret .... Lillian Conway

I note that Othello was originally announced for the 12th, but that a repetition of Sir Giles was substituted. Had *A New Way to Pay Old Debts,* Sir Giles in particular, made such a hit, or was the shift for other reasons? The *Brooklyn Eagle* would lend support to the first view, besides showing us some valuable stage-business:

E. L. Davenport began his engagement at the Brooklyn Theatre last evening with the promise of a fitting appreciation from our public. It was but last Saturday that one of the most experienced of our American managers, while deploring the poor support extended to amusements all over the South, Southwest and West, remarked that while it is evident people will not in these times pay present prices to see an ordinarily good performance, they will most cheerfully pay them to see anything extraordinarily good. If this be true, E. L. Davenport will certainly play one of the finest engagements ever played in Brooklyn.

Since Forrest, no actor has displayed in Brooklyn such a magnificent work of histrionic art as was the *Sir Giles Overreach* portrayed by Mr. Davenport at the Brooklyn Theatre last evening. The effect of the portrayal can perhaps be best described by reference to the kindred art of painting. The conception—and the execution carries out the conception with startling fulness—is purely that of a Rembrandt. The heavy sombre back ground of remorseless ambition, lighted only by lurid revelations of the

[29] Hutton, Diary, Vol. III, p. 131, checked by newspaper advertisements. Hutton misses September 30 unless the play announced was changed. (Brown, Vol. II, p. 538.)
[30] The playbill.

crimes through which it works towards the end that finally evades it, finds parallel in its effect nowhere else. From the very intensity of evil he evokes in the spectator a certain degree of respect—not unlike that which the reader of Milton is forced to yield to Satan, "the Archangel Ruined." What such a will and such a brain could have accomplished, had its aim been good in lieu of evil, expels contempt from the awe which the picture evokes; and as the bitterness of rage and disappointed wrath bring on the apoplectic death, while we are glad that *Overreach* dies baffled, we feel a certain satisfaction that *Overreach* did not live despised.

Were we to particularize any passage of peculiar excellence in a performance whose chief excellence lies in its entirety, we should point chiefly to the scene between *Overreach* and his daughter, the second scene of the second act, where *Overreach* advises his daughter to sacrifice her virtue in order to secure the aristocratic husband his ambition yearns to secure her. The Satanic gamester staking a maiden's virtue against a title, with the confidence of a Lucifer arming against Heaven, was so portrayed by Davenport as to curdle the blood in a man's veins. The passage itself is so powerful, so peculiarly written in Massinger's finest vein, that we cannot resist the temptation to quote it:

> "*Sir G*—He comes to woo you; see you do not coy it:
>   This mincing modesty hath spoiled many a match,
>   By a first refusal—
> *Margaret*—You'll have me, sir, preserve the distance that confines a virgin?
> *Sir G*—Virgin, me no virgin!
>   *I'll have you lose that name*—or you lose me,
>   I'll have you private—start not—I say private.
>   If you are *my* true daughter
>   You'll venture alone with one man, though he came
>   Like Jupiter to Semele; and come off too;
>   And therefore when he kisses you, *kiss close*."

It is fairly impossible to describe the devilish autocracy of vice over virtue, which Davenport throws into these lines. We have striven to mark his reading by the weak use of italics; but the fiendish despotism of his face, the iron positiveness of his tones as he commands his daughter to offer up her virtue to a man she has never even seen is as impossible to describe as the demoniac expression of his face when the last two words grate out between his teeth.

The self reliance of *Overreach* was not less finely rendered in his very next speech. Naturally, the girl's nature revolting at obedience to such a command, she ends by saying:

> "If to obey you, I forget my honor,
> He must and will forsake me."

When uttering the command to kiss close Davenport had bent toward her, now his form raised to his full height, his eyes flashing with the conscious power of a will never successfully opposed, he reveals in tone, look, gesture, pose, his apparently indomitable self reliance as he exclaims—

> "How! forsake thee!
> Do *I* wear a sword for fashion? Or is this arm
> Shrunk up or withered? Does there live a man,
> Of that large list I have encountered with,
> Can truly say I e'er gave inch of ground
> Not purchased with his blood that did oppose me?
> Forsake thee!—He *dares* not
> Though all his Captains, echoes to his will,
> Stood armed by his side to justify the wrong;
> Spite of his lordship, and his colonelship,
> *I* would make him render
> A bloody and a strict account, and force him,
> By marrying thee, to cure thy wounded honor.
> Meg—*I* have said it.

As Davenport ends the speech we see indeed what Massinger meant to draw—a human reflex of the devil himself: Intellect without principle—courage without honor.

To enumerate every passage in which Davenport reflects with equal force and truth Massinger's great creation would be to quote and describe his reading of almost every sentence of the part. One touch, however, we cannot pass over. It occurs near the end of the last act, after *Overreach* has found himself baffled by a mere petty stratagem of his daughter and the man she loves. Estopped in his attempt to kill his daughter, he turns on the Lord he schemed to have her wed, and in tones fraught with hate and quivering with defiance, hisses out his challenge, nervously twitching at his sword hilt: "Lead the way; let's quit the house, and change six words in private!"

The answer is quick, "I am ready."

Having heard it, Davenport exits, only to return in a minute finding the Lord has not followed. He leans against the wing, and with taunting contempt, and hate that conveys insult in every letter of the three words, says aloud, "Are you pale?"

From that moment the delirium seizes him, and the climax, reached in the fall and death, is a piece of acting certainly unique of its kind, and wholly unequaled by anything on our stage to-day.

Great in all he plays, Davenport is certainly greatest in this part. His *Richelieu,* which he will play to-night, is of the Macready type, a fine study, but it no where attains the sublimity of his *Sir Giles.* It is the best we have; but that, alas, has come to mean too little to be a compliment. It is finished with the minute care of a picture by Meissonier; but is too wholly intellectual to move as his *Sir Giles* moves or to haunt the mind as his *Sir Giles* haunts it. Next to *Sir Giles,* his best work is his *Hamlet.*

From Brooklyn to the Chestnut Street Theatre, Philadelphia, went Sir Giles, where he appeared in his old haunt on November 19 and 21. The bills show us that still another member of the Davenport family appeared in *A New Way to Pay Old Debts* this time, —the fourth, I believe,—when Miss May Davenport played Margaret:

Sir Giles Overreach	Davenport
Wellborn	Clarke
Lord Lovell	Nagle
Marrall	Vincent
Justice Greedy	Jack
Allworth	Norris
Lady Allworth	Miss Mary Maddern
Margaret	Miss May Davenport

Though in August Davenport had decided not to play Sir Giles for Daly, he apparently changed his mind. Daly was now in his second season at the New Fifth Avenue Theatre, in other words Apollo Hall made over. Here Davenport enacted Sir Giles from December 21 through December 26, or as the bills have it: "Every evening this week and Saturday matinee."[31]

[31] *The Honeymoon* was originally announced for Thursday evening December 24 and Saturday matinee but cancelled in favor of *A New Way to Pay Old Debts* on Wednesday, December 23.

Sir Giles Overreach .... Davenport
Wellborn .... Harkins
Lord Lovell .... Devere
Marrall .... Jennings
Justice Greedy .... James Lewis
Allworth .... H. Conway
Lady Allworth .... Miss Annie Graham
Margaret .... Miss Sara Jewett

Evidently Daly did not share the belief that Davenport would not draw. As a matter of fact, the finances of the new theatre were in a bad way, and the manager had sent some of his principals on tour so that he could bring in stars.[32]

Let us start slowly and work to the climax. The *Times* of December 22 is merely reportorial: the production is called "one of the best of the revivals which Mr. Daly has recently given to the public. . . . It is played in the old-fashioned way [reader, please note]. . . The merit of last night's performance consists, not so much of excellence in any isolated feature as in its general and equal merit. No doubt the exacting and strongly marked character of *Sir Giles Overreach* found a representative of rare ability in Mr. E. L. Davenport, and his fine rendition of that unscrupulous personage was the central object of interest, but at the same time all the other parts were played with an intelligence and appreciation of their requirements not usually distributed in such goodly proportions through a stock company. . . . Mr. Davenport's acting gained the old-time favor, and, in the last act more especially, he won the unrestricted applause of the house." The *Herald* of the same date is definitely cordial: "It is certain . . . that as Sir Giles Overreach Mr. Davenport has no rival on the stage. It is his finest part, and in saying this we must speak of it as one of the finest performances of the time. Mr. Daly has given the piece with unusual strength. . . . Strong, therefore as the piece was in the masterly impersonation of Mr. Davenport, it was still stronger in the admirable manner in which Mr. Daly put it on the stage and cast the minor characters. The scenery was worthy of the old revival times at Booth's, when the genius of Hamlet was lost in the splendor of upholstery and scenic effects. Mr. Davenport played Sir Giles with

[32] Daly, p. 184, calls Davenport's "one of the greatest impersonations of *Sir Giles Overreach* the stage had seen. . . ."

all his usual fire and skill. This really great actor never seemed in better heart and purpose, and as he reached the climax of the play he was tumultuously cheered and called before the curtain at the end of each act. Mr. Daly's revival of this famous old comedy is a theatrical event, and we welcome it as an augury, we hope, of a brilliant and successful season in this charming little theatre."

Two days later, alas, another paper, though frantic in the praise of Davenport, finds it necessary to criticize the theatre-going public for being unappreciative :[33]

There are performances, to describe which the average news-paper critic is sensible that his stock phrases of praise or blame, his petty tricks of style and manner, his commonplace compari-sons, must prove utterly flat and unprofitable. Such a performance is Mr. E. L. Davenport's *Sir Giles Overreach* which should, if anything could, inspire even the most mediocre mind to say something at least worthy the noble theme.

What satire upon our modern society is his grand impersona-tion. Here is a man, one of the most finished, artistic and powerful actors we have, scarcely able to command an audience of decent size when at rare intervals he appears at one of our leading metropolitan theatres. We have been prating about the immorality and viciousness of the French drama which has, nevertheless, taken such hold upon our people's affections; we have been con-demning certain managers for their production of inane and meretricious spectacle, we have been lifting up our voices to pray for the return of the legitimate drama to our stage, and yet, with all that, we permit Edwin Booth to go a bankrupt, and E. L. Davenport to play to half-empty benches.

We err not, mark it, when we say that it is a crying disgrace that the Fifth Avenue Theatre is not packed from floor to roof to witness such a play as Massinger's "New Way to Pay Old Debts," and such a *Sir Giles Overreach* as Mr. Davenport's. Has our love for good acting disappeared, and has a desire for scenery, misè en scene [*sic*], and display, taken its place? We scarcely dare confess the truth. . . .

There is about Mr. Davenport that peculiar magnetism, that majestic presence, which fills the stage the moment he appears upon it, and establishes a sympathy between himself and his audience which, with wondrous tact, he fits to his purpose till,

[33] I quote from an unidentified Harvard cutting.

ascending by firm and well-measured strides, he reaches the climax and carries all before him. We cannot describe the effect of his *Sir Giles Overreach* other than by saying it first interests by its quiet power, then startles by its wonderful force and intensity, and finally rouses to enthusiasm by its incomparable grandeur and majestic passion. . . .

The character of Sir Giles Overreach has been drawn by a master hand and we know no other in which ambition, greed for gold, lust of power, reckless bravery, force of character, and strength of mind are so admirably blended and illustrated. It has one difficulty as regards an audience. It has a strong tendency to become repulsive. Only a great actor could save it from being so. This Mr. Davenport does, and by the very intensity of his impersonation makes us forget for the moment that the man before us is a thing of loathing. In the last act where *Sir Giles* discovers that he has been cheated of his wealth by *Marrall,* and that he has been made the unwitting instrument of his daughter's recent marriage to *Allworth,* Mr. Davenport fairly rose to the grandeur of the occasion and presented a picture of baffled, impotent rage, wrecked ambition, lost hope, and fiendish malignity which will not easily be forgotten. . . ."

We have plainly the same old story: the critic's praise—the poor attendance. Is it any wonder that Davenport could ask feverish rhetorical questions? "Why is it? In Heaven's name, why is it? Can't I act any more? Am I no good? Have I outlived my usefulness? Is it time for me to retire?"[34] Peace, friend; you can still act with the best of them, but times are changing. Sir Giles, indeed, appears to some a little old-fashioned, too repulsive for the modern taste, very much alive, but passé. William Winter,[35] while commending Davenport's portrayal as "a sinister and grisly embodiment of worldly craft and insensate villainy," adds: "He was proud and justly so of his performance of *Sir Giles Overreach,* and he often expressed the intention of making a specialty of that character. He told me that it would one day become as popular in his hands as *Rip Van Winkle* had become in those of Jefferson. He forgot that *Sir Giles* is abhorrent to the human heart, and accordingly that the better it is acted the more it will be disliked, and the more it will be avoided. People can be startled, once and again, by

[34] Edgett, p. 117.
[35] *Life and Art of Edwin Booth,* pp. 90-1.

a superb exhibition of brilliant wickedness and horror, but they cannot be charmed by it. There is, to be sure, fascination in evil, and this sometimes is beautiful and potent. But it does not strike deep, and it does not endure. Humanity fears a monster the moment it realizes its presence, and what it fears it soon hates. The safety of the actor who embodies *Sir Giles, Richard the Third,* and *Pescara* is that his hearers do not apprehend the work as a fact. They see it as an illusion, and what they admire is the skill with which he converts a man into a fiend. Awful strifes of passion and awful depths of iniquity and suffering are suggestively laid open to their view by his art, and he therefore shines out as a wonderful, dreadful sorcerer. But the honors he wears are only for a day if he stops at that order of achievement and does nothing to captivate affectionate sympathy. Davenport went to his grave unsatisfied in his ambition as to *Sir Giles.* Everybody admired it, and everybody refrained as much as possible from seeing it."

We are nearing the end of Davenport's career; indeed as far as Sir Giles is concerned, we are through with New York City. We must follow him now to Providence, where at the Opera House, he presented the character for a Saturday matinee on February 27, 1875, and on the evening of June 2. For the first performance, a bill gives us the cast:

Sir Giles Overreach	Davenport
Wellborn	Burroughs
Lord Lovell	Cotter
Marrall	Smith
Justice Greedy	Norman
Allworth	Treville
Lady Allworth	Mrs. Pennoyer
Margaret	Miss Wilmot

On the day following the second performance, the *Daily Journal* shows that the city where he had made his début in the same play almost forty years before was not unappreciative of Davenport's power. Will the reader please note how well the review backs up the opinions of William Winter just quoted?

Massinger's fine old English play, "A New Way to Pay Old Debts," received a rare interpretation at the Opera House, last evening, with Mr. Davenport in the leading rôle of Sir Giles

Overreach. The powerful portraiture of the distinguished actor, in a presentation specially adapted to his dramatic genius, is so universally recognized and so fully appreciated by lovers of the histrionic art, that it is impossible to add new words of praise to the plaudits that have long been awarded in full measure to the portrayal. The picture was a painful delineation of a character wherein inborn rascality, stony hard-heartedness, boundless extortion, miserly acquisitiveness and fiendish malignity strive for mastery in a depraved nature, unredeemed by a single virtue. There were many points of special power in the presentation, as in the diabolical spirit manifested in the scene where Sir Giles instructs his daughter in the art of fascinating Lord Lovell; his gloating exultation when he hurries on the clandestine marriage, and feels convinced that his ambition for a titled son-in-law will be gratified; in the expression of the contemptible policy which leads him to patronize his nephew Wellborn, who has been ruined by his remorseless extortion; and in the culminating action of the fifth act, when the consequences of his evil deeds weave a network of retribution around him that he cannot escape, and an insane revenge takes possession of his whole being till death closes the tragic scene.

The portraiture in the last act was intensely thrilling and powerful. The audience manifested a fine appreciation of the tragic power of the artist, both in the breathless attention given to the presentation, and in the enthusiastic applause which twice demanded a repetition of the scene at the close of the play. A thorough admiration of his great effort was also manifested at the end of the third act, when the actor was twice recalled, while abundant proof of enjoyment was interspersed throughout the whole performance. Those who have never seen the Sir Giles Overreach of Mr. Davenport, have failed to witness one of the most soul-stirring portrayals of utter meanness and pure "cussedness" ever enacted on the American stage. Mr. Davenport brought vividly before us last evening, in many gestures and expressions, the acting of the elder Booth, whose memory we shall never cease to reverence. If the audience was not as large as we could wish, its full sympathy must have been a satisfactory tribute to the merits of the chief actor in the play. Though the house was but half full, we are sure that the smallness of the number in attendance was due more to the lateness of the season, than to any want of appreciation of the acknowledged ability of the dramatist.

Last scene of all—the Howard Athenaeum in Boston, where Davenport's Sir Giles gave up the ghost on the 7th, 8th, and 12th of June, the last a matinee. With the exception of Sullivan as Lord Lovell, the cast was the same as at the Providence Opera House, where, apparently, Davenport had been supported by the Howard company. For a year and a half longer Davenport continued to play, but for us his career is over. It is a pitiful fact to record that when he died on September 1, 1877, one of the finest actors of the nineteenth century was known to the younger generation of playgoers only as "the father of Fanny Davenport." The king is dead, long live the queen!

The comments and reviews which have been quoted in this chapter bear witness to the truth of the statement made by J. Ranken Towse[36] that Davenport's Sir Giles Overreach "was generally admitted to be the best upon the stage." Actors as well as critics agreed in the estimate. Besides those already mentioned, for example, Walter Leman says, "There was no man who so closely approached the grandeur of the elder Booth in the character of 'Sir Giles Overreach' as E. L. Davenport."[37] And yet both these statements must be qualified. It is plain that though there was a great deal of admiration for Davenport's portrayal, it was not, particularly toward the end of his career, popular with playgoers for reasons which I have already endeavored to make clear. And, in the second place, if Davenport's Sir Giles was the logical successor to the elder Booth's, it must constantly be borne in mind that his conception of the rôle was new and original. If Davenport belonged to the older school by reason of his extraordinary versatility and was out of place in the then modern cup-and-saucer comedy and adaptations from the French, he belonged in part to the new school in his complete lack of theatrical trickery and sensational acrobatics, emotional and otherwise. He lacked the animal magnetism and bravura airs of an earlier time, and substituted the quiet intensity and finished execution which stem not so much from inspired but irrational genius as from thought and intelligence. Though he always preferred the older emotional plays to drawing-room

---

[36] *Sixty Years of the Theatre,* p. 226.
[37] *Memories of an Old Actor,* p. 339.

chatter and polite wit, he presented the emotion through his mind. The Sir Giles of Kean and of Junius Booth were what we might expect from erratic Kean and mad Booth; it is equally true that the Sir Giles of Davenport was what we might expect from an extremely intelligent gentleman whose emotions were all the more real because they were not always on the surface to be seen, but were sensed and transmuted and deeply felt.

Before we come to the other Titan of this chapter, we must mention briefly a few performances of *A New Way to Pay Old Debts* which temporally precede his. None of them are of any particular importance except in showing the persistence of the play. At the Boston Museum on May 28, 1855, Sir Giles Overreach was acted by George Jamieson with a familiar support. I copy the cast from a bill:

Sir Giles Overreach .... Jamieson
Wellborn .... Keach
Lord Lovel! .... Davies
Marrall .... W. Warren
Justice Greedy .... W. H. Smith
Allworth .... Bascom
Lady Allworth .... Mrs. Vincent
Margaret .... Mrs. Rainforth

Since I cannot find any other presentations of Sir Giles by Jamieson, it is needless to estimate its worth or scope. Jamieson is unfortunately remembered primarily as the author of the Consuelo letter in the Forrest divorce case. The opinions reflected in memoirs and accounts are determined by the author's attitude towards Forrest. Rees accordingly calls him "unreliable, careless, and regardless of the proprieties, dramatic, social or moral," and finds retribution in the fact that he was run over by a Hudson River Railroad train in 1868. William Winter in his *Shadows of the Stage,* on the other hand, is friendly to the man and praises his acting. Somewhere in between is Walter Leman who says that Jamieson "possessed most wonderful and versatile mimic powers; with little effort and ordinary application, he could have rivalled Matthews." Born in New York he made his début at the Bowery Theatre in 1835 in his own farce, *The Chameleon,* playing five characters. He was subsequently connected with the National Theatre, New York, and the theatre of the same name in Philadelphia, acted with the elder Booth and Forrest, toured in England, and achieved perhaps his greatest hit as Pete in *The Octoroon* at the Winter Garden, New York.[38]

John Dyott too, apparently, acted Sir Giles only once, though we have found him acting in the play with Couldock at the Walnut Street Theatre, Philadelphia on May 23, 1851. His Overreach was presented at Burton's Theatre, New York on September 10, 1855. Odell notes that Lord Lovell was played by Leffingwell, Marrall by Burton, Lady Allworth by Miss Raymond, and Margaret by Kate Reignolds, who had made her début at this theatre five days before.[39] A playbill pasted in a Harvard prompt-book completes the cast of main characters with the information that G. Jordan acted Wellborn, Burke Justice Greedy, and Holman Allworth. Dyott was a good stock company actor but without the capacity for a star. Ireland says that he had good sense, correctness of conception, and genuine feeling to cover up deficiencies of person, grace, and memory.[40] Born in England, Dyott made his American début at the Park Theatre, New York, in 1844, and remained in the United States until his death in 1876. He who will may follow his career at the Bowery, Burton's, Wallack's, Laura Keene's and elsewhere through the indices of Odell.

Of even less importance in theatrical history, though more connected with *A New Way to Pay Old Debts,* was an actor with the imposing name of Boothroyd Fairclough, who came from out the West and made an Eastern début at the Bowery Theatre in New York in 1855. The date was November 14 and the part Sir Giles Overreach. Odell gives the Wellborn as Prior, the Marrall as Winans, and the Margaret as Mrs. Ward. The play was repeated on December 8.[41] Fairclough is hard to trace, but he seems to have been fond of the play; at any rate he and Mary Agnes Cameron included scenes of the play in their readings at Hope Chapel on April 22 of the following year. On June 7 he enacted Sir Giles again at

[38] Rees, pp. 355, 369-70; Winter, *Shadows of the Stage* (Second Series), p. 112, and *Brief Chronicles,* Part II, pp. 169-72; Leman, p. 181.

[39] Odell, Vol. VI, p. 432.

[40] Ireland, Vol. II, p. 428.

[41] Odell, Vol. VI, pp. 457-8, 500.

a regular theatre, this time the old Broadway, and a playbill gives
us the cast:

Sir Giles Overreach .... Fairclough
Wellborn .... C. Fisher
Lord Lovell .... Grosvenor
Marrall .... Chapman
Justice Greedy .... Whiting
Allworth .... Eytinge
Lady Allworth ....Mrs. Buckland
Margaret .... Mme. Ponisi

As far as I can discover, Fairclough's Sir Giles reappeared only
once more, though heaven knows how many times he played it in
the West and elsewhere. This once was on April 14, 1862, at Wallack's old Broome Street Theatre, now called, among other things,
Mary Provost's Theatre. Mary Provost indeed was announced to
play Camille on that date but fell ill, and *A New Way to Pay Old
Debts* was substituted. The *New York Daily Tribune* of the following day says "the house was desperately bad, and enough to
chill the actor. From what we saw we judge him to be a judicious
performer. . . ." Judicious let him be, so long as we forget him
as soon as possible, him and his Sir Giles. We cannot take time to
follow his long career further—he did not die until 1911 at the age
of eighty-six. I am not so interested in Fairclough, indeed, as I am
in the amateur performance of *A New Way to Pay Old Debts* at
the Brooklyn Athenaeum on January 22, 1856, by the New York
Dramatic Society.[42] Who, I wonder, entered the body of Overreach on this occasion?

If I followed exactly the plan outlined in my preface, whereby
the various representatives of Sir Giles Overreach are to be
studied in the order of their first appearances in that character,
Edwin Booth should in reality precede Davenport. Actually as we
shall see, he played the part two years before Davenport. I have
ventured in this instance, however, to depart from the prearranged
plan. We shall have a clearer picture of the nineteenth century
theatre in America if we place Booth in our minds along with and
after Davenport, who in many ways, as I have attempted to show,
belonged to an earlier school of acting. Moreover, though Booth

[42] Odell, Vol. VI, p. 508; Vol. VII, p. 417.

acted Overreach first, his connection with the play begins only in 1852, whereas Davenport had made his début in it in 1836; and Davenport played his last Sir Giles in 1875 while Booth continued with the part until 1886. To follow the order of first performances here would therefore be misleading.

In one sense Edwin Booth was the most popular actor of all those studied in this book—but only in one sense. He never aroused the enthusiasm which greeted Kean or the elder Booth; he never was popular in the sense of appealing particularly to "the people," the groundlings so to speak; he never was the critic's actor in the sense that Davenport was, with uniformly good newspaper notices; he never was exempt from the enmity of certain persons who were found to be unscrupulous in dealing with him. But Booth, if any man ever had, had a genius for friendship. Completely devoted to making art prevail, to giving his audiences what he thought best for them, living in the spirit, absolutely unselfish, intelligent, and loving, he evoked the most fervent admiration from the actors who worked with him and whom he helped, and the most devoted friendship of the finest men who were in any way connected with him. People like William Winter and Laurence Hutton and Lawrence Barrett communicate in their studies of him this whole-hearted love so effectively that it is impossible to put it down as over-praise and exaggerated enthusiasm. The more one searches for him, the more it is borne to mind that Edwin Booth was a truly noble figure.

Edwin Booth, the fourth son of Junius Brutus Booth, was born on his father's farm at Bel Air, Maryland, on November 13, 1833.[43] The two were devoted to each other; early, Edwin began to travel with the famous actor, and a little later to guard him from the influences which worked havoc with the mind of that strange genius, for he had more control over him than anyone else. It was natural that the son should be drawn to the stage; he made his début, somewhat unexpectedly perhaps, at the Boston Museum on September 10, 1849, in the part of Tressel in Cibber's version of *Richard III*; during the next years, his characters rapidly in-

---

[43] Unless otherwise noted, I follow William Winter's *The Life and Art of Edwin Booth*; Mr. Richard Lockridge's *Darling of Misfortune, Edwin Booth 1833-1893*, is a readable but somewhat breathless character-study; while it contributes some new information, it does not supersede Winter.

creased in number and importance. His début in New York was at the National Theatre on September 27, 1850, when he acted Wilford to his father's Sir Edward Mortimer. Early in April of the following year,[44] the Booths were again at the National, and the elder, ill or feigning to be ill to test his son's real calibre, shoved Edwin without warning into Richard III, his first star part; aided by John R. Scott, who was the Richmond of the evening, Edwin got through with some success. These were first steps, however; Edwin's real apprenticeship began when he accompanied his father to California in 1852. There and then began his connection with *A New Way to Pay Old Debts*. He had of course already seen his father's Sir Giles; now he was to act a part in the play.[45]

If we could draw the curtains of time and take our seats at the Jenny Lind Theatre in San Francisco on July 31, 1852, we should find that Massinger was the dramatist of the evening and that his most popular play was to be acted. More than that, we should find that Junius Brutus Booth was playing Sir Giles Overreach; Junius Brutus Booth, Jr., Lord Lovell; Mrs. Booth, Jr., Margaret; and Edwin Booth, Allworth.[46] All in all, it was something of a Booth evening. Report does not tell us how young Edwin fared as Allworth; we know only that the whole engagement of the elder Booth was very successful. Edwin and the younger Junius were members of the stock company which accompanied their father from San Francisco to Sacramento, where, however, they lost all the money they had just earned. In October the star departed for the East, leaving his sons to learn their art in California; they never saw him again, for he died in November under circumstances already related.

Edwin Booth's trials immediately began. When the news of his father's death reached him, he was hemmed in by a snowstorm at Grass Valley where he had been playing to bad business under D. W. Waller. He walked the fifty miles to Marysville in two days

[44] There is some doubt about the exact date; see Odell, Vol. VI, p. 43.

[45] On "Booth in California," see William Winter in the *New York Tribune Illustrated Supplement,* August 24, 1902, p. 12.

[46] The Lady Allworth was Mrs. Hamilton. *Edwin Booth: Playbills, Portraits, and Souvenirs,* Collected by William Cushing Bamburgh, in the Harvard Theatre Collection. Pp. 98-120 deal with a Chronology of the life of Edwin Booth. For this particular reference, a playbill at *The Players,* is cited.

and one night, and finally made his way to San Francisco; his brother had received a later message; their father had been buried in Baltimore; there was nothing they could do but stay on, and hope for good fortune. Junius, Jr., was now manager of a stock company playing at the San Francisco Hall, and Edwin was engaged for utility parts, but soon rose to a startling success as Richard III. And, as his father had done before him, he chose Sir Giles Overreach as the character to follow Richard. I cannot find the exact date; it was sometime between February and the end of April, 1853.[47] His second rôle too caused some popular excitement, and by the time he had played Macbeth, and finally his first Hamlet, Booth was a favorite with the theatre-going public. He was wise enough to know, however, how much he had yet to learn, and under his brother he continued to play all sorts of parts from star down to utility, "a lesson," he remarked later, "for crushed tragedians."

Booth next played briefly at the new Metropolitan Theatre under the managership of Catherine Sinclair (Mrs. Edwin Forrest), and then determined, in 1854, to go to Australia. It was a fantastic trip; did—I wonder—Sir Giles accompany him? With Laura Keene and D. C. Anderson, Booth played Sydney and Melbourne, and then, without the lady, on the way back, Honolulu for two months. John Roe played the heroines; the company slept in hammocks in the theatre; Booth posted his own bills. San Francisco was better than this—and better than the Samoan Islands and Tahiti—and Booth returned to act with Catherine Sinclair at the Metropolitan. Soon he was in Sacramento again, and then with a manager named Moulton into the mountains by wagon and brass band. Booth became renowned as The Fiery Star, because every village they visited seemed to catch fire as soon as they left. As soon as news of this got about, their personal safety was in question. The manager skipped out; Booth's horse was seized as security; penniless, the actor finally made his way back to San Francisco, determined now to return to the refinement of the

---

[47] See an article by G. C. Warren in *The San Francisco Chronicle* of May 12, 1929. He cites as source "W. F. Hooke's manuscript list of plays and players in San Francisco from October 1852 to December 1883, a volume that is in the library of the Bohemian Club, where I was permitted to inspect it. It is a record made from the files of the old daily, *Alta Californian*."

East. How many performances of Sir Giles I have missed during these vagrant years, I shall never know. I note only three more, all from rare bills. These were at the Sacramento Theatre, the first on May 3, 1856, for Booth's benefit; the others fell on the 20th and 21st of the same month:

Sir Giles Overreach .... Booth
Wellborn .... Venua
Lord Lovell .... Rand
Marrall .... Dumfries
Justice Greedy .... Mitchell
Allworth .... Moreland
Lady Allworth .... Miss Sophie Edwin
Margaret .... Mrs. Thoman

Enough money was collected from benefits in Sacramento and San Francisco to enable Booth to leave California in September of that year. What blows followed were of a different kind.

Booth made his first appearance after long absence in the East in Baltimore and followed this with a successful tour through the Southern circuit, Washington, Richmond, Charleston, New Orleans, Mobile, and Memphis. Fletcher notes a Sir Giles in Pittsburgh on December 23rd.[48] This was all very well, but Booth now wanted proof that he was a star, not a miscast stock actor. Boston to him was the test; if he were successful there, all was well; if not, back to stock. The character he chose for the ordeal was Sir Giles Overreach. How amazingly and persistently *A New Way to Pay Old Debts* dominates the lives of these actors: the triumph of Kean, the last performance of Cooke, the début of Davenport; back in 1816 the turning point in the career of Edwin's father, now in 1857 the determining point in his own. Booth looked forward to the performance with fear and trembling.

Booth's Sir Giles Overreach was presented to Boston at the Boston Theatre on April 20, 1857,[49] with the following cast:

[48] Fletcher, pp. 455, 580.
[49] From the playbill. The play was not repeated on May 4th, as given by Cruickshank (Edition), p. 137; on that date Matilda Heron played *Camille*; as a matter of fact Booth was playing Richard III at Burton's in New York.

Sir Giles Overreach .... Booth
Wellborn .... Belton
Lord Lovell .... Donaldson
Marrall .... John Gilbert
Justice Greedy .... John Wood
Allworth .... Cowell
Lady Allworth .... Miss Lizzie Emmons
Margaret .... Miss Emma Taylor

Let his sister tell the story:[50] "It was a cold dreary night, and he had a thin house. Many white-haired men were in the parquette, which contained more of the passing than of the present generation. On the entrance of *Allworth,* the modest personator of that character was startled by vigorous applause from the audience, which, with the laugh that followed on discovery of the mistake, succeeded in taking away his power of speech. When Sir Giles appeared loud and prolonged applause greeted him; then (as he described it) the people braced themselves, self-satisfied, in their seats, as if to say, Now, young man, let us see what you can do for yourself. The play proceeded quietly until the fourth act, when the player was on his mettle, for he felt that evening to be the turning point in his career. . . . This Boston indorsement was to decide his future; and with a nervous calm he reserved himself for the last great scenes. The effect was electrifying, the call genuine and spontaneous; he knew his power, and felt that he was safe. The next day his pronounced success was universally acknowledged, and the press was unanimous in his praise." William Winter was in the audience and testifies to his triumph:[51] "That night I saw him for the first time and saw his audience thrilled by his magnetic acting." "The principal event of the week," says a Harvard clipping from a Boston newspaper, "has been the début of Mr. Edwin Booth at the Boston Theatre. . . . From the first it was discovered that Mr. Booth possesses the true fire of histrionic genius, and gives promise of an actor worthy to wear the laurels worn by his father. . . . Mr. Booth's voice is good but not as full as it will become in maturer years. It falls a little short sometimes, of the requirements of very forcible passages,

50 *Elder and Younger Booth,* pp. 148-9.
51 *Vagrant Memories,* p. 152.

such for instance, as occur in the last act of Sir Giles Overreach. Some of the tones of his voice remind one of his lamented father's, and this circumstance told with thrilling effect upon the audience, on the first night of his engagement." Booth was henceforth a recognized star; he had passed the turning point.

Injudicious enthusiasm in the preliminary announcements of Booth's engagement at Burton's New (Metropolitan) Theatre made his first appearance in New York as a full fledged star a difficult task. He wished to open as Sir Giles Overreach, but Burton had already announced Richard and the audience expected that character. However, when he appeared on May 4, he was again triumphant, and as his engagement continued, he gained more and more applause—in short, his success was brilliant. Sir Giles Overreach was presented on May 6 and repeated on May 16, "by universal desire" says the playbill:

Sir Giles Overreach .... Booth
Wellborn .... C. Fisher
Lord Lovell .... Rainford
Marrall .... Mark Smith
Justice Greedy .... Setchell
Allworth .... Holman
Lady Allworth .... Mrs. A. Parker
Margaret .... Mrs. S. Stevens

On August 31, the opening of a new season, Booth again appeared as Sir Giles at this theatre with certain changes in the cast: the Lord Lovell was now J. L. Barrett, the Marrall Moore, and the Margaret Miss Susan Denin.[52] John Moore was the stage-manager of this company, and his book of the play with the part of Marrall written out in longhand with cues is in the Harvard Theatre Collection. Booth's success was repeated. The *Herald* of September 1 remarks: "Mr. Booth's Sir Giles is one of his very best impersonations, and in it he treads close upon the footsteps of his father, whose performance of the last act we have never seen equalled. Mr. Edwin Booth has the same electric flashes, the

[52] Cruickshank (Edition), p. 134, lists Burton's Theatre August 31, 1857 and just below it Tripler Hall, same date. Tripler (later Metropolitan) Hall burned on January 8, 1854. The Metropolitan was built on its site, and was inaccurately sometimes called Tripler Hall.

same marked inequalities, and achieves almost the same triumphs. He is an actor whose rise has been almost without parallel, and who, as we have said before, has his future in his own hands."

Boston, avid of the new star, beckoned Booth back in September, and again at the Boston Theatre we find his Sir Giles Overreach. The playbill of September 14 gives a cast for the play different enough from the preceding to justify printing all the major rôles:

Sir Giles Overreach .... Booth
Wellborn .... Howe
Lord Lovell .... Donaldson
Marrall .... John Gilbert
Justice Greedy .... Davidge
Allworth .... Cowell
Lady Allworth .... Mrs. Abbott
Margaret .... Miss Emmons

The South and the Middle West now saw Booth again, but I note no *New Way,* though the play was doubtless presented, and return again to the Boston Theatre for a performance on March 30, 1858, with the cast unchanged.

Sir Giles was back at Burton's again on April 8, 1858, accompanied by the Margaret of Mrs. Hudson Kirby, the rest as before —so the bill. "And now Booth," says Professor Odell[53] "paid the penalty of all who achieve sudden sensational success. Grown accustomed, the public and critics began to find flaws—probably to the great advantage of the young man's art." Perhaps New York did not yet appreciate him as much as Boston, for two performances of Sir Giles were necessary when he visited the Boston Theatre in October, one on the evening of the 27th, the other as a matinee on the 30th. The cast on the playbill is worth noting entire:

Sir Giles Overreach .... Booth
Wellborn .... Edwin Adams
Lord Lovell .... Horton
Marrall .... Dan Setchell
Justice Greedy .... George Holland
Allworth .... Selwin
Lady Allworth .... Charlotte Crampton
Margaret .... Mary Devlin

[53] Vol. VII, p. 15.

Note Mary Devlin there as daughter to Sir Giles but shortly to be the wife of Edwin Booth, his adored Mary all his life though she died less than three years after their marriage in 1860. He had met her first in Richmond on his southern tour earlier in the year, a sweet, charming, and talented girl; her influence on the tragedian was both deep and permanent. I wonder what were Booth's feelings when as Sir Giles he behaved so shamefully to her.

I note next Booth's Sir Giles at the Holliday Street Theatre, Baltimore, on October 2, 1860, by courtesy of a playbill of that date:

Sir Giles Overreach .... Booth
Wellborn .... C. Barton Hill
Lord Lovell .... Leak
Marrall .... Scallan
Justice Greedy .... Williams
Allworth .... Ringgold
Lady Allworth .... Miss Osborne
Margaret .... Miss Gray

In September of 1859 the theatre which had been managed by Burton reopened under the name of the Winter Garden, A Conservatory of the Arts, a theatre to be important in Booth's life. During the 1860-1861 season an extraórdinary succession of stars appeared there: Charlotte Cushman, Booth, Jefferson, Chanfrau, John Sleeper Clarke (Booth's brother-in-law), Mrs. John Wood, the W. J. Florences, and others too numerous to mention. During this triumphant year, Sir Giles trod the boards at least twice, on February 1, 1861, for Booth's benefit in curious companionship with Petruchio,[54] and on April 24. Fortunately there are bills for both performances. For the first the cast was as follows:

Sir Giles Overreach .... Booth
Wellborn .... Lingham
Lord Lovell .... Lawler
Marrall .... J. H. Stoddart

[54] Not on January 31 (Odell, Vol. VII, p. 316), when Booth's part was Richelieu.

Justice Greedy .... Davidge
Allworth .... George Stoddart
Lady Allworth .... Mrs. Duffield
Margaret .... Miss Ada Clifton

For the second performance Barton Hill succeeded Lingham as Wellborn. We know strangely little yet about Booth's Sir Giles, but I cannot help it if the war was the absorbing topic of the newspapers to the virtual exclusion of dramatic criticism. Of the performance at the Howard Athenaeum on June 1, 1861, a new Boston Theatre for Booth, I can give only the cast on the bill:

Sir Giles Overreach .... Booth
Wellborn .... Aiken
Lord Lovell .... John McCullough
Marrall .... Setchell
Justice Greedy .... Curtis
Allworth ....J. A. Smith
Lady Allworth .... Mrs. Rand
Margaret .... Miss Oriana Marshall

Shortly thereafter Booth sailed for England where, as we have seen in another section of this book, Sir Giles Overreach was one of the characters he presented—with no great success.

Booth's first Sir Giles after his return to this country was, with the inevitable question-mark, at the Boston Theatre on December 8, 1862. We have not had a Boston Theatre cast for four years, so I copy the playbill:

Sir Giles Overreach .... Booth
Wellborn .... Daly
Lord Lovell .... J. W. Lanergan
Marrall .... T. E. Owens
Justice Greedy .... W. H. Smith
Allworth .... Marlowe
Lady Allworth .... Miss Emily Mestayer
Margaret .... Miss Cross

Booth had, however, previous to this date, begun his famous connection with the Winter Garden in New York, a connection which with brief intermissions lasted from September 29, 1862, until March 23, 1867. It was here that Booth really achieved the popularity he deserved by presentations in excellent revivals of the recognized masterpieces of the theatre. I note, however, with some disappointment that *A New Way to Pay Old Debts* seems not to have been immediately called for. If my records be correct, indeed, Booth presented Sir Giles in New York only rarely from this time on.

On February 21, 1863, Booth's wife died very suddenly, and the shock to Booth was overpowering and permanent. Till this time he had been drinking not wisely but well; now he put the bottle from him with bitter self-reproach for his lapses. This sudden cessation along with the anguish of bereavement affected his nervous system and brought physical as well as mental exhaustion. Though he smoked to a dangerous, perhaps even fatal, excess, he was almost never hereafter under the influence of liquor again. With his wife's death, Booth bought a house in New York, gave up all thought of acting again, and retired into seclusion. On March 7 he wrote to the Rev. Samuel Osgood, who had performed the marriage ceremony, words which reveal so clearly his character and state of mind at this time that they cannot be omitted from any study of him:[55]

> When I was happy my art was a source of infinite delight and pride to me, because she delighted in my success and encouraged me in all I did; I had then an incentive to work, to achieve something great. But my ambition is gone with her; it can give me no pleasure to paint a picture of my grief and hold it up as a show for applause again.
>
> My agony will be too intense to render properly those passions of woe, and sufferings which till now I thought required years of study and practice, but which, alas! I have too quickly—too deeply learned.

Sincere and moving, however, as was this expression of Booth's feelings, he was too large a man to do nothing long. Lack of occupation soon became irksome, and when the opportunity arose, he joined his brother-in-law, the comedian John Sleeper Clarke, in two enterprises of considerable importance, the purchase of the Walnut Street Theatre, Philadelphia, and the management of the Winter Garden in New York. Booth's connection with the Philadelphia theatre lasted until 1870 when his partner bought

[55] Winter, *Booth*, pp. 29-30.

him out. In the Winter Garden management they associated themselves unfortunately with William Stuart, first agent, later lessee.
Booth made his first appearance under these conditions as Hamlet
on September 21, 1863, and played a popular and prosperous engagement. It was a year later that Booth acted Hamlet for the
extraordinary run of one hundred nights.

We return to Boston where Booth's Sir Giles, if I mistake not,
was most popular. There we find him at the Boston Theatre on
November 5, 1863, with a radically different company listed on
the bills:

Sir Giles Overreach .... Booth
Wellborn .... Whalley
Lord Lovell .... W. H. Hamblin
Marrall .... Scallan
Justice Greedy .... Curtis
Allworth .... N. T. Davenport
Lady Allworth .... Anna Cowell
Margaret .... Miss Cranston

After this emergence Sir Giles again disappears, partly explained
by Booth's second retirement in 1865 when the awful news came
to him that President Lincoln had been assassinated by his brother.
From this retirement, Booth returned to the stage only because
it was imperative to fulfil certain obligations already contracted;
otherwise he might never have acted again. Fortunately when
he reappeared in 1866, Booth had the sympathy of his audience,
and he was cordially welcomed.

In 1866, Booth played at the Walnut Street Theatre, Philadelphia, after an absence of two years from its stage. His first
presentation of *A New Way to Pay Old Debts* fell on June 11;
I take the cast from a bill:

Sir Giles Overreach .... Booth
Wellborn .... Charles Barron
Lord Lovell .... Chester
Marrall .... Fawcett
Justice Greedy .... Bailey
Allworth .... Taylor
Lady Allworth .... Mrs. Chester
Margaret .... Miss Graham

When the play was represented on October 16 and November 9, there were some changes in the cast: Barton Hill played his familiar Wellborn, and W. A. Chapman acted Marrall, Owen Fawcett being shifted to Justice Greedy and Bailey dropping out.

Ill luck and disaster continue to follow Booth when we accompany him back to the Winter Garden. The performances of Sir Giles Overreach on January 8 and 10, 1867, foreboded no trouble,[56] but on the morning of March 23, the Winter Garden burned to the ground. Just prior to the fire, Clarke had sold his interest to Booth for ten thousand dollars. In the building was uninsured property belonging to Booth valued at sixty thousand dollars or more. The Winter Garden, scene of the triumphs of Jenny Lind, Rachel, Burton, Brougham, Matilda Heron, Charlotte Cushman, Wallack, and Booth himself, was no more; and Booth, with financial security in his grasp, saw it fly swiftly away amid the smoke of the ruin. Almost immediately Booth began laying plans for the erection of a new theatre, this time to bear his name.

But this is a chronicle of Sir Giles as well as of Booth, and to find the two together again we must go to the Boston Theatre for performances on April 16 and 24, and May 6, 1867. Playbills show us a new cast:

Sir Giles Overreach .... Booth
Wellborn .... C. R. Thorne, Jr.
Lord Lovell .... Louis Aldrich
Marrall .... Hardenberg
Justice Greedy .... Walter M. Leman
Allworth .... Bascomb
Lady Allworth .... Mrs. Stewart
Margaret .... Mrs. Agnes Perry

Later in the year, in the fall to be more exact, Booth was acting at McVicker's Theatre in Chicago, and during this engagement he became betrothed to Mary McVicker, the stepdaughter of the manager. Apparently she accompanied him East, for Booth's sister says that she was the Margaret to Booth's Sir Giles when he

[56] Odell, Vol. VIII, p. 149, Winter, *Booth,* p. 44, errs in recording a performance in March.

played the part in Baltimore in the engagement which followed.[57]
This was the second time that Booth had played Sir Giles with
a fiancée as Margaret. Miss McVicker retired from the stage in
1869 when she became the actor's wife.

Booth's magnificent new theatre was opened on February 3,
1869, with *Romeo and Juliet* which ran for ten weeks, to be succeeded by *Othello* until May 29 when Booth finished his acting
season. He did not reappear on his own stage until January 5,
1870, when his Hamlet held the boards till March 19. His next
character was Sir Giles Overreach, and its comparative importance
in his mind and perhaps the public's may be found in the fact that
he played the part only three times, the 21st, 22nd, and 23rd of
March. This in spite of the fact that Hutton notes Sir Giles[58] was
"said by the critics to have been among the best of his representations." Before we look at the reviews, let us glance at the cast
which heads them:

Sir Giles Overreach .... Edwin Booth
Wellborn .... W. E. Sheridan
Lord Lovell .... Theo. Hamilton
Marrall .... Charles Hale
Justice Greedy .... D. C. Anderson
Allworth .... Augustus Pitou
Lady Allworth .... Miss Fanny Morant
Margaret .... Miss Blanche de Bar

We have not yet had any full-length portrait of Edwin Booth's
Sir Giles; I therefore take the liberty of introducing here the rele-
vant parts of three reviews from New York newspapers in the
hope that the picture will be clearer. Alas, we are in difficulties at
once. The critic in the *Times* of March 23 lays himself open to
suspicion at once by preferring Booth's Sir Giles to his Hamlet:

> Mr. Edwin Booth played *Sir Giles Overreach* on Monday, and
> achieved in the part an unequivocal success. So immeasurably
> superior is Mr. Booth's *Sir Giles* to his *Hamlet* that it seems
> almost incredible that the two should be those of the same man.
> . . . The essence of the one is vacillation; the essence of the other
> is intensity. Now, when Mr. Booth tries to depict vacillation, he

---

[57] *Elder and Younger Booth*, p. 108.
[58] In his Diary, Vol. I, p. 46, in the Princeton University Library.

gives us languid monotony. He gropes in the dark after what is foreign to his artistic nature. . . . But when he tries to depict intensity he has merely to reproduce himself. . . . Hence his *Hamlet* seldom rises above mediocrity, and hence his *Sir Giles* frequently ascends to greatness. . . .

We are glad to bear witness that in such parts as *Sir Giles* the time has gone by when Mr. Booth could be termed a mere copy of his father. He stands in this character at least, upon his own merits and the footing is trustworthy, and substantial. It is true that he has not in the part his father's massiveness, his savage hardihood, nor, to our memory, his physical power. But he has more subtlety, more elaboration and consequently more variety. There is indeed a fineness of perception, a delicacy of discrimination about his reading that on the surface seems incompatible with the coarse, brutal passions that are *Sir Giles'* most salient qualities. Only on the surface though; for the profound analysis of human character and motives that Massinger puts so freely into his hearer's mouth are possible for no common man. They lead us with little reflection to see that *Sir Giles* was not from the first what he afterward became, a cruel, rapacious monster, but a being with a noble and far-reaching intellect; and that we see in him a high nature perverted, not a low one carrying out its original instincts. We are of opinion that Mr. Booth has here thought more deeply than his father, and that he has wisely heightened the effect of his picture by touches of brilliancy, which, in this view of the character of *Sir Giles,* are fairly warranted. It should not be inferred from this that the representation lacks evenness, either in design or execution. On the contrary, the carefulness of its study is minutely reflected throughout in reading, action and business—the latter, by the way, being especially good and presenting several points of novelty. The dialogue with *Wellborn,* particularly from the passage beginning, "We worldly men," &c., is very fine, the great scene of the fourth act ending with the burst of "Joy! joy! all over!" that brings down the curtain, is magnificently acted, and the horrible passages of the conclusion give scope for what we must pronounce on the whole the finest histrionic display we have ever witnessed from this artist. Nothing can well surpass the stony amazement with which he discovers the obliteration of the deed, the overwhelming fury with which he afterwards turns on *Marrall,* the demoniac yell of rage and hate with which he hears of his daughter's froward marriage, or the agonies of the final paralysis, and the miserable, yet indomitable death. All this shows that Mr.

Booth possesses fine ability, judiciously turned to account; and, to our mind, there is more of genius in either of the scenes we have named than there is in the whole five acts of his *Hamlet*.

It is greatly to Mr. Booth's credit that, notwithstanding the elegance of detail at which we have hinted, his *Sir Giles* should still be so grandly picturesque. There is nothing in the least finical about it. The rugged, flinty and remorseless traits of the ambitious old usurer stand out none the less boldly because of the delicate filling in of the intermediate tints. The harmony of the picture renders it none the less striking. We feel throughout that it is well within the artist's means, and that respect for his vocation has prompted all his handling of it. This power and this spirit combined make possible great acting; and we rejoice to feel able to say that in his *Sir Giles Overreach* Mr. Booth so illustrates the combination that no intellectual spectator can refuse to award him the highest meed of praise.

The critic in the *Herald* (March 22) goes precisely in the other direction. After a string of theatrical reminiscences and comments on the elder Booth, he continues:

Enough that we express our convictions that Booth, the younger is not the peer of Booth, the elder, in the character of Sir Giles Overreach. The streaks of the elder's genius which occasionally flash through the younger's personations are too ephemeral and transient to establish his reputation upon so exalted a pinnacle as some of his over-zealous friends would erect for him. In the character of Sir Giles last night he was tame to positive weariness during the first two and part of the third acts. He did not come up to the standard of E. L. Davenport in other portions of the play, and in the final scenes, when the spasms of stage ranting are somewhat pardonable he was not so effective as the late Gustavus V. Brooke. The negative success of Mr. Booth last evening may be attributed to the lukewarmness of the audience, or to the fact that he was laboring under his long and successful impersonation of quite an opposite character—Hamlet. But certain it is that he failed to elicit more than one single round of hearty applause; and his repeated calls before the curtain were but compliments extended to the kind and genial man, and not the thrilling, startling and great actor. The play was otherwise [!] well cast, and put upon the stage in the usual elegant style that has won Booth's theatre a high reputation all over the country.

William Winter in the *Tribune* of March 22 comments on the "truth and taste" of the presentation but finds the play "dull and coarse":

> The character of *Sir Giles Overreach* is undeniably strong, but it is horribly repulsive. The opportunities which it affords for the manifestation of wild rage and animal excitement, thrilled through and through by intensely wicked purpose, have always commended it to tragedians. . . . Mr. Booth's performance last night was remarkable for quick transitions of feeling and manner, a continuous and fervent intensity, and, at the last, an electrical outburst of frenzy made awful by the coming on of death. He was much applauded and was several times called before the curtain. It is worthy of note that he dressed the character with accuracy— "which was not so before," according to our recollection. The iron-gray wig, the halting walk, the somber yet rich-colored costumes, harmonized with the essence of the character, and made the embodiment exceedingly picturesque. There was nothing however in the performance that very deeply stirred our admiration, except its magnetic violence. Mr. Booth's own nature is rich in qualities that are foreign to that of *Sir Giles*, and it is in precisely wherein those qualities appear that his personation becomes most enthralling to the imagination. He seemed, in many ways, an abler, finer, more poetic, and more human creature then the vile worldly-minded villain that Massinger has drawn. And yet his ideal of the character seemed perfectly accurate. After *Hamlet* it must be a rest to Mr. Booth's mind to play such a part as *Sir Giles*, which draws to a very great degree upon the commoner emotions and the physical resources. . . .

One thing at least is evident from these criticisms—that the reviewers did not get together and decide what to say. I have seldom come upon criticisms so entirely contradictory. One gets, among other things, impressions that Booth surpassed a weak Hamlet, was nowhere near as good as in Hamlet, was a distinctly weak Sir Giles; that he was admirably suited to the part, that he was woefully miscast; that the play is grand and thrilling, out-of-date for the new acting, low and repulsive. And what happens to our hope for a clear picture of Booth's impersonation? Unless we are careful, here is confusion worse confounded. Some conclusions can, I think, be drawn. The general tenor of the criticism in the

Times shows that much of it must be discounted. To think Booth's Hamlet bad was certainly exceptional. The reviewer in the *Herald* is plainly an adherent of the old school indulging in reminiscences misleading as to Booth's abilities in the part because he is thinking of the impersonation and manner of the elder Booth, of Brooke, and of Davenport. The *Tribune* is probably closest to the truth; it is not new to find the play no longer suitable, the character too vile to awaken the imagination; we have found this attitude in connection with the impersonations of Davenport. Booth's art and age had finer resources than could be displayed in Sir Giles. He seems to have played the part with intelligence and intensity, but Booth could play Hamlet and Hamlet was not Sir Giles. We do, however, manage to piece together fragments of these remains so as to give us a picture, even though that picture is blurred. Later comments will clarify and interpret the image.

It has been apparent that Booth, as his career progressed, played Sir Giles with decreasing frequency. We skip a year and a half, for instance, to the performance at the Boston Theatre on November 2, 1871, when the actors who took part were listed on the playbill as follows:

Sir Giles Overreach	Booth
Wellborn	Louis Aldrich
Lord Lovell	France
Marrall	Allen
Justice Greedy	Maguinnis
Allworth	Sullivan
Lady Allworth	Mrs. Charles Poole
Margaret	Mrs. J. B. Booth

And then Sir Giles vanishes from Booth's repertory for almost fourteen years! The reasons are not far to seek, for we have already seen the signs. "He discarded *Sir Edward Mortimer, Sir Giles Overreach,* and *Pescara,*" says Winter in his *Vagrant Memories,* "because he considered them too dark and repellent, and he told me that he was inclined to discard *Bertuccio* for the same reason." Another passage from the same book will give us a second explanation: "Edwin Booth was fortunate in coming later [than Forrest], when the culture of the people had increased and when the sledge-hammer style was going out, so that he gained almost without an effort the refined and fastidious classes."[59] Sir Giles is not a fastidious part. And in the third place Edwin Booth was now the actor of "the philosophic mind"—Booth was Hamlet.

It is not strange then that Booth dropped Sir Giles Overreach; what *is* strange is that he ever revived the part again. Much happened in the interval. In 1874 Booth's Theatre failed and the management passed out of his hands: Booth had no business sense, and though he attracted audiences without difficulty, he was an easy prey to unscrupulous men who did not share his unselfish artistic ideals. Weary in mind and body, he was literally forced out of his own theatre by following the injudicious advice of people actuated only by grasping self-interest. The whole pitiful tale deserves to be read in Winter's biography, but it cannot be included here. Booth never again took part in management; from this period he became a travelling star, allowing himself intervals for rest and retirement. In 1880 he visited Europe and was enthusiastically received. Most memorably, he acted at the Lyceum in London with Irving, whose generous hospitality gave him uninterrupted pleasure. After his return in 1881, Mrs. Booth died following a difficult domestic period in the actor's life. The next year he again sailed for England, fulfilling successful engagements in London and the provinces. In Germany he received extravagant testimonials of admiration and affection, one of the most delightful episodes in his career. He returned to the United States in 1883 and did not again leave these shores.

Why Booth revived Sir Giles Overreach is a problem which I have not been able to solve; one can think of many arguments for not doing so, few in favor of it. It is perhaps significant, however, that it was in Boston, the city where his Sir Giles had always been most popular, that the revivals of *A New Way to Pay Old Debts* first occurred. They were presented at the Boston Museum on March 4, 5, and 19, 1885.[60] The playbills give us the cast:

[59] pp. 182-4.

[60] Not the 16th, 17th, and 18th as given by Cruickshank (Edition), p. 137. Note Miss Robins, later a distinguished actress in the plays of Ibsen.

Sir Giles Overreach	Booth
Wellborn	Parks
Lord Lovell	Whytal
Marrall	Kent
Justice Greedy	Robertson
Allworth	Arden
Lady Allworth	Miss Regina Dace
Margaret	Miss Elizabeth Robins

and we note that the performances "achieved instantaneous and tremendous success and produced a profound impression upon the public." This popularity is surprising and we must go to the reviews for confirmation, and to fill out our yet shadowy impressions of Booth's Sir Giles. Some of the criticisms are not encouraging, though it is pointed out that the fault lies mostly with the play, now too old-fashioned to please. *The Boston Journal* (March 5) says: "Mr. Booth's acting last evening was of such histrionic power as to give a degree of warrant for the capabilities that have been attached to the rôle in popular esteem. Through the three or four somewhat tedious and uneventful acts that lead up to the culmination it was the intensity of Mr. Booth's conception and grasp of the character that sustained the spirit of the play, in spite of the author's platitudes. . . ." *The Boston Post* of same date is even more flatly disapproving: "It [the play] belongs to the past and should be brought out occasionally and after long intervals as a curiosity. . . . The character of Sir Giles Overreach does not give Mr. Booth the opportunities to display his powers." The play, says the *Daily Globe* of March 5, is "not one suited to be popular with audiences in these later days. . . . Mr. Booth's acting as Sir Giles Overreach is almost beyond criticism. . . . Within the limitations set by the playwright himself there could hardly be an improvement suggested in Mr. Booth's presentation of the character. . . ." There was, however, some difference of opinion about the play. The following is taken from an unidentified clipping in the Harvard Theatre Collection, dated March 1885: "On Wednesday and Thursday came Massinger's 'A New Way to Pay Old Debts' having in its old age all the health and vigor of youth. . . . Sir Giles is a man, real flesh and blood . . . and Mr. Booth's portrayal of the part is masterly. This is a revival that one might well hope to see turned into permanency. With hardly an instant where disapproval is possible, and filled full with illustrations of what, in the strict sense, is the most charming side of Mr. Booth's acting, the part of Sir Giles Overreach may fairly be regarded as one of the half dozen that Mr. Booth should always keep ready like a trusty weapon."

The three reviews which best reveal the details of Booth's acting all speak of the play with esteem. I make no apologies for quoting at length. The first is from *The Boston Herald* of March 5:

> There is yet more life in Massinger's comedy of "A New Way to Pay Old Debts," though it be in the third century of its age, than in countless dramatic works of more recent origin. The passions and emotions whose workings and effects it illustrates belong to no time, and influence humanity today with no less force than when the play was first produced "at ye Phoenix in Drury lane." Overdrawn as many of its characters are, none can justly be called a caricature; and all may be accepted as types. The dialogue, if it occasionally seem verbose to the ears of modern playgoers, is nevertheless instinct with poetic thought, not lacking in genuine humor, and often epigrammatic and quotable. But had it no other claims for popularity, the scope it gives for powerful acting in the character of Sir Giles Overreach would have kept it on the stage. The records of the triumphs of Kemble, Cooke, Kean, Brooke and the elder Booth in the part are still fresh and many lesser lights have gained distinction in it. To Edwin Booth's performance of Sir Giles at the Museum last evening more than ordinary interest attached, for it was in this rôle that he made his first appearance here as a "star" 28 years ago next month. . . .
>
> So much of reminiscence. Last night, . . . it was worthy of remark that "white haired men" were in the majority in the large audience, and doubtless not a few were present who witnessed Mr. Booth's Boston début as a star. However this may be, old and young together joined in giving him a hearty greeting when he stepped upon the stage. But they did not thereafter coldly sit in judgment. On the contrary, there was hardly a scene in which the tragedian appeared that did not bring him a round of applause, and the descent of the curtain was the signal for an enthusiastic call after the third, fourth and fifth acts.
>
> Of Mr. Booth's impersonation of the ambitious, scheming, miserly, heartless, passionate and domineering Sir Giles, little or

nothing that is new can be said. The character is not complex, nor does it require delicacy of treatment, and he depicts it with bold, forcible strokes, aiming to gain broad effects rather than finish in detail. Last night he acted in the closing scenes with unwonted fire and vigor. The outbursts of passion, the manifestations of baffled rage and bitter hate, the defiant but vain struggle against the advances of the fatal palsy which immediately precede the death of the wretched victim of his own plots, were portrayed with thrilling power, and the death scene was made realistic to a degree that must have impressed the most callous of playgoers.

Mr. Booth was well supported by the Museum company, and the performance as a whole was one of general excellence. . . .

The next revelation of contemporary opinion I take from the *Boston Transcript* of March 5. The bit about the music is too good to miss even though it has nothing to do with the case:

Philip Massinger's plays, with a single exception, are unknown to few besides those who have made a study of dramatic literature, especially of that which was produced in the Elizabethan period. . . . The single exception to the general oblivion that has overtaken his works is "A New Way to Pay Old Debts," and even that is unknown to the younger playgoers of today. Why it should be so rarely played cannot be explained except on the ground that the elder Booth's powerful impersonation of Sir Giles Overreach appalled his professional rivals, though there were some in his day that dared attempt the part. It was a part peculiarly adapted to Booth's picturesque and intense style, as it was to that of Edmund Kean, who, it was declared, had been Booth's model. Edwin Booth, nobly ambitious to follow in his father's footsteps, included the drama in the repertory of his earlier seasons as a star actor, but not in fifteen years (probably more) has he appeared as Sir Giles in Boston. It was next to impossible to avoid comparison with his first presentations of the character here, although memory alone could be depended upon to reproduce the vanished picture, and it was necessary also to make allowance for the sharpness of first impressions. Making, then, such mental comparisons as were possible, his Sir Giles appeared to be the result of a closer study both of human nature and of the dramatist's work. The knight is about as bad a man in thought and deed as one would wish to see. Still he has the social standing of a gentleman, and talks like a man of education. Furthermore, he is not entirely without love for his daughter, although his affection is so tempered by an absorbing ambition and a constant desire to see her advanced to the highest social position attainable, that he counsels her to unmentionable doings when there comes a chance that she will be courted by a nobleman. But his villany is chiefly made apparent to the spectator only, and excepting what is known of it by his creatures, Marrall and Justice Greedy, there is little of it revealed to the other characters of the drama, although they may have all the suspicion in the world. Therefore it seems that Mr. Booth's present picture of the grasping usurer who knows how to accomplish his purposes under the shield of the law is true to nature. Sir Giles is set before us in the guise of a typical Englishman, strong and alert, and with something more than the average quickness of perception and readiness of wit found among English country gentlemen. His very super-abundance of physical strength is the cause of his sudden death by apoplexy, and even in the presence of death, his strong brain urges him to defy the dreadful fate that his suddenly disordered vision opens up to him. Mr. Booth very properly reserved his powers for the catastrophe, but without a sacrifice of the picturesqueness that the character really demands. It was an effort that yielded results of the highest artistic value, and the spectators of the occasion, who gave constant evidence of their absorption in the performance, cannot soon forget it, even though one recalls the time when Mr. Booth played the part with more impetuosity. . . .

By a reversal of portions of the dialogue the play was made to end with the death of Sir Giles. The omission of parts of the dialogue succeeding left the audience in ignorance of the manner in which Wellborn's fortunes are repaired. There were played some bits of incidental music concerning which a word or two may be spoken. A minuet which had a Handelian flavor was entirely out of place. But to hear Mendelssohn's wedding march was a shock. . . .

Much the most interesting review, however, is that from *The Boston Daily Advertiser* of March 5, where the reviewer deals in full both with the play, and Booth's interpretation of Sir Giles:

If one were asked to name the greatest English play outside the productions of Shakespeare's unapproached genius, his only hesitation must be in deciding between two: "A New Way to Pay Old Debts," of Philip Massinger, and "She Stoops to Conquer," of Oliver Goldsmith. And between these two admirable productions, the choice must finally fall upon the former, which, inferior to the latter in richness of humor and delicacy of characterization, yet finds no rivals in fire and force except upon the pages of the creator of "Othello" and "Macbeth." Compared with Shakespeare, Massinger must often seem both rude and shallow, but measured with other dramatic authors he seems immense. Many of his lines would not discredit the master poet himself. . . . Most of all, who, besides these two great dramatists, could have conceived and produced such a character as *Sir Giles Overreach*? It is many years, we believe, since Mr. Booth has given a single representation of this part; it is certainly many years since the character has been included in his list for frequent performance. In his early days when he was comparatively "green in judgment," Mr. Booth with the reckless courage of youth essayed this part, as he essayed several others, which he afterwards dropped and did not again touch until his powers were solidified and his art was matured. It is an event worth chronicling now, as it is worth remembering, to see him once more grapple with the tremendous dramatic creation which has taxed the ability of the greatest English actors, and in the interpretation of which his illustrious father won some of his most brilliant triumphs.

No one who was with the large and critical audience at the Museum last night could doubt the ample wisdom of Mr. Booth's reëntrance into this old part. *Sir Giles Overreach,* though somewhat complex, is not a complicated character. Upon a large canvas, with great, strong, unfaltering strokes, Massinger has painted a nature of enormous potency for evil, a nature capable of craft, and intellectually endowed with the gifts which make for subtlety, but tending by its own interior impulse always towards accomplishing its innumerable purposes by force and arms; of vast physical plenitude and quenchless flame of spirit; ignorant of fear; supremely, consciously, consistently selfish; a keen observer, in his own way, of men and motives, and capable of being deceived only through the blind cynicism which cannot allow for the virtue in which it has no faith; boundless in ambition, devoid of compunction, of scruple, of decency, almost of human affection; a soul which has deliberately decided and frankly avows its intent to "jump the life to come," which is Mephistophelean in the completeness of its self-delivery to evil and yet differs from the fiend who "eternally denies" in this, that it honestly, sincerely, and with vast sensuous satisfaction, believes in the solidity of the ends which it seeks to compass—this is indeed a personage to tax the full strength of a very strong actor. And Mr. Booth proved himself last night fully equal to the great task which he had put upon his powers. His *Sir Giles Overreach* will take rank at once with the strongest and most effective of his impersonations. Differing from the late Mr. E. L. Davenport, and from some other of his predecessors, Mr. Booth has in no way idealized the character or removed it from among the ranks of men to the company of fiends. His *Sir Giles Overreach* is a red-blooded, strong bodied Englishman, rosy in face; full in habit, abounding in physical life and in the joy of physical energy, with a voice like a trumpet, an eye like a hawk, a hand like a pugilist. The vast vitality of the man as Mr. Booth represents him is such as to stir the spectator with a certain strange but keen joy in his presence, even when he is busied with the worst of his schemes. The hugeness and the frankness of his selfishness are made equally impressive; and the tireless strength both of his intellect and his will seem carried into every physical function: his walk, his face, his gesture, all show the unfaltering will, the unswerving purpose. His cruelty is as much and as naturally a part of him as his courage, or as the carriage of his head, and in his bearing towards every other personage there is an affluent insolence of prosperous selfishness, which is never veiled except when he, with difficulty, puts on the smoothness necessary for his plots. Mr. Booth's acting in the scenes with his daughter was also very fine; his feeling towards the girl is the only confusing element in a nature otherwise of colossal simplicity in evil, and Mr. Booth indicated with delicate exactness the genuineness of *Sir Giles's* regard for his own flesh and blood, and yet the complete subordination of his affection to his greed and ambition. The last act affords the crucial test. The passion of the man in the presence of defeat and disaster is so violent and so vast that few actors dare attempt to display it. Mr. Booth was adequate to the exacting scene, and with little or no rant, but with overbearing power, he displayed the fierce exultation, the rage, the frenzy of disappointment, the moment of despair, and the last malevolent rally of the evil soul of this wonderful man. Massinger's attempt in . . . part of *Sir Giles's* last speech . . . is to show the beginning of a hideous retribution, coming upon a man who has snapped his fingers in the face of the Almighty; and the terror stricken utterance of an awful fear, in language but slightly varied from that of deliberate bravado used in a previous act, is an intimation of the hell which the awakened conscience is to be, even in such a creature as *Sir*

Giles Overreach. At the very last his courage rises again for a moment, and he dashes his shipwrecked soul desperately against the divine purpose, but it is the last stir of a will which is even then breaking in the sight of eternity. Mr. Booth acted the entire scene in a most masterly fashion, expressing all these ideas and many more, and nothing more impressive in its kind is now to be seen upon our stage than his simulation of the effects of the short, sharp, touch of paralysis and the wonderful rally of *Sir Giles's* evil forces, through which he once more darts out defiance against his foes, and after the supreme effort drops dead almost in a moment. The effect, as a whole, was a noble piece of artistic work, equally self consistent, clear and strong, and it gave the highest satisfaction to a highly judicious audience. We think, however, that it ought to be said that Mr. Booth is too squeamish, not to say prudish, in his expurgations of the text, especially in his first scene with his daughter. *Sir Giles's* calculating coarseness is an important element in his nature, and might be indicated without offence or real impropriety.

In summary now, what facts become evident from a study of these reviews? In the first place, there is a very considerable disagreement as to the advisability of reviving so old a chestnut as *A New Way to Pay Old Debts,* but a majority opinion feels that the step has been wise, that the play still has in presentation something to say to a modern audience. On the other hand, let us not forget that a divided house does not speak too well for any long continuance of such a revival. In the second place, the critics are almost unanimous in praising Booth's interpretation and accomplishment in the rôle of Massinger's villain, finding therein especial intelligence, intensity, and variety. Verily both *A New Way to Pay Old Debts* and Booth seem to have triumphed over time; and Sir Giles Overreach whom many thought on the verge of his grave proves that the reports of his death had been greatly exaggerated.

On January 16, 1886, Booth again played Sir Giles Overreach at the Boston Museum. The cast has changed sufficiently to require its inclusion—I copy the bill:

Sir Giles Overreach .... Booth
Wellborn .... Mason
Lord Lovell .... Atkins
Marrall .... Kent
Justice Greedy .... Hudson
Allworth .... Whytal
Lady Allworth .... Miss May Davenport
Margaret .... Miss Blanche Thompson

and Froth by Miss Kate Ryan whose *Old Boston Museum Days* presents such interesting recollections of the company at that theatre. On this occasion *The Boston Herald* of the 18th is not so enthusiastic as heretofore: "This old play has little in it to hold the attention or excite the sympathy of a modern audience and whatever of interest attaches to it is created by the character of Sir Giles Overreach. . . ." The *Daily Advertiser* of same date says: ". . . In the great last act, where passion reaches its white heat, Mr. Booth is supremely great; for the moment he is transformed beyond the penetrating, but quiet, intensity usual with him, into a man completely possessed with a fierce frenzy of physical rage. . . ." *The Boston Evening Transcript* of May 18 is perhaps the most revealing: "The impersonation is one that will always remain in the minds of those who have ever witnessed it. Massinger's drama may not keep the stage after Mr. Booth has withdrawn from the theatre. At any rate there is living no other actor who includes the part in his repertory. The opportunity then to see this interpretation of a character that is almost unique in English drama, if not entirely appreciated now, will be remembered with grateful satisfaction when the play is permanently shelved. . . ." Clearly these reviews add little to our information; equally clearly, it is Sir Giles Overreach who is keeping the play alive. This is the last time that Booth played the part in Boston.

The next month, February 1886, Booth presented Sir Giles for the last time in New York. There were two performances of *A New Way to Pay Old Debts* at the Fifth Avenue Theatre on the 16th, and 17th, "for the first time in New York in many years." Booth was supported by the Boston Museum company with the cast as of January 16. Quite contrary to the Boston opinions about shelving the play, *The New York Times* of the 17th recommends a more careful revival and lauds Booth to the skies as Sir Giles Overreach. It is a most revealing criticism and just about completes the process of clarification upon which we have been concentrating:

Many years have elapsed since Edwin Booth has acted in New York the leading character in Philip Massinger's "New Way to Pay Old Debts." Those persons who saw his subtle, picturesque, and thrilling performance of Sir Giles last evening, and there were enough of them to completely fill the Fifth Avenue Theatre, will hope that he may be induced to give Massinger's play a high place in his repertory hereafter. In nothing that he has done of late has Mr. Booth's complete mastery of the resources of his art been more clearly exhibited, and, as in Pescara and Sir Edward last year, so as Sir Giles Overreach he again demonstrated that he entered into the spirit of characters with which he is comparatively unfamiliar with a zest and earnestness often lacking nowadays when he acts parts more closely associated with his fame. It is a mistake to infer that Mr. Booth's artistic work today does not possess both the strength and the finish that marked his earlier achievements. Some of the graces of youth are gone, to be sure; the Hamlet of 1886 is not, in outward aspect, the Hamlet of 1864; but the fire, passion, and vehemence of the tragedian's acting last evening in the scene of Sir Giles's discomfiture were never excelled by him in his young manhood. The death of the usurer was powerful and realistic; the effect of the stroke of paralysis falling suddenly in a moment of violent passion was vividly manifested. The voice which had been clear and resonant sunk into a hoarse whisper, the utterance of every word impeded by a palsied tongue; one of the eyelids drooped, there was a convulsive twitching of the muscles of the face. With a supreme effort, the baffled old man was himself again for an instant, and then he sank lifeless at the feet of his enemies, his power for doing evil gone forever. In the earlier scenes Mr. Booth's impersonation was equally remarkable; although Sir Giles was kept in his place among the other personages, and not thrust forward out of harmony with the rest of the picture. In make-up and costume the portrayal was, of course, admirable. Mr. Booth was not recognized when Sir Giles entered the home of Lady Allworth with his followers, so completely was the actor's personality hidden in the sturdy grey-bearded knight, richly and rather pretentiously attired. He showed Overreach throughout as a man confident of his own power, stooping to use the meanest craft to gain his ends, of course, but never losing the sense of his own dignity and vast importance. The cruel and heartless scene with Margaret, in which the knight commands his daughter to sacrifice her honor rather than fail to captivate the nobleman he desired her to wed, was carried forward with malignant intensity and a simulation of self-confidence that indicated the man without conscience or fear, content to be a law unto himself. In the scene of pretended reconciliation with his scapegrace nephew there was another fine bit, which deserves to be singled out in this hasty account of a memorable dramatic performance. . . . "A New Way to Pay Old Debts" would repay a careful revival with an appropriate setting and painstaking stage-management. . . .

Much as we may remember Booth's Hamlet, it is manifestly unfair to forget a characterization which calls forth such praise. It is not a little revealing of the actor's art that such remarks could be appropriate the last time he presented the character in New York, and almost thirty years after his first success in the rôle.

Booth's daughter, Edwina Booth Grossman, prints in her book[61] one of the actor's letters in which he refers to a performance of Sir Giles at Philadelphia in 1886. This was probably that at the Chestnut Street Opera House on March 6, to which I find reference in the announcement of an earlier program, but I have seen no bill for this date. He was announced to play Overreach at the Star Theatre (late Wallack's) on November 19 and 20 but illness prevented his acting so vigorous a rôle, and New York was deprived of seeing his interpretation of the part again.

Booth indeed, if I mistake not, played Sir Giles Overreach only once more, and on the other side of the continent. The tour during which this performance took place is described by Kitty Molony, a member of the company, who afterwards became the wife of George P. Goodale, the dramatic critic. *A New Way to Pay Old Debts,* she says, was played "but once this season." This was at the Baldwin Opera House in San Francisco, a city in which Booth had last presented Massinger's extortioner in 1853. I learn from an article by George C. Warren in the *San Francisco Chron-*

[61] *Edwin Booth: Recollections by his daughter Edwina Booth Grossman, and letters to her and his friends,* p. 68.

icle of July 14, 1929, that for this last Sir Giles of Booth, March 23, 1887, the receipts were sixteen hundred and fifteen dollars, much the smallest he had drawn in over two weeks "which showed the public wanted him in the familiar rôles." Be that as it may, this is a memorable performance, and we are glad that Mrs. Goodale has given us so full an account of it and of the effect of Booth's acting of Sir Giles on her and on his audience:[62]

> *A New Way to Pay Old Debts* had no part for me, so I was able to see from the audience Mr. Booth act a monster. He played Sir Giles but once this season. Mrs. Foster shone as Lady Allworth. I was impressed by the sweetness of her far-reaching voice and truly amazed by her appearance. At close range she was oldish and fat, but from the front as Lady Allworth she was in her prime and most attractive to look at. I liked her voice better than any on the stage except Mr. Booth's—always except Mr. Booth's —always!
>
> He did not give the impression of making the least effort to speak loud, yet his lowest tones carried to the limits of the theatre. In his bursts of passion each syllable was distinct. Not anger nor emotion marred his perfect elocution. About me people were saying, as the curtain fell, that his speaking voice gave as much pleasure as a great singer's. One marvelled at its beauty and his diction.
>
> Considered as a play I thought *A New Way to Pay Old Debts* old-timey, but Mr. Booth's acting was ageless art. His Sir Giles Overreach tore my nerves apart. He stung me to the quick. My skin felt as if it were shrivelling under acid burns. I knew there was someone walking on my grave all through the performance, from my constant shivering. Every one about me, too, was shrinking and trembling. Mr. Booth made not one appeal for sympathy. Uncompromisingly he let himself be written down a monster without one redeeming trait. He stripped the villain's soul naked. People slunk out of the theatre looking upon one another as victims who had for three hours been saturated with evil, had it injected into their veins. The amazement of it was that Sir Giles was filtered through the *mind of Edwin Booth,* and yet had come out wholly obnoxious. If there were a Sir Giles in that audience, he must have felt as if he were gazing at the head of Medusa and

[62] *Behind the Scenes with Edwin Booth,* pp. 197-8.

had a bad night of it later on. My own was quite bad enough. That monster mocked me for a long time!

His audience that night, if comments in the lobby and in the aisles meant anything, felt privileged for this opportunity to estimate Edwin Booth's versatility, to have a completer range of his powers, and broaden a realization that for him it was as easy to plunge into hell as to join in anthems of angels' choirs; that he was native to the universe, and the deeps of his genius were soundless.

It is not ill to close this chronological account of Booth's Overreach with so affectionate a tribute.

It is hardly necessary to say much of the rest of Edwin Booth's life. His alliance with Lawrence Barrett and with Mme. Modjeska, his failing health, the founding of The Players, his last performance on April 4, 1891, as Hamlet of course, his death in 1893 at the age of sixty, are all facts well known. But Booth's life cannot be written coldly with names and dates; it is written instead in his achievements as artist, in his fine honesty and pure spirit, in the love and admiration of his friends.

For many years, Edwin Booth had difficulty in avoiding too close a copy of his father's famous Overreach;[63] some of the reviews already quoted mention the resemblance, a great many inevitably compare the two actors. But Edwin was no servile imitator, and what he lacked of his father's vibrant energy and physical force, he made up in careful reading and delivery, in a more even balance between the first acts and the last, and in a quiet unsensational intensity which made the part less melodramatic but more real and human. It must constantly be remembered that though Sir Giles Overreach may have been the turning point in his career, it was not one of the parts which made him most famous or which were most suited to his nature. Moreover, Sir Giles was not a part which he played with anything like frequency; even granting, as I do, that I have failed to note many performances of the part, it is plain that there were intervals in his life in which he acted Sir Giles only rarely and never for any consecutive run such as distinguished his more memorable rôles, and at least one interval of almost fourteen years when he dropped the part en-

[63] Matthews and Hutton, Vol. III, p. 105.

EDWIN BOOTH, from a photograph with a lock of his hair

tirely because he felt the character too repulsive to please a modern audience, too unspiritual perhaps to please himself. He never apparently felt the attraction for Sir Giles which we have seen in E. L. Davenport.

Nevertheless we must not make the assumption that Edwin Booth's Sir Giles was of no particular importance, even that it was not a great Sir Giles. Ample testimony has already been given to refute such a view. William Winter, never a particular admirer of *A New Way to Pay Old Debts,* admits that he was "fine" in what he calls "the terrific" parts, Sir Giles included:[64] "His swift defiance to Lord Lovell, as Sir Giles, and indeed the whole mighty and terrible action with which he carried that scene—from 'What, are you pale?' down to the grisly and horrid viper pretence and reptile spasm of death—were simply tremendous. This was in the days when his acting yet retained the exuberance of youthful spirit, before 'the philosophic mind' had checked the headlong currents of the blood or curbed imagination in its lawless flight. . . . He needed, in that period of development, the more terrible passions to express. . . . But his Sir Giles was a consummate work of genius —as good then as it ever afterward became, and better than any other that has been seen since, not excepting that of E. L. Davenport." Certainly even in 1885 and 1886, the judgment of the majority of the criticism shows that his Sir Giles, though tempered, was still a work of genius. And though J. Rankin Towse seems to have preferred Davenport's creation, he does not deny the effectiveness of Booth's: "He rose . . . to a wonderful pitch of baffled wrath as Sir Giles Overreach in the last scene where the defeated schemer becomes the prey of his own savage passions. . . ."[65]

By far the best extended study of Edwin Booth's Sir Giles Overreach is to be found in a magazine article by the Boston dramatic critic, Henry A. Clapp. Curiously enough, the article— which I copy from a cutting in the Harvard Theatre Collection— persistently escapes identification; it is entitled "Edwin Booth" and deals with a series of his characters, but I do not know the

[64] Winter, *Shadows of the Stage* (First Series), pp. 76-8.
[65] *Sixty Years of the Theatre,* p. 193.

periodical from which it was taken, nor, accurately, the date of its publication.[66] An extended quotation from this study will serve best, I think, for fixing at the conclusion Booth's Sir Giles in our minds, and for keeping the lines and contours of the picture clear and bold:

Mr. Booth's impersonation of Sir Giles Overreach is as much greater than any of the others now under consideration as the character itself is greater than each and all of the others. "A New Way to Pay Old Debts" has some obvious faults and defects, but it is a wonderful play, full of force and fire and virile imagination. A drama two and a half centuries old can scarcely fail to be archaic in many ways to the temper of our time, and nothing short of the antiseptic power of true genius can have kept it sweet for the present taste. But genius was not wanting in Massinger. The diction of his plays is second among English pieces only to that of the master-poet himself; and Sir Giles Overreach is a personage whom Shakespeare might have been proud to own. The character is singularly original, and indeed almost unique. The immense temperamental force of the man's nature, his straightforward selfishness and frank avowal of the same, his deliberate refusal and rejection of the higher theory of life,—these traits, coupled with his passionate violence of spirit, which, ignorant of the name of fear, is submissive to no control except that of the tremendous will which may choose to subordinate temper to policy, make him a figure almost Mephistophelean, but for the huge relish with which he affirms, so to speak, his belief in himself. Sir Giles is a perfect exemplar of an utterly selfish materialist living up to the principles of his philosophy. He is utterly indifferent to the hatred of his fellow-men, except as it stands in the way of his projects for self-aggrandizement; towards the majority of those about him, indeed, his feeling is that of supreme contempt, as for a set of poor creatures who know not "how to love" themselves. His surname and one or two of the phrases in which he speaks of his delight in "dark and crooked ways" imply a capacity for intrigue, and that his nature is plastic enough for

[66] My perplexity is shared by the libraries of Harvard and Princeton, and by the Library of Congress, to all of whom acknowledgment is made for tireless but unsuccessful search.

a very large kind of hypocrisy, when a sufficient motive is presented, is made plainly to appear. But Massinger has been careful so to emphasize his force and courage and fierceness in pursuit as to indicate a nature much more inclined to violence than to chicane, where either will subserve its purposes. "Fawning" is "a stranger to" his "nature." Mr. Booth grasps the dramatist's idea in all its amplitude with keen and clear intelligence, and utters it with splendid imaginative breadth, with brilliant directness, with masterful ease of skill. The impersonation is strongly and freshly realistic, yet with the realism is fused a just ideality which sufficiently lifts the part into a high dramatic conception. The rough solidity and resonance of the earlier portion of the performance are highly impressive, and, as one might say, delightful. Mr. Booth's face and figure undergo an extraordinary transformation for the purposes of this character: his sturdiness of frame is like that of an oak; all the horizontal lines of his countenance and form seem lengthened and deepened; his mouth shuts as if his jaw were made of iron; every motion of his arms and every turn in his head have the certainty and decision of the man's will; his gait is equally unfaltering, elastic, and vigorous. The late E. L. Davenport, in his remarkable impersonation of this part, chose to represent the man as rather lean and very pallid. The face was that of one depleted of his blood by evil passions and ambitions. Mr. Booth makes Sir Giles Overreach a red-blooded, strong-bodied Englishman, "full in habit, abounding in physical life and the joy of physical energy"; he suffers from no remorse, is troubled by no forebodings, takes a huge, sensuous satisfaction in existence, and in the very insolence of his own prosperity. Mr. Booth's finest skill is displayed in the variations which he makes in Sir Giles's manner and manners towards the other persons of the play. To most of them he shows a careless roughness; to Marrall he is savagely tyrannical, the sharpest utterance of his cruel scorn being made in the scene in which he beats the cringing knave and then flings him a coin with the words, "There's a piece for my late blows," into the tone and manner of which as much contemptuous indifference is concentrated as it seems possible that language can be made to hold; the bluff *sans-façon* good-nature of his manner to his nephew, Wellborn, after the apparent lift in the young man's fortunes, is so displayed as to seem the absolutely subtle piece of hypocrisy which it really is; and his bearing towards Lord Lovell is a wonderful mixture of manly frankness with most flattering deference. One faint qualification of the greed of the character appears in Sir Giles's affection for his daughter, and it is difficult not to feel a momentary regard for the man, when, to Margaret's suggestion that Lord Lovell may conquer her "virgin scruples" and then forsake her, he replies:

> "How! Forsake thee!
> Do I wear a sword for fashion?"

Mr. Booth delivers this famous speech with exemplary force; but he is also careful to emphasize the selfishness which lies at the core of Sir Giles's desire for his daughter's advancement. To the last act and all its vast demands Mr. Booth is no less than adequate. His passion of rage and surprise when he discovers the disappearance of the writing of his deed is enormous, overbearing, overpowering. And the final spectacle of the man with all his wondrous potency for evil struck down in an instant by the lightning of paralysis, shrinking back appalled from a vision of the waiting hell which gapes within that "life to come" which cannot now be jumped, yet rallying at the last, under the impulse of an awful impious malevolence, is most startling, stirring, and impressive. If the facility and picturesqueness of the performance are admirable, its strength is more than admirable. And in all this we see the great progress which Mr. Booth has made during the years within which this part has remained untouched not only in plastic skill and ease, in smoothness and finish, but also in interior vivacity, and especially in that real power which makes itself felt without flourish or noise, which has its source and secret not in physical robustness but in mental and temperamental impetus and strength.

I must express my regret here, as I have already expressed it in another publication,[67] that Mr. Booth has chosen so to expurgate his lines that the calculating coarseness of Sir Giles Overreach and his infamous readiness to sacrifice his daughter's honor to his ambition are almost eliminated from an otherwise artistically perfect picture. A large part of the omitted language might, I think, be given without causing just offense to any listener. Yet, having said this, I cannot do better than to close my article by

[67] In the *Boston Daily Advertiser* of March 5, 1885?

thanking Mr. Booth for the service he has done to the theater and to the cause of pure art and good morals by the scrupulous refinement which he has long practiced in dealing with the text of all his plays.

No words can more aptly express both the affection in which Edwin Booth was held at his death and the characteristics which endeared him to all who shared his high ideals of life and art than Shakespeare's own, "Good night, sweet prince."

CHAPTER XI

THE OLD ORDER CHANGETH

EDWIN BOOTH was the last great actor to appear in *A New Way to Pay Old Debts* in America. Indeed the 1880's, when he presented his last Sir Giles, mark the close of a long period in the play's existence when it was regarded as a stock piece in which all actors worthy of the name of tragic stars must at least make an attempt, and, if successful, include in their repertory. Stock companies as a matter of course prepared the minor parts in anticipation of the star's visit. However, we have already seen signs, in spite of the critics' praise of Davenport's Sir Giles and the last surprisingly successful impersonations of Edwin Booth, that the play was diminishing in popularity, was indeed open to the charge of being what all of the drama of Shakespeare's age was except Shakespeare—old-fashioned. Few denied its power, but many thought it ready for the shelf, an interesting but uncomfortable antique revealing the period of its origin but otherwise having little to say to the modern theatre-goer who could see Bronson Howard and Tom Robertson and Sardou. Theatrical conditions were changing with the plays. The permanent stock company with the travelling star gave way first to the travelling stock company with its own stars, and then to the company presenting one successful modern play; in short, the age of the star and the stock company gave way to the age of the manager and the independent actor.

Since I have chosen to deal with the various impersonators of Sir Giles in the order of their first presentations of that character, we shall find that the conditions discussed in the first part of this chapter parallel those discussed in the last. But the parallel line will in this case be continued farther into the era when the production of *A New Way to Pay Old Debts* becomes an antiquarian revival. We shall see therefore what happened to the play after it went on the shelf, and how finally it was removed from the shelf and presented under entirely different conditions, for the acting play did not die with the passing of the older era. Let us first then scan some new faces under the old system; we go back to the 1850's.

I pass rapidly over a performance of *A New Way to Pay Old Debts* at the Boston Museum on June 22, 1857, for the benefit of W. H. Smith, in which according to the Harvard Boston list "Mr. Charles Jackson of Boston volunteered" to come to Barry Sullivan. Barry Sullivan indeed is not a new face, though new to this country. His first appearance here was as Hamlet on November 22, 1858, at the Broadway Theatre, New York, where the originality of his conception and reading of the lines provoked some comment.[1] Later in the season he was at Burton's, but New York, so far as I know, never saw his Sir Giles. His first American presentation of that character of which I have record was at the New Walnut Street Theatre in Philadelphia on February 7, 1859; I take the cast from a playbill:

Sir Giles Overreach .... Sullivan
Wellborn .... Perry
Lord Lovell .... Dubois
Marrall .... F. Drew
Justice Greedy .... Thayer
Allworth .... Bascomb
Lady Allworth .... Mrs. Perry
Margaret .... Mrs. Leonard

Two performances in Pittsburgh, April 6 at the Theatre, September 15 at the Apollo, precede one at the St. Charles Theatre in New Orleans in December of that year.[2] In the summer of 1860 he returned to England. He came over again, however, and played Overreach on the West Coast, though I note only one performance—at Baldwin's Academy of Music, San Francisco, on April 7, 1876. One finds with pleasure that the part of Furnace was to be acted by a young man named David Belasco.[3] "I had the advantage," says Belasco, "of private rehearsals . . . with this great tragedian in his room at the Baldwin Hotel. . . . The reason why he liked me, he said was that, with my pale face and

---

[1] For example, "I know a Hawk from a Heron—Pshaw!"
[2] Fletcher, pp. 476, 478, 584, 585. Sillard, Vol. II, pp. 23-4.
[3] Sillard, Vol. II, pp. 170-6; Winter, *Belasco*, Vol. I, pp. 87-9; Vol. II, p. 482.

blue-black hair, I reminded him of a little priest who had been a chum of his in Ireland."[4] I wish I could find the cast for this production, for the company is replete with interest; it contained among others the names of James A. Herne, Louis James, William H. Crane, and James O'Neill. Crane indeed contributes an anecdote which is too good to omit, though it leaves us less certain who did play Furnace:[5]

> Another piece in the repertoire of Sullivan was *A New Way to Pay Old Debts*. His Sir Giles was a wonderful performance. It may seem silly, but I didn't like the idea when they cast me for the small part of Order, the leader of the servants. I had been first comedian all along and had made, if I may say so, something of a hit in California. I therefore refused to accept the assignment. James A. Herne, the stage manager, said to me quietly, with a smile: "You're a long way from home." "I wouldn't care if I was in China," I said hotly. "You had no right to cast me for Order."
>
> They put Dave Belasco, who was an actor then, in the rôle, and I sat out front at the opening performance with Mrs. Crane and Alice Harrison. When Belasco, who was a charming, bad actor, came out, I flew out of the building and around to the stage door. I went to Herne and shook my fist in his face and said: "You had your nerve to cast me for that part."
>
> "But you didn't play it," said Herne, quiet as ever. "It was not that you were cast for the part, but seeing Belasco play it that has upset you."

I should like to know more than I do about Sullivan's Sir Giles. Though rough and vehement in the originality of his methods, he is spoken of with some enthusiasm by his contemporaries as a performer of great ability. Without much education, he relied chiefly on vigorous action and forcible declamation, both of which are necessary to Overreach. He claimed to have played Hamlet more than thirty-five hundred times.

On March 14, 1865, Walter Grisdale "from the London Theatres" followed a début at the New Bowery Theatre, New York, with Sir Giles Overreach: "First time in this theatre of Mas-

---

[4] "The Story of My Life," *Hearst's Magazine*, March 1914-December 1915.
[5] *Footprints and Echoes*, p. 74.

singer's Innmense [*sic*] Play of a New Way to Pay Old Debts,"
says the playbill:[6]

Sir Giles Overreach	Grisdale
Wellborn	Marden
Lord Lovell	Thompson
Marrall	Brookes
Justice Greedy	Glassford
Allworth	Lingard
Lady Allworth	Mrs. Phillips
Margaret	Miss Hyatt

The performance was repeated on August 3.[7] After a short starring engagement Grisdale became leading man at the Bowery, evidence, I suppose, of a certain amount of success, though he soon
drops out of sight. The newspapers were much too occupied with
the activities of General Sherman to notice those of this new-
comer, and I confess to sharing the indifference, "eminent tragedian" though he may be marked on the bills.

In the case of Charles Dillon the puff changed from "eminent"
to "truly great," of course in capitals. Born in Suffolk in 1819,
Dillon made a provincial reputation for himself before his presentation of the title-part of the now forgotten *Belphegor* at Sadler's
Wells in the spring of 1856, the character upon which his reputation chiefly rests and which he played in America in 1861. A sojourn in Australia was followed by another trip to the United
States, this time with a more varied repertory. He returned to
England in 1868 and was for a time successful in London, but
his acting degenerated, and after 1873 he was primarily in the
provinces until his death in 1881.[8] I strongly suspect that he had
played Overreach in the minor theatrical centers of Great Britain
before he came over here,[9] and very possibly in Australia, but the
only performances of which I have record took place during his
two visits to North America. During the first Dillon played Sir

---

[6] Cruickshank (Edition), p. 134, wrongly gives the part to George C. Boniface
who had concluded his engagement there a few days before; Parker, p. 569,
gives the date wrongly as the 13th.

[7] Odell, Vol. VIII, p. 40.

[8] For Dillon, see Pascoe, pp. 103-11; Marston, Vol. II, pp. 180-93.

[9] See Carados in *The Referee* (September 10, 1922).

Giles at Montreal on September 4, 1861.[10] I do not find a repetition until the second trip. The next performance was at the Albany Academy of Music, during an engagement which began on January 29, 1866; Sir Giles was the third character there impersonated.[11] Back in Montreal Overreach was one of Dillon's parts during an engagement which began on June 25.[12] The last occurred on November 30 of the same year for his farewell benefit at the Broadway Theatre, New York; during this engagement J. W. Lanergan provided chief support, but I do not know the cast for Massinger's play.[13] In New York Dillon was successful, though he did not please in some parts, and "great" was modified to "good." *The New York Herald* of December 1 comments as follows: "Mr. Dillon took his farewell benefit last night, and it is to be regretted that he had not a better house to testify their appreciation of his careful endeavor to place legitimate drama before the New York playgoers. The performances commenced with Massinger's comedy 'A New Way to Pay Old Debts' in which Mr. Dillon took the character of Sir Giles Overreach. His acting throughout the piece was good, and in the last act was truly excellent. He was very successful in his representation of the rage consequent upon the defeat of the well laid plots which are developed in the course of the previous acts. He was vociferously called before the curtain at the close of the piece." Dillon's style was distinguished by naturalness of manner, simplicity of method, and intensity of feeling; his acting was uneven because he was moody, his life uneven because he drank to excess.[14]

Though Frederic Robinson occasionally played starring engagements, he is best remembered as a capable stock actor, and many are the companies and players with which he was associated. Born a Londoner in 1832, he appeared first at York, Liverpool, and

[10] Graham, p. 130.

[11] Phelps, pp. 348-9.

[12] Graham, p. 149.

[13] J. S. G. Hagan, "Records of the New York Stage," *The New York Dispatch,* December 5, 1875; advertisements in the newspapers.

[14] Another actor who starred at the Broadway Theatre this season was James Stark, a favorite in California. Hagan in *The New York Dispatch* of December 5, 1875, says that he was at one time good as Sir Giles, doubtless on the West Coast; I have, however, no record of any performances.

Edinburgh; he made his London début under Phelps at Sadler's Wells in 1857 where he took part in the various Shakespearean revivals for which that house was noted. In 1865 Wallack engaged him for his company, and he appeared successfully in New York. Apparently his only performance of Sir Giles Overreach was that at Wallack's Theatre on March 27, 1867, for his own benefit. Two days before Wallack had announced in the *New York Daily Tribune*: "Mr. Robinson has won a distinguished position in comedy, and much curiosity must naturally be felt to see him in a tragic character—especially one so difficult and so famous as Sir Giles." Be that as it may, the bills show that Wallack afforded him the most distinguished support:

Sir Giles Overreach	Robinson
Wellborn	Charles Fisher
Lord Lovell	Norton
Marrall	Young
Justice Greedy	John Gilbert
Allworth	Ringgold
Lady Allworth	Miss Fanny Morant
Margaret	Mrs. Clara Jennings

Since Sir Giles was obviously not one of Robinson's usual characters, I shall follow the example of the newspapers in not reviewing it. Robinson later played with Charlotte Cushman, Janauschek, Lawrence Barrett, Booth, Jefferson, and finally Irving before he retired from the stage. According to all accounts he was an able and accomplished gentleman.[15]

With the exception of E. L. Davenport, Charles Barron was for a time perhaps the most versatile actor on the stage; he graced over five hundred different plays, in many of them enacting the leading part, and yet somehow managed to make each characterization separate and distinct. Born in Boston in 1840, he was for the greater part of his life a Boston actor, and always a popular one. After appearing in Portland, Maine, and Providence, he was engaged by Davenport for his company at the Howard Athenaeum, where he made his first appearance in 1861 in support of Edwin Booth. The following year he joined the Davenport-Wallack com-

[15] For Robinson, see Clapp and Edgett, Vol. III, pp. 310-11.

bination, leaving it to play leads at Grover's Theatre in Washington and the Chestnut Street Theatre, Philadelphia. From 1869 to 1889 with exceptional intervals he was leading man with the famous Boston Museum company, with which his name is usually associated.[16] All his performances of Sir Giles Overreach, indeed, seem to have taken place at the Museum, though they are scattered over fourteen years; with one exception, the second, all were on the occasion of his benefits. *A New Way to Pay Old Debts* seems a peculiarly apt title for a benefit performance. Barron first presented his Overreach to Boston on December 10, 1869, when the cast of the play was as follows—I follow the bills throughout:

Sir Giles Overreach	Barron
Wellborn	Hardenbergh
Lord Lovell	Salisbury
Marrall	Warren
Justice Greedy	McClannin
Allworth	Murdoch
Lady Allworth	Mrs. Vincent
Margaret	Miss Clarke

The performance was repeated on December 16 because the play had been "received with Great Applause" at its previous representation. I do not find Barron repeating Sir Giles thereafter until January 22, 1875, when W. H. Crisp played Wellborn, Stevenson Allworth, and Burrows Lord Lovell, the rest as before. Two years later, January 27, 1877, the cast has changed sufficiently to require tabulation:

Sir Giles Overreach	Barron
Wellborn	Barr
Lord Lovell	Cotter
Marrall	Warren
Justice Greedy	McClannin
Allworth	Carlos
Lady Allworth	Miss Phillips
Margaret	Miss Cary

[16] Clapp and Edgett, Vol. I, pp. 26-8; Herbert I. Jackson in *Boston Evening Transcript,* July 26, 1930.

The last performance but the "First time in many years" took place on December 29, 1883:

Sir Giles Overreach	Barron
Wellborn	Mason
Lord Lovell	Burrows
Marrall	Wilson
Justice Greedy	Hudson
Allworth	Whytal
Lady Allworth	Miss Dace
Margaret	Miss Robins

A transcript of an article in the *Boston Globe* of the following day will show how the performance was received, as well as making a fitting close to the popular Barron's representations of Overreach:

That Mr. Charles Barron has a host of admirers in this city was manifest last evening by the large audience which assembled at the Museum on the occasion of his annual benefit. Mr. Barron selected as the bill for the occasion the five-act play, "A New Way to Pay Old Debts," the leading character of which, Sir Giles Overreach, furnished unusual advantages for the display of his marked talents as an actor. The plot of the play is too well known to need repetition in these columns. Every part was well cast and well played, and it is not often the case that all the members of a cast are so equally competent as in the performance of last evening. Mr. Barron naturally led in the evening's honors, and the applause accorded him during the performance was certainly due from the excellent manner in which he essayed the character, one of the best in his extensive repertoire. At the close of the fourth act, Mr. Barron was twice called before the curtain, and, although he made several attempts to get the curtain between himself and the audience, was unable to do so, owing to the continued applause and calls for a speech. He finally succumbed to the inevitable, and, with a voice choked with emotion, thanked his friends. . . .

Like Barron, Walter Montgomery played Sir Giles at the Boston Museum, but, unlike Barron, he acted the part only once, on May 18, 1871; with the exception of Norris as Allworth, the cast was the same as on Barron's first Overreach there.[17] As far

[17] Cruickshank (Edition), p. 137, wrongly gives this performance to Davenport, who was acting the same part at the Globe Theatre (May 8, 9, 12, 13, 22, 23).

as I know this was the only time that Montgomery played the part in America, though I suspect all sorts of omissions. His London Sir Giles was presented later in the same year. Montgomery's real name was Richard Tomlinson; he shot himself through the head on September 2, 1871, a few days after his marriage to a beautiful but unscrupulous woman who, not content with one husband, wanted Montgomery as well. He was a handsome actor of considerable promise; Cecil Howard says he was excellent as Sir Giles Overreach.[18]

Neil Warner (William Burton Lockwood) had a roving disposition; it makes his performances difficult to follow. Born in London in 1830, he was encouraged by Brooke and soon won favor at the minor theatres and in the provinces. He had played most of Great Britain, including Australia, before he came to America, and I have little doubt that his Sir Giles Overreach antedates his arrival, though he has not been included in the first section of this book because I could find no definite record.[19] His performances of the part over here are scattered across the continent. He made his first appearance in New York in 1869 as Othello, subsequently becoming leading man in Mrs. F. B. Conway's company in Brooklyn. In Montreal he was manager of the Theatre Royal and the Academy of Music before he headed a company to California. Back East, he was engaged by Augustin Daly, but the contract was cancelled by mutual consent. While with Kate Claxton he suffered an apoplectic stroke which brought his career to a close; he died in 1901. Warner was an educated man with a handsome stage-presence and considerable powers. For a while he was reckoned as one of the best of Shakespearean actors, though his love of travel prevented his achieving any great local reputation in the established centers.[20]

W. Fraser Rae in his book *Westward by Rail* describes a trip from New York to San Francisco which began in the latter part of 1869. Several chapters have to do with a visit to the Mormons in Salt Lake City, where he went to the theatre built by Brigham

18 In a footnote to Scott and Howard, pp. 400-1.

19 See, however, *The New York Dramatic Mirror*, December 15, 1900.

20 For Warner, see *The New York Dramatic Mirror*, December 15, 1900, and June 22, 1901.

Young in 1862, on whose stage many great actors have trod in plays which run all the way from *Robert Macaire* to *The Shanghai Gesture*. One of the plays he saw there was *A New Way to Pay Old Debts*:[21]

> . . . The occasion was a special one, it being a "Grand complimentary benefit tendered by the citizens of Salt Lake to the Great Tragedian Neil Warner." This actor was described in the advertisements as a "great English tragedian." In what part of England he acquired his fame I am ignorant, yet I must admit that his physical power was extraordinary. He roared and gesticulated through the part of Sir Giles Overreach with a robust vigor and fire altogether exceptional and he performed a death scene in a manner which perfectly exemplified the difficulty of dying naturally upon the stage. When recalled after the fall of the curtain, he apologised for not making a lengthened speech, on the ground that no man could be expected to have much breath or any voice left after exertions like those through which he had gone. None of the regular members of the company, some of whom acted in a way that was truly praiseworthy, were summoned before the curtain. Although the audience testified by loud and prolonged applause their admiration for the strength of Mr. Warner's lungs and for the vehemence of his gestures, yet I heard remarks made by individuals which were not wholly complimentary to him, and these remarks lead me to think that a few Mormons are judges of good acting. The newspaper critics were as greatly pleased with the performance as modern dramatic critics are with theatrical performances of a sensational type. In the *Salt Lake Daily Telagraph* of the following morning it was said that Neil Warner "is the greatest actor we have ever seen and a splendid career awaits him." The *Deseret Evening News* wrote that the delineation of the part of Sir Giles Overreach "was a perfect triumph, and we think could not possibly be excelled." It seems clear, then, that Salt Lake City is a blissful abode for English actors with powerful lungs and boundless pretensions.

From such supercilious contempt we turn next to performances of Sir Giles Overreach at the Bowery Theatre, New York, on the 4th and 5th of November, 1872,[22] with Grace Rawlinson as Mar-

---

[21] pp. 109-10.

[22] Advertisements in *The New York Herald*; not 1873, as given by Parker, p. 569.

garet. For the second of these nights Mr. William B. Freligh, the manager, arranged to have the election returns reported from the stage. The *Herald* of November 6 carries an amusing article, hardly a review, describing what happened:

> . . . It is not every one who would think of treating such a matter as the election of a President as a kind of *entr'acte* to the ancient comedy, A New Way to Pay Old Debts. However there may have been something particularly appropriate in the connection, and it certainly required the possession of no ordinary genius to enable a man to invent such an excellent device for filling his house on a night when political excitement would in all probability have drawn away his *clientele*. In spite of the foresight displayed on this occasion the patrons of the intense drama were not to be won from the delights of the tar barrels and the bonfires which blazed in every direction. Perhaps they failed to comprehend the luxuries prepared for them. Neil Warner, as Sir Giles Overreach, strutted his brief span on the classic stage and brought all the resources of his tremendous wit to bear on the susceptibilities of his audience. They, however, were laboring under conflicting emotions, and failed to recognize in anything like a hearty manner the fine points of the actor.

To the best of my knowledge, this is the only time since he was Sir Giles Mompesson that Overreach got into a political conflict, and I am positive that this is the only time he ran against Ulysses S. Grant. He appeared only once more in New York in Warner's impersonation, at Mrs. Conway's Theatre on September 16, 1873.[23]

Neil Warner was closely connected with the theatres in Montreal, and following his début there was a popular citizen of that city for fifteen years. He made his bow to a Montreal audience for the first time on December 7, 1874, as Sir Giles Overreach, and Graham lists that character among his "great rôles" with the comment that "had he been at all ambitious, [he] could have been a great actor." I note his Sir Giles there again, at the Academy of Music, on January 1, 1876.[24]

The last time I catch sight of Warner's Sir Giles Overreach is at the Baldwin Theatre, San Francisco, on August 11, 1889.[25] This

23 Odell, Vol. IX, p. 485.
24 Graham, pp. 175, 221.
25 Not Tuesday, the 13th, as Cruickshank states (Edition), p. 132.

is the latest date I have found for *A New Way to Pay Old Debts* as a stock play, the latest date for Overreach by a travelling star of the old type. How tattered and spent the old piece seemed to the audience is made clear by a review in the *Call* of August 13:

> Mr. W. Neil Warner took his farewell of the stage and his good-by of San Francisco at the Baldwin Theatre on Sunday evening last in that strictly legitimate and great play of Philip Massinger, "A New Way to Pay Old Debts." The presentation of such a drama was like opening the doors of a wine-cellar and letting in the morning breeze. The wine in the bins was old and choice, but its place is with the mold and cobwebs of age, and the free, fresh air was only a disturbance. Nobody present at the benefit seemed to understand the play. The serious purposes of life which it conveyed, the tremendous will power of the principal character as expressed in the text and action, were unheeded, and the applause that came freely enough, with the recalls before the curtain, were more in the nature of personal compliments to Mr. Warner than in recognition of the acting ability he displayed. And how splendidly this veteran actor discharged himself of the responsibilities of that great creation, Sir Giles Overreach! It is not to be wondered at that the small people in the cast drew aside in a huddle when the closing scene of the last act was on, and watched the usurer equally as awe-stricken as the audience watched Warner in the agonizing throes of disappointed ambition and despair, in which the life of the strong and unscrupulous Sir Giles went out. We had here a picture of one of the old masters in the dramatic art, but in all the audience there were but few to realize the beauty of it, or to accord it fitting praise. The public appreciation is confined to dramatic chromos just now. There is no audience, no recognition for such wares as Mr. Warner has to offer. . . .

If this is the farewell of Neil Warner, it is also very near to being the farewell of Sir Giles; it is almost twenty years before he is heard from again on the stage, and when he does appear, it is only because of a radical change in the attitude of the revivalist and the audience. It was a close thing for Sir Giles, but he escaped with his life, a little awkward from the stiffness in his joints and a bit uncomfortable to have to exhibit his passions to an age which he did not entirely understand.

If Warner, however, was the last to play Sir Giles as a stock part in the United States, he is not the last on our list since his first performance of the rôle preceded that of W. E. Sheridan. The latter's presentations of Sir Giles were on the other hand few and far between. Sheridan was an able product of the stock system, and as a stock actor, starring was generally not in his province. He was born in Boston in 1839, and made his début in that city at the Howard Athenaeum in 1858. The next two seasons he played "heavies" at Pike's Opera House, Cincinnati, after which he distinguished himself in the Civil War as a captain in the Sixth Ohio Volunteers, and as signal officer in West Virginia. He was wounded in 1864 at the battle of Resaca, but an operation restored the use of his fractured arm. He reappeared then at Pike's Opera House, and his subsequent history is primarily a list of the major stock companies of which he was a member: these include the companies at the Olympic Theatre, St. Louis; Booth's Theatre, New York; and the Chestnut Street Theatre, Philadelphia, where perhaps he was most popular; at the last two he played "leads," being second only to the star. He did a deal of trouping, however, and when he died in 1887, he was in Sidney, Australia. Hagan says he "merits more than mere passing notice," was indeed "a manly and capable actor" who "appears to advantage in everything he undertakes."[26]

We have already found Sheridan playing Wellborn at Booth's Theatre in 1870, but no doubt this was only one of many parts in Massinger's play which he had acted during his career as stock player. I find no Sir Giles Overreach, however, until 1880; on November 15 of that year, Sheridan opened as star at the Baldwin Theatre, San Francisco. One of his parts was the extortioner, and according to David Belasco, then employed there, it "increased his popularity." William Winter, in his biography of Belasco, is not surprised: "He was a sterling actor and richly deserved success. I knew him and liked him much."[27] An unidentified and by me unidentifiable Harvard clipping says that Sheridan played Sir Giles in Philadelphia after his California trip, but I cannot be more

---

[26] Hagan in *The New York Dispatch,* August 15, 1875, from which most of the above sketch is taken.
[27] Winter, *Belasco,* Vol. I, pp. 221-4.

precise. Quite definite, though, is his performance of the part at the Star Theatre, New York (once Wallack's), on December 15, 1883. Alas, a successful New York stock actor might be a successful star in California, but it did not follow that a successful star in California would find equal popularity in New York. *The New York Herald* of December 16 makes the point sufficiently clear:

> As two performances in one day have evidently become too severe a strain for Mr. Booth to bear, the Saturday nights of his engagement will be given up to the representations of Mr. W. E. Sheridan. On the latter, it would seem, after witnessing his performance last night, that no strain could be too severe. As Sir Giles Overreach, in which part he last evening made his first appearance at the Star Theatre, he spared himself in no way. Never did actor throw himself into his work with greater earnestness than did Mr. Sheridan. But his earnestness never rises to the heights of passion, nor even to intensity. It is merely spasmodic vehemence. His voice is sepulchral and apparently incapable of modulation, his gestures are frequent, but frequently devoid of meaning, and his look is never otherwise than baleful in the extreme. All this was not exactly pleasant to contemplate and listen to. What conception he had of the *rôle* it would be difficult to decide. It was ill defined, and his Sir Giles suggested by turns a fiend, a bedlamite, and again a man who, for the amusement of his fellow creatures, assumed the ways and manners of a tragedian. Nothing could have been more vague. In the provinces Mr. Sheridan has won the suffrages of his audiences in the most emphatic manner, and his work has there been likened only to that of the greatest artists of the day. Unless, however, Mr. Sheridan prove himself more the true artist than he did as Sir Giles Overreach, it is not likely that such opinion will be echoed, even in the faintest way, by local theatre goers.

Was Sheridan so bad, I wonder? Was the contrast with Booth too great? Or was it that *nobody* in 1883 was able to convince a New York audience as Giles? I suspect that Sheridan, though an admirable stock actor, had not and *could* not have the resources to make Overreach clear and convincing to an audience who already found the character a relic of the dim past, and therefore not clear and convincing anyway.

This is Sir Giles's last appearance in this book as a stock figure. In that capacity his life in this country had been long, from Chalmers's first inconspicuous portrayal in 1795, through the more sensational exhibitions of Cooke and Kean and the elder Booth, through the less electric but no less artistic performances of E. L. Davenport and Edwin Booth, the last great representatives of the rôle, through a period of waning popularity and minor stars to the final eclipse with Neil Warner in 1889, when Sir Giles as a stock part vanished from the continent, after a career no less than amazing. But this is not Sir Giles's obituary. Like Rip Van Winkle, he only slept and grew older and more tattered and a little puzzled. When he awakes, he no longer enters the accustomed halls; the theatre as he knew it in the old and happy days no longer exists. There are new faces who look at the strange figure in bewilderment and pass on and forget. And Sir Giles, sick at heart, stumbles on and on, and at last finds refuge in the strangest place, where he discovers to his utter amazement that his past *is* known, a place which finds to *its* astonishment that he is still very much alive, the American college.

The honor of extending a welcome greeting to Sir Giles Overreach after his long sleep of almost twenty years must go to Princeton University, where *A New Way to Pay Old Debts* was presented in Alexander Hall on March 20, 1908. By a curious coincidence Sir Giles was impersonated by Mr. Van Winkle of the Class of 1910. The presenting organization was the English Dramatic Association, then in its second season; the stage direction was in the hands of Mr. George L. Sargent. The major characters were played by the following:

Sir Giles Overreach	C. Van Winkle
Wellborn	P. H. Stitt
Lord Lovell	F. C. Laubach
Marrall	W. Schroeder
Justice Greedy	E. A. Brennan
Allworth	L. F. H. Lowe
Lady Allworth	H. C. Burr
Margaret	R. S. Barr

The performance was a success and the play was repeated on May 22 with Mr. F. S. Niles as Lord Lovell, the rest as before. *The Princeton Bric-a-Brac* says that Mr. Van Winkle "gave a powerful presentation,"[28] and *The Daily Princetonian*, issues of March 21 and May 23, is properly laudatory of the production as a whole and of the skill with which practical difficulties were surmounted. There was, however, apparently no realization of the importance of the occasion in the life of Sir Giles Overreach.

Since the Princeton production, at least three other college organizations have presented *A New Way to Pay Old Debts*. The Zelosophic Society of the University of Pennsylvania came next with a performance at the New Century Drawing Rooms on January 15, 1909; a search of the archives of the society reveals no program or comment except that it was the society's second annual play.[29] A little over a year later, the College of the City of New York joined the ranks of reception committee to Sir Giles with a production on March 18, 1910. I learn from *The New York Herald* of the next day that "the play, done after the Elizabethan manner, was produced in the Gothic Great Hall of the College, before about two thousand spectators. The hall, the stage settings and the costumes harmonized remarkably to produce the desired Elizabethan effect. Mr. Charles Weisbord, 1910, was the star of the production as Sir Giles Overreach." The cast was as follows:

Sir Giles Overreach .... Charles Weisbord
Wellborn .... Arthur M. Courtney
Lord Lovell .... Lester M. Brown
Marrall .... Leonard J. Matlow
Justice Greedy .... Irving Fern
Allworth .... Samuel C. Kohs
Lady Allworth .... Harrison M. D. Frerichs
Margaret .... Sidney Adams

The Elizabethan manner was also preserved in the production of the play by the Yale Chapter of the Fraternity of Alpha Delta Phi on March 16, 1921, on which occasion—so I learn from the program—the following took part:[30]

28 Vol. XXXIV, p. 91.
29 I am indebted to Professor Arthur Hobson Quinn for this information.
30 Cruickshank (Edition), p. 133, says March 15.

Sir Giles Overreach .... Oscar Davisson
Wellborn .... Edward Emerson
Lord Lovell .... John E. Holland
Marrall .... Wendell W. Anderson
Justice Greedy .... George M. Barker
Allworth .... Yates G. Smith
Lady Allworth .... Thomas F. Robertson
Margaret .... Walter A. Donahoe

The college revivals of *A New Way to Pay Old Debts* are plainly antiquarian in spirit, produced either to illustrate reading done in the field of Renaissance drama or to show on the stage an admittedly powerful but unfashionable play of a strange and romantic era, now long past. A good deal of the accent is decidedly literary, for *A New Way* is revived along with plays like *Doctor Faustus, The Silent Woman,* and *The Knight of the Burning Pestle,* which though read as masterpieces of Elizabethan drama have no extraordinary stage-history, and indeed are produced partially because they are not to be seen in the regular theatre. Marlowe and Jonson, perhaps wrongly, are now of the library, and Massinger is included with them because he is of the library, not because *A New Way to Pay Old Debts* has been triumphantly of the theatre.

But *A New Way to Pay Old Debts* has recently also been revived in America by professionals, and here the accent, though decidedly antiquarian, is also decidedly unliterary and theatrical. The attempt is to show the glory of the theatre of the past. The first project for the professional reappearance of Sir Giles Overreach never reached the stage. In the summer of 1921 Mr. William Seymour was commissioned by David Belasco to make a prompt-book for a proposed revival in the old-fashioned manner, not Elizabethan, but in the style of the nineteenth century theatre, the style of the productions in which the great stars trod the boards amid sliding scenery and painted backdrops. The book was accordingly made, but the project never achieved fruition. It remained for Mr. Walter Hampden to reintroduce Massinger's extortioner to the professional audience.

It seems peculiarly fitting that Mr. Hampden should have been the man to revive *A New Way to Pay Old Debts,* for he is in a sense in the great tradition, a star with a more or less permanent company, a trouper unafraid of the road. He is now president of The Players, which Edwin Booth was instrumental in founding; like Booth, he is untiring in his exertions for the best interests of the theatre, and unselfish in his aims; a natural leader, his best work, like Booth's, is in the revival and dispersion of the masterpieces which have been landmarks in the past and which will continue to stand in spite of the threats of time and the half-tolerant patronizing of some of the newspaper critics who feel that anything which is dated necessarily lacks significance in the modern theatre. Mr. Hampden's disinterested enthusiasm and his fine intelligence mark him as an important influence in the modern American theatre.[31]

It is characteristic of Walter Hampden that his revival of *A New Way to Pay Old Debts* was of the nature of an experiment. He expected no unusual financial return, was even willing if necessary to lose some money in the venture. He was chiefly interested in finding out why the ancient play had so long held the stage, whether it would still hold an audience as it had in the days of Kean and Booth, and whether Sir Giles could still be made a vivid and terrible figure. I shall let the reviewers answer these questions, and since this is the most important modern production in the new spirit, I shall deal with it in some detail and at some length.

Mr. Hampden rehearsed Massinger's play in San Francisco in the spring of 1922, but was dissatisfied with the result and put off immediate production until certain difficulties could be surmounted. It finally reached the boards on November 1, 1922, on a stage whose name will ring familiar to readers of this history, the Walnut Street Theatre, Philadelphia. I now efface myself, except for occasional comments, behind the reviews which accompany Mr. Hampden's tour; in each case, the criticisms unless otherwise noted appeared the day after the performance. The cast for the entire tour was as follows:

[31] It is hardly necessary to sketch the career of Walter Hampden, since information is so easily available; see for example *Who's Who in the Theatre*, 8th ed., pp. 731-2.

Sir Giles Overreach	Walter Hampden
Wellborn	Ernest Rowan
Lord Lovell	William Sauter
Marrall	Edwin Cushman
Justice Greedy	P. J. Kelly
Allworth	Charles Brokaw
Lady Allworth	Mary Hall
Margaret	Elsie Herndon Kearns

Perhaps the best review of the Philadelphia performance appeared in the *Evening Ledger,* which calls it "a brilliant revival":

There is nothing weighty or ponderous in this tale of a villainous usurer, scoundrel and seventeenth century sharp, who finally met his "come-uppance." It is frankly a combination of rollicking low comedy and old-fashioned romance; but, given a splendid production and acting that counts down to the smallest rôle, it becomes something alive and warming to the spirit.

One notices the lack of poetic beauty in the lines, and more superficiality in the thoughts expressed as compared to the finer Shakespearian comedies; but the characters are drawn with a vivid, if not most careful, hand, and the story has a dash and a culminative power that well merits revived stage representation. Structurally, too, it can bear close scrutiny, and although Mr. Hampden has not been able to solidify the action and eliminate unnecessary scene changes, as he has in the case of certain other plays in his repertoire, the version he presents is shorn of superfluous details and proceeds to its stunning climax smoothly and with fire.

Mr. Hampden is seen as Sir Giles Overreach, the evil individual mentioned above, and it is not until the end of the play that one realizes why he chose to re-create such a rôle. His final scene is the answer; in it he holds the center stage in a frenzy of rage and madness, which this star makes not only palatable, but strikingly forceful. As a part, Sir Giles is not to be classed with certain other of Mr. Hampden's rôles, but he forces it up to their level by the sheer power of his ever mounting ability.

For fully two-thirds of the play there was another who definitely shared (if not stole) honors with Hampden. That was Ernest Rowan in the appealing rôle of Wellborn. . . . Rowan's acting was superb. . . .

The rest of the cast was always adequate. Many of them were cast in the rôles of servants, as the play depends in its comedy

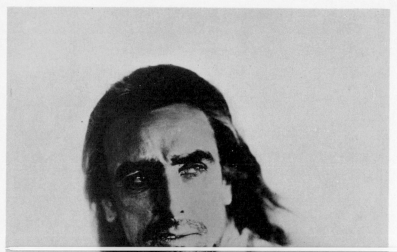

WALTER HAMPDEN as SIR GILES OVERREACH, from a photograph
by Strauss-Peyton Studios

on the antics of menials. Outdoing even "The Shrew" in this respect, the buffoonery of Furnace, Amble, Order and the rest became deadly monotonous and the lamentations of the ever-hungry Justice Greedy were overdone in a manner in which Shakespeare was seldom guilty.

The stage settings with one exception (that of an old-fashioned painted back-drop) were outstanding. . . .

Other Philadelphia reviews may be quoted more briefly. The *Record* says that the revival "was given . . . very creditably with respect to individual enactment, and especially enthralling because of the portrayal of Sir Giles by Hampden. His scene of frenzy . . . was a deeply impressive presentation. . . . Hampden's interpretation of Sir Giles' rôle was in heroic fashion, and the company, despite an evident unfamiliarity with the lines, gave a worthy performance of a quaint and interesting old play. . . . It is of course a stilted drama, but it has its frequent suggestion of Shakespeare in his comedies of English life." The *Bulletin* speaks of Mr. Hampden's "excellent portrayal of Sir Giles Overreach." The play "is mounted in the simplified style in which Mr. Hampden does his Shakespearean performances, draperies and a few essential settings serving in place of the traditional full sets of scenery, though the effect of the acting is not lessened." The last scene "enabled Mr. Hampden last evening to rise to splendid heights and partly to redeem the shortcomings of a performance for which there had not been sufficient preparation." The *Morning Ledger* points out that the play "is not particularly endowed with literary flavor, nor does it contain much of verbal beauty. . . ." Sir Giles's "death scene in the last act is a genuine dramatic tour de force. . . . Mr. Hampden acted it with wonderful effect and throughout the play he was the dominating figure," though the other parts "were in the main capably filled. . . . The play, however, is rather more interesting as an archeological specimen than as drama to enchant the taste of the modern ear and intelligence." (I should think it might be rather difficult to enchant the taste of an ear anyhow!) Agreeing with this estimate, the *American* notes that *A New Way to Pay Old Debts* is "a play with little matter, but presented with a great deal of art. . . . Mr. Hampden's portrait of the principal character was by far the most interesting thing

about the performance and his changes of mood from the haughti-
est pride to cringing servility for those stationed in rank far above
him were delineated with exquisite fineness. . . . The chief quality
lacking in the production seemed to be abandon and tautness, but
the fact that this was the first presentation may have been the
reason for this. . . ."

From Philadelphia, the company went to Syracuse where the
play was presented at the Wieting Theatre on November 7. The
Post-Standard thought Hampden "especially fine. Sir Giles, like
Shylock, is a terrible and repellent, and yet a magnificent character,
as Mr. Hampden plays the part; with all the personal charm which
this admirable actor has, all the beauty of voice, bearing and
manner, it is the nobility of the character of Sir Giles, not his
hatefulness that impresses us." The next stop was Pittsburgh with
Sir Giles vivid on November 18, but I find no reviews of the play
as it was presented at the Shubert-Pitt Theatre. The same applies
to the presentation at the Shubert-Teck Theatre, Buffalo, on
November 25. The next localization was His Majesty's Theatre,
Montreal, and the date December 4. Here the *Gazette* is laudatory:
"As played by Mr. Hampden and his admirable company of associate players, the old comedy is not only diverting in its unfolding
but presents a virile and lifelike group of human beings. . . . In
depicting this rôle, Mr. Hampden carefully builds up the character
bit by bit, with all the vanity, venality, cruelty, and vulpine craft of
Sir Giles brought out skilfully, until the overtoppling of his scheme
culminates in a passionate outburst of foiled rage, followed by
madness. It is a lifelike portrait, and further performances should
round it into a perfect similitude of the rôle as the author conceived
it . . . and as noted histrions of the past have played it. The
performance owes much of its entertaining quality to the gusto
with which the enactors of the broad comedy rôles approach their
tasks."

By far the ablest and most revealing criticism, however, came
from the pen of the veteran J. Ranken Towse of *The New York
Evening Post,* after he had witnessed the performance of *A New
Way to Pay Old Debts* at the Montauk Theatre, Brooklyn, on
December 16, 1922.[32] Since other road engagements prevented,

[32] *The New York Evening Post,* December 18, 1922.

Brooklyn was as near as Sir Giles came to Broadway. The head-line of the review reminds us of older days in the play's history: "Stirring Performance That Set a Somewhat Apathetic Brooklyn Audience to Cheering." Since Mr. Towse displays his usual acumen, I make no apology for quoting his remarks in full:

In the Montauk Theatre, Brooklyn, on Saturday evening, Mr. Walter Hampden brought to a triumphant close his week's engagement, one of the most remarkable that has been played in this country for many years. New York City, apparently, if one may judge by the absence of public records, has been unaware of it. The final feature was a revival of Massinger's famous old play, "A New Way to Pay Old Debts," which attracted a large, and in the end, hotly enthusiastic audience. They had witnessed a bit of vivid melodramatic acting which had not been excelled, or equalled, upon the local stage in this generation, and it woke them up very thoroughly.

This piece scarcely comes under the category of great drama, though abounding in vigorous characterization and written in robust and pregnant English; but it does provide opportunities for great acting, as our forefathers well knew. The plot, drawn on the simple and primitive lines of its period, seems to modern eyes somewhat childish, transparent, and awkward but for all that it is one of the models upon which most of the more recent melodramas have been patterned. Here we have, in their primary form, the wicked baronet, the greedy and corrupt judge—Greedy is supposed to embody a satirical attack upon Sir Giles Mom-pesson of infamous memory [*sic*]—the shyster lawyer, the Lady Bountiful, the virtuous youth and the prodigal, the angelic heroine, and the comic servants. Doubtless they were more life-like in their own day than they now appear to be in ours. In the old days the sentiment was more florid, luscious, and treacly, the virtue more transcendent and self-assertive, the passions more lurid, the vice blacker, and the humor broader than in our more artificial times. The dramatists dealt in unadulterated and unmodi-fied types. But their characters had the red blood of life in them, were human, ran true to form, and, in their own unreasonable way, were consistent.

And to make them credible and effective, upon the contem-porary stage, they have to be played after the fashion in which they are moulded. It is of no use trying to express them by modern methods. They need, for their proper representation, a larger, freer, bolder style in speech and action than is required in or is appropriate to our modern drama of artificial social life. Our players had the secret of it up to forty or fifty years ago, but lost it through want of practice, and now find it exceedingly difficult to recover. But recovered it must be, or the older drama—Shakespeare and the rest—which constitutes the greater part of the literary treasure of the theatre, the main foundation, indeed, upon which the whole artistic structure rests—will be found only in the library. That is why so much depends upon individual endeavors to restore some of our stage classics to the footlights and especially upon the work of a man like Hampden, who has studied and practised his profession in the best of schools and now assumes the leadership in the fight for the literary and poetic drama, fully qualified for the post by experience, ambition, and executive ability.

The courage with which he has struggled to the front in spite of difficulties, obstacles, and discouragements of every kind, is sufficient assurance that he will maintain the foothold which he has gained and reach the goal to which he aspires. It is impossible to doubt that he, in the not distant future, will, like Edwin Booth, of whom he is the legitimate successor, be at the head of his own theatre in New York, and inasmuch as he is a good business man as well as the best actor of his day, there may be no fear of his loosing hold of it as did his illustrious forerunner. Meanwhile he is engaged upon the formidable task of creating a competent repertory company out of what is for the most part practically raw material, and he is well on the way to the accomplishment of it.

Already his associate players show the good results of sound instruction and example. They speak out well, cooperate nicely in sustaining the general action of the scene and fall naturally into picturesque and living groups. Some of them exhibit more zeal than discretion or intuition, but their work has the merit of animation and is often exceedingly effective in scenes of strife or rapid movement. Here is no case of a star and a bundle of sticks. They did not shine brilliantly in the closing representation of Massinger's play, but did quite as well, perhaps, as could reasonably have been expected. They were evidently conscious of being in a strange atmosphere and environment. Some of them made the mistake of trying to tone down the strong coloring to soften extravagances of humor, sentiment, and satire, and so deadened the spirit of the scene, without making it more natural. The

Marrall, the Greedy, and the Lovell, all lost innumerable opportunities. All the characters in the play are sketched in the boldest outlines, and should be given their fullest significance, as they are designed to be appropriate foils to Overreach, who himself is a monstrosity. They are all of them extreme types and when any of them are modified the play loses its proper balance. In this case the artistic need is full and adequate expression rather than timorous repression.

But this representation is still in the rehearsal, or experimental, stage, and doubtless will improve with repetition. It was received by a large audience with interest and great cordiality. Hampden, as might have been foreseen, was its life and backbone. His Overreach is not yet the finished portrait that it will be, but it is a vivid, bold, and expressive sketch. The character, of course, does not call for the exercise of those superior faculties essential to a satisfactory interpretation of Hamlet, Macbeth, or Othello. There is nothing of the vague, subtle, or indefinite about it. The picture is one of consummate and unscrupulous villainy, avarice, hatred, and the basest sycophancy delirious in success and rabid in defeat. It was the opportunity which it affords for the delineation of the darker passions, and especially the final scene of maniacal and futile fury and despair, that made it a favorite with such actors as Edmund Kean, Cooke, Phelps, Davenport, and Edwin Booth. It is, perhaps, more of a test of the physical resources involved in energetic utterance, than it is of the intellectual conception—the emotions are all expressed are entirely savage and ignoble [*sic*]—but it is one that can be met only by an actor possessed of the full tragic equipment. Mr. Hampden rose to it with an astonishing power and with a realism that was thrilling—the use of the stronger word appalling might be permissible. After it the house, awed for a moment or two into silence, broke into cheers, a fitting end to a memorable week.

From New York Sir Giles took the long-familiar trip to Boston, a city in which he had almost always been enthusiastically received. He made his first appearance there at the Boston Opera House on December 28, 1922, and discovered somewhat to his chagrin that one critic at least not only did not extend the welcome he expected, but frankly felt his presence in Boston an affront to the city. Since the whole truth must be told, I dare not omit the review in the *Boston Transcript* by Mr. H. T. Parker. The review will do little harm to Sir Giles; it shows a misunderstanding so complete as to convict Mr. Parker out of his own mouth, and forms a neat contrast to the discerning criticism of Mr. Towse, who making no great claims for the play does show that it has a meaning and a place. No one doubts that the play is theatrically old-fashioned; no one asserts that it can be put beside Shakespeare's masterpieces. Yet Mr. Parker makes these statements as if they were great discoveries, and then feels it necessary to refute the opposites, to refute so warmly indeed that he overstates his case.

"To revalue Shakespeare, revive Massinger." This terse tag, over which no copyright is spread, might be recommended to Mr. Walter Hampden when next that proven disciple of the Great Elizabethan is tempted to stray from his chosen master. Indeed Mr. Hampden's resuscitation of "A New Way to Pay Old Debts" at the Opera House last evening did not so much honor to his able and searching desire for variety of repertory as it accomplished discredit to Massinger. The fault of the old play in its new dress and manners is not entirely a result of comparison with mightier contemporary names. Massinger was a crude workman with regard to plot. The frankly amateurish Marlowe, the overburdened Webster, the turgid Ford and the tenuous Tourneur could not voluntarily have put together such an intricate and disingenuous patchwork as "A New Way to Pay Old Debts." The drama of intrigue is no modern discovery. Neither was it exactly a novelty in Elizabethan times, all plots partaking of the nature of intrigue. Yet the beefy Massinger handles situations as though they were appalling mysteries, the very thought of which dumbfounded him. As the piece comes to being on the twentieth century stage, it is distressing to witness his awkward juggling of episode and climax with which Sacha Guitry or Avery Hopwood would have made short and tidy work.

There is no need to indulge in painful analysis. The point is simply this, that this cumbrous old play exists, and indeed was probably written, for one thing alone, that final convulsive speech which caused the Byronic "convulsion fit." . . . For this rot of grandiose make-believe, Mr. Hampden, fine scholar that he is, has neither the aptitude nor the gift. . . . His intelligence is mate for big matters, not for small. So when he desperately seeks to enkindle the blown ashes of Massinger, there remains nothing but scattered dust and the falling echoes of an overdriven voice, noble organ though it be when it play on adequate themes.

The sweeping condemnation expressed in Mr. Parker's review is not reflected in other accounts. The *Globe* is highly complimentary, though it contributes nothing especially revealing. The *Post* remarks that "to the piece Mr. Hampden brought all the rich store of emotional art that is his to bestow. He dominated, he plotted, fought, and schemed, and fought again with the subtle deviltry of a fiend. His performance was by far one of his best contributions of his present visit, something to be long remembered." *The Christian Science Monitor* in the person of E. C. S., it is true, finds the play frankly out of date, but does not stop there: "Sir Giles belongs utterly to the so-called grand style of acting that has passed and with it has passed Massinger's hollow Elizabethan play. Although the sincerity and skill of Mr. Hampden's company made it live again spasmodically last evening in the intenser emotional scenes, in truth it must be said the chief interest was historical rather than dramatic. Historically, however, the performance had an absorbing interest for the playgoers who had possibly read the play and wondered how it could possibly have been acted with any semblance of conviction. . . . Hampden has performed wonders in its revival, or, shall we say, his galvanization of it. . . . Without 'cleaving the air with horrid speech,' Mr. Hampden attained to the effect of the traditional grave style of acting. Playgoers last night who had seen Booth were heard to exclaim that they had never expected to see that style again. . . ." The *American* adds that "his performance bore out the past evidences of the genius which seems to touch almost any play and make it a masterpiece." Philip Hale in the *Herald* brings up the question of the stage alteration of one scene, a point considered elsewhere in this book:

It is a question whether Massinger's making Wellborn whisper to Lady Allworth his one suit is not more effective than the spoken scene which has been substituted, written by one not named. Massinger excited the curiosity of the audience. The wonder at Lady Allworth's behavior thereafter was the greater. The substituted open dialogue seems laborious, an underrating of a spectator's intelligence.

The play is a virile melodrama and it should be played in rattling melodramatic spirit. . . . Perhaps Mr. Hampden takes too intellectual a view of the character; puts too much weight on the spoken word and does not let himself go until the end. . . . No one can be "moved" by an actor playing this part; the spectator must be overpowered. . . . Mr. Hampden made a brave endeavor . . . [but] the play should be performed in a more reckless spirit by all.

Mr. Hampden is to be thanked for reviving this old play. Well contrived for performance, written in sturdy English, a play by a man who deserved better than the study by Arthur Symons.

It is plain, I think, that Mr. Parker's opinions are not echoed by his colleagues, and that Sir Giles, once over the shock of being treated as an unwelcome visitor, continued to flourish in the repetitions of January 1, 6, and 10.

As he had often in the days of Junius Booth, Sir Giles went from Boston to Providence where he made public appearances on January 16 and 20 at the Shubert Majestic Theatre. Here, according to the *News,* he was "well received by a critical and expectant audience. . . . No character portrayal has been seen here recently in which such tragedy and emotion has been expressed to such an extreme that the rational element of man is completely lost to the beastly passion that envelopes Sir Giles. . . . [The play] should certainly attract lovers of things artistic and fine acting." The *Journal,* on the other hand, points out that times have changed, that there is no longer observable any Byronic convulsion in the audience. The play seems stilted, and the characters are neither human nor psychologically right. Still it is "interesting to watch as a relic of an outmoded theatrical manner and method." The *Tribune,* however, proclaims that "Mr. Hampden scored another success. . . . While it is rather dull and the plot progresses slowly, despite the many scenes, it is amusing in spots and affords an excellent opportunity for acting. Mr. Hampden and his players take every advantage of this opportunity and last night they gave an admirable performance. Mr. Hampden rose to great heights in the final scene and his work brought forth a long outburst of applause." At Parson's Theatre, Hartford, on February 2, Sir Giles was even more triumphantly successful. Both the *Times* and the *Courant* were enthusiastic, the latter headlining "Sir Giles Lives Once More. Walter Hampden in Superb Performance."

The next city visited was Baltimore, where *A New Way to Pay Old Debts* was presented at The Auditorium on February 5

and where according to the *News* Hampden portrayed Sir Giles
Overreach exactly as the rôle should be played. Norman Clark's
review is too breezy to have much meaning, but it brings out that
Hampden in the last scene "busts loose." The *Sun* (J. O. L.) is
more critical in both senses of the word:

> The work was played throughout by Mr. Hampden's associates
> with an admirably light touch and a kind of sincere romanticism
> that was delightful, while the famous character of the evil Sir
> Giles Overreach, a kind of prototype of all evil uncles since plays
> were written, Mr. Hampden himself approached in something of
> the grand manner of the old theatre, tempering his performance
> however with a certain glint of comedy that made this portrayal
> very interesting. It is of course impossible to make Sir Giles very
> real. He is inherently a creature of the theatre, epitomizing as he
> does all the uncontrolled temper that ever was since drama was,
> and the old-fashioned actors who used to portray this part so
> dynamically that the spectators became terrified as they watched
> the performance probably gave the rôle certain theatric values
> that Mr. Hampden's more restrained and "modern" manner of
> reading the part failed entirely to suggest, although even so, he
> finely dominated the scene for all that his portrayal never at any
> time was what may be described as devastating. It was, however,
> extremely thoughtful always, arresting and consistently pic-
> turesque, an important addition to the player's gallery of stage
> portraits. . . .

Washington received Sir Giles with open arms when Mr.
Hampden presented the character at the Garrick Theatre on
February 13. The *Herald* reports that "Mr. Hampden rises
magnificently to the occasion. The storm of passion, striking in
on a personality that could not conceivably be subdued, leads to a
scene that surpasses in stress and vigor even the stormiest episodes
of Shakespeare's tragedies." "It's a rich part," says M. McK. in
the *News*; "there's no belying that Overreach is a rôle fit to caress
the vanity of any actor, full of volcanic outbursts of temper, fine,
sonorous lines, unreasoning passions. But Hampden does not stop
with a superb reading. He exhausts every physical artifice to carry
his creation across the footlights." And the *Post* presents a scene
which recalls other days: "Let those who assert that the repressed
manner of modern acting has forever put to rout the declamatory

style of the past heed the ovations which the large audience paid at the end of the second act and again at the play's close, refusing to accept the lighting of the auditorium as any hint of cessation."

Having gone North and South, Sir Giles now went West, first to the Cox Theatre, Cincinnati, where he raged on the 28th of February. Russell Wilson in the *Times-Star* contents himself largely, however, with a history of the play. The next stop was the Shubert-Jefferson Theatre, St. Louis, March 7, and here again there were words of high praise. Harry R. Burke in the *Times* says: "A portrait of towering authority was added to his gallery last night when Walter Hampden . . . essayed the rôle of Sir Giles Overreach. . . . It calls for powerful acting in the old broad way. Hampden is one of the few with the physical force in America today to attempt it. In it, I think, he hurls a gauntlet at the theatre. It is his challenge. Is he or is he not to be the artistic successor to Edwin Booth in the history of the American stage? . . . Of physical acting, Sir Giles is itself a tour de force. Hampden makes it more. . . . This representation has thought and intellect behind it." Richard L. Stokes in the *Post-Dispatch* also finds Hampden's acting more than physical: "We do not remember having seen Mr. Hampden play any part with such vigor and excellence as that of Sir Giles Overreach. Though his rascality reached the point of monstrosity, it still preserved an illusion of life and reality so that the tremendous explosion of the mad scene was not merely retribution upon a rogue, but in some sort a spiritual tragedy."

Three more cities, and we bring this chronicle to a close. The first is Indianapolis where Mr. Hampden represented Sir Giles at the Murat Theatre on April 4; the second Cleveland, the theatre being the Hanna and the date April 11. In neither of these places are the reviews of any significance. At Detroit, however, there is a newspaper explosion. *A New Way to Pay Old Debts* was presented at the Garrick Theatre on April 24. The next day the review in the *News* bore the following headlines: "Play Proves Dull Antique. Massinger's New Way to Pay Old Debts Revived, But Who Knows Why?" Mr. Al. Weeks, the critic, finds the revival a "ghastly exhumation. . . . What motive prompted Mr. Hampden to drag this musty manuscript from its merited grave is beyond understanding. . . . Massinger must be dragged forth with his soliloquies and his asides, with his intricate and insincere plotting, with his bombastic rhetoric and his feeble wit." Mr. Ralph Holmes in the *Times* does his bit by calling the play "a creaky drama with one big scene," but adds: "Those who love the history of the stage and are willing to meet such an undertaking halfway will find real enjoyment in this tragi-comedy, in spite of the hollowness of its characters and the creakiness of its mechanics."

This brings to an end a tour during which Sir Giles Overreach visited sixteen cities. I wish for Sir Giles's sake that it could have ended on a happier note. That there was difference of opinion about him has been obvious from the very beginning; that he should be applauded in one city and scorned in another will surprise no one who knows anything about the vagaries of the road. That he has been observed to be somewhat old-fashioned in dress and language was to have been expected; that his story is somewhat wild and extravagant we knew in advance. Yet withal, there can be no doubt that considering the times and the circumstances Sir Giles triumphantly vindicated himself. The creation of a minor Elizabethan dramatist three hundred years before, Sir Giles was still vital and vivid enough in spite of his age to evoke cheering in a theatre for the gentleman who interpreted him.

Since Walter Hampden's production, Sir Giles has not been much in public. For one evening, Christmas Eve, 1928, he did appear for a while to an audience who watched him eagerly at Chevy Chase School, Washington, D.C. On this occasion he entered the body of Mr. Theodore Hardy, who directed his movements and those of his fellows. For the semi-professional cast, I am indebted to Mrs. F. E. Farrington, who sent me a program:

Sir Giles Overreach .... Theodore Hardy
Wellborn .... Leslie D. Waudby
Lord Lovell .... Maurice Jarvis
Marrall .... Arthur B. White
Justice Greedy .... J. Martin Scranage
Allworth .... Teddy Tenley
Lady Allworth .... Lenore W. Smith
Margaret .... Caroline McKinley

At the moment Sir Giles is on vacation. He seems to prefer quieter haunts than the bustling theatre can afford him. If one is careful, it is not difficult to catch him lurking in the stacks of various libraries, only occasionally to be coaxed out of his seclusion by someone energetic enough to persuade him to talk over old, unhappy, far-off things, and battles long ago. It is not that he has put off his boldness to become shy, but that he finds comparatively few who are really interested in him, few to whom he wishes to reveal himself. To wheedle his personality out of books is not easy. Several times a year, however, he does present himself for an hour or so in the classrooms of various colleges and universities. He somehow feels it his duty to help educate the aspiring and perspiring mind of the young disenchanted. But he is usually hurt and disappointed, for it happens often that he is not taken seriously, and then, wondering perhaps why he has lost some of his old power, he skulks back to the bookshelves where at least he is sure of a certain immortality, Tithonus-like though it may be. In the light of his past refulgence, however, it would be dangerous to prophesy his complete retirement, and I have small doubt but that he will in the future occasionally forget his inferiority complex, throw off his torpor, and appear all the more splendid because of the infrequency of such occasions, if not among the huge gatherings to which he has been in the past accustomed, at least to a limited public of special admirers who still appreciate him and honor his years.

Part III

A NEW GLANCE
AT *A NEW WAY TO PAY OLD DEBTS*

CHAPTER XII

LIGHT FROM THE BURNING

THE reasons for the stage-life of *A New Way to Pay Old Debts* have so far been given merely by implication; it remains to account definitely for the remarkable theatrical success which the play has enjoyed. Why of all the non-Shakespearean plays of pre-Restoration days has *A New Way to Pay Old Debts* alone been acted almost continuously from Garrick to Hampden? What is there about it that made it one of the greatest successes of Edmund Kean? Why did E. L. Davenport act in it more than five hundred times? Before I turn to the more obvious answers to these questions, answers which may be arrived at by scanning the play itself, let me first glance over the history of its revivals for reasons which lie at least partially outside the drama in the realm of circumstance. External and internal reasons for the life of the play are of course inextricably bound up together, but the separation if artificial is at least convenient.

I must assume from the start, before giving my reasons for the assumption, that *A New Way to Pay Old Debts* is worthy of revival. That being the case, a glance backward will, I think, show us other reasons to account for its stage-life. The popularity of the play before the Puritan interregnum need not detain us, nor need I spend useless time in accounting further for the lack of revivals in the Restoration era. But why did Garrick revive the play? It is hard to believe that he recognized it as a masterpiece, for he did not seize the opportunity to act in it himself. On the other hand he certainly did not think it worthless or the play would not have been revived at all. Garrick put Massinger's drama on the boards again, I think, at least partially because it was in line with his program of Elizabethan revival, the result of the reaction from the immorality of the Restoration, and the increasing knowledge of the drama of the antecedent era. Moreover the play was a fit vehicle for the natural acting which Garrick advocated. Here are reasons which lie outside the play itself which may account for its reappearance.

Poorly cast and poorly acted, the Garrick revivals proved to be failures. As I have previously suggested, too, perhaps the time was not ripe for this grim comedy. But then came John Henderson, and whatever brought the play to his attention, he forced it upon the attention of others by his success as Sir Giles Overreach, and originated the tradition according to which subsequent actors looked at this part as an important rôle. Shortly afterwards Kemble must try his hand at it, and though Sir Giles was not one of his best characterizations, he certainly succeeded in keeping the part before the public eye. What more natural than that Kemble's chief rival, Cooke, should seize upon it, and peculiarly adapted to it as he was, score heavily in the rôle? Sir Giles Overreach was now alive again, not only in London, but in the provinces, and somehow it reached the obscure country tragedian, Edmund Kean. Kean had only to play the rôle in London to have Massinger compared favorably with Shakespeare, and Sir Giles became a stock character. One night when Kean was scheduled to act Massinger's extortioner at Brighton, he failed to appear, and at the last minute, Booth was thrust into the part and made a success of it. When the latter came to London, he was for a short while at least Kean's chief rival, and therefore quite naturally continued to play the character. And so it went. Sir Giles became one of the parts by which an actor was estimated. Vandenhoff and Elton did not dare leave it alone, Charles Kean must follow his father, Phelps and Brooke hazarded comparison with the older actors, and younger actors than they had to try their parts. Until about 1880 *A New Way to Pay Old Debts* continued to be a stock play, and then lapsing because of changing theatrical conditions and the influence of the "new" drama, it became the subject of antiquarian revival. And so we find other elements outside the play contributing to its theatrical life: first, the impetus of theatrical success, and second, the natural rivalry of actors.

The same reasons hold for the revivals in the United States, where the early performances of *A New Way to Pay Old Debts* were of course derivative. Chalmers and Hodgkinson inherited Sir Giles Overreach from England; neither was successful enough to bring it to any great attention in America. But Cooke shocked New York as Massinger's villain, Bibby imitated Cooke in the rôle, Maywood tried it, and then Edmund Kean showed American actors the importance of the character. It was not Kean, however, but his rival, Junius Brutus Booth, who really gave impetus to the vivification of Sir Giles in the United States, and Booth played the part for thirty years, passing it on to Scott and the various minor actors mentioned in the text. English actors playing in America, Charles Kean, Vandenhoff, and Brooke increased interest in the rôle. Davenport and Edwin Booth inherited the Sir Giles tradition, and he became in America, as in England, a stock part to be attempted by every great tragic actor who would attain success. Finally the stock companies broke down, the interest in the old plays dwindled, and *A New Way to Pay Old Debts* passed over into the hands of colleges and little theatres.

I cannot help thinking therefore that external circumstances over and above the play itself had something to do with the theatrical vitality of *A New Way to Pay Old Debts*. Chosen as a fitting Elizabethan revival by a man whose reputation is in part due to his interest in the pre-Restoration drama, Massinger's play swept on through the years impelled by a tradition of its own creation, a tradition caused by the successes of various actors in the rôle of Sir Giles Overreach, and by the histrionic rivalry which forced a man to play the popular parts in which his contemporaries starred, if he were to prove his worth. The one proved the importance of the play as an acting vehicle, the other stimulated an actor to outdo his fellows in the rôle.

But even though there exist external circumstances which may have contributed to the popularity of *A New Way to Pay Old Debts,* they pale before the importance of certain elements in the play itself, and of these the chief is obviously the character of Sir Giles Overreach. The histrionic opportunities offered by this character constitute the primary reason for the theatrical vitality of Massinger's drama. If we knew nothing of its stage-history, a hurried reading could not but present the idea that it is a one-part play. When to this we add our knowledge of its extraordinary success and read the criticisms evoked by its performance, the fact becomes indubitable. Now when I say that *A New Way to*

Pay Old Debts is a one-part play, I do not imply unfavorable criticism. In the same sense *Hamlet, Lear, Macbeth* are also one-part plays. I do not mean that the other *dramatis personae* are weak, colorless, and unimportant, for they are not, but that one character, Sir Giles Overreach, is so much more important than the other rôles that he dominates the play. It is distinctly a star-part for a star-actor. Garrick did not realize this, and the play failed; but Henderson, Kemble, Cooke, and Kean recognized it and started the play on its trail of glory. It became a success in revival because stars wanted to enact Sir Giles Overreach; it is to the potentialities of the rôle that we owe its amazing stage-history.

If *A New Way to Pay Old Debts* has held the stage chiefly because of the opportunities it presents to a star, what is there about the character of Sir Giles Overreach that attracts the actor and offers scope for his talents? In the first place Sir Giles is strong willed, and strong will, other things in the play being of sufficient merit to escape censure, makes for dramatic character. With a strong will, conflict is almost inevitable, and though conflict is not the essential of drama, it stimulates the actor and evokes the enthusiasm of an audience. There is nothing weak and vacillating about Sir Giles; he is heroic in his villainy, triumphant in his success, unrepentant in his downfall. Throughout the play, no matter how he fares, his purpose is unswerving. He is an out-and-out scoundrel of the blackest hue, mean, cruel, snobbish, selfish, taking pride in his own wickedness and with not the slightest sense of moral values. What a tremendous opportunity for the actor who grasps the picture! What a chance for slashing, brutal strokes of characterization, for telling thrusts of portrayal! But Sir Giles is no coldly intellectual villain, and this brings me to my second point. He is on fire with emotion, emotion which the actor can transform for his audience into an almost hysterical suspense. Sir Giles is a part for a romantic actor. No wonder that Kemble could not convince in the rôle. It is the part for Cooke, for Kean, for Booth. Sir Giles is emotionally mad, and the actor must be able to feel and communicate this quality. The audience must be swept off its feet, and I have quoted sufficient testimony to show that it often was. One can admire the intelligent portrayal of an intellectual

character, but one does not get excited about it. But here was
this part, alive with feeling, interpreted by emotional actors at
the very time when the shackles of classicism had been broken and
when passionate feeling became popular. Cato was dead, long
live Sir Giles! Gothic novels, itinerant Don Juans, Sir Giles Overreach—all releases from the conventional and plunges into the
emotional. Kean's audiences were horror-struck—and delighted.
Indeed it is only that elusive quality of vitality which keeps Sir
Giles from being melodramatic. One other fact at least recommended the part to romantic actors; it is a display of will, it is
emotional, it is also athletic. It offers an opportunity for the display of unusual physical powers. No weakling could act Sir Giles.
We have seen that Kean in his last years was unable to play the
rôle as he had previously played it, because his physique was no
longer equal to the task; and we have noted too that Brooke lapsed
into a coma which baffled a physician after a particularly strenu-
ous interpretation of the character. A little man could act it but
not a puny one. Now coupled with the natural tendency to the
spectacular in everyone, the romantic actor had a particular liking
for exhibiting his physical strength. Feeling was the emotional
release from the classicism of the eighteenth century; athleticism
was the physical release from the convention of dignified art.
Hence it is not surprising to discover how popular were such
plays as *Richard III, Virginius,* and the countless melodramas,
all of which permitted the actor, in theory at least, to be artistically
acrobatic. The last act of *A New Way to Pay Old Debts* falls distinctly into this group, and again Sir Giles becomes the very part
for the emotional, romantic star. Beyond and above these qualities are indefinables which vary with the personal equation, but
they sum up to the conclusion: "Here is the history of Sir Giles
Overreach; he must be great, for see how he has lived!"

If I were writing a general criticism of *A New Way to Pay Old
Debts,* I should have to spend considerable time in a discussion
of the minor characters; since I am merely interpreting its stage-
history, that duty does not devolve upon me. The space allotted
in contemporary notices to a treatment of the lesser *dramatis personae* shows how little they counted in imparting to the play its
vitality as an acting vehicle. What few remarks there are on the

subject show merely that these characters are adequate to carry
the plot and set off the character of Sir Giles Overreach. I am not
accusing Massinger of hasty or sloppy character drawing; indeed
Wellborn, Marrall, Justice Greedy, Lady Allworth are remarkably well projected. I mean simply that the minor characters do not
require interpretation in the light of the stage-history of the play,
that they are not responsible for its continued success, though they
are of sufficient merit not to retard the impetus given by the protagonist. In other words, the lesser figures of the drama may be
regarded as a constant factor which has neither hindered nor
advanced the stage life of the play.

The history of *A New Way to Pay Old Debts* does show us,
however, that certain sections of the play have had a theatrical
value over other sections of the play. Of these it is natural that
those scenes in which Sir Giles is dominant would be most impressive to an audience, since they are precisely those which afford opportunity to the star to exercise his talents. It is easily
explicable for example that Kean, on certain benefit nights when
he chose to play one act of five different pieces, picked the last act
of *A New Way to Pay Old Debts*. Merely a cursory glance backward will show that it is on the last act that the reviews particularly dwell, that it is in the last act that the star has the best chance
of sweeping the audience off its feet. Here occurs the tremendous
peripeteia, which is not only *per se* dramatically effective, but which
also gives to the actor his great opportunity to run the gamut of
emotions from joy to grief. Sir Giles, exultant in the apparent
success of his diabolical schemes, discovers that everything has
turned against him, seeks to avenge himself, and becomes a raging lunatic who must be forced or carried off the stage. Indeed
some actors, as we have seen, interpret his final insensibility as
death. The inherent power of this last scene and the scope allowed
the individuality of the actor have had much to do with keeping
A New Way to Pay Old Debts on the stage.

If the last scene has been the most theatrically effective scene in
the play and that to which reviewers have devoted most space,
there are at least two other scenes of *A New Way to Pay Old
Debts* to the importance of which the stage-history of Massinger's
drama testifies. In both of these, as might be expected, Sir Giles

Overreach figures largely. The first is that portion of Act III, scene ii (in the standard text) which deals with the extortioner's admonition of and advice to his daughter. The reader will recall that here Sir Giles tells Margaret of the expected arrival of Lord Lovell, reveals to her his hopes of their marriage which will make her "right honorable," and commands her to gain that end by methods which savor considerably more of the bagnio than of the drawing-room. It is not a pleasant scene, and it is not intended to be; its purpose is to show to what shocking degradation Sir Giles can stoop, and to arouse in the audience moral indignation against him so strong as to preclude any thought of later sympathy. It is as artistically revolting a piece of work as any scene in Elizabethan drama, and it is no wonder that there has been much comment on it. The contrast between Sir Giles's utter lack of principles and the maidenly modesty of his daughter is admirable; it is a contrast which affords considerable scope to the players of both rôles. This is Margaret's big scene; it is also one of Sir Giles's big scenes, and naturally the star makes the most of it. The reviews already quoted show that here Edmund Kean, the elder Booth, Charles Kean, Brooke, and others evoked admiration by their playing. In the study the scene calls forth our praise; in the theatre its effect on the audience is much more pronounced.

If we were asked to read carefully *A New Way to Pay Old Debts* and to pick out that scene which is weakest, most out of character, and most improbable, the majority of us would select, I think, Act IV, scene i. Here Sir Giles reveals to Lord Lovell his true character, promises to obtain for him by fair means or foul whatever he wishes as dowry, acknowledges that all his possessions have been gained by the oppression of the weak and the poor and by the vilest kind of extortion from the rich, and admits his own insensibility alike to the pleas for mercy and the curses of the families made wretched by his sinister practices. The result is that Lord Lovell is horrified and disgusted with the "blasphemous beast" with whom he is dealing, and doubles his efforts to confound him. I confess that a reading of this scene has until recently always made me wonder why Massinger wrote it. Why have Sir Giles give himself away so completely? If the dramatist felt that the exposure was necessary for the audience, why did he put the scene on the stage? Why did he have Sir Giles deliberately alienate the very person on whose favor he counted? It was therefore surprising to discover that this scene, so improbable in the study, was the third which the stage-history of the play has marked as especially effective in the representation. It shows clearly to my mind the futility of literary criticism of the drama, and the unreason of finding fault with a man of the theatre without having seen his plays presented. When we read the reviews of Cooke, Kean, Booth, and even lesser actors, we cannot but see that our judgment has been wrong, that the scene is not weak, not out of character, not improbable. Our error is due to a too casual view of Sir Giles, largely inevitable because we have not seen him to the life. In the first place we have failed to recognize that, steeped in immorality as he is, Sir Giles cannot understand morality in others. In the second place we have not seen that Sir Giles, to use Scott's words, has "learned to pique himself even upon his own atrocious character." The perspicuous Hazlitt, after seeing Kean's Overreach was aware of aspects of the character which are not obvious to us who live a hundred years too late:[1] "His steadiness of purpose scarcely stands in need of support from the common sanctions of morality, which he intrepidly breaks through, and he almost conquers our prejudices by the consistent and determined manner in which he braves them. Self-interest is his idol, and he makes no secret of his idolatry: he is only a more devoted and unblushing worshipper at this shrine than other men. Self-will is the only rule of his conduct, to which he makes every other feeling bend: or rather, from the nature of his constitution, he has no sickly, sentimental obstacles to interrupt him in his headstrong career. He is a character of obdurate self-will, without fanciful notions or natural affections; one who has no regard to the feelings of others, and who professes an equal disregard to their opinions. He minds nothing but his own ends, and takes the shortest and surest way to them. His understanding is clear-sighted, and his passions strong-nerved. Sir Giles is no flincher, and no hypocrite; and he gains almost as much by the hardihood with which he avows his impudent and sordid designs as others do by their caution in concealing them." These traits are not so discernible in the study;

[1] Waller and Glover, Vol. V, p. 267, n. 1.

in the theatre apparently they are clear or at least sensed. If we grant these postulates, the scene becomes not an anomaly but an impressive depiction of character by no means out of keeping with the rest of the play. And studded as this scene is with some of the most effective rhetoric in the play, it is no wonder that Cooke and Kean and Booth made the most of it and called forth such hearty praise from the theatrical critics.

Other scenes in the play are effective too, but it is not my business to point them out. The three I have mentioned are those which are from the point of view of stage-history most important; these are the three which have drawn out the actors to special theatrical effectiveness, and which therefore have contributed towards keeping *A New Way to Pay Old Debts* on the stage. It is not therefore remarkable that almost all the quotations in the reviews are from these three scenes, and that when the critics linger with admiration upon sections particularly striking and dramatic, it is these three scenes which they describe.

One more paragraph and I shall have finished with the interpretation of the stage-history of *A New Way to Pay Old Debts*. I would simply point out that Massinger's play was by no means out of keeping with the drama produced in the early part of the nineteenth century. I am quite willing to admit that certain portions of the play, particularly the spectacular last act, verge on melodrama, the play of violent and improbable action. Such being the case it would be more popular than not with the audiences who enjoyed Gothic extravaganza, pseudo-Elizabethanism, and the wild German and French importations which flooded the stage. Moreover in general *A New Way to Pay Old Debts* does not rely upon subtlety but on broad effects, easily translatable in the huge, clumsy theatres of the early nineteenth century.

Other elements of *A New Way to Pay Old Debts* do not, I think, need interpretation from stage-history. It is all very well to say that the play is well constructed—and it is; to point out that the dialogue is intelligent, dramatically fitting, and at times poetically beautiful; to mention that some of the scenes are humourous if not funny; but these qualities hardly kept the play on the stage, are to be found in any number of Elizabethan plays. Like the minor characters, they may be considered as constant qualities; the play was not revived for these reasons and did not stay in the theatre for these reasons; they are outside my province.

But one thing remains to be done: to give an obvious answer to an obvious question. Granted that *A New Way to Pay Old Debts* has had an extraordinary vitality on the stage, granted that it is theatrically effective; is it really good drama, an important work of art? Is it a *Hamlet* or an *Abie's Irish Rose*? My answer is simply this: no play which was *merely* good theatre has ever held the stage over so extended a period of time. *Abie's Irish Rose, Chu Chin Chow, Lightnin', Charley's Aunt,* in spite of their amazing consecutive runs, will soon be as dead as *The Stranger,* and *The Marble Heart.* Yet here is a play that almost three hundred years after its original production still sets foot in the theatre, if not alongside of Shakespeare, at least not very many paces to the rear. And Sir Giles Overreach, his cloak now old-fashioned, his words antiquated, but his face as young, and his heart as vile as ever, still stands forth, a bit puzzled at the furor he has created, but as little moved

> " . . . as rocks are
> When foamie billowes split themselves against
> Their flinty ribs."

Hail Sir Giles: *morituri nos salutamus!*

Appendix A

THE STAGE VERSIONS
OF *A NEW WAY TO PAY OLD DEBTS*

I T should be plain that I have not been primarily interested in the question of adaptations of *A New Way to Pay Old Debts,* though I have devoted to literary borrowings a few pages of the section which deals with the play during the Restoration.[1] Quite another matter, however, theatrical rather than literary, is the acting text of Massinger's play. If it is not a subject which deserves exhaustive treatment—to list the endless minor variations in the stage versions would be pure pedantry—it will be important to find out in large the nature of the changes which managers and actors thought it necessary to make to render the play suitable for stage performance. I have not consulted all the published acting texts, nor do I think it necessary to do so; I have, however, examined the major collections—Dibdin, Inchbald, Oxberry, Cumberland, etc.—as well as all versions known to me which are early enough to have been determinative factors in the make-up of what might be called a standard acting text. It is distinctly to be understood that such are not in any sense "new" plays; indeed in most instances I do not know how or by whom they were made. Though the title-page usually makes it clear that they are acting versions and not standard texts, they bear no other title than *A New Way to Pay Old Debts* and Massinger's name always appears as the playwright.

In the first place, I have no evidence that any acting version of the play was published before the nineteenth century, which is natural enough when we remember that it was not until then that *A New Way to Pay Old Debts* began its great era of theatrical popularity. In 1744 Robert Dodsley published the first text of the play since the Quarto of 1633; it was included along with four others by Massinger in the eighth volume of *A Select Collection of Old Plays,* and was not republished in later editions of

---

[1] See pp. 27-30 above.

this anthology; it was also issued separately in 1744 and 1748. The text is a reprint of the Quarto with some modernization of spelling and punctuation, and a few insignificant editorial changes. The pedigree of the literary editions continues with the inclusion of the play in the third volume of the two issues of the four-volume *Dramatic Works of Philip Massinger,* edited by Thomas Coxeter, and published first by Dell in 1759 and then by Davies in 1761.[2] In 1770 appeared an edition of *A New Way to Pay Old Debts* which apparently scholars have heretofore failed to note. The play was in that year printed separately for James Dodsley, who had in 1759 succeeded his elder brother as bookseller and publisher. The copy in the New York Public Library bears the autograph of T. Harris, Esq., probably Thomas Harris, the Covent Garden manager under whom the play was presented on April 18, 1781, for the benefit of Quick, Henderson being the Sir Giles. The title-page carries the statement, "Acted at the Theatres Royal," but this is not a stage version of the play. It is plainly based on the R. Dodsley text of 1744; there are a few minor variations, of which a good many are misprints. In 1779 appeared the four-volume Massinger edited by J. Monck Mason, *A New Way to Pay Old Debts* in the third volume. The play was not again printed as a literary text until Gifford's *Plays of Philip Massinger* in 1805. From this point the familiar version proceeds through the re-editions of Gifford, Hartley Coleridge, and Cunningham, down to Symons, Deighton, Stronach, Sherman, and A. H. Cruickshank, and needs no further comment here. So much for what will hereafter be called, regardless of the editor, the standard text.

In the light of my previous statement that no stage versions of the play were published in the eighteenth century, it is necessary to comment on an edition which has been curiously misdated.[3] This bears the following title-page: "A NEW WAY TO PAY OLD DEBTS. /A/ COMEDY./ [Double rule.] /WRITTEN, BY/ PHILLIP MASSINGER, GENT./ [Double rule.] /With the

---

[2] "In the year 1751 Proposals were printed for a new Edition of Massinger's works with Notes and Observations in five volumes . . . but the Subscription went on so slowly that the Project was dropt." (*Some Account of the Life and Writings of Philip Massinger,* London, 1779.)

[3] It is listed by Chelli, *Étude,* bibl., p. 285.

Variations in the/ MANAGER's BOOK./ AT THE/ Theatres Royal./[Ornament consisting of the letters J. B.] /LONDON:/ Printed by BARKER and SON, Dramatic Repository,/ Gt. Russell-Street, Covent-Garden." In the British Museum Catalogue the year of publication is given as [1780?].[4] Now this date is very early for a text which has plainly been altered for stage purposes, and it therefore becomes necessary to inquire into the matter more closely. The activities of the Barkers have curiously escaped the notice of historians of British typography and bookselling. J. Barker, whose "dusty treasures" are extolled by Charles Lamb in the delightful essay on Old China, though primarily a theatrical bookseller, participated in the publication of the 1805 and 1813 editions of Gifford's *Massinger*. From 1779 until sometime in 1798 his shop was located in Russell Court, Drury Lane. He then removed to 19 Great Russell-Street. During the year 1801 the firm name was changed from J. Barker to Barker and Son. About 1807-1808 it reverted to J. Barker.[5] It would be reasonable to suppose then that an undated edition of Massinger's *A New Way to Pay Old Debts* bearing the imprint of Barker and Son must have appeared between 1801 and 1808. All this I learned while waiting for a photostatic copy of the book in the British Museum. When it arrived, the *terminus a quo* was proved beyond all doubt: on the *verso* of the title-page was printed the cast of the production in which George Frederick Cooke appeared as Sir Giles at Covent Garden on March 28, 1801. The Barker and Son text therefore, stage version though it is and the British Museum notwithstanding, belongs not in the eighteenth century but in the first decade of the nineteenth, and will accordingly be reserved for discussion in its proper chronological order.

Though no stage alteration of *A New Way to Pay Old Debts* was printed in the eighteenth century, the first one of which I have record was actually made about 1780.[6] This was the work of

---

[4] Mr. Sellers of the British Museum writes: "There is no indication of date beyond the appearance of the typography, from which we have guessed 1780."

[5] On J. Barker I am indebted to Mr. Martin A. Roberts of the Library of Congress for a lengthy report, which is a model of painstaking and ingenious research. The above data were arrived at primarily from a consultation of London directories and the title-pages of books bearing the Barker imprint.

[6] See p. 43, n. 13, above.

the actor, John Philip Kemble, and I may say at once that to Kemble goes the credit of preparing what becomes the standard acting version of the play. It was printed in 1810, "adapted to the stage by J. P. Kemble; and now first published as it is acted in the Theatre Royal in Covent Garden. London. Printed for the Theatre." That the version published in 1810 was identical with that prepared in 1780 is doubtful, for plays have a way of changing during continued production as improvements are suggested and new exigencies arise, but I think it is fair to assume that the essentials of the adaptation published in 1810 were well known in the theatre somewhat earlier than that date and could therefore easily be incorporated, at least in part, in such versions as were printed in the first decade of the century and which pretended to represent the play as it was then acted.

We are now in a position to compare the Kemble version with the standard text:[7]

Act I, scene i.

To deal only with the more noticeable variations, one finds at once certain modifications of language. Wellborn's question (l. 1), "No bouze? nor no Tobacco?" becomes in Kemble, "No credit, nor no liquor?" Tapwell's speech beginning l. 9 is shortened and ends, "Your threadbare, tattered. . . ." instead of "Your tattered, louzie. . . ." Tapwell's speech beginning l. 29 is shortened and modified, and the amount of Sir John Wellborn's estate is omitted. At l. 25 Tapwell's comment on Wellborn's mistresses is made a statement of their existence instead of an estimate of their temperature. Ll. 56-8 do not appear. The scene is shortened by the entire omission of ll. 62-84 and 133-43. There are other minor omissions and changes too trifling to be worthy of mention.

Act I, scene ii.

In this scene the dialogue of the servants is somewhat cut down, notably by the omission of ll. 25-33, and a few speeches are slightly rearranged for a more even distribution of the parts. The waiting-woman and chambermaid who enter with Lady Allworth are called Abigail and Tabitha. Ll. 55-9 are omitted, probably lest Furnace seem too presumptuous. After the servants leave, Kemble

[7] Line numbers refer to the Cruickshank edition.

cuts to l. 68. Lady Allworth's speech beginning l. 105 is rearranged and in part omitted.

Act I, scene iii.

This, in the Kemble version, is still part of scene ii, there being only two scenes in his first Act. The change is only nominal, however, since the setting of both scene ii and scene iii of the standard text is Lady Allworth's house. The first fifty-two lines are practically identical. Abigail's and Tabitha's comments on Wellborn's odor are made less odorous. Ll. 62-5 are omitted because not clear to a modern audience. Lady Allworth enters alone. There are some omissions, notably ll. 80-4, in her dialogue with Wellborn. Beginning l. 120 there is a change important enough to require the printing of Kemble's conclusion to the scene:

Well. Madam, on no terms:
    I will not beg nor borrow sixpence of you,
    But be supplied elsewhere, or want thus ever.
    One only suit I make.—'Pray, give me leave.—
        [*Lady* ALLWORTH *signs to the Servants, who retire*
            out of hearing.]
    I will not tire your patience with relation
    Of the bad arts my uncle Overreach
    Still forg'd, to strip me of my fair possessions;
    Nor how he now shuts door upon my want,
    And my low, hopeless state.—Hopeless, indeed;
    But that in your kind courtesy I spy
    A hope to raise it:—Would you but vouchsafe
    To your dead husband's friend,—as well you may,
    Your honour still left free,—but such feign'd grace,
    As might beget opinion in Sir Giles
    Of a true passion tow'rds me, you would see,
    In the mere thought to prey on me again,
    When all that's yours were mine, he'd turn my friend;
    And, that no rub might stay my course to you,
    Quit all my owings, set me trimly forth,
    And furnish'd well with gold:—which I should use,
    I trust, to your no shame, lady; but live
    Ever a grateful debtor to your gentleness.

Amb. See, see, she weeps.

Lady. What? nothing else?

> [*Offers her Pocket-book again.*]

Well. Nothing:—Unless you please to charge your servants,
To throw away a little respect upon me.

Lady. All you demand is yours.—

> [*She beckons the Servants, who advance a little.*]
> Respect this gentleman,
> As 't were myself.—Adieu, dear master Wellborn,—
> 'Pray, let me see you with your oft'nest means:
> I am ever bound to you.

> [*Going, and* WELLBORN *waiting on her.*]

Ord. What means this, I trow?

Fur. Mischief to us, if he has malice in him.

Well. Your honour's servant.   [*Kisses her hand.*]

> [*Exit Lady* ALLWORTH.

All the Servants. [*Coming up to* WELLBORN *with Bows and Cringes.*]

> Ah, sweet sir,—

Well. Nay, all's forgiven, all forgotten, friends:
And, for a lucky omen to my project,
Shake hands, and end all quarrels in the cellar.

All the Servants.

> Agreed, agreed.—Still, merry master Wellborn.

> [*Exeunt all the Servants.*

Well. Faith, a right worthy and a liberal lady,
Who can at once so kindly meet my purposes,
And brave the flouts of censure, to redeem
Her husband's friend! When, by this honest plot,
The world believes, she means to heal my wants
With her extensive wealth, each noisy creditor
Will be struck mute; and I, thus left at large
To practise on my uncle Overreach,
May work, perhaps, the measure to redeem
My mortgag'd fortune; which he stripp'd me of,
When headlong dissipation quell'd my reason:—
The fancy pleases: If the plot succeed,
'T is a New way to pay old debts, indeed.

> [*Exit.*

END OF ACT I

It will be plain that the major alterations here consist in the addition of two long speeches to Wellborn's part. Instead of whispering to Lady Allworth as in the standard text, Wellborn explains in the hearing of the audience the stratagem by which Sir Giles is to be overreached. The explanation is reinforced by the addition of the soliloquy which concludes the act. I reserve comment until the end of this scene-by-scene analysis.

Act II, scene i.

There are practically no changes in this scene. Wellborn's introduction of himself (ll. 90-1):

> Sir your Wifes Nephew
> Shee, and my Father tumbled in one belly.

is changed for obvious reasons to:

> I am your nephew; call me what you will, sir.

The second half of l. 109 is omitted and "Abram-men" (l. 131) is changed to the more familiar "gipsies" for the better understanding of the audience.

Act II, scene ii.

The first twenty-six lines of this scene, where the waiting-women converse with Allworth, are entirely omitted. Otherwise there are no alterations of any importance. There are some few omissions and changes in the dialogue of the servants, partially that they may not seem presumptuous, partially because the speeches are longer than necessary, partially because of allusions no longer familiar (e.g. Ram Alley).

Act II, scene iii.

There are no important alterations in this scene. Ll. 2-6 are cut down, ll. 25-30 omitted, as well as a few scattered lines and phrases *passim*.

Act III, scene i.

Kemble omitted about forty-five lines of this scene, the most notable being Lovell's speech characterizing his treatment of Allworth (ll. 20-9), Allworth's praise of Lovell (ll. 41-9), and the rhetorical description of Margaret (ll. 61-5, 68-78, 87-91, and 95-8) which Gifford thought "in very bad taste."

Act III, scene ii.

Although Greedy's part is fattened by a few speeches and some additional business, there is more than compensation in the omission of the grosser sections of Sir Giles's charge to Margaret. After l. 3, Kemble inserts a prose speech for Greedy: "It does, indeed, Sir Giles; I do not like to see a table ill-spread, poor, meagre, just sprinkled o'er with salad, sliced beef, giblets, and pig's pettitoes. But the substantials! Oh, Sir Giles, the substantials! The state of a fat turkey, now! the decorum, the grandeur he marches in with! Oh, I declare, I do much honour a chine of beef! Oh, I do reverence a loin of veal!" The longer omissions are ll. 34-8, 54-6, 87-9, 122-8, 129-35 (with alteration), 193-4, 209-14, 256-9. Words and lines here and there are made less offensive to delicate sensibilities. At what would be the end of the standard text scene, another prose speech, similar in nature to that quoted above, is inserted for Greedy.

Act III, scene iii.

As in the first Act, the second and third scenes of the standard text are made one. Again the change is of no importance since there would be no change of setting. Ll. 18-31 are cut down and altered, largely to omit Sir Giles's nasty comments about Lady Allworth. The walk in the garden is dispensed with, Lovell is deprived of his parting kiss, and "a thousand pounds" is changed to the indefinite "wherewithal."

Act IV, scene i.

Allworth enters without servants; consequently the Kemble version does not have ll. 169-76 (Exeunt Amble and Woman). Lady Allworth's remarks to Lovell are cut down by the omission of ll. 184-9, 191-9, and for ll. 210-27 there are substituted two lines:

> And 'tis my resolution ne'er to wed
> With the rich Margaret, Overreach's daughter.

Instead of the last line of the scene, Kemble's text has:

> *Lady.* Affected coyness might deny your suit;
> But, such your honour, frankness shall become me,
> And bid my tongue avow my honest heart:
> I shall attend your lordship.

Lov. My heart thanks you.

There are other omissions and alterations too minor to deserve notice.

Act IV, scene ii.

In Kemble l. 10 is omitted, ll. 11-16 are given to Froth instead of Tapwell, and ll. 18-19 are dismissed as too outspoken. In general the ensuing dialogue is cut down. Words are softened throughout (e.g. bawde > quean; whore > thief! (l. 57)). Ll. 70-6 are omitted from Greedy's speech, and two lines substituted at l. 82 to fit his humour. For obvious reasons the surgeon is absent from the creditors (ll. 98-104), and ll. 106-10 also disappear.

Act IV, scene iii.

The omissions in this scene, though they are fairly numerous, are in most cases too brief to catalogue; exceptions are ll. 36-44 and 101-4. Characteristically, passages left out are not necessary to the action of the scene, or are too plainspoken for taste, or make allusions which would be imperfectly understood.

Act V, scene i.

For purposes of discussion the scene may be divided into two parts at the entrance of Parson Willdo. Until that point the alteration is much as heretofore. Lady Allworth's first speech is cut down by the omission of ll. 4, 6-13. Ll. 30-4 also disappear. For ll. 38-63, there is a substitution of three lines:

Lady. The young ones have my warmest wishes with them.
Lov. Oh, gentle lady, prove as kind to me!
        You've deigned to hear, now grant my honest suit.

Overreach does not enter until l. 95, the preceding dialogue with Marrall being given off-stage while Wellborn, Lovell, and Lady Allworth comment on-stage. Other omissions and minor alterations to the entrance of Willdo need no comment.

At this point the departure is radical enough to make it necessary to print Kemble's ending of the play:

            Enter two of Sir GILES's *Servants.*
Lady. Whom have we here?
Sir G. After these storms,
        At length a calm appears.—My chaplain comes.—
        Enter Parson WILLDO, *with a Letter in his Hand.*

Welcome, most welcome!
There's comfort in thy looks!—Is the deed done?
Is my daughter married? Say but so, my chaplain,
And I am tame.

Will. Married? Yes, I assure you.

Sir G. Then, vanish all sad thoughts!
My doubts and fears are in the titles drown'd
Of my honourable, my right honourable daughter.

[*Sir* GILES *whispers* WILLDO.]

Mar. [*To* WELLBORN] What think you, sir?
Was it not quaintly done,
To turn his wicked arts upon himself,
And snare him thus in his own springe?

Sir G. Instantly be here?—
To my wish, to my wish.—Now, you that plot against me,
And hop'd to trip my heels up, that contemn'd me,
Think on't, and tremble.

[*Musick.*]

They come!—I hear the musick.—
A lane there for my lord:—

Well. This sudden heat
May yet be cool'd, sir.

Sir G. Make way there for my lady and my lord.

[*Musick.*]

Enter MARGARET *and* ALLWORTH.

Marg. Sir, first your pardon, then your blessing, with
Your full allowance of the choice I've made.
As ever [*Kneeling.*] you could make use of your reason.
Grow not in passion; since you may as well
Call back the day that's past, as untie the knot
Which is too strongly fasten'd:—Not to dwell
Too long on words, this is my husband.

Sir G. How?

Allw. So, I assure you: all the rites of marriage,
With every circumstance, are past:
And, for right honourable son-in-law, you may say
Your dutiful daughter.

Enter LOVELL *behind.*

Sir G. Devil!—Are they married?

Will. Do a father's part, and say, Heaven give 'em joy!

Sir G. Confusion and ruin! Speak, and speak quickly,
Or thou art dead. [*Seizes* WILLDO.]

Will. They're married.

Sir G. Thou hadst better
Have made a contract with the king of fiends,
Than these.—My brain turns!

Will. Why this rage to me?
Is not this your letter, sir? and these the words,—
Marry her to this gentleman?

Sir G. It cannot;
Nor will I e'er believe it, 's death! I will not,
That I, who never left a print
Where I have trod, for the most curious search
To trace my footsteps, should be gull'd by children!—
Baffled and fool'd, and all my hopes and labours
Defeated, and made void!

Well. As it appears.
You are so, my grave uncle.

[WILLDO *retires.*]

Sir G. Village nurses
Revenge their wrongs with curses: I'll not waste
A syllable; but thus I take the life
Which wretched I gave to thee.

[*Offers to kill* MARGARET.]

Lov. [*Stopping him.*] Hold, for your own sake!
If charity to your daughter have quite left you,
Will you do an act, though in your hopes lost here,
Can leave no hope for peace or rest hereafter?
Consider; at the best, you're but a man,
And cannot so create your aims, but that
They may be cross'd.

Sir G. Lord! thus I spit at thee,
And at thy counsel; and again desire thee,—
And as thou art a soldier,—if thy valour
Dares show itself where multitude and example
Lead not the way, let's quit the house, and change
Six words in private.

Lov. I am ready.

Lady. Stay, sir:
Contest with one distracted?

Well. You'll grow like him,
Should you answer his vain challenge.

Sir G. Are you pale?
Borrow their helps; though Hercules call it odds,

I'll stand 'gainst all, as I am, hemm'd in thus.—
Say, there were a squadron
Of pikes, lin'd through with shot, when I am mounted
Upon my injuries, shall I fear to charge 'em?
No: I'll through the battalia, and, that routed,
I'll fall to execution.—
                    [*Attempts to draw his Sword.*]
Ha! I'm feeble:
Some undone widow sits upon mine arm,
And takes away the use of't; and my sword,
Glued to my scabbard with wrong'd orphans' tears,
Will not be drawn.—
            [*Sinks into the Arms of his two Servants.*]
Ha! what are these? Sure, hangmen,
That come to bind my hands, and then to drag me
Before the judgement-seat.—Now, they are new shapes,
And do appear like Furies, with steel whips,
To scourge my ulcerous soul.—Shall I then fall
Ingloriously and yield? No: spite of fate,
I will be forc'd to hell like to myself;
Thus would I fly among you.—
        [*He rushes madly towards his Servants, and is
                carried off by them.*]
            [*Exeunt Lady* ALLWORTH's *Servants.*

Marg. O, my poor father!—
Allw. Nay, weep not, dearest;—though it shows your pity,
        What is decreed above we cannot alter.
Mar. Was it not a rare trick,
        An't please your worship, to make the deed nothing?
Well. What arts didst use to rase out the conveyance?
Mar. They are mysteries,
        Not to be spoke in publick:—Certain minerals,
        Incorporated in the ink and wax.—
        Besides, he gave me nothing; but still fed me
        With hopes and blows; and that was the inducement
        To this conundrum.—If it please your worship
        To call to memory, this mad beast once caus'd me
        To urge you or to hang, or drown, yourself:
        I'll do the like to him, if you command me.
Well. You are a rascal: He that dares be false
        To a master, though unjust, will ne'er be true
        To any other. Look not for reward,

Or favour, from me; till thou hast learn'd to mend
Thy wicked life.

Mar. Give me the means to do't,
I'm ready for a better.

Well. I will with joy: Anon, I'll speak with you.—
Not a word now, but instantly begone.

[*Exit* Marrall.

Lov. Here is a precedent to teach wicked men,
That, when they leave religion, and turn atheists,
Their own abilities leave them.—'Pray you, take
comfort;—[*To* Margaret.]
I will endeavor, you shall be his guardians
In his distractions:—And for your land, Wellborn,
Be't good or ill in law, I'll be an umpire
Between you, and this the undoubted heir
Of Sir Giles Overreach:—For me, here's the anchor
That I must fix on. [*To Lady* Allworth.]

Allw. What you shall determine,
My lord, I will allow of.

Well. 'Tis the language
That I speak too; but there is something else,
Beside the repossession of my land,
And payment of my debts, that I must practise:
I had a reputation, but 't was lost
In my loose course; and, until I redeem it
Some noble way, I am but half made up:
It is a time of action; if your lordship
Will please to confer a company upon me
In your command, I doubt not, in my service
To my king and country, but I shall do something
That may make me right again.

Lov. Your suit is granted,
And you lov'd for the motion.

Well. Nothing then [*To the Audience.*]
Now wants, but your allowance:—and in that
Our all is comprehended; which if you
Grant willingly, as a fair favor due
To the poet's, and our labours,—as you may,

For we despair not, gentlemen, of the play,—
You may expect, the grace you show to-night,
Will teach us how to act, our poets how to write.

> *[Exeunt.*

THE END.

Briefly to summarize now the major aspects of this altered conclusion, it will be plain first that Justice Greedy does not appear at all, and that in place of his first speech three lines are given to Marrall. From l. 309 Kemble jumps to ll. 358-74. This means that Sir Giles's two long speeches are telescoped into one, and that he is not absent from the stage until he leaves it for good and all. From l. 374 Kemble then goes back to ll. 319-42, which are followed by ll. 380 to the end of the play, including the partially altered epilogue. Therefore whatever explanations of the action are necessary, ll. 309-19 and 342-58 being dropped entirely, follow Sir Giles's single exit, instead of coming both between and after his two exit-speeches in the standard text.

A word now about Kemble's alteration as a whole. Massinger's play was evidently too long to be accommodated in an evening which was to include, according to custom, farce and pantomime besides. Therefore dialogue which in general involved minor characters or which seemed not important to the action of the play was omitted. Such allusions as were no longer intelligible to the general also disappeared, as well as words and lines which might offend the public taste. What additions were made were usually short substitutions for lengthy omitted passages. Greedy's part, however, was slightly fattened that the comedian who acted him might engineer more laughter out of his humour; and the two female attendants of Lady Allworth were dignified with names. Some violence was necessarily done to the poetry of the play. Florid and rhetorical passages which had little dramatic importance were pretty much cut. For the rest, Kemble is not unsuccessful in keeping the swing and meter of the verse, but apparently does not bother about incomplete lines. It must be remembered that the poetry of the play in general was not one of the reasons for its revival. Scenes of the play where the setting did not change were in two cases acted continuously.

The most important changes, however, occur at the end of the first and at the end of the last acts. The first consists in the addition of two speeches for Wellborn, one in substitution for the whispering with Lady Allworth, the other as a concluding soliloquy, and both that the plan by which Overreach is gulled may be made plain to the audience. It is not without interest to find that Professor Garrod and Mr. Walter Pritchard Eaton both criticize Massinger for failing to let the audience in on the secret.[8] There is justice in this attitude, and Kemble's alteration here seems to me a wise one. Our pleasure in the play lies not so much in an uncertain or surprising ending as in seeing the proud and villainous Sir Giles, all unwittingly, becoming gradually entangled in his own snares. The suspense consists of the conflict between the hope that he will be circumvented by plans which we see in process, and our knowledge of the terrible cleverness and ruthless cruelty of a character who may discover and thwart those plans and visit with punishment the persons with whom we are in sympathy. And it must not be forgotten that this alteration seemed necessary to an actor and manager of long experience in the theatre, and that it was adopted by others and became the standard ending for the first act of the theatre text.

Less comment is necessary on the change at the end of the fifth Act, nor can I quarrel with Kemble for making it. He succeeds in reducing the bulk of the dialogue by the omission of unnecessary comment and explanation with the effect of concentrating the attention on Sir Giles. This concentration is even more fully achieved, however, by the transpositions which keep the leading character in the center of the stage as long as he appears on it, so that the actor may build up to a romantic *crescendo* of emotion uninterrupted by less important motifs. On the Caroline stage the play was probably more comic than in revival, and Massinger may have felt it necessary to temper the inherent seriousness of the action by means of Sir Giles's first exit and the ensuing level dialogue before his final reappearance and outburst of insanity. With the change in spirit which emphasized the serious and emotional side of the play, however, Kemble aspired as much as pos-

[8] Garrod, *Profession of Poetry,* p. 233; Eaton, *Drama in English,* p. 148.

sible to harrow the feelings of his audiences that they might leave the theatre with awe as well as relief.

What now of the later history of the Kemble text? First published in London in 1810, it was reissued by John Miller in 1814 with Kemble's name on the title-page. In 1818 it reappeared in Vol. I of *"The New English Drama.* Edited by W. Oxberry, Comedian. London. W. Simpkin and R. Marshall. . . . Being the only Edition existing which is faithfully marked with the Stage Business and Stage Directions. As performed at the Theatres Royal."* Kemble's name is not mentioned here or hereafter, and subsequent editions of Kemble's adaptation follow the Oxberry text which differs from Kemble in three unimportant respects: it is slightly shorter, it has fuller stage-directions, and at the end of the fifth Act some of the minor dialogue is slightly rearranged. It is introduced with "Remarks" by W. H. [William Hazlitt], and was reissued in 1824, and in the United States two years earlier. The Oxberry text is identical with that contained in Vol. II of *The London Stage,* published by Sherwood, Jones & Co., no date [1824-1827], in four volumes. It reappears in 1826 in Vol. VII of *"Cumberland's British Theatre,* with Remarks, Biographical and Critical, by D.—G. [George Daniels]. Printed from the acting copies . . . London. John Cumberland."* In the United States in its slightly modified Oxberry form, it appears as No. XIV of Lopez and Wemyss's Edition of *"The Acting American Theatre* . . . carefully corrected from the prompt books of the Philadelphia Theatre, by M. Lopez, Prompter,"* Philadelphia and New York [1827-]; and as Vol. V of *Modern Standard Drama,* edited by Epes Sargent, and published by Taylor, New York, in 1847. To return to England, Thomas Hailes Lacy became the proprietor of *Cumberland's British Theatre* and from it took the text of *A New Way to Pay Old Debts* for *Lacy's Acting Edition of Plays,* published 1849-1873, where it is to be found in Suppl., Vol. I. We have it again in Vol. II of *The British Drama,* published in London by John Dicks in 1867. Finally—for me at least—when Lacy retired in the spring of 1873, his business was transferred to Samuel French, New York and London, from whom the play in the acting guise given it by Kemble can still be procured as No. XXXIII of

French's Standard Drama. The Kemble stage text therefore extends in a more or less straight line from its first publication in 1810, through Oxberry, Cumberland, Lacy, and the rest, to the present day, and represents the form in which the play was usually presented throughout the nineteenth century.

We must go back now, however, to the first decade of the nineteenth century to consider more briefly certain other versions which though probably influenced by the Kemble alteration are not identical with it. The first of these is the Barker and Son text which I have shown could not have appeared before 1801 and probably did not after 1808. This text is practically identical with that contained in Vol. II, Part I of *"The British Drama* comprehending The Best Plays in The English Language. London. Published by William Miller, Old Bond-Street. Printed by James Ballantyne, Edinburgh. 1804.", a collection in three volumes, bound in five. The Barker text differs from the Miller text in a few minor respects: (1) the scenes, though indicated, are not numbered; (2) the stage directions are not absolutely identical; (3) it has some misprints; and (4) the original contractions are retained. For example the Barker text takes over from J. Dodsley (1770), "There's *no* law to cure our bruizes" (Act I, scene i, l. 98) while in the Miller the "no" is properly absent; where Barker has "'em," "for't," Miller expands to "them," "for it," etc. Since there seems to be small reason why a stage version should accept an earlier corrected misprint or deliberately return to the original contractions, there is strong presumption for believing that the Barker text is earlier than the Miller, and that the latter corrected the misprints and expanded the contractions. The Barker text therefore was very likely published between 1801 and 1804.

What now of the peculiarities which differentiate the Barker text from the as yet unpublished but certainly, in its main aspects, already familiar Kemble adaptation? At the end of the first act it has, like Kemble, the concluding Wellborn soliloquy, but, unlike Kemble, it retains the whisper of the standard text. In its major aspects the fifth Act agrees with Kemble, but Greedy's part remains, Marrall is not allowed a chance to reform, and the epilogue is given as in the original. Like Kemble it has only two scenes to Act III, but unlike Kemble it has three to Act I. Unlike Kemble, the waiting-women are entirely dropped. In language, the Barker version, while definitely showing the influence of the Kemble text, is somewhat closer than the latter to what Massinger wrote. Since this text was not apparently reprinted after 1804, though it may have been the basis of other versions, it is not of much importance and it hardly seems worth while to go into the matter more fully, but on the basis of cursory examination I should gather that it represents a partially independent alteration of the standard text by someone who plainly has had some kind of access to Kemble's version. Whether this access was merely auditory or whether it implies actual familiarity with Kemble's (or another's) theatre manuscript, which was then imperfectly reproduced, I do not venture to say. All sorts of possibilities arise, one of which is of course that the theatre text was still in a transitional form. I have learned too much of published stage alterations, however, to give great weight to the statement on the title-page that it entirely embodies "the Variations in the Manager's Book at the Theatres Royal."

Two other versions of *A New Way to Pay Old Debts* exhibit variations not found in either of the types already discussed. The first of these is contained in Vol. VI of *"The British Theatre,* or A Collection of Plays which are acted at the Theatres Royal, Drury-Lane, Covent Garden, and Haymarket. Printed under the authority of the managers from the prompt books, with Biographical and Critical Remarks by Mrs. Inchbald, in twenty-five volumes. London: Printed for Longman, Hurst, Rees, and Orme, Paternoster Row. 1808." This collection was later reissued, no date, London and Edinburgh, but picture dated 1816, and in a new edition in twenty volumes, "Printed for Hurst, Robinson, and Co.; 1824"; in 1810 Mrs. Inchbald's text of *A New Way to Pay Old Debts* was printed in Philadelphia by Stephen Cullen Carpenter in the first volume of the periodical which he edited, *The Mirror of Taste and Dramatic Censor.* To return now to the 1808 edition, we learn from the separate title-page of Massinger's play that it was printed "as performed at Covent Garden, printed under the authority of the managers from the prompt book." Now the reins of Covent Garden were in the capable hands of John Philip Kemble, but, curiously enough, the Inchbald version, supposedly printed under his authority, is in many respects closer to the Barker type than to the alteration which bears his name. It has, for example, three scenes to Act I, two to Act III; it keeps the whispering at the end of Act I, but has the Wellborn soliloquy; Greedy appears in the last scene, and Marrall does not reform. On the other hand, like the Kemble version, it keeps the waiting-women, but calls them Bridget and Barbara in the list of *dramatis personae* (not in the text). The second half of the epilogue differs from all other versions, proclaiming that

> . . . honest Massinger himself, to night
> Shall teach our modern witlings how to write.

And the language, while plainly following in its essential order the Kemble alteration, differs to a degree from both Kemble and Barker.

The problem is complicated still further by the text of the play published in Vol. XVIII of *"The London Theatre*, A Collection of the Most celebrated Dramatic Pieces. Correctly given, from copies used in the theatres, by Thomas Dibdin of the Theatre Royal, Drury Lane. London. Printed for Whittingham and Arliss, Paternoster Row. 1816." This text was in a slightly modified form reprinted in Vol. I of *"The British Drama*. A Collection of the Most Esteemed Tragedies, Comedies, Operas and Farces in the English Language. Two Volumes. London. Jones & Co. 1824." This differs from the Dibdin text only in an occasional wording, and in that the two waiting-women, here called Tabitha and Abigail as in Kemble, appear in Act II, scene ii for a total of three lines. The Jones & Co. text was published under the same title by J. J. Woodward in Philadelphia in 1832, and by Lippincott in 1859. The characteristic features of the Dibdin text are in some respects those of the Barker: the waiting-women are entirely cut; there are three scenes to Act I, but only two to Act III; and the epilogue is given as in the standard text. On the other hand, like the Kemble text and no other, at the end of Act I it has both the Wellborn speeches with the whispering discarded. And the wording differs, though not very significantly from all other versions!

Are we to understand now that the Dibdin text is to be associated with that played at Drury Lane, while the Inchbald represents Covent Garden? And if so, how are we to explain the variations between the latter and the Kemble version, also from Covent

Garden? Like Sir Giles Overreach, I can say with all sincerity, "My brain turns!" Exhaustive examination, however, does not seem to me to be indicated. The obvious explanation for these mysteries must be either that we have a series of partially independent revisions, or that the theatre texts were in a constant state of flux as words and business changed to suit individual requirements.

Whatever the reasons, however, for the divergencies in the four types I have discussed, they are less important than the similarities. All pare down the standard text so that the play may fit into a long and varied evening. In the process of modernization are omitted allusions no longer pertinent, words and phrases which might offend, and such lines and dialogue in general as do not contribute much to the acting qualities of the play. All the alterations change the end of the first act either by including Wellborn's soliloquy of explanation or by adding as well a speech to take the place of the whispered colloquy with Lady Allworth. And finally all the versions revamp the end of the last act by a transposition and compression of the dialogue. From these data, and a reminder that the Kemble text both because of its priority and its later development is much the most important of the acting alterations, the form in which *A New Way to Pay Old Debts* was presented in the theatre during the nineteenth century should now be clear.[9]

[9] It may be well here to list certain other scattered data on the matter in hand. *The Times* (London) of October 26, 1827, objects to the alteration of the play presented the day before at Covent Garden with Edmund Kean as Sir Giles. Unless it be due to a misprint or the incapacity of the critic, I have no explanation for the fact that the *New York Mirror* of September 11, 1830, reviewing Charles Kean at the Park Theatre, implies an alteration in three acts. See also *The Theatrical Times* of November 14, 1846. The text of the play in Vol. XV of "*Sharpe's British Theatre* . . . London . . . John Sharpe . . . 1805" is standard. That in Vol. III of "*The Modern British Drama*. Five Vols. London. William Miller. 1811" edited by Sir Walter Scott, is also a standard text and is not to be confused with the earlier issue by Miller in 1804. The fifth act is given in "*Beauties of Massinger* . . . London . . . John Porter . . . 1817." An expurgated version of the play appeared in Vol. III of "*The Plays of Philip Massinger*. Adapted for family reading. . . . London: John Murray. 1831" and in Harper's edition of the same, New York, 1831. The standard text is printed in John S. Keltie's *The Works of the British Dramatists* published by Nimmo in Edinburgh and by Simpkin in London, 1870, and an expurgated standard in H. Macauley Fitzgibbon's *Famous Elizabethan Plays*, London, W. H. Allen &

In conclusion it may be not without interest to show how the play was altered for a more modern production. Mr. Walter Hampden has kindly allowed me to use the text which he prepared for his presentation of *A New Way to Pay Old Debts* in 1922-1923. The basic authority was Gifford, but French was consulted for purposes of condensation and occasionally of wording, and the familiar acting change at the end of Act I was adopted. Mr. Hampden's arrangement of the play is in a prologue and three acts, and it is most noteworthy in the changes that have been made in the order of scenes and parts of scenes.

Co., 1890. Later anthologies it is hardly worth while to list or examine; all I have seen print the standard text. I have not examined the following copies of *A New Way to Pay Old Debts*:

(a) "As performed at the Theatres Covent Garden and New York from the Prompt Book," New York. D. Longworth. At the Dramatic Repository. December, 1810.

(b) "With the variations in the manager's book at the Theatre royal Drury-Lane," London, Printed for W. Lowndes, 1816.

(c) "Printed from the acting copy with remarks biographical and critical by D.—G. As performed at the Theatres Royal, London. . . . London. G. H. Davidson," n.d.

(d) *English Theatre. Comedies.* Vol. I. London. Printed for John Bumpus. 1821.

(e) "Correctly given as performed at the Theatres Royal," London. T. Hughes. 1822.

(f) "Correctly given as performed at the Theatres Royal with remarks." London. Printed by and for D. S. Maurice. Sold by T. Hughes, n.d.

(g) *The London Stage.* Vol. II. "accurately printed from the acting copies." London: G. Balbe [1824].

(h) Duncombe's edition. "The only edition correctly marked . . . from the prompter's book. . . . As performed at the London Theatres." J. Duncombe and Co. [1825].

(i) *The Acting Drama.* . . . London, at the National Library Office [1830?].

(j) *The Acting Drama.* . . . London. . . . Mayhew, Isaac, and Mayhew. . . . 1834.

(k) "Modern Standard Drama, No. 33." Edited by Epes Sargent. New York. Douglas, 1848.

(l) *The New York Drama.* Vol. V. "A choice collection of tragedies, comedies, farces, etc. . . . New York. H. T. Cornett [1880].

(m) *British Drama.* Vol. I. . . . Henry Lee. n.d.

(n) "Adapted for Theatrical Representation; as performed at the Theatres Royal, Drury-Lane and Covent Garden. Regulated from the Prompt Books, by permission of the managers."

(o) Printed by and for J. Roach. London. n.d.

(p) Zwei Meisterwerke des altenglischen Dramas: Neues Recept, alte Schulden zu zahlen, . . . zum erstenmal bühnengerecht für das deutsche theatre bearbeitet, von S. Gatschenberger. London. . . . Wohlbauer, 1874.

PROLOGUE.

Scene i. Before an alehouse.

The play opens with the dialogue between Wellborn and All-worth from the latter part of Act I, scene i, beginning, "Sent to your mother?" (p. 498),[10] and goes to the end of the scene, at which point exit Allworth "to my Lady Allworth," while Well-born enters the alehouse. Enter Sir Giles and Marrall. The dia-logue which follows is from Act II, scene i (p. 518), where Sir Giles complains that Wellborn has lived too long; he gives Marrall money to cause the tapster to turn Wellborn out. Exit Marrall to inn. Enter Greedy. The ensuing conversation between Sir Giles and Greedy, dealing with Greedy's appetite, is partially from Act III, scene ii (p. 551), partially from Act IV, scene i (p. 563). Marrall enters and reports success. Wellborn is ejected from the alehouse, followed by Tapwell and Froth. The succeeding dialogue between Wellborn and Sir Giles is from Act I, scene iii (p. 510) and Act II, scene i (p. 520). Wellborn is upbraided and disowned by Sir Giles, who with his henchmen, Greedy and Marrall, leaves the scene. Now follows the first part of Act I, scene i. Wellborn is refused credit by Tapwell and Froth, who enter the alehouse laughing as Wellborn begins to lose his temper. Wellborn closes the scene with a soliloquy, "Howso'er blind fortune . . . ," from the end of Act I (p. 502). By his arrangement Mr. Hampden has been able to bring Sir Giles on the stage earlier than in the standard text and to give a good deal of exposition without change of scene.

Scene ii. A room in Lady Allworth's house.

Discovered Lady Allworth and servants, including Tabitha and Abigail. The scene begins with Lady Allworth's order to "sort those silks well" from Act I, scene ii (p. 505). Furnace upbraids her for not eating. Exeunt Lady Allworth and women. Now comes the conversation of the male servants from the beginning of Act I, scene ii (p. 502). Enter Sir Giles, Greedy, Marrall, and Act I, scene iii (p. 508) follows. Allworth enters and is snubbed by Sir Giles, who leaves with Greedy. Allworth is welcomed by the servants as in Act I, scene ii (p. 505); the servants are dismissed

---

[10] Pagination refers to Gifford text, second edition.

at the entrance of Lady Allworth. Now follows dialogue between Lady Allworth and Allworth (p. 506). He is warned to avoid Wellborn. Exeunt. Enter servants and Wellborn, and we return to Act I, scene iii (p. 510) and conclude the scene as in French with the conversation between Lady Allworth and Wellborn and their agreement. For the whispering is substituted the speech of explanation.

ACT I.

Scene i. A room in Sir Giles Overreach's house.

The play proper begins with Act II, scene i (p. 515) except what has already been used. Sir Giles charges Marrall to tempt Wellborn, who invites Marrall to dinner. This is followed by a portion of the dialogue between Sir Giles and Margaret from Act III, scene ii, but supplemented by Hampden. Overreach greets Margaret as "Your ladyship," asks her about her new woman, Lady Downfallen, tells her that he has barred Allworth from the house as unsuitable for her and that he plans to have her marry Lord Lovell. The Greedy interruptions and the direct charge to Margaret do not appear here. "How to let Allworth know!" Enter Lady Downfallen who is rated by Sir Giles for her lack of ceremony. The women leave the room, frightened and weeping. Sir Giles, *solus,* laughing with a kind of mad glee, turns to table, picks up pipe, sits and smokes, murmuring, "My honorable, my right honorable daughter!", as the curtain falls.

Scene ii. A room in Lady Allworth's house.

This scene is composed of Act II, scenes ii and iii, up to the entrance of Overreach (p. 534): that is, the dinner scene, followed by Marrall's offer to help Wellborn, played here indoors after the others leave the room.

Scene iii. Outskirts of Lady Allworth's park.

This is Act III, scene i, with Gifford language but French omissions, and some transposition of speeches. Lovell promises to help Allworth and to respect his love for Margaret.

ACT II.

Scene i. A room in Sir Giles Overreach's house.

Marrall discovered. He looks around, puts hat on table, sits, looks at paper. Enter Sir Giles. This is Act II, scene iii (p. 534) beginning, "Ha! Marrall! Is he conjuring?", where Marrall tells Overreach of his experience at Lady Allworth's house with Wellborn. Then follows with some omissions Act III, scene ii, Sir Giles giving orders for Lovell's reception. Enter Margaret (p. 543). The dialogue between Sir Giles and his daughter is made up of the speeches not already used in Act I, scene i of this alteration. Here occur the advice to Margaret on how to conduct herself with Lovell and the Greedy interruption, the arrival of Lord Lovell and his plot with Margaret, the appearance of Lady Allworth and Wellborn to dinner, and the relegation of Greedy to eating with the servants. Act III, scene iii follows without interruption, but somewhat rearranged and cut down. Sir Giles, exultant, is jeered at by Marrall. Enter Lovell, Margaret, Allworth, Wellborn, and Lady Allworth together. Lady Allworth, Allworth, and Lovell leave by coach, Wellborn remaining at Sir Giles's request. Wellborn accepts the latter's offer of assistance. Curtain.

Scene ii. A room in Lady Allworth's house.

This is Act IV, scene i (p. 561) with slight omissions. Lovell dismisses Allworth with the letter for Margaret. Sir Giles, with Greedy and Marrall, enters in time to give Allworth his ring so that he may have free access to Margaret. Greedy leaves with Allworth. Sir Giles reveals his character to Lovell and promises him anything he wants. Exit. Enter Lady Allworth. She and Lovell arrive at mutual explanations. Curtain.

Scene iii. A room in Sir Giles's house.

Enter Margaret, who looks around and beckons to Allworth. This is Act IV, scene iii (p. 577). Their love scene is interrupted by Sir Giles, who packs them off to Parson Willdo with the usual letter. The scene ends with Sir Giles's soliloquy.

Act III.

Scene i. Before an alehouse.

Enter Tapwell and Froth from the alehouse. This is Act IV, scene ii (p. 570) with some omission and transposition. They bewail their folly. Enter Wellborn, Greedy, Marrall, and creditors.

Some of the last present petitions and are paid. Wellborn accepts Marrall's application for the position of bailiff. Tapwell and Froth have their license revoked. Other creditors are paid. All but Marrall and Wellborn leave the stage. Wellborn is told by Marrall to require Sir Giles to produce the deed by which his property has been made over to Overreach. A dialogue at the end of the scene in which Marrall explains why he does not wear his hat is taken from Act II, scene iii (p. 532). Curtain.

Scene ii. A room in Lady Allworth's house.

This is Act V (p. 582). The scene follows Gifford fairly closely except that portions of the dialogue at the end are transposed. The love scene between Lady Allworth and Lovell is interrupted by the arrival of Wellborn, who thanks her. Sir Giles drives in Marrall as Lovell and Wellborn retire out of sight but within hearing. Lady Allworth says she does not know where Margaret is. Enter Wellborn. Sir Giles demands his money or security, and Wellborn refuses unless he produce the deed, which turns out to be blank. Marrall refuses testimony. Parson Willdo enters and to Overreach's joy announces his daughter's marriage. At the entrance of Margaret, Allworth, and Lovell, however, he learns the truth and challenges Lovell. Exit Sir Giles. Wellborn dismisses Marrall. Lord Lovell grants Wellborn's request for a company. Sir Giles enters, mad, attempts to kill his daughter, and falls exhausted, as Lovell comforts Margaret. The transposition gives Overreach the final curtain.

Mr. Hampden's judicious arrangement succeeds admirably in rendering the play suitable for the modern stage. The thirteen scenes of five acts have been telescoped into the ten scenes of a prologue and three acts; and they have been so ordered as to make the changing of the sets a comparatively simple matter. Such omissions as have been made do not require lengthy exposition, and the few additions to business and dialogue are in keeping with the tone of the play, and the character of Overreach. Sir Giles, as befits his importance to the play and the actor, is introduced to the audience earlier than in the original, and his personality dominates like thunder-clouds the dramatic landscape until the final curtain. It must be remembered that in revival at least the spirit of the play is definitely serious, and is prevented from being tragic only by our lack of sympathy with Sir Giles. His discomfiture brings a sigh of relief with a wondering shake of the head that such persons can be, as we depart joyfully for sunnier climes of the imagination.

ADDENDA

D URING the preparation of this manuscript for the press, information about additional performances of *A New Way to Pay Old Debts* came to hand. Whenever possible, this was incorporated into the text; in a few instances, this new matter would distort the arrangement or was too unimportant to necessitate further rewriting, and has therefore been relegated to an appendix. Unless otherwise noted, playbills are the source of information for all performances in Great Britain; Philadelphia entries are from A. H. Wilson, *A History of the Philadelphia Theatre, 1835 to 1855*; Pittsburgh entries from E. G. Fletcher's unpublished Harvard doctoral dissertation, quoted with his kind permission.

I. *A New Way to Pay Old Debts* in Great Britain:

Date	Theatre	Sir Giles Overreach
December 3, 1816	Theatre Royal, Hull	Fitzgerald
December 27, 1816	Theatre Royal, Chester	C. Crisp
November 7, 1817	Theatre Royal, Chester	C. Crisp (bt.)[1]
December 1817	Crow Street Theatre, Dublin	T. Cobham[2]
July 14, 1827	Theatre Royal, Liverpool	E. Kean
July 31, 1829	Theatre Royal, Manchester	Waldron
August 12, 1829	Theatre Royal, York	Stuart
April 30, 1830	Theatre Royal, Manchester	Waldron
May 5, 1831	Theatre, South Shields	E. Kean
September 26, 1831	Theatre, Hastings	Younge (bt.)
September 11, 1832	Theatre, Bridgewater	H. Lee
September 16, 1833	Theatre, Leeds	Waldron
September 5, 1834	Theatre, Leeds	Barton
September 10, 1834	New Theatre, Shrewsbury	Clinton
October 7, 1836	Theatre, Morpeth	Bertram
October 26, 1836	Theatre Royal, Cheltenham	Anderson
November 2, 1838	Theatre Royal, Leeds	Creswick

[1] "By desire of the Worshipful Master, officers and brethren of the Royal Chester Lodge of Free and Accepted Masons."

[2] *Oxberry's Dramatic Biography*, Vol. I, n.s., London, 1827, pp. 8, 16.

Date	Theatre	Sir Giles Overreach
July 30, 1839	Theatre, Leeds	H. Hall[3]
October 27, 1840	Theatre, Leeds	Mude
May 11, 1843	Theatre Royal, Birmingham	Lyon
May 15, 1843	Theatre Royal, Manchester	C. Pitt
August 9, 1850	Sadler's Wells	Cowper
July 7, 1851	Theatre Royal, Manchester	T. Swinbourne
September 29, 1856	Queen's Theatre and Opera House, Edinburgh	T. Swinbourne[4]

II. *A New Way to Pay Old Debts* in America:

Date	Theatre
February 19, 1835	Walnut Street Theatre, Philadelphia
May 31, 1836	Walnut Street Theatre, Philadelphia
September 12, 1836	Walnut Street Theatre, Philadelphia
December 10, 1836	Pennsylvania Theatre, Philadelphia
December 19, 1836	Walnut Street Theatre, Philadelphia[5]
February 3, 1837	Walnut Street Theatre, Philadelphia
June 26, 1837	Walnut Street Theatre, Philadelphia[6]
July 12, 1837	Walnut Street Theatre, Philadelphia
November 17, 1837	Walnut Street Theatre, Philadelphia
July 10, 1838	Walnut Street Theatre, Philadelphia
September 11, 1838	Chestnut Street Theatre, Philadelphia
June 29, 1839	Walnut Street Theatre, Philadelphia
December 12, 1839	Chestnut Street Theatre, Philadelphia
December 17, 1839	Theatre, Pittsburgh
June 16, 1840	Walnut Street Theatre, Philadelphia
June 25, 1840	Theatre, Pittsburgh[6]
December 23, 1840	Walnut Street Theatre, Philadelphia
March 3, 1841	Walnut Street Theatre, Philadelphia
May 3, 1841	Arch Street Theatre, Philadelphia
June 29, 1842	Walnut Street Theatre, Philadelphia
January 22, 1844	Arch Street Theatre, Philadelphia
March 19, 1844	Walnut Street Theatre, Philadelphia
June 3, 1844	Walnut Street Theatre, Philadelphia
September 6, 1844	Arch Street Theatre, Philadelphia

[3] Last act only, "in imitation of Mr. Kean."

[4] "Carados" in *The Referee*, September 10, 1922, mentions performances by Dillon, Creswick, Pennington, Vezin, and Montgomery. All except Pennington are treated in the text; he took part in the charge of the light brigade, went on the stage early in the '60's, was patronized by Gladstone, and lived until 1923.

[5] Overreach: Denvil.

[6] Act V only.

Date	*Theatre*
October 22, 1844	Walnut Street Theatre, Philadelphia
November 21, 1845	Arch Street Theatre, Philadelphia
March 26, 1846	Theatre, Pittsburgh[7]
May 19, 1846	Arch Street Theatre, Philadelphia
May 17, 1847	Theatre, Pittsburgh[8]
November 6, 1850	Theatre, Pittsburgh[9]
May 5, 1851	Theatre, Pittsburgh[10]
May 27, 1851	Arch Street Theatre, Philadelphia
September 8, 1852	Chestnut Street Theatre, Philadelphia
April 18 1853	Arch Street Theatre, Philadelphia
January 12, 1855	Theatre, Pittsburgh[11]
May 23, 31, 1855	City Museum, Philadelphia
October 11, 1856	Theatre, Pittsburgh[12]
April 22, 1858	Foster's New National Theatre, Pittsburgh[13]

[7] Overreach : Morris.
[8] Overreach : Oxley (bt.).
[9] Overreach : McBride.
[10] Overreach : Oxley.
[11] Overreach : Couldock?
[12] Overreach : Roberts?
[13] Overreach : Bennett?

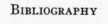

BIBLIOGRAPHY

BIBLIOGRAPHY

THIS bibliography does not represent the reading necessary for the investigation of this or any similar field; it includes only such books, periodicals, and articles as are cited in the text or footnotes. Entries are in the alphabetical order of the authors' or editors' names, except where the documentation is to title. In a few cases where confusion might result, I have indicated in brackets following the entries the short titles or names used in the notes. Thus, Wemyss, without title, refers to his autobiography; Wemyss, *Chronology*, refers to his *Chronology of the American Stage*. Acting editions of *A New Way to Pay Old Debts* are given in Appendix A. Editions of plays mentioned casually in the body of the book have not been included in cases where any convenient edition is satisfactory for the purpose. In the interests of economy of space, the location of playbills and other fugitive material, unless unique, has not been indicated; consult *Theatre Collections in Libraries and Museums* by Rosamund Gilder and George Freedley, New York, 1936.

Adams, Joseph Quincy (ed.). *The Dramatic Records of Sir Henry Herbert, Master of the Revels, 1623-1673* (Cornell Studies in English III). New Haven, 1917.   [*Herbert*]

Adams, Joseph Quincy. *Shakespearean Playhouses; a History of English Theatres from the Beginnings to the Restoration*. Boston and New York, 1917.

Adams, W. Davenport. *A Dictionary of the Drama . . .* , Vol. I, A-G. Philadelphia, 1904.   [*Dictionary*]

Albion; a Journal of News, Politics and Literature. New York, 1822-1875.

Alger, William Rounseville. *Life of Edwin Forrest, the American Tragedian*. 2 vols., Philadelphia, 1877.

Allen, Percy. *The Stage Life of Mrs. Stirling: with some Sketches of the Nineteenth Century Theatre*. With an Introduction by Sir Frank R. Benson. New York [1922].

Appleton's Cyclopædia of American Biography. . . . 12 vols., New York, 1887-1931.

Archer, William. *William Charles Macready*. New York, 1890.

Athenæum; a Journal of Literature, Science, the Fine Arts, Music and the Drama. London, 1828-1921.

Aubrey, John. *Natural History of Wiltshire,* edited by John Britton. London, 1847.

Baker, H. Barton. *History of the London Stage and its Famous Players (1576-1903).* London, 1904.

Balch, Marston Stevens. *The Dramatic Legacy of Thomas Middleton.* (Unpublished Harvard doctoral dissertation, 1931.)

Ball, Robert H. "Massinger and the House of Pembroke," *Modern Language Notes,* June 1931, Vol. XLVI, pp. 399-400.

Baltimore News. Baltimore, 1872-.

Barrett, Lawrence. *Edwin Forrest.* (American Actor Series, edited by L. Hutton), Boston, 1881.

Baynham, Walter. *The Glasgow Stage.* Glasgow, 1892.

Belasco, David. "The Story of My Life," *Hearst's Magazine,* March 1914-December 1915.

Biographia Dramatica; or, A Companion to the Playhouse . . . by David Erskine Baker, . . . Isaac Reed, . . . Stephen Jones. 3 vols., London, 1812.

Blackwood's Edinburgh Magazine. Edinburgh and London, 1817-.

Blake, Charles. *An Historical Account of the Providence Stage.* . . . Providence, 1868.

Boaden, James. *Memoirs of the Life of John Philip Kemble.* . . . 2 vols., London, 1825.

Booth, Edwin. *Junius Brutus Booth.* [See Matthews and Hutton.]

Booth, Edwin. Recollections by His Daughter, Edwina Booth Grossman. . . . New York, 1894.

Booth, John. *The "Old Vic."* London, 1917.

Borgerhoff, J. L. *Le Théâtre Anglais à Paris sous la Restauration.* Paris [1912].

Boston American. Boston, 1904-.

Boston Daily Advertiser. Boston, 1813-1929.

Boston Daily Courier. Boston, 1824-1864.

Boston Daily Globe. Boston, 1872-.

Boston Evening Transcript. Boston, 1830-.

Boston Herald. Boston, 1846-.

Boston Journal. Boston, 1833-1917.

Boston Post. Boston, 1831-.

Boyd, Frank. *Records of the Dundee Stage.* . . . Dundee, 1886.

Broadbent, R. J. *Annals of the Liverpool Stage.* . . . Liverpool, 1908.

Brooklyn Daily Eagle. Brooklyn, 1841-.

Brown, T. Allston. *History of the American Stage*. . . . New York
[1870]. [*American Stage*]
————. *A History of the New York Stage from . . . 1732 to 1901.*
3 vols., New York, 1903. [Brown]
Bunn, Alfred. *The Stage: both before and behind the Curtain.* . . .
3 vols., London, 1840.
Burley, T. L. G. *Playhouses and Players of East Anglia*. . . . Norwich,
1928.
Byrne, M. St. Clare. "Stalls and Places in the Orchestra," *Times
Literary Supplement,* November 24, 1932, p. 888.
Byron. *The Works of Lord Byron; with his Letters and Journals, and
his Life,* by Thomas Moore. 17 vols., London, 1832-1833.
————. *The Works of Lord Byron.* Letters and Journals, edited
by R. E. Prothero. 7 vols., London and New York, 1898-1918.
*Calendar of State Papers, Domestic Series, of the Reign of James I.
1623-1625* . . . edited by Mary Anne Everett Green. . . . London,
1859.
Call-Bulletin. San Francisco, 1856-.
[Carpenter, Stephen Cullen]. "Sketch of the Life of the Late Mr.
Hodgkinson," *The Mirror of Taste and Dramatic Censor,* Vols.
I and II. Philadelphia, 1810.
Carr, William. "Sir Francis Michell," *Dictionary of National Biogra-
phy,* Vol. XXXVII, pp. 331-2.
Carson, William G. B. *The Theatre on the Frontier; the Early Years
of the St. Louis Stage.* . . . Chicago [1932].
*Catalogue of engraved British Portraits preserved in the Department
of prints and drawings in the British Museum,* by Freeman
O'Donoghue. . . . 6 vols., London, 1908-1925.
Catalogue of Prints and Drawings in the British Museum, Division I,
Political and Personal Satires. . . . 5 vols. in 6, 1870-1935.
Chelli, Maurice. *Le Drame de Massinger.* Lyon, 1923. [Chelli]
————. *Étude sur la collaboration de Massinger avec Fletcher et
son groupe.* Paris, 1926. [*Étude*]
Child, Harold. "Revivals of English Dramatic Works, 1901-1918,
1926," *Review of English Studies,* April 1927, Vol. III, pp.
169-85.
Christian Science Monitor. Boston, 1908-.
Cincinnati Times-Star. Cincinnati, 1840-.
Clapp, John Bouvé, and Edgett, Edwin Francis. *Players of the
Present.* 3 vols., The Dunlap Society, New York, 1899-1901.
Clapp, William W., Jr. *A Record of the Boston Stage.* Boston and
Cambridge, 1853.

Clarke, Asia Booth. *The Elder and the Younger Booth.* (American Actor Series), Boston, 1882.

Coad, Oral Sumner, and Mims, Edwin, Jr. "The American Stage," *The Pageant of America*, Vol. XIV. New Haven, 1929.

Cole, John William. *Life and Theatrical Times of Charles Kean.* . . . 2 vols., London, 1859.

Coleman, John, and Coleman, Edward. *Memoirs of Samuel Phelps.* London, 1886.

Coleman, John. *Players and Playwrights I Have Known.* 2 vols., London, 1888.

Coleridge, Hartley. *The Dramatic Works of Massinger and Ford,* with an Introduction by Hartley Coleridge. . . . London . . . , 1840.

[Colman, George]. *Critical Reflections on the Old English Dramatic Writers.* . . . London . . . , 1761.

Columbian. New York City, 1809-1820.

Cotton, William. *The Story of the Drama in Exeter.* . . . London and Exeter, 1887.

Cowell, Joe. *Thirty Years Passed Among the Players.* . . . 2 vols. in 1, New York, 1844.

Coxeter, Thomas (ed.). *The Dramatic Works of Philip Massinger.* . . . 4 vols., London, 1761.

Crane, William H. *Footprints and Echoes,* with an Introduction by Melville E. Stone. . . . New York [1927].

Creswick, William. *An Autobiography: A Record of Fifty Years of the Professional Life of the Late William Creswick.* London, n.d. [*c.* 1889].

Critical Review; or Annals of Literature. London, 1756-1817.

Cruickshank, A. H. (ed.). Massinger's *A New Way to Pay Old Debts,* Oxford, 1926.   [Edition]

Cruickshank, A. H. *Philip Massinger.* Oxford, 1920. [Cruickshank]

Cumberland, Richard. *Memoirs of Richard Cumberland, Written by Himself* . . . with illustrative notes by Henry Flanders. Philadelphia, . . . 1856.

Cunningham, Lt. Col. Francis (ed.). *The Plays of Philip Massinger.* . . . London [1871].

Daily Princetonian. Princeton, 1876-.

Daily Telegraph. London, 1855-.

Daly, Joseph Francis. *The Life of Augustin Daly.* New York, 1917.

Dana, Richard Newry. *Poems and Prose Writings.* Boston, 1833.

[Davies, Thomas]. *A Genuine Narrative of the Life and Theatrical Transactions of Mr. John Henderson, commonly called the Bath Roscius,* third edition. London, 1778.

Davies, Thomas. *Some Account of the Life and Writings of Philip Massinger.* London, 1789 [1779].

Deighton, K. (ed.). Massinger's *A New Way to Pay Old Debts.* . . . London, 1893.

Dibdin, James C. *The Annals of the Edinburgh Stage.* . . . Edinburgh, 1888. [*Edinburgh Stage*]

Dibdin, Thomas. *The Reminiscences of Thomas Dibdin, of the Theatres Royal, Covent-Garden, Drury-Lane, Haymarket, &c.* . . . 2 vols., London, 1827. [*Reminiscences*]

Dodsley, Robert (ed.). *A Select Collection of Old Plays,* Vol. VIII. London, 1744.

Doran, John. *"Their Majesties Servants": Annals of the English Stage.* . . . Edited and revised by Robert W. Lowe. 3 vols., London, 1888.

Downes, John. *Roscius Anglicanus* . . . edited by the Rev. Montague Summers. London [1928?].

Dramatic Censor, or Weekly Theatrical Report. London, 1800-1801.

Dramatic Mirror. New York, 1879-1922.

Drew, John. *My Years on the Stage*; with a foreword by Booth Tarkington. New York [1922].

Dunlap, William. *A History of the American Theatre.* New York, 1832.

——————. *Memoirs of the Life of George Frederick Cooke.* . . . 2 vols., New York, 1813. [Dunlap]

Durang, Charles. "The Philadelphia Stage from 1749 to 1821," *Sunday Dispatch.* Philadelphia, 1854-.

Eccles, Mark. "Arthur Massinger," *Times Literary Supplement,* July 16, 1931, p. 564.

Edgett, Edwin Francis (ed.). *Edward Loomis Davenport.* . . . The Dunlap Society, New York, 1901.

Edinburgh Evening Courant. Edinburgh, 1705-?

Ellen Terry and Bernard Shaw, A Correspondence, ed. by Christopher St. John. New York, 1931.

Era. London, 1838-.

Evening Bulletin. Philadelphia, 1847-.

Evening Public Ledger. Philadelphia, 1914-.

Fletcher Edward Garland. *Records and History of Theatrical Activities in Pittsburgh, Pennsylvania, from their Beginning to 1861.* (Unpublished Harvard doctoral dissertation, 1931.)

Francis, John W. *Old New York: or, Reminiscences of the Past Sixty Years.* . . . With a memoir of the author, by Henry T. Tuckerman. New York, 1866.

Fraser's Magazine. London, 1830-1882.

Gaisford, John. *The Drama in New Orleans.* New Orleans, 1849.

Gardiner, Samuel R. *History of England from the Accession of James I. to the Outbreak of the Civil War 1603-1642.* . . . 10 vols., London, 1899-1901.

————. "The Political Element in Massinger," *Contemporary Review,* August 1876, Vol. XXVIII, pp. 496-507.

[Genest, John]. *Some Account of the English Stage, from the Restoration in 1660 to 1830.* . . . 10 vols., Bath, 1832.

Gentleman's Magazine. London, 1731-1907.

Gifford, William (ed.). *The Plays of Philip Massinger.* . . . 4 vols., second edition, London, 1813.

Gilliland, Thomas. *The Dramatic Mirror.* . . . 2 vols., London, 1808.

Goedeke, Karl. *Grundrisz zur Geschichte der Deutschen Dichtung, aus den Quellen,* Vol. III. Dresden, 1881.

Goodale, Katherine. *Behind the Scenes with Edwin Booth* . . . with a foreword by Mrs. Fiske. Boston and New York, 1931.

Gould, Thomas R. *The Tragedian; an Essay on the Histrionic Genius of Junius Brutus Booth.* New York and Cambridge, 1868.

Graham, Franklin. *Histrionic Montreal. Annals of the Montreal Stage with Biographical and Critical Notices of the Plays and Players of a Century.* Montreal, 1902.

Grosart, Alexander B. "Literary Finds in Trinity College, Dublin, and Elsewhere," *Englische Studien,* 1899, Vol. XXVI, pp. 1-19.

Guardian. London, 1846-.

Hagan, J. S. G. "Records of the New York Stage," *New York Dispatch,* February 21, 1875-July 30, 1876.

Hannam-Clark, Theodore. *Drama in Gloucestershire (the Cotswold Country; some account of its Development from the Earliest Times till To-day.* . . . Gloucester [1928].

Harby, Isaac. *A Selection from the Miscellaneous Writings of the late Isaaac Harby, Esq., arranged and published by Henry L. Pinckney and Abraham Moise, for the benefit of his family.* . . . Charleston, 1829.

Harrison, Gabriel. *Edwin Forrest, the Actor, and the Man.* . . . Brooklyn, 1889.   [*Forrest*]

————. *History of the Progress of the Drama, Music, and the Fine Arts in the City of Brooklyn.* Brooklyn, 1884.   [*History*]

Hartford Courant. Hartford, 1837-.

Hartford Times. Hartford, 1841-.

Harvard Boston List. [A record of Boston performances compiled by J. B. Clapp, now in the Harvard Theatre Collection.]

Hawkins, Frederick. "About a Picture at the Garrick Club," *The Theatre* (London), August 1, 1895.

Hawkins, F. W. *The Life of Edmund Kean*. . . . 2 vols., London, 1869.

Hazlitt, W. Carew (ed.). *Poetical and Dramatic Works of Thomas Randolph*. . . . 2 vols., London, 1875.

Hazlitt, William. *The Collected Works of William Hazlitt* . . . edited by A. R. Waller and Arnold Glover. . . . 12 vols., London, 1902-1904.

Henderson, John. *Letters and Poems by the late Mr. John Henderson with anecdotes of his life by John Ireland*. London, 1786.

Hillebrand, Harold Newcomb. *Edmund Kean*. New York, 1933.

Hitchcock, Robert. *An Historical View of the Irish Stage to 1788*. . . . 2 vols., Dublin, 1788, 1794.

Hodgkinson, John. *Narrative of his Connection with the Old American Company . . . by John Hodgkinson*. New York . . . , 1797.

Hornblow, Arthur. *A History of the Theatre in America from its Beginnings to the Present Time*. 2 vols., Philadelphia and London, 1919.

Hotson, J. Leslie. *The Commonwealth and Restoration Stage*. Cambridge, 1928.

Hunt, Leigh. *Critical Essays on the Performers of the London Theatres*. . . . London, 1807.

Hutton, Laurence. Manuscript Dramatic Diary. 6 vols., 1870-1883. [Princeton University Library: HTN 3794.8.368]   [Diary]
——————. *Plays and Players*. New York, 1875. [*Plays and Players*]

Illustrated London News. London, 1842-.

Indianapolis News. Indianapolis, 1869-.

Indianapolis Times. Indianapolis, 1888-.

Ireland, Joseph N. *Records of the New York Stage from 1750 to 1860*. . . . New York, 1866-1867.

Irving, Henry. *The Drama; addresses*. . . . Boston [1892].

James, Reese Davis. *Old Drury of Philadelphia*. . . . Philadelphia, 1932.

Jefferson, Joseph. *The Autobiography of Joseph Jefferson*. New York and London [1890].

Kemble, John Philip. *Fugitive Pieces*. . . . York, 1780.

Knickerbocker; or New York Monthly Magazine. New York, 1833-1865.

Knight, Joseph. "William Creswick," *Dictionary of National Biography*, Suppl. Vol. II, p. 88.

——————. "Edward William Elton," *Dictionary of National Biography*, Vol. XVII, pp. 337-8.

Knight, Joseph. "John Henderson," *Dictionary of National Biography,* Vol. XXV, pp. 399-401.

————. "Charles Kean," *Dictionary of National Biography,* Vol. XXX, pp. 255-8.

————. "John Vandenhoff," *Dictionary of National Biography,* Vol. LVIII, pp. 98-9.

————. *Theatrical Notes.* London, 1893.

Knights, L. C. *Drama and Society in the Age of Jonson.* London, 1937.

Koeppel, Emil. "Quellen-Studien zu den Dramen George Chapmans, Philip Massingers und John Fords," *Quellen und Forschungen zur Sprach- und Culturgeschichte der Germanischen Völker,* Vol. LXXXII. Strassburg, 1897.

Lamb, Charles. *The Dramatic Essays of Charles Lamb,* edited . . . by Brander Matthews. New York [1891].

Langbaine, Gerard. *The Lives and Characters of the English Dramatick Poets.* . . . First begun by Mr. Langbain, improved and continued down to this time, by a careful hand [Charles Gildon]. London [1699].

Lawrence, W. J. *The Life of Gustavus Vaughan Brooke, Tragedian.* . . . Belfast, 1892.

Lee, Sidney. "Sir Giles Mompesson," *Dictionary of National Biography,* Vol. XXXVIII, pp. 141-3.

Leman, Walter M. *Memories of an Old Actor.* San Francisco, 1886.

Levey, R. M., and O'Rorke, J. *Annals of the Theatre Royal, Dublin.* . . . Dublin, 1880.

Literary Gazette; or, Journal of criticism, science, and the arts. . . . Philadelphia, 1821.

Lockhart, John Gibson. *Life of Sir Walter Scott.* 8 vols., Edinburgh, 1902.

Lockridge, Richard. *Darling of Misfortune, Edwin Booth: 1833-1893.* New York [1932].

London Weekly Paper. London, 1852.

London Weekly Times. London, 1847-1912.

Ludlow, N. M. *Dramatic Life as I Found It.* . . . St. Louis, 1880.

McAfee, Helen. *Pepys on the Restoration Stage.* New Haven, 1916.

McIlwraith, A. K. "On the Date of A New Way to Pay Old Debts," *Modern Language Review,* October 1933, Vol. XXVIII, pp. 431-8.

McManaway, James G. "Philip Massinger and the Restoration Drama," *Journal of English Literary History,* December 1934, Vol. I, pp. 276-304.

Manuscript Sloane 1900. British Museum.

Manuscripts of the Corporation of Rye, Thirteenth Report of the Royal Commission on Historical Manuscripts. London, 1892.

Manuscripts of the Earl Cowper, K.G., preserved at Melbourne Hall, Derbyshire, Historical Manuscripts Commission. 3 vols., London, 1888-1889.

Manuscripts of the House of Lords, Fourth Report of the Royal Commission on Historical Manuscripts, Part I. London, 1874.

Marston, Westland. *Our Recent Actors. . . .* 2 vols., London, 1888.

Mason, John Monck (ed.). *The Dramatick Works of Philip Massinger. . . .* 4 vols., London . . . , 1779.

Matthews, Bache. *A History of the Birmingham Repertory Theatre.* London, 1924.

Matthews, Brander, and Hutton, Laurence (eds.). *Actors and Actresses of Great Britain and the United States. . . .* 5 vols., New York [1886].

Matthews, Brander, and Lieder, Paul Robert (eds.). *The Chief British Dramatists. . . .* Boston and New York [1924].

Molloy, J. Fitzgerald. *The Life and Adventures of Edmund Kean, Tragedian, 1787-1833. . . .* 2 vols., London, 1888.

Monthly Mirror: Reflecting Man and Manners; with Strictures on their Epitome, and the Stage. London, 1795-1811.

Montreal Gazette. Montreal, 1778-.

Morning Advertiser. London, 1804-.

Morning Post. London, 1772-.

Moses, Montrose J. *The Fabulous Forrest; the Record of an American Actor. . . .* Boston, 1929.

————. *Famous Actor-Families in America.* New York [1906].

Mowatt, Anna Cora. *Autobiography of an Actress; or, Eight Years on the Stage. . . .* Boston, 1854.

[Munden, Thomas Shepherd]. *Memoirs of Munden, Comedian, by his Son.* London, 1846.

Murray, John Tucker. *English Dramatic Companies, 1558-1642.* 2 vols., Boston, 1910.

New England Palladium and Commercial Advertiser. Boston, 1793-1840.

New Monthly Magazine. London, 1814-1884.

New Statesman. London, 1913-.

New-York American. New York, 1819-1845.

New York Clipper. New York, 1853-1924.

New York Herald. New York, 1835-1924.

New-York Journal. New York, 1784-1793.

New-York Mirror: A Weekly Gazette of Literature and the Fine Arts. New York, 1823-1842.

New York Post. New York, 1801-.

New York Times. New York, 1851-.

New York Tribune. New York, 1841-.

News, A Weekly Paper. . . . London, 1805-1839.

News Chronicle. London, 1930-.

Newton, H. Chance. *Cues and Curtain Calls* . . . with an Introduction by Sir Johnstone Forbes-Robertson. . . . London [1927].

Nicoll, Allardyce. *A History of Late Eighteenth Century Drama 1750-1800.* Cambridge, 1927.   [*Late Eighteenth Century Drama*]

—————. *A History of Restoration Drama 1660-1700.* Cambridge, 1923.   [*Restoration Drama*]

Nungezer, Edwin. *A Dictionary of Actors . . . in England before 1642* . . . (Cornell Studies in English, XIII). New Haven, 1929.

Odell, George C. D. *Annals of the New York Stage.* 9 vols., New York, 1927-.

Oulton, W. C. *A History of the Theatres of London.* . . . 5 vols., London, 1796, 1818.

Owl. London, 1831.

Oxford Mail. Oxford, 1928-.

Page, Eugene R. *George Colman the Elder, Essayist, Dramatist, and Theatrical Manager 1732-1794.* New York, 1935.

Parker, John. "A New Way to Pay Old Debts," *Times Literary Supplement,* September 7, 1922, p. 569.

—————. "Herman Vezin," *Dictionary of National Biography,* Second Suppl., Vol. III, pp. 557-8.

—————. *Who's Who in the Theatre* . . . , eighth edition. London, 1936.

Pascoe, Charles Eyre. *The Dramatic List: A record of the principal performances of living actors and actresses of the British stage.* . . . Boston, 1879.

Passages, Incidents, and Anecdotes in the Life of Junius Brutus Booth (The Elder), By His Daughter. New York, 1866.

Penley, Belville S. *The Bath Stage: a History of Dramatic Representations in Bath.* London, 1892.

Pennsylvania Packet, and Daily Advertiser. Philadelphia, 1771-1790.

Phelps, Henry P. *Players of a Century. A Record of the Albany Stage.* . . . Albany, 1880.

Phelps, W. May, and Forbes-Robertson, John. *The Life and Life-Work of Samuel Phelps.* London, 1886.

Philadelphia American. Philadelphia, 1919-1924.

Philadelphia Record. Philadelphia, 1870-.

Piozzi, Mrs. *Autobiography, Letters and Literary Remains of Mrs. Piozzi (Thrale)* . . . edited . . . by A. Hayward, second edition. 2 vols., London, 1861.

Pollock, Sir Frederick (ed.). *Macready's Reminiscences, and Selections from his Diaries and Letters.* . . . 2 vols., London, 1875.

Pollock, Thomas Clark. *The Philadelphia Theatre in the Eighteenth Century.* . . . Philadelphia, 1933.

Porter, Henry C. *The History of the Theatres of Brighton, from 1774 to 1885.* . . . Brighton, 1886.

Post-Standard. Syracuse, 1854-.

Princeton Bric-a-Brac, Class of 1910, Vol. XXIV. Princeton.

[Proctor, Bryan Waller]. *The Life of Edmund Kean.* . . . 2 vols., London, 1835.

Providence Journal. Providence, 1829-.

Providence News. Providence, 1891-1929.

Providence Tribune. Providence, 1880-1929.

Public Ledger. Philadelphia, 1836-1934.

Rae, W. Fraser. *Westward by Rail.* New York, 1871.

Rees, James (Colley Cibber). *The Life of Edwin Forrest.* . . . Philadelphia [1874].

Referee. London, 1877-1928.

Repertory and General Advertiser. Boston, 1811-1827.

Report of Receipts Bowery Theatre (1845-47). [In the Harvard Theatre Collection.]

Reynolds' Weekly Newspaper. London, 1850-.

Robinson, Henry Crabb. *Diary, Reminiscences and Correspondence of Henry Crabb Robinson,* . . . edited by Thomas Sadler, second edition. London, 1869.

Rosenfeld, Sybil. "The Players in Norwich, 1710-1750," *Review of English Studies,* July 1936, Vol. XII, pp. 129-38.

Ryan, Kate. *Old Boston Museum Days.* Boston, 1915.

Ryley, S. W. *The Itinerant, or Memoirs of an Actor.* . . . 9 vols., London, 1808-1827.

St. James's Chronicle; or British Evening Post. London, 1761 ?-1799?

St. Louis Post-Dispatch. St. Louis, 1878-.

St. Louis Times. St. Louis, 1895-1932.

Saintsbury, George (ed.). *The Best Plays of Thomas Shadwell* . . . (Mermaid Series). London and New York [1907?].

San Francisco Chronicle. San Francisco, 1865-.

Scott, Clement, and Howard, Cecil. *The Life and Reminiscences of E. L. Blanchard.* . . . 2 vols., London, 1891.

Seilhamer, George O. *History of the American Theatre.* . . . 3 vols., Philadelphia, 1888-1891.

Sherman, Lucius A. (ed.). *Philip Massinger* (Masterpieces of the English Drama). New York [1912].

Sherson, Errol. *London's Lost Theatres of the Nineteenth Century* . . . with a foreword by Mrs. Kendal. . . . London [1925].

Sillard, Robert M. *Barry Sullivan and his Contemporaries.* . . . 2 vols., London, 1901.

Simpson, Percy. "Two Poems of Philip Massinger," *Athenæum,* September 8, 1906, pp. 273-4.

Sinclair, G. A. "A Successor of David Garrick," *Scottish Historical Review,* Vol. I, pp. 306-13.

Smith, Sol. *Theatrical Management in the West and South for Thirty Years.* . . . New York, 1868.

Spectator. London, 1828-.

Spirit of the Times. New York, 1841-1861.

Stephenson, Andrew. "The Maddermarket Theatre," *Theatre Arts,* July 1923, Vol. VII, pp. 203-12.

Stirling, Edward. *Old Drury Lane.* . . . 2 vols., London, 1881.

Stoddard, James H. *Recollections of a Player.* . . . New York, 1902.

Stoker, Bram. *Personal Reminiscences of Henry Irving.* 2 vols., New York, 1906.

Stone, Henry Dickinson. *Personal Recollections of the Drama or Theatrical Reminiscences.* . . . Albany, 1873.

Straus, Ralph. *Robert Dodsley, Poet, Publisher and Playwright.* London, 1910.

Stronach, George (ed.). *A New Way to Pay Old Debts.* . . . (The Temple Dramatists), London, 1923.

Summers, Montague. *A Bibliography of the Restoration Drama.* London [1934].   [*Bibliography*]

Summers, Montague (ed.). *The Complete Works of Thomas Shadwell.* 5 vols., London, 1927.   [*Shadwell*]

Sun. Baltimore, 1837-.

Sun. London, 1798-1876.

Sunday Dispatch. Philadelphia, 1848-.

Sunday Mercury. Philadelphia, 1851-1891.

Sunday Times. London, 1822-.

Symons, Arthur (ed.). *Philip Massinger* (Mermaid Series). 2 vols., London, 1887-1889.

Theatre; or Dramatic and Literary Mirror. London, 1819.

Theatre, a Weekly Review and Magazine. London, 1877-1897.

Theatrical Inquisitor and Monthly Mirror. London, 1812-1820.

Theatrical Journal. London, 1839-1873.

Theatrical Looker-On. Birmingham, 1822-1823.

Theatrical Observer, and Daily Bills of the Play. London, 1821-1876.

Theatrical Times; a Weekly Magazine of Thespian Biography. . . . London, 1846-1851.

Thespian Dictionary, or Dramatic Biography of the Present Age. . . . London, 1805.

Times. London, 1785-.

Tit for Tat, Etc., The First Season (and second) of Mr. G - - - - - k's Management. [Manuscript in the Harvard Theatre Collection.]

Tompkins, Eugene, and Kilby, Quincy. *The History of the Boston Theatre, 1854-1901.* . . . Boston and New York, 1908.

Towse, John Ranken. *Sixty Years of the Theatre; an Old Critic's Memories.* New York and London, 1916.

United States Gazette. Philadelphia, 1789-1847.

[Vail, James T.]. *The Actor; or, a peep behind the curtain. Passages in the lives of Booth and some of his contemporaries.* New York, 1846.

Wagner, Bernard M. "George Jolly at Norwich," *Review of English Studies,* October 1930, Vol. VI, pp. 449-52.

Wallack, Lester. *Memories of Fifty Years.* With an Introduction by Laurence Hutton. New York, 1889.

Walsh, Townsend. *The Career of Dion Boucicault.* The Dunlap Society, New York, 1915.

Ward, Adolphus William. *A History of English Dramatic Literature to the Death of Queen Anne.* . . . 3 vols., New York, 1899.

Warner, George Frederick. *Catalogue of the Manuscripts and Muniments of Alleyn's College of God's Gift at Dulwich* . . . , London, 1881.

Washington Daily News. Washington, 1921-.

Washington Herald. Washington, 1906-.

Washington Post. Washington, 1877-.

Weekly Dispatch. London, 1804-1928.

Wemyss, Francis Courtney. *Chronology of the American Stage, from 1752-1852.* . . New York [1852].   [*Chronology*]

————. *Twenty-Six Years of the Life of an Actor and Manager.* . . . New York, 1847.   [*Wemyss*]

Wilkinson, Tate. *Memoirs of His Own Life.* . . . 3 vols., Dublin, 1791.   [*Memoirs*]

————. *The Wandering Patentee; or, a History of the Yorkshire Theatre.* . . . 4 vols., York, 1795.   [*Wandering Patentee*]

Willard, George O. *History of the Providence Stage, 1762-1891.* . . . Providence, 1891.

Willis, Eola. *The Charleston Stage in the XVIII Century, with Social Settings of the Time.* . . . Columbia, 1924.

Wilson, Arthur Herman. *A History of the Philadelphia Theatre, 1835 to 1855.* Philadelphia, 1935.

Wilson, John Harold. *The Influence of Beaumont and Fletcher on Restoration Drama.* Columbus, 1928.

Winter, William. "Booth in California," *New York Tribune Illustrated Supplement,* August 24, 1902.

————. *Brief Chronicles.* The Dunlap Society, 3 parts, New York, 1889-1890.

————. *Life and Art of Edwin Booth.* New York, 1894. [*Booth*]

————. *Life and Art of Joseph Jefferson.* New York, 1894.
[*Jefferson*]

————. *Life of David Belasco.* 2 vols., New York, 1918.
[*Belasco*]

————. *Shadows of the Stage.* Three series, New York, 1892-1895.

————. *Vagrant Memories.* . . . New York, 1915.

Wood, Anthony à. *Athenae Oxonienses . . . To which Are Added the Fasti . . .* , edited by Philip Bliss. . . . 5 vols., London, 1813-1820.

Wood, William B. *Personal Recollections of the Stage.* . . . Philadelphia, 1855.

World. New York, 1860-1931.

[Wright, James]. *Historia Histrionica: An Historical Account of the English Stage.* . . . London, 1699.

Wyndham, Henry Saxe. *The Annals of Covent Garden Theatre from 1732 to 1897.* 2 vols., London, 1906.

INDEX

INDEX

The index is confined to proper names, but certain listings are analyzed in order to provide convenient tables. For example, under "Overreach" is a list of the actors who have played Sir Giles; under "*A New Way to Pay Old Debts*" is a table of places and dates of productions. Entries in this table are confined to cities except for London and New York, where the theatres are indicated. Under each city in the index will be found a list of the theatres where the play was presented. Authors or editors whose names appear in the footnotes and bibliography do not reappear in the index unless referred to as individuals rather than as writers, or for some special reason. Considerable time has been spent in the identification of actors listed in the playbills and the text by surnames only. Full names or initials have been given when a reasonable certainty was felt; probabilities are indicated by question marks; when neither of these obtained, only the surname followed by the word "actor" has been given. It is to be noted that when the description is "actor or actors," more than one individual may be meant; and "actors" lists all individuals of a given surname, otherwise unidentified. Amateurs are not included unless they played Sir Giles. Allowance must be made for variation in spelling. Playbills were carelessly composed, often by ear: "Aickin" may appear as "Aiken," "Grey" as "Gray," and so forth; in some cases there is no certainty which spelling is correct. There is only one entry for each name, followed by a list of variants in parenthesis; those who use this index as a catalogue of actors should in doubtful cases search under several headings.